Spanish Romanticism and the Uses of History: Ideology and the Historical Imagination

LEGENDA

LEGENDA, founded in 1995 by the European Humanities Research Centre of the University of Oxford, is now a joint imprint of the Modern Humanities Research Association and Maney Publishing. Titles range from medieval texts to contemporary cinema and form a widely comparative view of the modern humanities, including works on Arabic, Catalan, English, French, German, Greek, Italian, Portuguese, Russian, Spanish, and Yiddish literature. An Editorial Board of distinguished academic specialists works in collaboration with leading scholarly bodies such as the Society for French Studies and the British Comparative Literature Association.

MHRA

The Modern Humanities Research Association (MHRA) encourages and promotes advanced study and research in the field of the modern humanities, especially modern European languages and literature, including English, and also cinema. It also aims to break down the barriers between scholars working in different disciplines and to maintain the unity of humanistic scholarship in the face of increasing specialization. The Association fulfils this purpose primarily through the publication of journals, bibliographies, monographs and other aids to research.

Maney Publishing is one of the few remaining independent British academic publishers. Founded in 1900 the company has offices both in the UK, in Leeds and London, and in North America, in Boston. Since 1945 Maney Publishing has worked closely with learned societies, their editors, authors, and members, in publishing academic books and journals to the highest traditional standards of materials and production.

Spanish Romanticism and the Uses of History

Ideology and the Historical Imagination

DEREK FLITTER

LEGENDA

Modern Humanities Research Association and Maney Publishing
2006

Published by the
Modern Humanities Research Association and Maney Publishing
1 Carlton House Terrace
London SW1Y 5DB
United Kingdom

LEGENDA is an imprint of the
Modern Humanities Research Association and Maney Publishing

Maney Publishing is the trading name of W. S. Maney & Son Ltd,
whose registered office is at Hudson Road, Leeds LS9 7DL, UK

ISBN 1 900755 97 1 / 978-1-900755-97-9

First published 2006

Printed in Great Britain

Cover: 875 Design

Copy-Editor: Sarah Newton

CONTENTS

ACKNOWLEDGEMENTS

This book has been a long time, some would say far too long a time, in the making, and there are a lot of people I wish to thank for their contribution to it in its various phases of preparation. In the first place, I am grateful to my colleagues in Oxford and Birmingham for listening dutifully, at our regular seminars, to my preliminary outline sketches for this book, when the ideas contained in it were at a very unformed stage to say the least. In the early days of the project, which now seem so long ago, first drafts of some chapters were read by my friend and colleague David Gies, of the University of Virginia, who provided me with a shrewd, thoughtful and honest appraisal and some valuable suggestions. At Birmingham I was lucky enough to be able to discuss part of the focus of what often appeared a dauntingly specialised topic with Ceri Crossley, who has furnished us with such an illuminating study of French historians of roughly the same period. I was able to develop some of my ideas further thanks to the invitations extended to me by Carol Tully, in her workshop on 'Romantik and Romance' at the Institute of Romance Studies, and by Milagros Fernández Poza, in her stewardship of the conference 'Fernán Caballero, hoy' at El Puerto de Santa María. The material on interpretations of the Peninsular War benefited greatly from my participation in the conference on 'La ilusión constitucional: pueblo, patria, nación' at the Universidad de Cádiz in May 2002, and I should like to thank the organisers, and especially Alberto Ramos Santana, Alberto Romero Ferrer and Marieta Cantos Casenave, for allowing me to be part of that colloquium and for their customary generous and hospitable welcome. At different moments in time I have spoken, both on matters of detail and on ones of general theoretical approach, with Brian Dendle, Javier Fernández Sebastián, Salvador García Castañeda, Nicholas Griffiths, Craig Patterson, Leonardo Romero Tobar, Donald Shaw, Philip Silver and Eric Southworth. As the project neared completion, I was fortunate indeed to be dealing with such a sympathetic and helpful editor as Graham Nelson, who has guided me most affably and patiently through the minefield of final preparation.

On a more personal note, I am hugely indebted, now as ever, to John Rutherford, who had enough faith in my ability to recommend me for a place at The Queen's College, Oxford, and who could not have proved a more admirable role model as teacher and mentor. Ron Truman, my excellent postgraduate supervisor, showed me, most formidably at times, what it took to be a serious student of the history of ideas, and any valuable expertise I may have acquired in that area is principally the result of striving determinedly to follow his example. Finally, I could not say anything meaningful about revisiting the past without reminding Martine what a special person she has always been and will continue to be; she knows why.

INTRODUCTION

The Changeful History of Spanish Romanticism

The diverse political tyrannies of the twentieth century have left modern civilization no doubt as to the potential rewriting or reordering of history for ideological ends. Régimes such as that of Hitler in Germany, Stalin in Russia, or, more pointedly in the Spanish context, that presided over by General Franco between 1939 and 1975, employed a skewed and slanted account of the historical relationship, in both national and international terms, between past and present. Each of their respective rewritings is familiar to us as a form of self-justification, as a putative source of doctrinal truth, or as the revelation of an appointed destiny. We make a grave error, however, if we conceive of such a process as a strictly contemporary phenomenon; as Hayden White noted in his seminal analysis of the nineteenth-century historical imagination, most of the significant theoretical and ideological disputes occurring and developing in Europe between the time of the French Revolution and the Great War involved conflicting claims to the definitive or 'realistic' representation and explication of the current historical moment.[1] White is especially interested, he declares in the introduction to his *Metahistory*, in alternative interpretations of the same set of historical events and in differing notions of the nature of historical reality.[2] White's 'ideological dimension' in fact stems directly from the assumption, by the historian, of a particular perspective on the nature of historical knowledge and on the implications that may be drawn from the study of the past for the understanding of the present.[3]

Romantic historiography was to cohere in a period acutely subject to such ideologically significant narratives of past events. The political thrust of the Congress of Verona lay in a collective and corporate affirmation of a new Europe, predicated upon an alliance between the various European monarchies calculated both to preserve their own traditional rights and to function as a buttress against possible changes in political structures and in popular representation. Study of the past, as José Vila Selma avers, was thus enlisted as a particularly appropriate means by which to countervail revolutionary change, and one which led to an enhanced apprehension of the intimacies of historical events and processes. Historical writing was intended implicitly to revise and effectively to discard the equally revisionist Enlightenment perspective, which the proponents of this metaphysically orientated Romantic historiography would consistently dismiss as superficial empiricism. Vila Selma therefore identifies as keynotes of post-Napoleonic ideology the principle of royal legitimacy and, secondly, what he calls the desire to comprehend the world as a harmonious and unified whole, the conservative desire for a reassuringly integrated cosmological vision; this last was the ideological matrix of the work that he is here prefacing and one of the salient examples of the historical vision that he summarizes: Juan Donoso Cortés's trenchant *Ensayo sobre el catolicismo, el liberalismo y el socialismo* of 1851.[4]

What follows is a study of the Romantic historical imagination in Spain within the context of these defining ideological parameters. It is intended as a critical exploration of what, if we follow the promptings of Giovanni Allegra, we might interpret as an intellectual culture of conservative retrenchment. In Spain, as Allegra has forcefully indicated, a conspicuous defence of national cultural heritage targeted at hearts as well as minds had repeatedly baulked the dissemination of characteristic Enlightenment premises regarding the ordering of society, the workings of the individual psyche, or indeed regarding any form of philosophical speculation or aesthetic inclination. The end result was a marked refusal to countenance any of what the Italian critic designates the myths of our own time: in other words, the secular, rationalistic and democratic intellectual promptings that we associate with the modern age.[5] The reactionary struggle is itself articulated, he asserts, according to a conception of the world that denies modernity, and is aided and abetted by theories of art and literature that project and contain a justificatory reappraisal of Spain's distinctive historical culture. He depicts then a conscious return to that cultural legacy which the Enlightenment, in the shape of its French master practitioners and their Spanish adherents, had scorned and depreciated, to a tradition that, as he put it, had been placed in the dock and subjected to the arrogant and cynical interrogation of the *Encyclopédie*.[6]

The *casticista* campaign of cultural reclamation detailed by Allegra, as much as the strategies of historical legitimation highlighted by Vila Selma, broadly coincide in time and space, as the latter acknowledges, with Romanticism in its multifarious literary, philosophical and artistic forms.[7] We are consequently led to a further source of conflicting and conflictive interpretation, to what Iris M. Zavala, with particular reference to Spain, describes as a cultural production acutely susceptible to 'interpretaciones antagónicas' [antagonistic interpretations]; Romanticism figures in Spanish literary history, she observes, beneath the sign of the paradox.[8] We might indeed postulate, therefore, a second, superimposed, ideological dimension, one projected backwards from our own day upon the work of the Romantics themselves. Leonardo Romero, within the overview contained in his *Panorama crítico del romanticismo español*, makes what is a fundamental connection; referring to those 'componentes ideológicos' [ideological components] present in any and every scrutiny of the recent past, he contends that where Romanticism is concerned they go so far as to constitute a diagnostic test of the researcher's own affiliations.[9] Philip Silver, in his own revisionary thesis, stresses that perspectives on Spanish Romanticism have long been ideologically charged, and specifies one significant misreading: that of modern critics who, failing to find Spain's essentially conservative, *moderado*-led Romanticism to their liking and acutely conscious of the political events of their own day, 'imagined a liberal political and literary romanticism that had not in fact been there'. What they failed to take duly into account, he continues, was the series of interrelationships between historical Romanticism, the continuing bourgeois revolution of their own day, and the Romantic historiography of the period between 1840 and 1870, which went a long way towards defining our own present view of both mediaeval and modern Spanish history.[10]

Silver's candid reference to a 'substantial, politically interested, albeit conservative' Romanticism reinforces, from a different methodological angle, the thesis I put forward in my earlier polemical study of the reception of Romantic aesthetics in Spain.[11] Part of the original research for that book, but a component part that swiftly outgrew the dimensions that might have been assigned to it within the published volume, concerned the interpretation of history enunciated by Spanish intellectuals of the Romantic period, and particularly in the decade of the 1840s, when historical study possessed to a marked degree the kind of ideological dimension identified and defined by Hayden White. As Inman Fox declares in another recent assessment of nineteenth-century intellectual history, the construction of Spain's national cultural identity was essentially historico-political in nature; he subsequently cautions that such constructs are not always concerned with the elucidation of truth but more often contain the mythification or outright falsification of given moments in history.[12]

One problem with Inman Fox's assessment, as I see it, is his exclusion from discussion of those general histories of Spain published in the 1840s, which not only antedate but consistently anticipate, most crucially in their theological coordinates, the construction of national identity he feels to have been embarked upon from the mid-century. Concomitant with literary Romanticism and possessing many profound points of contact with it, the historical outlook of the period prior to 1850 is best characterized by what Ana-Sofía Pérez-Bustamante Mourier calls the unqualifiedly conservative slant taken by forms of *casticismo* from the writings of the political and religious reactionaries of the late eighteenth century and after, a cultural nationalism implanted from the higher intellectual echelons of Spanish society but thriving among the population at large as a result of its encapsulation of an instinctively felt and intimately desired populism.[13] Within a period she defines as the germination of modernity, Pérez-Bustamante Mourier specifies a retrenched and defiant cultivation of *lo castizo* at an historical moment when not just popular imaginative identity but also an entire 'sistema integralista nacional' [integrationist national system] was perceived to be under serious threat.[14]

Just how closely these comments dovetail not just with my own analysis of Spanish Romantic literary theory and criticism and with Philip Silver's depiction of a triumphant historical Romanticism, but also, much more specifically, with the dominant interpretative tenor of Romantic historiography, will become increasingly clear as the wider picture I am constructing here begins to emerge. Deserving of notice at this stage, as a signally clear portent of the intellectual context in which my study will be immersed, is Pérez-Bustamante Mourier's assertion that such populist affirmations of a distinctive national identity are especially marked in moments of historical crisis or uncertain transition, at those critical junctures when 'fuerzas cohesionadoras' [cohesive forces] are invoked in the face of revolutionary encroachment. In this way, she continues, the consciously intellectual culture of the Enlightenment generates a broad-based conscious reaction in which *lo castizo* constitutes a relentless and uncompromising attack upon those allegedly subversive ideas that threaten to corrode the prevailing integrationist model. *Casticismo* is, then, within Pérez-Bustamante Mourier's terms, a movement in defence of the national past corresponding to a *Volksgeist*-dominated Romanticism, one that re-fashions popular tradition in a manner that is essentialist and metaphysical in its emphases.[15] Similarly, much of nineteenth-century intellectual history is characterized by the calculated manipulation of *casticista* prescriptions by the forces of ideological reaction.[16]

It goes without saying, therefore, that I shall be especially concerned, like Hayden White, with those histories that contain, as well as data, 'theoretical concepts for "explaining" these data, and a narrative structure for their presentation as an icon of sets of events presumed to have occurred in times past'.[17] Antonio Gil y Zárate, in embarking upon an expansive introduction to modern history ('modern', as the Romantic period understood it, as referring to the entire period from the fall of the Roman Empire), professed his task to lie in probing the causes of events and the relationships between them, and to uncover, in a word, their interdependence.[18] As the cultural historian José Amador de los Ríos put it in 1845, the nineteenth-century mind had imprinted upon the study of history the hallmark of philosophy; it was prompted to investigate earlier processes of both cause and effect, in order not just to avoid any repetition of deleterious examples of the former but also to extract salutary lessons from an intimation of the latter.[19] Historical writing thus involved a search for what the philosopher and historian Tomás García Luna, writing in 1847, called the intimate correspondence between apparently unconnected events and for a founding principle by which to explain them, a search that he felt had been made possible by Vico's *Scienza nuova*.[20] Spanish Romantic historiography, to cite Emilio Castelar's Ateneo lectures of 1858, much more than a narrative of events comes to be an exposition of a systematic philosophy in which 'los hechos vienen a ser la forma de las ideas' [factual events become the formal expression of ideas], a system defined by 'leyes incontestables' [unanswerable laws];[21] it therefore subscribes, within Hayden White's conceptual pattern, to the 'Organicist' mode of historical writing that is characterized by transcendent aspiration.

Again like White, but with more specific application to Spain, within rather less ample theoretical referents, and with rather closer regard to the anatomy of a single intellectual generation, I aim to probe that level of consciousness on which a writer chooses such conceptual strategies by which to explain or represent history.[22] It is a task not heretofore undertaken with reference to the period of Spanish Romanticism proper: Manuel Moreno Alonso's panoramic *Historiografía romántica española* is, as its sub-title implies, conceived as a broad introduction to the general tenor of nineteenth-century historical study, and does not include within its professed remit any close analysis of the kind of ideological dimension I have begun to identify here;[23] Inman Fox, meanwhile, elects end-dates that preclude the integration of Romantic historiography into an intellectual focus that is otherwise much nearer to my own. The lack of a thoroughgoing study, with specific reference to Spain, of the Romantic historical imagination is all the more striking when we bear in mind that historical thinking in the Romantic period is acutely marked by what White describes as the degree of theoretical self-consciousness with which historians researched the past and subsequently constructed their narrative accounts of events.[24] We are dealing, after all, with decades that saw the rigorous modern implantation within Spain of the philosophy of history as a key intellectual and theological concern; those historical studies that will form the bedrock of my thesis are ones in which, again in White's terms, 'the element of conceptual construct is brought to the fore, explicitly set forth, and systematically defended, with the data used primarily for purposes of illustration or exemplification'.[25]

For the sake of clarity and with a view to the construction of an original thesis with appropriate and transparent connections, I have isolated six principal areas of investigation. Firstly, I deal with the intellectual parameters of the Romantic 'mediaeval revival', a broad artistic phenomenon that, within Spain, is a prevalent factor both quantitatively and in terms of its ideological content. An idealized view of the Middle Ages, particularly the Spanish Middle Ages, imaginatively recalled as a stable and reassuring moral universe via specifiable and ideologically significant emphases that stem directly from the dominant Schlegelian pattern, provides, more than any other area of historical inquiry, the fundamentals of the Spanish Romantic response to the past. Chapters two and three are then concerned with conflicting and politically laden sequential interpretations of history. Guizot's 'elementary' and progressive formula, together with Vico's cyclical and providentialist account, with their respective ideological labels firmly attached, represent the battleground upon which politically interested interpretations of history struggle for intellectual supremacy. The prevalent reliance upon Vico's pattern as a discourse of order and authority reveals much of the psychological intimacy of the intellectual moment, and anticipates a substantial part of the language and rhetoric of the dominant historical perspective on the recent past. Assessments of the contemporary moment, in the wake of the perceived collapse of Enlightenment premises, the cataclysm of the French Revolution and the uncertainties of Spain's turbulent nineteenth century, are predicated upon a desired return to established scales of value and an unconditional adherence to Catholic tradition, and, accordingly, upon a trenchantly conservative, *casticista* historical reading that draws much of its inspiration from the earlier religious reactionaries and their committedly Manichaean narrative of history. Chapter four examines the rejection of Enlightenment formulae and the primitive fear of an absent but pyschologically potent Revolution, while the following chapter moves on to consider historical diagnoses of nineteenth-century reality within the prism of the 'Two Spains' and to postulate the prevailing emphases of the *década moderada*. Chapter six then appraises the *casticista* credentials of Romantic literary history, focusing upon its acute reiteration of the kind of cultural nationalism contained in Schlegelian Romantic theory and upon its exclusion from its chosen canon of both neo-Classical formalism and radical, principally French, manifestations of Romanticism. The concluding chapter seeks to relocate Romantic thought within Spanish intellectual history by cementing its connections both with earlier reactionary formulae and the later historical prescriptions of the distinguished cultural historian Marcelino Menéndez Pelayo. It aims also to chart the consecutive processes of historical transference, whereby successive generations relate the prevailing thought and response of their own age to those of their historical predecessors. Such transferential readings constitute the most fundamental continuity within modern Spanish history.

In the broadest terms, what I have sought to do is to provide a convincing explication of Spain's Romantic historical imagination and its increasingly conservative drift in the twenty or so years preceding and immediately following the mid-century. For, as is now widely acknowledged, the triumph of a liberal Romanticism after 1833 was precarious and short-lived: Vila Selma's assertion of the 'coincidencia triunfante' [triumphant coincidence] of literary Romanticism and political liberalism throughout western Europe, as a result of which those more conservative forms of Romanticism surrendered both popularity and imaginative potential,[26] like so many similar proclamations delivered within the last thirty years, is deceptive and unreliable, and effectively discards not just the majority of the Spanish movement's creative output but also, and most crucially in the present context, the apprehension of the relationship between past and present upon which that output was largely founded.[27] Only a thoroughgoing consciousness of the extent and significance of diverse forms of *casticismo* enables us to reconcile the ultimate direction of literary Romanticism in Spain with its conflictive historical moment and with the interpretative tenor of contemporary assessments of the past.

Notes to the Introduction

1. *Metahistory: The Historical Imagination in Nineteenth-Century Europe* (Baltimore, 1973), p. 46.
2. *Metahistory*, p. 13.
3. *Metahistory*, p. 22.
4. See Vila Selma's introduction to his annotated edition of the *Ensayo sobre el catolicismo, el liberalismo y el socialismo* (Madrid, 1978), pp. 13–14.
5. *La viña y los surcos. las ideas literarias en España del XVIII al XIX* (Seville, 1980), p. 13.
6. *La viña y los surcos*, pp. 13–14.
7. Donoso Cortés, *Ensayo*, 'Introducción', p. 13.
8. *Romanticismo y realismo. Primer suplemento*, Historia crítica de la literatura española, ed. by Francisco Rico, 5.1 (Barcelona, 1994), p. 25.
9. *Panorama crítico del romanticismo español* (Madrid, 1994), p. 74.
10. *Ruin and Restitution: Reinterpreting Romanticism in Spain* (Liverpool, 1997), p. xiii.
11. *Spanish Romantic Literary Theory and Criticism* (Cambridge, 1992); it was followed by a Spanish version, *Teoría y crítica del romanticismo español* (Cambridge, 1995).
12. *La invención de España: nacionalismo liberal e identidad nacional* (Madrid, 1997), pp. 12–14.
13. 'Cultura popular, cultura intelectual y casticismo', in *Casticismo y literatura en España* ed. by Ana-Sofía Pérez Bustamante Mourier and Alberto Romero Ferrer (Cadiz, 1992), pp. 125–62 (148–49).
14. 'Cultura popular, cultura intelectual y casticismo', p. 150.
15. 'Cultura popular, cultura intelectual y casticismo', pp. 150–51.
16. 'Cultura popular, cultura intelectual y casticismo', p. 152.
17. *Metahistory*, p. ix.
18. *Introducción a la historia moderna; o, Examen de los diferentes elementos que han entrado a constituir la civilización de los actuales pueblos europeos. Lecciones dadas en el Liceo Artístico y Literario de Madrid* (Madrid, 1841), p. 7.
19. 'Estudios históricos: el rey don Pedro', *El Laberinto*, 2 (1845), 150–51 (p. 150).
20. '¿Cuál es el provecho que puede reportarse de las investigaciones históricas acerca de Grecia y Roma? ¿Por qué es reciente la filosofía de la historia?', *Revista Científica y Literaria*, 1 (1847), 378–82 (p. 381). García Luna was an influential figure in Spanish philosophical circles whose *Manual de historia de la filosofía* was to become a textbook at almost every national university.
21. *La civilización en los cinco primeros siglos del cristianismo. Lecciones pronunciadas en el Ateneo de Madrid*, 3 vols (Madrid, 1858), III, 55.
22. *Metahistory*, p. x.
23. Manuel Moreno Alonso, *Historiografía romántica española: introducción al estudio de la historia en el siglo XIX* (Seville, 1979). Moreno Alonso's study, together with Allegra's *La viña y los surcos* and Javier Herrero's *Los orígenes del pensamiento reaccionario español*, has nevertheless proved an invaluable documentary source and remains an excellent point of departure for the specialist.

24. *Metahistory*, p. 39.
25. *Metahistory*, pp. 427–28.
26. Donoso Cortés, *Ensayo*, 'Introducción', pp. 16–17. Only thus can he categorically state at the outset that 'Donoso jamás fue romántico' [Donoso was never a Romantic] (9), an imprudently sweeping declaration that is at odds with a great deal of the textual evidence.
27. A perspective comparable to that adduced by Vila Selma can be found, for example, in Susan Kirkpatrick, 'Spanish Romanticism', in *Romanticism in National Context*, ed. by Roy Porter and Mikuláš Teich (Cambridge, 1988), pp. 260–83. Kirkpatrick attempts to subordinate all of the material evidence to a formulaic Marxist definition, programmatically accounting for the historical development of Spanish Romanticism — as much the uncertainty of its hold as its precisely fixed heyday and its alleged attenuation after 1843 — with reference to 'the erratic progress of Spain's liberal revolution'(pp. 262–66).

CHAPTER 1

The Meaning of the Mediaeval Revival

The most prominent feature of Romanticism's imaginative vision of the historical past, what John B. Halsted has called the historicizing of Europeans' thought, was unquestionably the revival of creative and intellectual interest in the Middle Ages; Halsted himself highlighted the Gothic revival in art and architecture, the historical view of their own work expressed by the German Romantic theorists, and their dating of the beginnings of the modern era to the end of the Roman Empire.[1] All of these, but perhaps most pointedly in the present context the last, reveal how Romantic historicism provided nineteenth-century Europe with an entirely new perspective on the past. Voltaire and Enlightenment historians generally had mapped out, in their respective overviews of historical development, what amounted to a sequence of peaks and troughs, of brilliant civilizations — signally Classical antiquity and the European Renaissance — alternating with more extended periods of dissolution and savagery. Romantic writers, on the other hand, preferred to see the period between the fall of Rome and the Renaissance not as a barbaric Dark Ages but as an historical epoch superior in every sense to the Classical age, particularly in its celebration of a transcendent religion and in its nurturing of the elevated values of the chivalric ideal. This 'mediaeval revival', or cultural reclaiming of the Middle Ages as a period of extraordinary and unsurpassed human dynamism and sublimity, came to be a broad-based and pervasive influence affecting many diverse aspects of art and life. Mediaevalism in all areas of creative art and study acquired overtly sentimental and elegiac terms as a lament for a more noble past, one imaginatively endowed with a legendary or even supernatural mystique that allowed it to transcend what now came to be seen as the brutalizing prescriptions of philosophical rationalism and rampant materialism. Chateaubriand epitomized the imaginative effect of a Gothic church by stating that as one contemplated it 'L'ancienne France semblait revivre' [the France of old seemed to come back to life],[2] while Jules Michelet memorably evoked his researches in the Archives du Royaume in recounting that 'Je ne tardai pas à m'apercevoir dans le silence apparent de ces galeries, qu'il y avait un mouvement, un murmure qui n'était pas de la mort [...] Tous vivaient et parlaient' [It did not take me long to perceive that in the apparent silence of those galleries there was a movement, a murmuring that was not of death [...] Everything lived and spoke].[3]

Spain was no exception to this Romantic preference for the Middle Ages. What effectively began with the espousal and dissemination, by Johann Nikolaus Böhl von Faber, Agustín Durán, and others, of the mediaevalizing tenets of Schlegelian

Romantic theory became further popularized with the translation and imitation of the works of Walter Scott.[4] The trend, extended and accentuated after the Romantic 'explosion' of 1834–37, saw historical novels and dramas, verse narrative *leyendas*, and prose *cuentos*, all conspire to produce a literary ferment that extended to many other areas of writing. Magazines and periodicals carried numerous commentaries on characters and episodes from national history, from folkloric and religious traditions, and from earlier periods of Spanish literature, while potted accounts of the best examples of native architecture, religious and secular, normally accompanied by reference to famous events connected with each of them, as well as far more extensive projects such as Parcerisa and Piferrer's *Recuerdos y bellezas de España*, furnish untold evidence of this striking popular interest in the national past. In its first five weeks of publication, Mesonero Romanos's *Semanario Pintoresco Español*, which was to run under a series of editors from 1836 to 1857, carried features on San Lorenzo del Escorial, Fernán González, Westminster Abbey (a piece written by Mesonero himself under the heading 'Abadía de Westminster'), the Alcázar de Segovia, the Palacio de Buenavista and Gonzalo de Córdoba.[5]

In intellectual terms, a return to the Middle Ages became, as Alice Chandler cogently expressed it, a way of reorganizing humanity into a closely knit and organically harmonious set of structures that could engage emotions and loyalties with a wealth of traditions and customs.[6] As modern Europe faced a chaotic period of radical social upheaval and political instability (and Spain was certainly no exception here) the Middle Ages were increasingly idealized and viewed nostalgically as a desirable alternative to the traumas of recent experience. As I have shown elsewhere, a return to the literary traditions of the national past was consistently regarded by Spanish Romantic critics as a means of inspiring broader collective improvement.[7] This 'regenerationist' view of national literary tradition had proved a characteristic feature of the new sensibility as expressed by the German theorists so influential in determining the course of Romanticism in Spain. Moreover, as Siegbert Prawer has shrewdly reminded us, that new sensibility went hand in hand with endeavours to make history serve a purpose different from any envisaged by the Enlightenment; both art and history were perceived as enabling elements in the regenerative process, holding up to the present images of an idealized past that might help to shape future development.[8] At a period of crisis intensified by the far-reaching breakdown of religious beliefs and established values for which the Enlightenment was increasingly held responsible, the harmonious and unitary belief-system and cultural patterns of the mediaeval period began not just wistfully to be eulogized and imaginatively to be evoked but ideologically to be reasserted. The vogue enjoyed by things mediaeval, that is the intrinsically sentimental appeal of a vague romantic attachment, was thus no more than a surface image; once we scratch that surface, we become aware of much more fundamental intellectual processes at work.

Hayden White identifies as common denominators of historical consciousness in the first half of the nineteenth century an antipathy for Enlightenment rationalism and 'a sympathy for those aspects of both history and humanity which the Enlighteners had viewed with scorn or condescension'.[9] The aspirations of historical study, he goes so far as to claim, are best characterized 'in terms of what it objected to in its eighteenth-century predecessors', most specifically the essential irony of their outlook and the scepticism of their cultural reflection.[10] Manuel Moreno Alonso, whose broad introduction to nineteenth-century Spanish historiography remains the best starting point for any specialized scrutiny, similarly underlines as one of the salient trends of the Romantic period its harsh criticism of the historical studies produced by the preceding generation, which, it alleged, had neither taken the Middle Ages properly into account nor ascribed to that period its true worth.[11] The point is amply borne out by any number of sources; as just one example Fermín Gonzalo Morón, in the introduction to what began as a series of lectures delivered in Valencia and Madrid in 1840 and 1841 and subsequently became one of the most extensive general histories of Spain to be written in the 1840s, bemoaned the indifference and general disdain that 'los filósofos del siglo XVIII' [eighteenth-century philosophers] had, with few exceptions, bestowed upon historical study. Voltaire in particular he decried, claiming that his appraisal of the feudal system, of chivalry, and of the entire political order of mediaeval Europe, had been 'casi siempre superficial y muchas veces inexacta y falsa' [virtually always superficial and often false and inaccurate].[12] At much the same time, Antonio Gil y Zárate was asserting that until the end of the previous century modern Europe had laboured under the yoke of 'los recuerdos antiguos' [memories of ancient times]; the models of Classical antiquity, he argued, had dominated artistic and literary production as they had public institutions, and had been seen to represent exclusive standards of perfection, so much so that eighteenth-century reformers, in their desire to promote civil liberties, had, regrettably, used the examples of 'famosas repúblicas' [famous republics] that were 'nada aplicables al estado actual de las sociedades' [by no means applicable to the current state of human societies].[13] In referring to 'las dos grandes divisiones que constituyen la historia universal' [the two great component parts that together make world history], he regretted the fact that Europe in the modern age had not until recent years been accorded the attention nor the privileged position it undoubtedly merited; in particular, he specified the relative neglect in historiography of the period following the collapse of the Roman Empire, an historical age that had remained largely unknown, set aside as merely 'siglos de ignorancia y barbarie' [centuries of ignorance and barbarism]. It had nonetheless proved, he now contended, the cradle of the modern nation-states of Europe and the birthplace of contemporary institutions; it had passed on to later times the cultural legacy of language and artistic heritage, while the noble families of modern Europe all claimed descent from 'nuestra edad heroica' [our heroic age]. In the midst of that 'caos informe' [shapeless chaos], he continued, resided the germ of a new order of things, of 'una nueva civilización de todo punto superior a la civilización antigua, y más digna de la naturaleza divina del hombre' [a new civilization superior in every respect to that of the ancients and more worthy of man's divine nature].[14]

Rafael Mitjana, writing in 1845, agreed with Gonzalo Morón and Gil y Zárate that the previous age had not accorded the mediaeval period its due. He credited more recent scholarly investigation into the cultural history of the Middle Ages with having cast new light on that period, with the result that far from being the primitive and barbarous era that it was often casually labelled, the twelfth and thirteenth centuries in particular had outshone the most brilliant ages in all of those areas of knowledge where human dignity and idealism are customarily most evident.[15] The art historian José Caveda, writing later in the decade, would view the whole issue in similar terms. In describing the inspiration of thinkers and creative writers of the Enlightenment, he observed that by comparison with the magnificent artistic contribution of the Classical world, that of the Middle Ages seemed to them lacking in worth and less deserving of their attention, although it was from the latter period that were derived 'las modernas sociedades, y su religión, y sus leyes, y su nacionalidad y sus costumbres' [modern societies, their religion, their laws, and their diverse nationhood and social custom]; this misreading he felt to be a fatal error.[16] As he saw it, then, 'las exigencias del clasicismo y el orgullo enciclopédico' [the demands of Classicism and the vanity of the *Encyclopédie*] had led to a deviation from historical truth, which had been lost from sight. He further explained his interpretation of events by asserting that the eighteenth century had placed undue trust in 'vanas teorías' [vacuous theories], and had allowed itself to be influenced more by what he labels 'escepticismo intolerante de la época' [the intolerant scepticism of that age] than by 'las tradiciones y venerables recuerdos de nuestros padres' [the traditions and venerable reminders of our forebears].[17] An ostensible result of this erroneous perspective had thus been, he went on, that any one of his eighteenth-century predecessors, seduced by the dogmas professed by 'los preceptistas' [preceptists], would necessarily have failed to comprehend mediaeval architecture and would accordingly have perceived examples of it as no more than the inspiration of uncultured and primitive peoples.[18] Eventually, however, had come the historical opportunity to put an end to this exclusivist Classicism; only then and for the first time had men of learning begun seriously to examine a Middle Ages that had previously lain in darkness and that was now, instead and by contrast, 'enaltecida con sus tradiciones, con la importancia de sus colosales empresas, con sus castillos góticos y espléndidos torneos, con el espíritu caballeresco de sus héroes y paladines, con sus leyendas misteriosas y sus trovas' [set on high with all of its traditions, with the greatness of its colossal undertakings, with its Gothic castles and splendid tourneys, with the knightly spirit of its heroes and its paladins, with its mysterious legends and the poetry of its troubadours].[19]

Caveda's text may be said to contain all of those structural dichotomies that were so forcefully to characterize the Romantic historical imagination in Spain. On the one hand, the historical overview predominant at the time of the Enlightenment is disparaged wholesale as a product of that intellectual arrogance typically pertaining to adherents of the *Encyclopédie*, as a set of spurious notions prompted by the intolerant scepticism of preceptists blinded by their own dogma, something that had distorted and misled in a perversion of historical truth. On the other, we find imaginatively exalted the sacred traditions of a God-fearing society underpinned by stable and enduring values, an historical age that had inspired humanity with the sublimity of its magnificent deeds and with the idealism of its chivalric enthusiasm. Caveda's insistence upon the mediaeval origins of 'religión', 'leyes', 'nacionalidad' and 'costumbres', meanwhile, provides an intimation of the *casticista* ideological prism that was to prove the hallmark of Romantic conceptions of early Spanish history.

José Amador de los Ríos, by 1850 an established academic at the University of Madrid, was as scathing as any of his colleagues when it came to the alleged prejudices of Enlightenment historians against the Middle Ages. The *Ilustración* [the Enlightenment] had, in his view, unjustly maligned with the repulsive and unjustifiable label of 'barbaric' everything that was great, everything that was beautiful and everything that was sublime in the art and literature of the mediaeval era. He now went so far as to depict a form of historical conspiracy in which the efforts of rhetoricians, artists and poets had been harnessed in a calculated attempt to consign a set of precious but undervalued treasures to historical oblivion.[20] The Enlightenment idea of a 'Dark Ages', he insisted, was belied by the evidence (he singled out here the sublimity of mediaeval cathedrals), and he once again imputed to eighteenth-century cultural historians a blind Classicist prejudice: had it not been ludicrous to expect that feudal barons, heroic crusader knights and the Spanish warriors of the Reconquest should have felt and acted like Greek and Roman heroes? Since the two ages could not possibly have been united in their expression of feeling, in their systems of belief, and in their political and civil institutions, why had historical commentators been unable duly to appreciate the imaginative depiction of these great warriors 'con su verdadera fisonomía, con su brillante colorido?' [with their true features, in their brillant colouring].[21]

   As irresistibly suggested by a number of the above citations, Romantic historians in Spain as elsewhere in Europe did not wish merely to redress the perceived imbalance between the respective views of Classical antiquity and the mediaeval period that had previously obtained. It became a systematic part of their procedure to underscore the superiority of the Christian Middle Ages over the pagan societies of Greece and Rome. As Gil y Zárate expressed it, the last days of Rome were ones in which a 'civilización estacionaria' [static civilization] was sliding inexorably into barbarism; at such a moment it was indispensable that 'nuevos elementos' [fresh elements] breathe new life into an expiring society that had lost all of its vitality and vigour. These new elements of civilization were provided, he declared, firstly by the nature of the Christian faith and secondly by 'las instituciones germánicas' [the Germanic institutions] — a characteristic contemporary reference to the social organization of the tribes of northern Europe — 'que obraron en la caduca sociedad romana una revolución completa' [which worked an utter revolution upon the decaying society of Rome].[22] Gil y Zárate's account, like so many others written during the period in question, assumes something of a programmatic quality in asserting that, with the preponderance of Christianity, 'una religión espiritual reemplazaba a otra que se fundaba en el materialismo; sentimientos y deseos de nueva especie agitaban poderosamente los ánimos, y les comunicaban un extraordinario impulso' [a spiritual religion was now replacing one that been founded on materialism; feelings and aspirations of a new kind were working feverishly upon hearts and minds and lending to them an extraordinary urgency]. Christianity therefore attained, in Gil y Zárate's lectures as in those much earlier ones delivered in Vienna by A. W. Schlegel, the pre-eminent status of 'regenerador del mundo antiguo y creador de otro mundo nuevo' [regenerator of the ancient world and creator of a new and different one].[23] This essential dualism is maintained as the Spanish writer subsequently observes that since Classical antiquity had depicted only 'el hombre exterior' [outer man], it contained no true conception of the spiritual nature of the inner man, 'ni esa lucha de las dos naturalezas del hombre que ha sido introducida por el cristianismo, y que ha arrojado tanta variedad en las literaturas modernas' [nor that struggle in mankind's dual nature that had been brought into being by Christianity and which had sown such variety in modern literatures].[24] Gil y Zárate is again close to the first of A. W. Schlegel's Vienna lectures, where the German theorist stipulated that without both a conscious and unconscious religion, man would be a mere surface with no internal substance. The implications of this analogy, both for the emphases commonly found in Romantic accounts of the past and for contemporary judgements of broader historiographical method, are legion: the perceived superficiality not just of the civilizations of Classical antiquity but also of Enlightenment history and indeed of any predominantly rationalistic historical scrutiny was to prove a systematic and ideologically weighted feature of the Romantic historical imagination as expressed in Spain.

Gonzalo Morón, for example, would himself adduce a similar perspective while introducing an extremity of language not found in Gil y Zárate's text, vehemently asserting that 'Todo era sensual, grosero y material en la sociedad pagana, y el cristianismo vino a restablecer el espíritu sobre el imperio de la materia' [In pagan society everything belonged to the gross materialism of the senses, and Christianity came to restore what is spiritual in displacing the sovereignty of matter].[25] The former's historical narrative in fact contains a calculatedly scriptural dimension; in the fall of the Roman Empire, the ancient world is seen to meet its inevitable destiny, 'condenado a desaparecer de una tierra que mancha con sus crímenes, y un nuevo diluvio debe sumergir a la raza envilecida y degradada' [condemned to vanish from an earth that it had stained with its crimes, and a new Flood must submerge a vile and degraded race of men]. The events evoked are then programmatically ordered within an overtly Providential design: 'Esta misión se cumple por la irrupción de los Bárbaros, segundo hecho que con el cristianismo constituye la civilización moderna' [This mission was accomplished by the invasion of the barbarian tribes, the second factor which, together with Christianity, constitutes our modern civilization].[26] Eugenio de Tapia, whose four-volume general history of Spain appeared in 1840, a year earlier than the first volumes of Gonzalo Morón's even more weighty project, was similarly dismissive of the pagan religion of Classical times, contemptuously categorizing it as a purely sensual religion whose objects of adoration were adulterous gods and fair prostitutes. The 'buenos filósofos' [good philosophers] of antiquity (and, unsurprisingly, he singles out the transcendent emphases of Plato for special praise under this heading) had themselves desired, stated Tapia, a belief-system 'más conforme a la razón y a los principios de la sana moral' [more commensurate with reason and with the principles of a healthy morality].[27] This process of evaluation, in which the worship of the gods and goddesses of the mythological canon figured as intrinsically inferior to the metaphysical parameters of the later Christian tenets of faith, conditioned the overwhelming bulk of contemporary historical judgements. As Gervasio Gironella put it in 1839, with the sack of Rome had come the historical collapse of 'el antiguo mundo, la idolatría, la religión de la materia' [the ancient world, idolatry, the worship of matter]; in their stead Europe would see a score of disparate nations, barbarous in material terms but true heirs to the future. In his subsequent words we again note how a single defining principle, the unprecedented spirituality of the Christian credo, in inculcating a new and heightened sense of the sacred and its pre-eminence over the profane, made this later age immeasurably superior in all other senses:

> Una religión divina, con su cruz, signo de libertad y de victoria, reemplazará al viejo culto del capitolio; y después, según los profundos designios del Criador, se levantará del seno de la barbarie un estado social mejor que cuanto había podido presumir a soñar la humana filosofía.

> [A divine religion, with its cross, the symbol of freedom and victory, was to replace the ancient shrine upon the Capitoline hill; and then, according to the mysterious designs of the Creator, there was to be raised out of the very bosom of barbarism a society superior to anything that the human mind had been able to conceive in all of its philosophy.]

If Voltaire had perceived the Middle Ages as an extended 'historia bárbara de pueblos bárbaros, que no se volvieron mejores por haberse hecho cristianos' [barbaric history of barbaric folk, of peoples who became no better for becoming Christian], then he could only disagree.[28] Pedro de Madrazo, writing several years later in the magazine *El Renacimiento*, also made this kind of programmatic distinction. In his terms:

> El paganismo, glorificando la forma, ennobleció la materia, y produjo la mayor belleza posible en el orden de las ideas finitas; la edad media, glorificando el espíritu, extenuó la materia destruyendo la morbidez sensual de sus contornos, y produjo la más completa enseñanza posible en el orden de las ideas infinitas.

> [Paganism, in glorifying form ennobled matter, and produced the greatest possible beauty in the order of the finite; the Middle Ages, in glorifying spirit, exhausted matter by destroying its morbidly sensual outlines, and produced the most complete model of instruction possible in the order of the infinite].[29]

While many other passages cited provide reminiscences of the general prescriptive tenor of A.W. Schlegel's framework, Madrazo's words are little more than a re-casting of comments found in the first of the Vienna lectures.[30]

Such was the prevailing mood that Gonzalo Morón, in writing his 1844 *Ensayo sobre las sociedades antiguas y modernas*, could go so far as to claim that the societies of Classical antiquity had possessed, in their totality, 'un carácter mezquino y restrictivo' [a mean and reductive nature], that it had been a deplorable time when 'falsas y groseras ideas dominaban al mundo' [false and coarse ideas dominated the world]; only with the coming of Christianity, he insisted, had there been implanted 'nueva moral, nuevo orden político, nuevos pueblos, y distintos hombres' [a new morality, a new political order, new peoples, and a very different set of men].[31] In putting an end to pagan society, Gonzalo Morón here continued in phrasing reminiscent of François Guizot, the barbarian tribes and the Christian ideal had asserted themselves as 'los elementos constitutivos de la moderna' [the constitutive elements of modern society]. More than that: 'en las costumbres de los primeros se hallaban los gérmenes de aquellos sentimientos, que enlazados después con los religiosos, debían dar un carácter tan poético y sublime a los tiempos feudales y caballerescos' [in the social customs of the former could be found the seed of those feelings which, afterwards bound together with religious feelings, had eventually to lend such a poetic and sublime nature to the feudal and chivalric age].[32] Given the Spanish writer's admiration for A. W. Schlegel,[33] it is perhaps not coincidental that he echoes premises contained in the first of the Vienna lectures: after Christianity, the German theorist had stressed, the character of modern Europe had been shaped from the beginning of the Middle Ages by the race of northern conquerors, while chivalry had then originated in the conjunction of their rough but honest heroism with the sentiments of a spiritual religion. Of some interest in the present context, meanwhile, is that Gonzalo Morón should make further application of the systematic evaluatory distinction between sensual and transcendent, matter and spirit, in asserting that the decay and dissolution suffered by Europe between the fifth century and the eighth were not of a moral kind but merely of a material one.[34]

Moreno Alonso indicates, then, with some justification, that the Middle Ages emerge from the work of Spanish historians of the Romantic period as a negation of Classical antiquity and as the effective point of departure of modern history: modern, as the texts I have cited clearly reveal, understood as referring to the Christian civilization which arose from the ashes of the Roman Empire but which remained imperfectly formed until several centuries later. The status of the mediaeval period as a determinant of modern civilization, not duly recognized by the Enlightenment, accounted for, in Moreno Alonso's words, 'su *trascendencia* en cuanto a la mentalidad romántica' [its *transcendent* status in the Romantic mind], and made it the era most highly favoured by Romantic historians.[35] The term I have chosen to stress is a particularly apt one in its encapsulation of the attractions afforded by the Middle Ages not just on a sentimental level but on a more intellectually rigorous epistemo-logical plane.

One of those numerous writers favouring the Middle Ages was Fernando de Madrazo, who again took a swipe at Enlightenment France in declaring his preference. It had often been claimed by eighteenth-century historians, and even by some commentators at the beginning of the present century, he stated, that the invasion of the barbarian tribes had been 'un torrente devastador' [a torrent of devastation] which, in sweeping away all vestiges of the civilization of ancient Rome, shrouded the whole of Europe in a fearful chaos; laws, literature, monuments, fine art, everything had perished in a communal shipwreck. So erroneous a judgement he himself regarded as no more than a direct consequence of 'las teorías filosóficas a la sazón sustentadas' [the philosophical notions which were then commonly professed]; Classical civilization, in his view, had itself been incomplete 'por no constar sino de un elemento' [since it had possessed but a single element]. With the historical genius of Charlemagne, on the other hand, he felt that the mediaeval period had compensated for this lack, since it added to the Classical conception of citizenship 'otra consideración de más elevada esfera, origen de toda acción generosa, fuente del heroísmo y del más noble enajenamiento' [a different and more elevated factor, the origin of every generous action, the source of all heroism and of the most noble transcendent feeling]. The reference to transcendent ennobling processes contained in the terms is entirely representative of the preferred Romantic evocation; this apprehension is reinforced when Madrazo depicts the chivalric ideal as projecting a sense of personal honour unknown to the societies of antiquity.[36] Indeed he makes an even more direct historical connection in claiming that, with a new conception of loyalty, spiritual love for woman and personal honour, the allegedly barbarian invasion of the Roman world had produced a new dawn: 'la aurora de la radiante caballería que iba a ser la señora del universo' [the dawning of that brilliant world of chivalry that was to be sovereign lady of all].[37] If these words encapsulate the extraordinary Romantic idealization of the Middle Ages, such a process of idealization was just one expression of much more fundamental underlying ideological concerns. Some of the essential connections begin to emerge when we consider, for example, Rafael Mitjana's profession of the strongest conviction that the barbarian tribes, and in Spain the Visigoths, significantly affected the temperament of entire peoples, preparing the ground for their reception and assimilation of the sublime imaginative life of the northern peoples; on this account, he went on, Spain's 'genuina literatura' [authentic literature] had much more in common with that of England and Germany than with that produced by the Mediterranean cultures of ancient Greece and Rome or modern Italy and France.[38]

His last comment inevitably leads us back to the Schlegelian Romantic assertion of the cultural independence and originality of early Spanish literature; the point here made by Mitjana is in fact contained in the twelfth of the Vienna lectures, that best known in Spain since it had occasioned, via Böhl von Faber's translation and commendation of A.W. Schlegel, both the initial polemic surrounding Calderón and the ongoing theoretical dispute that had grown out of it and which had led to the dissemination of Romantic theory within Spain.[39] While the published lectures had provided an almost unqualified eulogy of the entire Spanish cultural tradition, of more specific importance in the present context is August Wilhelm's comment that 'the spirit of chivalry has nowhere outlived its political existence so long as in Spain' and Friedrich Schlegel's similar contention that 'The general spirit of chivalry, and the poetry connected with it, was preserved here [Spain] much longer than in any other country of Europe'.[40] Both the physiognomy of the chivalric life as propounded by the Schlegels and the sublimation of the Spanish literary tradition contained in their respective lectures had proved a determining influence on Spanish Romantic views of the Middle Ages: in Agustín Durán's 1828 *Discurso*, for example, we read that Spain's quintessentially Romantic theatre had proceeded 'de las costumbres caballerosas adoptadas en la nueva civilización de los siglos medios, de sus tradiciones históricas o fabulosas y de la espiritualidad del cristianismo' [from the chivalric customs adopted in the new civilization of the Middle Ages, from its historical and imaginative traditions and from the spirituality of the Christian religion], while Durán, in arguing his case, had praised 'algunos sabios alemanes' [certain wise Germans] for their earlier efforts in propounding it.[41]

This perspective on the poetical and spiritual qualities inherent in the mediaeval period and specifically in the ideals of chivalry, in which Spain figured pre-eminently as the chivalric — and therefore Romantic — country par excellence, was to be restated on countless occasions in the twenty years or so following the publication of Durán's *Discurso*. Indeed, this work itself turned out to be one of the most influential by any standards in the first half of the nineteenth century. Juan Eugenio Hartzenbusch, effectively paraphrasing the Schlegelian perspective, argued that the enterprising and warlike spirit that had inspired the deeds of countless generations of Europeans during the Middle Ages — described as 'la parte maravillosa y heroica en los anales del mundo moderno' [that most marvellous and heroic part of the chronicle of our modern world] — 'quizá en nación ninguna tuvo un origen más justificado y noble que en nuestra España' [in perhaps no nation had a more noble and justifiable origin than in this Spain of ours].[42] Making precisely the same point, Gonzalo Morón commented that the Middle Ages had possessed throughout Europe features that were highly poetic and dramatic, but nowhere so intensely as in Spain; of all European countries, the ideals of religion, love and honour 'han existido en España con más fuerza, intensión [sic] y sublimidad' [have remained alive with the greatest force, intensity and sublimity in Spain].[43] José Ferrer y Subirana, meanwhile, depicted the culminating period of Spanish nationhood under the Catholic Monarchs in the most lavish of ways, underscoring the period as the historical pinnacle of the chivalric ideal:

> Enérgica por su índole, poética en sus maneras, exaltada en sus sentimientos, poderosa y eficaz en sus efectos; la religión y la monarquía, la caballerosa e hidalga nacionalidad española alcanzó hazañas e hizo prodigios que ningún pueblo había hecho ni alcanzado

> [Energetic in its very nature, poetic in its ways, exalted in its feelings, potent and efficacious in its deeds; religion and monarchy, and the chivalric and noble nationhood of Spain, made a reality of heroic feats and prodigious enterprises such as no other people had achieved before.][44]

Ferrer y Subirana evokes then, in quintessentially *casticista* terms, a discernible and distinctive Spanish national identity based upon the twin pillars of throne and altar and imaginatively accessible as a superior common and collective impulse; the Spanish *pueblo* in its guise of conservative imaginative subject that was to prove so eminently serviceable to traditionalists.

Gonzalo Morón, in an extensive 'Examen filosófico del teatro español' published in numerous instalments in the magazine *El Iris* in 1841, delineated the mediaeval age within the same parameters already noted, the elevated spirituality of that period transcending its material deficiencies. At the time of San Fernando (Ferdinand III of Castile), who, for Gonzalo Morón as for Fernán Caballero and numerous other writers, was the epitome of the chivalric life, the Spanish *caballero* had been motivated, he claimed, by the most elevated concerns and committed to turn into reality 'las magníficas y esplendorosas ilusiones' [the magnificent and splendid ideals] of his imaginative sentiment. Religious devotion, Gonzalo Morón then reiterated, had made a crucial contribution to human development in the age of chivalry: whenever and wherever this spirit of piety had been intimately and profoundly seated (as it had been in mediaeval Spain above all other places in Europe), it contained 'algo de vago, de abstracto, de indefinido y de sublime' [something that was elusive, insubstantial, undefined and sublime], something capable of producing the most heroic deeds and 'las más románticas aventuras' [the most Romantic adventures].[45] Another element naturally present in his account, given its lyrical restatement of the ideals of chivalry, was courtly love; Gonzalo Morón described this 'ideal y sublime respeto' [ideal and sublime respect] extended to women by knightly gentlemen in the midst of a more generally coarse and barbarous way of life as one of the most characteristic features of that age and as having prompted 'el romanticismo y el carácter altamente poético y dramático de la edad feudal' [the Romanticism of the feudal age and its elevated poetic and dramatic nature].[46] In the concluding section of his series he then summed up like this:

> Toda la poesía de la Europa moderna se halla en la edad media, en la época del feudalismo, en estos tiempos de desorden y anarquía material, pero en que la religión, el amor y el honor prestaban un impulso uniforme a las acciones de los hombres, y producían los sacrificios más heroicos, las situaciones más profundas y trágicas, las aventuras y proezas más extrañas y singulares.[47]

> [All of the poetry of modern Europe is to be found in the Middle Ages, in the era of feudalism, in times of disorder and of anarchy in material terms, but in which faith, love and honour lent a single shared stimulus to the actions of men, and produced the most heroic sacrifices, the most tragic and intense moments, the most singular and unwonted adventures and feats of arms.]

Precisely the same vision of mediaeval times dominated Gonzalo Morón's general history of Spain, the first volumes of which appeared at almost exactly the same time as his articles in *El Iris*. The feudal system, he professed in the former:

> elevó la dignidad del hombre, creó la sublime pasión del honor, excitó poderosamente los sentimientos de lealtad, rindió un culto poético y casi divino a la mujer, y fue origen de la caballería y de todos los grandes hechos y singulares aventuras, que han dado una fisonomía tan poética y dramática a la edad feudal.

> [created a more elevated sense of human dignity and a sublimely passionate conception of personal honour, provided powerful expression for feelings of loyalty, professed a poetic and almost divine adoration for women, and was the origin of the chivalric ideal and of all those splendid deeds and singular adventures that have supplied the feudal age with features that are so poetical and dramatic].[48]

He likewise used the familiar trinitarian model — the phrase is perhaps not inappropriate, for Amador de los Ríos, writing of the Spanish Reconquest, proudly stated that 'la patria, la religión y el amor, formaron pues, la trinidad ideal de aquella inmensa cruzada' [homeland, faith and love formed then the ideal trinity of that great crusade] — [49] to depict the inspirational elements of the later Middle Ages, insisting that these ideals were profoundly rooted in the hearts of Christians and had given rise to the most heroic and singular of deeds.[50] Again privileging Spain in his account of the formation of the chivalric ideal, he named Bernardo del Carpio, El Cid, and Fernán González as the three great figures of the Spanish Middle Ages;[51] the Cid especially he considered the ideal model of chivalry.[52]

The unmistakable intentionality residing in such accounts of the Middle Ages, making them rather more than a sentimental and idealized representation of a more noble and heroic past, is transparent in most if not all of the passages cited. What best defines Gonzalo Morón's evocation, like so many others, is what we might call its discourse of transcendence: the insistent stress on the spiritual, the elevated and sacred as higher spheres than those of the secular and profane; the idea of a chivalric world-view existing on some higher experiential plane and infinitely superior to the sensual and mundane; above all else, the metaphysical qualities of an historical period regarded as intrinsically and incalculably greater not just than Classical antiquity but also than the Renaissance and the Enlightenment. Gonzalo Morón's recurrent dualistic pattern acquires the most suggestive terms and, I would argue, reveals the real motivating factors underlying its employment, in his declaration that:

> No eran tiempos de razón, de cálculo, ni de filosofía: mas en nombre de la religión, de la lealtad y del pundonor, un corto número de hombres en vuelo de su fantasía consumaba los más atrevidos y grandiosos hechos y dejaba muy atrás el heroísmo de los bellos días de Grecia y de Roma.

> [They were not times of reason, of calculation or of philosophy: but rather in the name of religion, of loyalty and of a scrupulous personal honour, a small number of men, flying upon the wings of their fantasy, accomplished the most audacious and splendid deeds and left far in their wake the heroism of the most glorious days of Greece and Rome.][53]

The Classical world, as I have intimated, is not the only historical age to suffer by comparison with the mediaeval age; the references to 'razón' and 'filosofía' irresistibly indicate that Gonzalo Morón is also placing the mediaeval achievement above that of later ages, which had attempted to re-invent antiquity and which had adopted the Classical epoch as their cultural model and historical inspiration. Not surprisingly, then, in throwing down the gauntlet to those who might question the historical reality of his lyrical evocation of the chivalric Middle Ages, Gonzalo Morón consciously defends an entire cultural tradition that the Enlightenment, and in most cases the Renaissance as well, was felt unfairly to have disparaged: let critics and philosophers dispute to their heart's content the reality of the chivalric ideal in Europe, he contended, but as far as Spain was concerned,

> apenas hay crónica, romance, comedia, ni anécdota que no muestre evidentemente que la lealtad, la nobleza de proceder y todas las virtudes caballerescas, no sólo fueron una verdad en España, si que formaron sus costumbres, su nacionalidad, sus glorias y su literatura.

> [there is hardly a chronicle, a ballad, a play or any apocryphal tale that does not provide ample evidence that loyalty, noble conduct and every chivalric virtue were not just an historical truth in Spain but intimately shaped its social custom, its nationhood, its glories and its literature].[54]

The location of the *romance* and the *comedia* in this patriotic cannonade not merely implies the Schlegelian provenance of Gonzalo Morón's account, but reminds us also that the defence of the native literary tradition was so often complementary to positive contemporary accounts of the feudal age, of monarchy and religion, and of the traditional Providentially ordered universe that the Middle Ages had taken for granted. Similarly, vilification of the mediaeval period as a Dark Ages conventionally went hand in hand with a preference for Enlightenment ideals of reason and progress. Gonzalo Morón addressed this point too in notably direct fashion; on turning imaginatively towards those past centuries, he commented, in which the elevated chivalric dedication of an idealistic élite transcended the more general climate of barbarism and primitive living, we could not but passionately feel the most lively indignation and contempt for

> los filósofos y demagogos, que en nombre de la fría y material razón y proclamando el dogma de la igualdad han ridiculizado y arrastrado por el suelo instituciones

respetables, dejándonos tras sí abundante cosecha de miserable cálculo, de baja ambición, y de grosero e insufrible egoísmo.

[those philosophers and demagogues who, in the name of a cold empirical reason and proclaiming the dogma of equality, have ridiculed and dragged through the mire institutions deserving of respect, and who have bequeathed to us a plentiful harvest of mean and calculating views, of low-minded personal ambition, and of coarse and insufferable egoism.][55]

The heart of the historical issue for Gonzalo Morón, in asserting the reality of the age of chivalry, was then the defence of the religious devotion and metaphysical certainties of that age against the perceived cold reasoning that he felt had since produced an age of scepticism and metaphysical questioning, an age that was catastrophically earth-bound and secular in its most intimate motivation and aims.

Finally, and I do not wish to leave Gonzalo Morón's text without underlining this point, the reader will have noted that within the defining parameters of this historical overview, the spiritual certainties of the mediaeval period had bred Romanticism and had lent a shared common purpose to the aspirations and deeds of men. Literary Romanticism, then, for Gonzalo Morón as for the majority of his Spanish contemporaries and as much earlier for the brothers Schlegel, was essentially the imaginative expression of a Christian and chivalric ethos: this had been its meaning for Johann Nikolaus Böhl in his early exposition of Schlegelian ideas; this was later to be its meaning for Ramón López Soler, Agustín Durán, and other critics of the 'Ominous Decade' of 1823–33; in the hands of Alberto Lista, Juan Donoso Cortés, and many others, this was again to prove its agreed meaning in the 1830s and 1840s, when Romantic radicalism had briefly appeared only to be summarily rejected by the prevailing tide of literary opinion. Furthermore, Gonzalo Morón's account reminds us that what Spanish writers now found attractive about the mediaeval period was not just its expression of spiritual awareness but also its essential homogeneity, the unifying effects of its authoritatively conceived and expressed transcendent world-view. While the period had contained its philosophical tensions, it had not suffered the spiritual anxieties later occasioned by widespread heterodoxy and religious dissent, by disturbing metaphysical doubt and, in a word, by secularism. Nineteenth-century Spanish historians were now turning to this earlier and, as they saw it, infinitely more noble age, in a calculated attempt to purge their own of contemporary demons brought to life principally by the Enlightenment but also, as we shall see, by the Reformation. As Jaime Vicens Vives succinctly expressed it, traditionalists were to use mediaevalism as a strategy of legitimation, finding support for their own projects and actions by resurrecting a supposedly admirable mediaeval way of life.[56]

Confirmation of just how representative was Gonzalo Morón's position is easily obtained from even a cursory reading of some of the original texts. Gervasio Gironella, for example, as editor of the *Revista de Madrid* an influential player in this discussion, placed a similar emphasis on the transcendent concerns of mediaeval man and in so doing allowed at least a hint as to the meaning of the mediaeval age for his own: quite aside from their knightly reliance upon physical and moral strength and courage, mediaeval men, he asserted, revealed in their lives a passionate ardour for all that was sublime and 'la profunda veneración por todo lo sagrado' [a deep-seated veneration for all that was sacred], which together rendered the history of that age so immensely attractive. This idealism and sense of gallantry had made possible, he continued, the appearance of the chivalric ideal, one of the most admirable features of the entire Middle Ages.[57] Just like Gonzalo Morón, Gironella contrasted the transcendent values of the mediaeval period with the lamentable rationalism of contemporary times: 'El ardor religioso de la edad media hizo llevar a cabo cosas que nuestro siglo positivo y lógico apenas puede comprender' [The religious ardour of the Middle Ages made possible the accomplishment of things which our own age of positivism and logic is barely able to comprehend]. The reductively pejorative specification of the contemporary age as 'positivo y lógico', as a period inclined towards the empirical and quantifiable, has a representative quality that will soon become more fully apparent. Gironella here set it against an earlier age of chivalresque enthusiasm and Christian piety that had necessarily been, he roundly declared, a supremely poetic age greater than any other; men of those times were more susceptible to poetry than either those that had preceded them or those that were to come after.[58]

For Gironella, it should be noted, the mediaeval period was historically demarcated by, on the one hand, the fall of the Roman Empire in the West, and, on the other, the Lutheran reforms of established religion. As he subsequently comments: 'La reforma vino a cerrar la edad media. Era, según se decía al principio, para su felicidad; mas más tarde se ha conocido que en vano se había creído' [The Reformation drew the Middle Ages to a close. Initially this was said to have been a change for the better; but more recently it has come to be seen that such a belief was vain].[59] Cayetano Rosell, meanwhile, writing slightly later on the creation of the Orden de la Banda, lavishly described the sublimity of the courtly love ideal; it plainly demonstrated, he claimed, that women had always enjoyed, in Christian society, 'una especie de culto que nunca podrá alcanzar con la quimérica emancipación de la filosofía moderna' [a kind of adoration that shall never be realized by the chimerical notions of emancipation found in modern-day philosophy].[60] As a final example, Amador de los Ríos's review of the first volumes of Modesto Lafuente's mammoth *Historia general de España* coincided forcefully with Gonzalo Morón's earlier texts in decrying what he called the spirit of carping contrariness that had been introduced by Voltaire and his followers, something that had in the eighteenth century perverted philosophy and historiography alike. This fundamentally impious stance, he continued, 'minó las tradiciones populares que se fundaban en el sentimiento religioso, con injustificable desdén; y pasando de la indiferencia al desprecio, acabó por despojar a la nación española de sus más brillantes glorias' [undermined, with unjustifiable disdain, those popular traditions founded upon devout religious feeling; and, passing from indifference to outright contempt, it finally stripped the Spanish nation bare of all its greatest glories]. It had admitted nothing, he concluded, that stood outside of its own prescriptive and reductive dogma.[61]

The reference made by Amador to 'las tradiciones populares' is of some significance. Voltaire, it is worth reminding ourselves, had maintained that the application of common sense and reason made it a simple task to distinguish between the true and the false in history, a task effected by discarding the fabulous elements of any historical record and thus by excluding the contents of popular tradition and legend as historical data. Yet, as Hayden White comments, this was to neglect 'that aspect of the past which such bodies of data directly represented to the historian trying to reconstruct a life in its integrity and not merely in terms of its most *rationalistic* manifestations'. The Enlighteners, he goes on, devoted to reason and interested in establishing its authority against the superstition, ignorance, and tyranny of their own age, saw the legendary and fabulous as simply 'testimony to the essential irrationality of past ages' despite the status of these as 'documents in which those ages represented their truths to themselves'.[62] Romanticism was committed to a revalidation of precisely those elements which Voltaire and the Enlightenment generally had refused to countenance as reliable historical testimony. It had been Vico, who was to prove an enormously influential figure in the development of the Romantic historical imagination in Spain, as we shall see in succeeding chapters of this study, who had much earlier testified to the role of what White designates 'human imaginings' in the construction of social and cultural institutions, while Herder had questioned whether a nation possessed anything more precious than the treasure-house of its early literature, which he regarded as a source of the most profound knowledge of ages and peoples, of their aspirations and inclinations.[63] Within the *casticista* rhetoric that Schlegelian Romanticism was to acquire in Spain, such 'tradiciones', particularly religious ones, would be endowed with a sense of the sacred.

This veneration for the greatest glories of Spain's cultural tradition or inalienable features of Spanish nationhood was intended to counterweight something which, only too characteristically, the perversely irreligious cultural model of the French Enlightenment was felt wilfully to have disparaged in the pursuit of its own malignant ends. The centrality of religious commitment to the view of the world that had typified mediaeval Spain would in fact be underscored by commentators not commonly known for their fanaticism. Gabriel García y Tassara, for example, saw it like this: Spanish nationhood had been founded in the aftermath of an internal crusade against Muslim occupation; consequently, devout religious feeling was a major factor in Spain's intimate makeup. Accordingly, he went on, 'llevábamos ardiendo en nuestro corazón el principio que grabamos más tarde en nuestras banderas' [we bore ardently in our hearts the principle that we would later engrave upon our banners].[64] Men like Gonzalo Morón and Amador de los Ríos were characteristically less circumspect. The former identified, after the Moorish invasion, two things left to Spain, designated the two seeds of its nationhood, that he described as having prompted and facilitated the Reconquest; these were 'el sentimiento religioso [...] y el valor e indomable energía de los pueblos del Septentrión de España' [religious feeling […] and the courage and indomitable energy of the peoples of the North of Spain].[65] He therefore transposes with specificity to Spain the two most potent elements he considered to have engendered modern European civilization. Amador, in tracing the physiognomy of Spanish chivalry, saw concomitantly religion and monarchy emerging as twin pillars of Spanish society; he made the essential connections in the following way:

> Así el amor, la lealtad y el honor llegan a ser entre los castellanos las prendas de más estima, formando el triple dogma caballeresco y sirviendo de base a las costumbres, al fundirse en los dos grandes principios que eran la piedra angular del edificio político y religioso.

> [Thus love, loyalty and honour come to be esteemed among the Castilians as

jewels of the highest price, forming the triple dogma of chivalry and serving as the foundation of social custom, fusing together into those two great principles that were to be the cornerstone of our religious and political edifice.][66]

The 'Throne and Altar' interpretation of the national past, which will assume much greater importance in the course of this study, is thus transparent.

Taking into account much of the textual evidence adduced here, Moreno Alonso is surely right to emphasize that Spanish historians of the Romantic period judged the country's mediaeval past subjectively, as they fondly imagined it to be rather than how it had really been.[67] Philip Silver, much more bluntly but hardly less appropriately, labels the phenomenon a kitsch mediaevalism disguising reactionary longings for literary, social and political reform.[68] To put this Romantic mediaeval revival into perspective, we might make some interesting comparisons with judgements expressed by the previous generation. Juan Pablo Forner, no friend of 'filosofismo' [philosophizing], could write in his *Reflexiones sobre el modo de escribir la historia de España* that the Middle Ages, a primitive period prejudicial to human development, had stunted the historical possibilities of later centuries; moreover, its evil consequences were still felt, so that 'Nos duran aún por nuestras desgracias muchos restos de la edad media' [Unfortunately for us, many remnants of the Middle Ages still survive].[69] José Gómez de la Cortina, meanwhile, as late as 1829 in his *Cartilla historial*, was scornful of idealizations of chivalry: if some accounts were to be believed, he observed, 'no respiraba más que religión, virtud, honor y humanidad' [the air was full of faith, virtue, honour and humanity]; if this were true, then we should regard mediaeval knights as having been 'tanto más extraordinarios, cuanto que florecieron en tiempos en que la barbarie, la relajación y el latrocinio tiranizaban a la Europa entera' [so much more extraordinary for having flourished at a time when barbarism, moral laxity and pillage held the whole of Europe in thrall]. Rather than subscribe to this view, he declared it to be surely unnatural to suppose such elevated qualities in men who had been ignorant and superstitious fanatics, whose only code of conduct had been physical force and personal courage and who had hardly been in a position to consult with the forces of law and order before committing themselves to any enterprise.[70] These comments are of course a far cry from even those less sentimental evocations of chivalry found two decades later. By 1847, the pen of Antonio Alcalá Galiano, not normally given to florid excess, would nonetheless express pretty broad agreement with its more lyrical contemporaries in asserting of Spanish chivalry that 'Su espíritu había comprendido el del siglo rudo pero generoso, idealista y romántico, y en armonía con él fundó sus estatutos' [Its spirit had embraced that of the roughly hewn but generous, idealistic and Romantic age, and in harmony with that spirit had its statutes been founded].[71] It is only rarely, in the 1840s, that we encounter a caveat such as that voiced by Martínez de la Rosa in warning that, if the Middle Ages were to be viewed 'en su disforme realidad' [in its misshapen reality] rather than through the prism of the novels of Walter Scott, he believed that 'se desvanecerían muchas de nuestras ilusiones' [many of our fond illusions would be dispelled].[72]

If the ideals of chivalry were widely felt to have been in harmony with the overall spirit of the age which had produced them, then the same might be said of the relationship between those same ideals and the literature which they had in their turn inspired. Joaquín Sánchez de Fuentes offers an admirable summary of the basic Romantic position: chivalric enthusiasm for religion, beauty, and virtue, he asserted, had aroused in countless sensitive hearts those delicate and sublime feelings that were so much admired in his own day. At such a time of 'bellas acciones' [beautiful actions] and 'hechos sorprendentes' [striking deeds], was it not inevitable that mediaeval poets should celebrate, in alternately passionate and melancholy verses, their beautiful queens, the victors of their tourneys, lovers' complaints, the arduous life of crusader knights and their journeying to the Holy Land: '¡Cuánta poesía no encierra la edad media, cuán poética no es de suyo la caballería!' [What store of poetry do the Middle Ages contain, how poetic by definition is the chivalric ideal!] Morally, he insisted, the influence of chivalry had been such that to it alone civilization owed the preservation of 'las sanas y sublimes ideas' [commendable and sublime ideas] in the midst of 'la oscuridad más espantosa' [the most fearful darkness] and 'la más absoluta abyección' [the most unremitting wretchedness].[73]

Gonzalo Morón would write in similar vein in the instalments of his 'Examen filosófico del teatro español', evoking a time when knightly examples of valour, loyalty and piety were engraved upon the minds of men, were celebrated by poets and minstrels, were recorded for posterity in chronicles and verses, and, importantly, served as inspiration to 'las más arrojadas empresas' [the most daring enterprises]; they had lent to ordinary life, he professed, 'ese tinte tan dramático y romancesco' [that colouring so dramatic and so Romantic] that had distinguished mediaeval Spain.[74] He subsequently reiterated, the lyricism of his vision blinding him to the possible dangers of repetition, that:

> la religión, el amor y el honor habían animado la vida y la nacionalidad de Europa en esta época, dado un tinte poético a las costumbres, creado el drama religioso, y excitado fuertemente la imaginación de los hombres para sentir las bellezas y encantos de la poesía.
>
> [faith, love and honour had energized life and nationhood throughout Europe in this era, had lent a poetic colouring to social custom, had created religious drama, and had forcefully aroused the imagination of men and turned it towards the beauties and charms of poetry.][75]

As a result, he claimed, social interaction in feudal Europe had been characterized by its essential variety and by its Romanticism, so that 'la literatura y las bellas artes, lejos de ofrecer el monótono cuadro de la sociedad antigua, debieron presentar el diverso, animado y dramático reflejo de la sociedad moderna' [literature and the fine arts, far from offering the monotonous picture of ancient society, had perforce to be the varied, lively and dramatic reflection of modern society].[76] In one of the later volumes of his general history of Spain, he emphasized the literary inspiration prompted by the spirituality of love, his tone again proving notably effusive as he declared that human love, 'divinizado por la religión y el honor' [deified by faith and honour], had become a profound and mysterious passion , 'tan ideal y romancesca, como parecía imposible concebirle a seres mortales' [of such an ideal and Romantic kind that it seemed to mere mortals impossible to conceive]. Consequently, chivalric idealism had radiantly enlightened the dark canvas of that coarse and semi-barbarous society and had lent the aforementioned poetic and highly dramatic colouring to the age, so that 'la más bella literatura de Europa es la que se ha inspirado del espíritu maravilloso y romancesco de tan singulares días' [the most beautiful European literature is that which has been inspired by the wonderful and Romantic spirit of such extraordinary times].[77]

Gervasio Gironella expressed much the same view, stating that the poetry of the troubadours had reflected the essential character of society, while alongside the mediaeval lyric stood narrative verse that was 'enteramente llena de la esperanza de un mundo mejor, penetrada de sus secretos' [entirely filled with the hope of a better world, permeated with its secrets]; this mediaeval epic, he continued in words that paraphrase the position of the Schlegels and their earlier Spanish adherents, 'es preciso distinguir de la epopeya antigua con la designación de romántica' [it is necessary to distinguish from the ancient epic by the designation Romantic].[78]

One of the clearest examples of this Schlegelian perspective on mediaeval literature, and specifically mediaeval Spanish literature, is the speech made by José Caveda on his reception into the Spanish Academy in 1852, a text which exemplifies the pre-eminent status still enjoyed by Schlegelian Romantic theory in the middle years of the century. Poetry had always been indicative, Caveda felt, of the society that had produced it, of that society's defining features and of the historical flowering and decline of its culture and civilization. The popular verse forms of the oral tradition he therefore regarded as a solemn testimony to 'aquella nacionalidad ingenua y sencilla, pero robusta y enérgica' [that simple and naïve but dynamic and robust nationhood] that lived and breathed in their poetic imagery and description.[79] National poetry in the Middle Ages, he subsequently commented, inevitably responded to an intimate collective need: this he defined as 'la de expresar las inspiraciones de su lealtad caballeresca, de su respeto al trono, de su espíritu eminentemente religioso, de su valor y constancia' [that of giving expression to inspiring ideals of chivalric loyalty, of respect for the throne, of a spirit eminently religious in inclination, of gallantry and constancy of purpose].[80] Once more, we detect the unmistakable organic connection between the desirable values of mediaeval society exemplified by the chivalric ideal, the essential qualities of its literary expression, and the intimate and unconditional adherence to monarchy and religion on which the entire culture, thought-patterns and belief-system of the Middle Ages were seen to be founded. The Spanish *romance*, then, in Caveda's account, 'concuerda admirablemente con el carácter de la época, y recibe su carta de naturaleza de la lealtad castellana, del misticismo religioso, del entusiasmo guerrero, y del respeto y el apoyo concedidos a la beldad inocente y desvalida' [is admirably attuned to the character of its age, its distinctive credentials being Castilian loyalty, religious mysticism, enthusiasm for the warrior life, the respect and assistance offered to beauty and innocence in their distress].[81] Similarly Alfonso X's *Crónica general de España* is here described as a 'mezcla singular de la fábula y de la historia, del espíritu caballeresco y de la crédula afición a todo lo maravilloso' [singular mingling of historical reality and literary fantasy, of the spirit of chivalry, and of a ready and eager belief in everything marvellous]; as such, Caveda went on, it offered a faithful depiction of its age and a 'cumplida idea de su carácter y sus costumbres' [thoroughgoing idea of its character and way of life]. No other text, Caveda went so far as to say, recreated more imaginatively nor more accurately the reality of mediaeval Spain.[82] Likewise, he claimed, those popular beliefs extracted from the old ballads, although embellishing reality with poetic fiction, contained as characteristic features 'descripciones felices en que respira el genio de la edad media' [felicitous passages of description that live and breathe with a distinctive mediaeval genius]. Indeed, such evidence he felt to be more appropriate to our imaginative reconstruction of the mediaeval period than the more accurate but dry and sterile recording of events found in many chronicles that provide nothing in the way of insight or instruction. The Middle Ages had after all been, he insisted, an 'época de fe robusta y pura, de acontecimientos extraordinarios, que hacían probables hasta los imposibles, y de sinceridad y honradez caballeresca' [era of robust and pure faith, of extraordinary happenings that made even impossible things seem probable, of chivalric sincerity and honour].[83] Summing up the position he had established, and concisely expressing in the process the view of mediaeval literature propounded by the German Romantic theorists, Caveda commented that:

> costumbres, ideas, civilización, cuanto constituye el carácter de un pueblo, cuanto concurre a determinar su originalidad y darle una fisonomía propia, se encuentra en esas ficciones, hijas de sus creencias, nacidas de altas y arrojadas empresas, alimentadas en la prosperidad y la desgracia por el espíritu nacional y grandes y memorables recuerdos.

> [social custom, ideas, civilization, all that goes to make up the character of a people, all that helps to determine its originality and to give it a distinctive set of features, is to be found in these fictions, born of intimate beliefs, inspired by elevated and daring deeds, nurtured in periods of prosperity and misfortune alike by the spirit of nation and by great and memorable reminders of its past.][84]

Consequently, he was in no doubt, and here too he was unconsciously echoing Herder, that poetry enables us to reach a more exact estimate of the nature of the past than history itself; on this account, and according popular traditions their due rather than pronouncing upon them in a way that was 'incrédula y presuntuosa' [sceptical and arrogant] as the eighteenth century had done, he asserted that historical evidence could be sought and found not just in archaeological remains or surviving chronicles but also 'en los monumentos de las artes, en los prodigios del romance, en la sencillez de los cantos populares, en la poesía nacional consagrada por la admiración o la gratitud pública a los héroes y sus empresas' [in artistic treasures, in the prodigious verses of the mediaeval ballads, in the simplicity of popular song, in that national poetry made sacred by public admiration for or gratitude to its heroes and their deeds].[85] He concluded on this most suggestive note, entirely in accord with the long-expressed position of historical Romanticism: we should not only see in the old ballads and in our national drama their fertility of invention, their charms of feeling and their harmonious rhythm: we ought to consider them also as 'fieles auxiliares de la historia' [faithful aids to history] and as 'un precioso depósito de documentos para ilustrarla' [a precious depository of documents by which to illuminate it].[86]

In responding to Caveda's speech, Pedro José Pidal effectively reiterated the same point; without a thoroughgoing knowledge of mediaeval poems, he observed, it was impossible to come to know the thought-patterns of the society and age that had produced them; without them it was impossible to know the Middle Ages. If Homer revealed more about Greek society than Herodotus, Xenophon, or Thucydides, then equally in the literature of mediaeval Spain could be found the nature of those different periods in the life of Castile and the principles upon which had been founded its 'nacionalidad fuerte y robusta' [forceful and robust nationhood]; among these he specified what he designated the most characteristic and enduring features of the Castilian people: 'su profunda religiosidad, su fidelidad a los Reyes, su elevado amor a las libertades públicas' [its intense religiosity, its loyalty to its kings and queens, its high-minded love for public freedoms]. Summing up, he declared that national history and tradition still live and breathe in these songs, poems and popular ballads.[87] Pidal was just one of countless writers sounding the by now axiomatic Herderian proposition that popular tradition communicated 'lo que hubo más íntimo y profundo en la vida y en la historia de los pueblos' [the most intimate and mysterious aspects of the life and history of peoples].[88] For Eugenio de Tapia as for so many others, the poems of mediaeval troubadours were the greatest historical monuments of those times,[89] while his description of the *romances* as poetry that was expressively revealing of the virtues and defects of society, a poetry that must be known in order to 'formar un juicio cabal de las costumbres, ideas y sentimientos de aquella edad' [form an accurate judgement of the customs, ideas, and feelings of that age] was again entirely representative.[90] In designating the Spanish *romance* 'la verdadera poesía nacional, la legítima expresión de los sentimientos, hábitos y cultura de la sociedad' [our true national poetry, the legitimate expression of the feelings, habits, and culture of our society],[91] he was echoing one of the principal tenets of Romantic historicism; the *Romancero* was proudly hailed, as the Duque de Rivas expressed it in the prologue to his *Romances históricos* of 1841, as 'nuestra verdadera poesía castiza' [our authentic true-blooded poetry].[92] At the same time, the prevalence of the typically Schlegelian distinctions between ancient and modern and of the historical judgements of literature and society prompted by them is evidenced by Salvador Bermúdez de Castro, writing in *El Iris* in 1841: 'nos hallamos íntimamente persuadidos que la edad feudal es la edad poética de los modernos; que las cruzadas son para la Europa lo que la guerra de Troya fue para Homero y los poetas griegos' [I am intimately persuaded that the feudal age is the poetical age of the moderns; that the crusades are to Europe what the Trojan War had been to Homer and the Greek poets]. This view of the feudal period as the prime literary inspiration of modern Europe contrasts sharply with Bermúdez's reaction to neo-Classicism; the tragedies of Racine and Voltaire, he reported, produced for his age a sense of weakness and monotony, since they were no more than a faithless parody of the Greek tragedies.[93] The inference is clear: to attempt to resurrect the world of ancient Greece in modern times was an historical and artistic anachronism that subverted the harmonious connection between literature and society in adopting cultural models that were no longer applicable. What Bermúdez and so many others did not realize, or at least were reluctant to acknowledge, is that the kind of programmatic positions they were defending were ultimately as prescriptive and as reductively intolerant as the previous models they sought historically to bury.

If it is possible, as I have tried to show here, to trace a line of continuity between, on the one hand, the work of the German theorists and their earliest Spanish adherents, and, on the other, the nature of the mediaeval revival fully consummated in the 1840s, then a parallel case might be made for Romantic interpretations of Gothic architecture.

Rafael Mitjana's description of Gothic architecture as the perfect expression of Christian sensibility,[94] written in 1845, provides evidence of the essential link between Chateaubriand's *Le Génie du christianisme* of 1802, an incalculably influential work in the period of Spain's overwhelmingly conservative historical Romanticism, and the fundamentally similar outlook of Gustavo Adolfo Bécquer's evocation of San Juan de los Reyes, Toledo, written for the *Historia de los templos de España* of 1857.[95]

In commencing his prefatory remarks, Bécquer famously asserted that 'La tradición religiosa es el eje de diamante sobre el que gira nuestro pasado' [Religious tradition is the diamantine axis upon which turns our past]; far less commonly cited are the concluding words of the same general introduction, in which Bécquer, in referring to a sensitive and intuitive artistic reconstruction of an earlier magnificent age, one which 'herida de muerte por la duda, acabó con el último siglo' [mortally wounded by doubt, expired in the last century], directly reproduces one of the most celebrated phrases found in Chateaubriand's own preface to *Le Génie du christianisme* in proclaiming: 'Acaso, cuando ya reunidos sus fragmentos, pongamos en pie al coloso de las creencias, sus gigantes proporciones humillen y confundan la raquítica babel de la impiedad' [It may be that, when its fragments have been reassembled and we are able to raise up that colossal figure of our beliefs, its gigantic proportions dwarf and confound the rickety tower of Babel that is impiety].[96] The French nobleman's emblematic encapsulation of the *Encyclopédie* as an unwarrantable human challenge to divine authority is therefore echoed in the Spanish poet's attack upon a related historical target. Moreover, in the later section on San Juan de los Reyes entitled 'Reflexiones sobre sus ruinas' [Reflections upon its ruins] and in apostrophizing the holy remains, Bécquer attempts to 'personificar la sensación que me causáis' [personify the feelings you create in me] by imaginatively projecting on to them the figure of a monk, the hood of whose habit is thrown back from his head and who wears in its place a warrior's helmet, a monk whose habit in turn conceals chain mail and spurs. He thus conjures up the quintessential Romantic idealization of the Middle Ages, what he calls 'la idea mística y caballera' [the mystical and chivalric idea], insisting that 'tan completamente se ha fundido en un solo pensamiento, marcial y santo a la vez, el espíritu religioso y conquistador de vuestros fundadores' [so entirely has been melded into a single conception, at one and the same time warlike and holy, the devout and conquering spirit of your founding fathers].[97]

In addition, we are left, on reading Bécquer's evocative prose, with the very feeling so often detected in a plethora of other historical material: namely, that intellectual, philosophical, and artistic judgements of even a remote past are coloured by more recent historical experience. As Giovanni Allegra put it, the Romantic preference for the Christian Middle Ages contained at its nucleus a nexus of ideas and values that had been eroded 'por el siglo libertino y por la revolución' [by the age of libertines and revolution].[98] When Bécquer refers to the fundamental changes in architectural preference wrought by the Renaissance, we therefore sense that more modern historical issues are at stake: he writes of a time when Classical taste, in the form of the Renaissance, 'inundó a las otras naciones' [flooded into all other nations], of an age when 'profanáronse los más caprichosos pensamientos de nuestra arquitectura propia a la que apellidaron bárbara; diéronse a los templos la matemática regularidad de las construcciones gentílicas' [the most fanciful expression of our native architecture was treated with profanity, and labelled barbaric; our places of worship were given the mathematical regularity of pagan buildings];[99] it is hard to reject the sensation that the fervent young admirer of Chateaubriand is in fact here transposing on to a different but comparable historical moment the idea of the ravaging of a sublime past tradition by the Age of Reason. His words, moreover, and this would appear beyond dispute, exemplify the general tenor of the mediaeval revival as admirably synthesized by Allegra, who summarizes this Romantic evocation of an heroic and holy era whose annals were written into the very stones of the churches of Spain. As the Italian critic continues, the belligerent Catholicism of 'las décadas antifrancesas' [the anti-French decades] can be considered part of a larger religious and aesthetic whole, one which rediscovered salvation in the soul of the people in the face of a conscious intellectualism that had dug up spurious Classical ideals of harmony and balance and invented pie-in-the-sky republican notions of natural societies. Allegra's terms, which I have recreated here, are themselves enormously suggestive.[100]

The *Historia de los templos de España*, as Rubén Benítez has elucidated, sits in profound harmony with Bécquer's artistic traditionalism, which viewed legendary and folkloric sources as invaluable historical testimony; following Chateaubriand's profoundly Romantic conception of 'reconstrucción artística del mundo espiritual del pasado' [the artistic reconstruction of a past spiritual world], Bécquer's method was impregnated with a Herderian sense of history: he did not solely use archive material, but relied more closely upon 'las creencias, las ideas, los sentimientos de la época' [the beliefs, ideas and feelings of that age].[101] Benítez continues, citing Bécquer's 'Solar de la casa del Cid en Burgos', by averring that in his defence of tradition there can be found a reiterated protest against a rationalistic and 'philosophical' form of historical scholarship which placed an exaggerated reliance upon mere documentation; what Bécquer significantly labelled 'esa incrédula hija de nuestra época' [that unbelieving daughter of our age] had only a contemptuous sneer for the 'brillante cimiento' [shining mortar] that held together the annals of the national past.[102] The poetic historian, as Bécquer saw it and as Philip Silver has recently reminded us, 'would focus on just such traditional sources, inasmuch as they were the genuine repositories of Spanish values'.[103] Silver comments, in words that allow us to make a close connection between Bécquer's work and much of the material examined here: 'the politically conservative purpose of the *Historia* was to celebrate, and to invite meditation on, the spiritual force of the high points of Spain's national-Catholic past'.[104] As Benítez observes, meanwhile, for Bécquer as much as for Mariana and Chateaubriand history was the working out of divine Providence, justifying his own earlier comment that it was only logical, in 1860 and when he was known principally for the *Historia de los templos* project, that Bécquer should have been considered a neo-Catholic writer;[105] José Pedro Díaz was likewise to underline Bécquer's powerful traditionalist adherence to Catholicism and monarchy.[106]

Little wonder then that the waning of the Middle Ages, that is in the present context the historical decline of the chivalric ideal, the abandonment of the Gothic style, and the perceived slow but inevitable disintegration of homogeneous societies founded upon metaphysical certainties was seen by Spanish historians as calamitous for the history of western Europe. Caveda, in terms that were to be echoed by Bécquer, typically compartmentalized the changing thought-patterns that had brought new historical emphases, claiming that, with the European Renaissance, 'Sustituyéronse entonces la imitación a la originalidad; las investigaciones arqueológicas a los arranques de la inspiración; la erudición al atrevimiento del genio' [Imitation replaced originality; archaeological investigations took the place of snatches of inspiration; erudition occupied that of audacious genius].[107] The new humanism he therefore saw as an enlightening regeneration but one hostile to enthusiasm and feeling, something that had systematically stripped western Europe of its most cherished illusions. For him, it had sounded the historical death-knell of those glorious ideals of honour, valour and piety that had constituted a 'caballerosidad poética y sencilla' [simple and poetical code of chivalry]. Within his still programmatic narrative, 'Una razón severa, un progreso inflexible como sus miras' [An austere reason, a vision of progress as inflexible as it was reductive] would demolish a world of fantasy whose dreams and aspirations were nonetheless not entirely lost to sight. What he saw as remaining to the sensibility and the imagination, it should be noted, was precisely that which Romanticism had by his own time effectively rehabilitated: 'esa edad de los castillos feudales, de los monumentos religiosos, de los torneos y de los trovadores, del misticismo y de las leyendas misteriosas, de las creencias y de las tradiciones' [that era of feudal castles, of monuments of religion, of tourneys and troubadours, of mysticism and mysterious legends, of beliefs and traditions].[108]

Manuel Cañete, writing in the same year, explicitly connected the slow death of the national literary tradition with the concomitant decline of the chivalric values that had intimately informed it; crucially, he saw recent optimistic signs of a return to that tradition as linked in similar fashion to an imaginative recovery of the Middle Ages. Within his perspective, true Spanish poetry perished together with the decline and disappearance of 'el caballeresco espíritu indígena' [the native chivalric spirit]; after a barren period of one hundred and fifty years it had experienced rebirth, as nineteenth-century literature turned its gaze once more to that long-dead chivalric world, reawakened 'las heroicas y romancescas costumbres de la edad media' [the heroic and Romantic customs of the Middle Ages], and —and this is crucial— began to divest itself of pagan attire in order to clothe itself in the pure garb of Christianity.[109] The Cuban writer Domingo del Monte, in an article also published in 1848, if somewhat less rhetorical in his style offers a much more acute sense of how the motivating factors behind the development of Romantic theory were now being evaluated. In recalling the physiognomy of Spanish society in the fifteenth and sixteenth centuries — referring to that society as 'un compuesto de fraile y de soldado' [a composite of monk and soldier] — he found it entirely predictable that the exponents of literature and the arts, like the population in general, should have professed 'las opiniones monárquicas y católicas' [Monarchist and Catholic opinions]. As he then remarks, and I have chosen to stress what seems to me the most telling phrase:

> El estupendo espectáculo de *esta homogeneidad de ideas*, en una nación grande y poderosa, sorprendió la imaginación de Guillermo Schlegel, y la tuvo por la más grandiosa obra de la religión católica, y a Calderón como al primero de los poetas del mundo, porque la reflejaba en sus dramas con la mayor viveza.

[The stupendous spectacle of *this homogeneity of ideas*, in a great and powerful nation, captivated the imagination of Wilhelm Schlegel, and he took it to be the most splendid achievement of the Catholic religion, and Calderón to be the foremost writer in the world, since he reflected those ideas with the greatest verve in his drama].[110]

Del Monte then, besides displaying his knowledge of A. W. Schlegel's role in rehabilitating the Spanish literary tradition, indicates with considerable clarity not just what had singularly attracted the German theorist in Spanish culture of the Middle Ages and the *Siglo de Oro*, but also what it was that had led so many later Spanish writers to make the mediaeval period their greatest historical inspiration.

Within this larger perspective, it is possible to discern a widespread commitment to what D. L. Shaw designates, in a brief but illuminating contextual approach to Rivas's *Romances históricos*, a myth of the past that exalted the traditional, organic, and hierarchical conception of society, brandished as an antidote to the abstract and mechanistic one characteristic of the Enlightenment.[111] The point is reinforced if we take into account also one rather later text, the speech made by the conservative politician Antonio Cánovas del Castillo on entering the Real Academia Española in 1867. The merits of Romanticism, he here asserted, had been to 'restablecer el olvidado sentido de las cosas de la Edad Media' [re-establish the forgotten meaning of things mediaeval] , to 'reproducir el concierto de los dogmas cristianos con las artes góticas' [reproduce the accord between Christian doctrine and Gothic art and architecture], and, finally and perhaps most significantly, to 'restablecer la unidad perdida' [re-establish the lost unity] of European nations.[112]

This retrospective assessment of the Romantic mediaeval revival itself highlights some of the issues seen here that will resurface later in the present study: the sense of modern Europe's being beset by a form of fragmentation or rupture that the homo-geneous spectacle presented by the Middle Ages — the noun 'concierto', to intimate a deep-rooted harmony or profound accord, is surely not casually chosen — might offer the opportunity to redress; the neglect previously suffered by the mediaeval period at the hands of the Enlightenment, which had judged it only superficially and in consonance with its own lack of a thoroughgoing transcendent principle; the belief in an integrated and distinctive national collective imagination that justified the intellectual adherence of the Romantic mind; and, most elusively but ultimately most importantly, the desire for order, meaning, and authority, consciously or unconsciously communicated here in the specification of 'sentido', 'concierto', and 'unidad'. Any view of the Middle Ages as barbaric, we might then more broadly extrapolate in conclusion, could only have been based upon a superficial apprehension of material or external factors in history — hence the kind of shortcomings consistently imputed to Voltaire and later, as we shall see, to Guizot — and, consequently, upon a view of history itself that lacked any conception of transcendent processes conducive to some determined supernatural end. In Hayden White's terms, the majority Spanish proponents of an 'Organicist' historical interpretation, confident of the teleological purpose behind historical events, decried what they regarded as the limitations of a more fundamentally rationalistic 'Contextual' historiography. The extension of precisely this distinction into every significant interpretative area of Spanish Romantic historiography, and the over-arching ideological implications of its application, will become more fully apparent in ensuing chapters.

Largely missing from this Romantic apprehension of the Middle Ages, meanwhile, is the 'afirmación municipalista' [affirmation of local autonomy] which, as José María Jover Zamora underlines, was part and parcel of a *progresista* project also rooted in mediaeval history but which sought to differentiate itself from the very different historical model tenaciously brought to fruition by conservative liberals by means of their epic poem of unification and centralization.[113] It is possible to trace this more radical form of mediaevalism directly back to the reforming prescriptions of the Cadiz parliament — with their justification of the Spanish Middle Ages on account of the historical freedoms apparent therein — and forward, as Jover Zamora intimates, into the second half of the century. Yet within the Romantic period proper, a majority conservative historiography rejected this alternative vision of a decentralized Spain which, especially between 1854 and 1873, was to prove a parallel myth for democrats, republicans, and federalists.[114] It was instead what Jover Zamora designates a retrospective nationalism intimately related to other openly ideological forms of *casticismo* that was to dominate historical writing of the 1840s.

Even José Luis Abellán, who, in common with Ricardo Navas Ruiz and others, makes an unduly prescriptive association between literary Romanticism and political Liberalism, is forced to concede the existence of this powerful current of ideas antagonistic to what he regards as more authentic forms of Romantic expression. He describes it as a traditionalist conservative 'Throne and Altar' Romanticism nostalgic for the Middle Ages and for earlier scales of value.[115] Abellán thus identifies a series of concerns central to the thought processes of the period, some of which I have begun to deal with here and some of which will be more fully explored and, I hope, clarified in subsequent chapters. A full appreciation and analysis of the intimate detail of such thought processes will not just confirm the accuracy of Abellán's brief delineation but also, and this is ultimately far more important, call into question the essential thesis upon which his and many other modern commentators' interpretation of the intellectual bases of Spanish Romanticism is seen to rest. Navas Ruiz, meanwhile, and perhaps unwisely, went even further than Abellán in roundly declaring that a conservative Romanticism had never really existed, that it had been a political project doomed to failure from its inception that had left behind it no meaningful literary legacy whatever.[116] The first part of this assertion is, I would suggest, effectively belied by the considerable evidence to the contrary already furnished here. If the existence of a conservative Romanticism, as more recent judgements somewhat more impartial than that of Navas Ruiz have tended to conclude, is no longer in any doubt, I shall go on to address the more fundamentally challenging second element of his observation by closely charting the extent, underlying motivation, aims and consequences of both conservative and progressive Romantic responses to history.

The intellectual processes I have been examining here are crystallized, arguably better than in any comparable text, by Amador de los Ríos in concluding a series of short pieces entitled 'Tradiciones populares de España: Rodrigo Díaz de Vivar' and written for the magazine *El Laberinto* in 1845. Amador sets the seal on the Romantic mediaeval revival as it had cohered in Spain, renders transparent its meaning, and anticipates for us some of the most crucial historical emphases and ideological implications to be explored later in this study in declaring that

> Un pueblo que no puede volver la vista atrás para gozar en sus antiguas glorias, no espera en modo alguno un porvenir venturoso. Lo pasado es nada para él: lo presente le ofrece sólo mil calamidades; y el porvenir es un abismo insondable, en que ha de hundirse infaliblemente. ¡Dichosa España que cuenta con tantos recuerdos, y que por entre el desastroso presente que la abruma, entrevé un porvenir de felicidad y bienandanza!

> [A people that is unable to turn back with delight to the vision of its past glories can hope for no happy future. The past for such a people is nothing: the present can offer it only a thousand calamities; and the future is a fathomless abyss into which it must needs fall. How fortunate is Spain in that it can count upon so many memories, and in that amidst the catastrophic present that enshrouds it it can yet glimpse a happy and prosperous future!] [117]

What might not be immediately evident is that the Spanish writer here paraphrases comments given by Friedrich Schlegel (a writer upon whom Amador would closely rely, as we shall see, in constructing his *Historia crítica de la literatura española*) in his Vienna lectures of 1812. [118] This edifying and ennobling appeal of past tradition, or apprehension, in *casticista* terms, of a priceless and enduring *Volksgeist*, felt by the great German writer to be indispensable to the whole intellectual existence of a nation, reveals how retrospective and how nostalgic were the dominant contemporary prescriptions for the political, philosophical, and cultural reorganization of Spain. As José Escobar has indicated, inherent in such prescriptions was the idealized vision of a pre-revolutionary world, one which had not known the systematic dehumanization of contemporary society. [119] At the heart of the larger process, therefore, would be the traditionalist tenets of the Romantic historical imagination, of which the mediaeval revival that I have sought to interpret here was to be just one representative part.

Notes to Chapter 1

1. John B. Halsted (ed.), *Romanticism: Selected Documents* (London, 1969), 'Introduction', p. 30.
2. Cited by Stephen Bann, 'Romanticism in France', in *Romanticism in National Context*, ed. by Roy Porter and Mikuláš Teich (Cambridge, 1988), pp. 240–59 (p. 249).
3. Cited by Douglas Johnson, 'Historians', in *The French Romantics*, ed. by D. G. Charlton, 2 vols (Cambridge, 1984), II, 274–307 (p. 290).
4. For documentary information on Spanish translations of Scott, see José F. Montesinos, *Introducción a una historia de la novela en España en el siglo XIX* (Madrid, 1966), pp. 239–40.
5. All contained in the weekly *Semanario Pintoresco Español*, 1 (1836), and published between the first issue, dated 3 April, and that of 1 May.
6. *A Dream of Order: The Medieval Ideal in Nineteenth-Century Literature* (London, 1971), p. 5.
7. See chapter 7, 'The Perception of Literature's Role in Society', in my *Spanish Romantic Literary Theory and Criticism*, pp. 130–50, and also my article 'Zorrilla, the Critics and the Direction of Spanish Romanticism', in *José Zorrilla, 1893–1993: Centennial Readings*, ed. by Richard A. Cardwell and Ricardo Landeira, (Nottingham, 1993), pp.1–15.
8. *The Romantic Period in Germany*, ed. Siegbert Prawer (London, 1970), 'Introduction', p. 11.
9. *Metahistory*, p. 38.
10. *Metahistory*, p. 47.
11. *Historiografía romántica española*, p. 333.
12. *Curso de Historia de la civilización de España, lecciones pronunciadas en el Liceo de Valencia y en el Ateneo*

de Madrid en los cursos de 1840 y 1841 por el profesor de historia en ambos establecimientos literarios, 6 vols (Madrid, 1841–46), I, 7–8, 22.

13. *Introducción a la historia moderna*, p. 11.

14. *Introducción a la historia moderna*, p. 10. Gervasio Gironella, though more circumspect, had made much the same point as Gil y Zárate in highlighting cultural differences which, he at least felt, made absolute comparisons inappropriate:

> En cuanto a constituciones, fuera tal vez cuerdo no admirar ni condenar a ninguno, sino relativamente. Tal forma de gobierno conviene a un siglo, a un pueblo, que no pudiera ser admitida en otro tiempo y en otra nación [...] De consiguiente, si el feudalismo se estableció y reinó durante siglos en toda Europa, conozcamos que aquel gobierno era entonces el único conveniente y posible, atendido el estado de las costumbres, de las ideas y de la inteligencia humana. ('La historia considerada como ciencia de los hechos', *Revista de Madrid*, 2nd series, 1 (1839), 36–66 (p. 59), 222–37)).

> [As far as political constitutions are concerned, it might be wiser to refrain from either admiring or condemning any one of them, unless in relative terms. A given form of government is suited to a particular age and people, and might not be applicable to another different time and nation [...] Consequently, if feudalism came to be established and exercise domination for centuries in every part of Europe, let us frankly state that such a form of governance was then the only possible and practicable one, if we bear in mind the prevalent state of society's customs, thought-patterns and knowledge.]

The majority of contemporary accounts would nonetheless be far more programmatic; it is perhaps significant, then, that Gironella's piece was a translation from a French original.

15. 'Estudios históricos sobre las bellas artes en la edad media. Arquitectura: siglos XIII–XIV–XV', *El Siglo Pintoresco*, 1 (1845), 163–68, 193–202 (p. 199).

16. *Ensayo histórico sobre los diversos géneros de arquitectura empleados en España desde la dominación romana hasta nuestros días* (Madrid, 1848), pp. vi–vii.

17. *Ensayo histórico*, pp. xi–xii.

18. *Ensayo histórico*, p. 25.

19. *Ensayo histórico*, pp. 269–70.

20. *Oración pronunciada en la solemne apertura del curso académico de 1850 a 1851, de la Universidad de Madrid, por el Doctor Don José Amador de los Ríos, catedrático de literatura española en los Estudios superiores de la Facultad de Filosofía* (Madrid, 1850), pp. 13–14.

21. *Oración pronunciada en la solemne apertura*, p. 17.

22. *Introducción a la historia moderna*, p. 41.

23. *Introducción a la historia moderna*, p. 213. The great German cultural historian had affirmed as a determining principle, in the first of his Vienna lectures, that Christianity had proved a sublime and beneficent religion regenerating the ancient world from exhaustion and debasement, and a guiding principle in the history of modern nations: see *A Course of Lectures on Dramatic Art and Literature*, tr. John Black, 2 vols (London, 1815).

24. *Introducción a la historia moderna*, p. 193.

25. *Curso de Historia*, III, 227.

26. *Curso de Historia*, I, 160.

27. *Historia de la civilización española, desde la invasión de los árabes hasta la época presente*, 4 vols (Madrid, 1840), I, 15.

28. *Revista de Madrid*, 2nd series, 1 (1839), pp. 56–57.

29. 'Bellas artes: génesis del arte cristiano', *El Renacimiento*, 28 March 1847, pp. 17–18. A further piece by Madrazo, entitled 'Bellas artes: sobre una de las causas de la decadencia del arte antiguo', followed in a later issue of the same periodical. In it, the author remarked that 'Sería de desear y lo deseamos con todo nuestro corazón, que los que, olvidados de la ley eterna de perfectibilidad que rige al mundo, sólo ven barbarie y decadencia en los primeros siglos, que con su clara luz alumbró el Evangelio de Cristo, pensaran con alguna detención en la historia de los últimos siglos de la edad pagana, para que se convenciesen del gran beneficio que hacía a la sociedad aquel cristianismo, al parecer rudo e incivil, moralizándola a pesar de los más grandes obstáculos, a pesar de la doble muerte que le amagaba: de la muerte material, con los suplicios, tormentos y persecuciones, de la muerte moral, con las herejías y el escepticismo': *El Renacimiento*, 18 April 1847, pp. 41–43.

[It is a desirable goal, and we desire it with our whole heart, that those who, forgetful of the timeless law of perfectibility that governs this world, see only a barbaric and degraded state of affairs in those earliest centuries upon which shone the true light of Christ's gospel, seriously reflect upon the history of the final stages of the pagan age, and convince themselves of the benefits worked upon society by that Christian ethos, seemingly coarse and lacking in civility, which nonetheless brought morality to that society despite all the most considerable obstacles, despite the twin deathly threats that menaced it: of physical death, in the form of torture, punishment and persecution; and of moral death, in the form of heresy and scepticism.]

30. According to the German writer, Greek culture cultivated a beauty of no higher character than that of a refined and ennobled sensuality.

31. *Ensayo sobre las sociedades antiguas y modernas y sobre los gobiernos representativos. Por Don Fermín Gonzalo Morón, Profesor del Ateneo y autor de la Historia de la Civilización de España* (Madrid, 1844), p. 16.

32. *Ensayo sobre las sociedades antiguas y modernas*, pp. 19–20.

33. See Chapter 6 below.

34. *Ensayo sobre las sociedades antiguas y modernas*, p. 21.

35. *Historiografía romántica española*, pp. 336–37.

36. 'Filosofía de la historia: Caballería', *El Laberinto*, 2 (1845), 118–20 (pp. 119–20).

37. *El Laberinto*, 2, (p.120).

38. *El Siglo Pintoresco*, 1 (1845), p. 196.

39. See my *Spanish Romantic Literary Theory and Criticism*, pp. 10–11; the first of Mitjana's comments, meanwhile, parallels a section of the tenth lecture, where A. W. Schlegel writes: 'The charm of the Spanish poetry consists, generally speaking, in the union of the sublime and enthusiastic seriousness of feeling, which peculiarly descends from the North, with the lovely breath of the South'.

40. A.W. Schlegel, *A Course of Lectures on Dramatic Art and Literature*, trans. by John Black, 2 vols (London, 1815), I, 342; F. Schlegel, *Lectures on the History of Literature, Ancient and Modern*, trans. by John Gibson Lockhart, 2 vols (Edinburgh, 1818), II, 91.

41. Durán's celebrated *Discurso sobre el influjo que ha tenido la crítica moderna en la decadencia del teatro antiguo español y sobre el modo con que debe ser considerado para juzgar convenientemente de su mérito peculiar* is reproduced in *El romanticismo español: Documentos*, ed. by Ricardo Navas-Ruiz (Salamanca, 1971), 54–100; the citation from p. 85. For a full examination of the ideas contained in it, see David T. Gies, *Agustín Durán: A Biography and Literary Appreciation* (London, 1975); for the specific framework of ideas discussed here, see my *Spanish Romantic Literary Theory and Criticism*, pp. 34–38.

42. 'Trozos del retrato histórico de don Enrique de Aragón, Marqués de Villena', *El Laberinto*, 1 (1843–44), 114–15 (p. 114).

43. *Curso de Historia*, III, 12; Gonzalo Morón again more or less paraphrases A. W. Schlegel's Vienna lectures, where we find the following: 'If the feeling of religion, true heroism, honour, and love, are the foundation of the romantic poetry, born and grown up in Spain under such auspices, it could not fail to assume the highest elevation': *A Course of Lectures*, trans. by Black, I, 344.

44. 'De la nacionalidad', *La Civilización*, 2 (1842), 61–72 (p. 67).

45. *El Iris*, 2 (1841), 135.

46. *El Iris*, 2, 121.

47. 'Examen filosófico del teatro español, relación del mismo con las costumbres y la nacionalidad de España', *El Iris*, II (1841), 281.

48. *Curso de Historia*, IV, 13.

49. 'Costumbres caballerescas de la edad media: El Paso Honroso', *El Laberinto*, 2 (1845), 217–19 (p. 217).

50. *Curso de Historia*, V, 184.

51. *Curso de Historia*, V, 192.

52. *Curso de Historia*, V, 206.

53. *El Iris*, 2 (1841), 121.

54. *El Iris*, 2, 153.

55. *El Iris*, 2, 154.

56. See David T. Gies (ed.), *El romanticismo* (Madrid, 1989), p. 163; given in English by Philip Silver, *Ruin and Restitution*, p. 10.

57. 'La edad media', *Revista de Madrid*, 2nd series, IV (1840), 117–32 (pp. 118–19).

58. *Revista de Madrid*, 2nd series, 4, (1840), 124–25.

59. *Revista de Madrid*, 2nd series, 4, 117, 132.

60. 'Creación de la Orden de la Banda', *El Laberinto*, 1 (1843–44), 255–58 (p. 258).

61. 'Crítica literaria: *Historia general de España desde los tiempos más remotos hasta nuestros días*, por D. Modesto Lafuente, Madrid, 1850 y 1851', *Eco Literario de Europa*, 1 (1851), 226–40 (p. 237).

62. See *Metahistory*, pp. 51–52, on which I have here freely drawn. White subsequently summarizes as follows: 'Poetry, myth, legend, fable — none of these was conceived to have real value as historical evidence. Once recognised as products of fantasy, they testified only to the superstitious nature of the imagination that had produced them or to the stupidity of those who had taken them for truths. For this reason the historical accounts of remote ages produced by the Enlightenment tended to be little more than condensations of (or commentaries on) the accounts of the historical works actually produced by those ages': *Metahistory*, p. 53.

63. See my *Spanish Romantic Literary Theory and Criticism*, pp. 13–14.

64. 'De la influencia social de Francia en España', *El Pensamiento* (1841), 255–58 (p. 257).

65. *Curso de Historia*, III, 185.

66. *Oración pronunciada en la solemne apertura*, pp. 18–19.

67. *Historiografía romántica española*, p. 338.

68. *Ruin and Restitution*, p. 11.

69. *Reflexiones sobre el modo de escribir la historia de España* (Madrid, 1816), pp. 69–72 (quotation, p. 72).

70. *Cartilla historial o método para escribir la historia* (Madrid, 1829), p. 32.

71. Antonio Alcalá Galiano, 'Reflexiones sobre la influencia del espíritu caballeresco de la edad media en la civilización europea', *Revista Científica y Literaria*, 1 (1847), 193–202 (p. 198), 267–79.

72. '¿Cuál es el método o sistema preferible para escribir la historia?', *Revista de Madrid*, 2nd series, 2 (1839), 531–39 (pp. 533–34).

73. Joaquín Sánchez de Fuentes, 'Preliminares al estudio del derecho público', *Revista de España y del Extranjero*, 9 (1844), 267–86 (pp. 274–75). Here he was concurring with Eugenio de Tapia's view that chivalry 'influyó favorablemente en las costumbres' [exerted a favourable influence upon contemporary customs]; while it flourished, stated the latter, 'fueron frecuentes los rasgos de heroísmo, de noble desinterés, de amparo a los desvalidos, de pundonorosa galantería con el bello sexo' [there were numerous and characteristic examples of heroism, of noble selflessness, of help offered to the defenceless, of scrupulous gallantry with regard to the fairer sex]: *Historia de la civilización española*, II, 258.

74. *El Iris*, 2 (1841), 56.

75. *El Iris*, 2, 184.

76. *El Iris*, 2, 282.

77. *Curso de Historia*, V, 184–85.

78. *Revista de Madrid*, 2nd series, 4 (1840), 125.

79. The speech, entitled 'La poesía considerada como elemento de la historia', was printed in full in the *Eco Literario de Europa*, 2 (1852), 361–77; the above citations from p. 363.

80. *Eco Literario de Europa*, 2, 366–67.

81. *Eco Literario de Europa*, 2, 367.

82. *Eco Literario de Europa*, 2, 368.

83. *Eco Literario de Europa*, 2, 370–71.

84. *Eco Literario de Europa*, 2, 372.

85. *Eco Literario de Europa*, 2, 373.

86. *Eco Literario de Europa*, 2, 377.

87. Pidal's reply similarly appeared in the *Eco Literario de Europa*, 2, 378–91; the citations from pp. 380–81. He had himself much earlier expressed the fundamental prescriptions of Romantic historicism in an expansive piece dealing with the literature surrounding the figure of El Cid. Here Pidal stipulated the need to 'estudiar en las producciones literarias el espíritu y la índole de cada pueblo y de cada época, y descubrir por este medio las máximas y sentimientos que en ellos dominaban y prevalecían' [study, in literary works, the spirit and nature of the age and people that had produced them, and by such means discover the feelings and principles dominant therein]; he defined literature as 'la expresión más pronunciada de las ideas, sentimientos y creencias de la época a que se refiere' [the

most pronounced expression of the ideas, feelings and beliefs of the age to which it belongs]. Pidal asserted that 'Un canto, un romance, un cuento popular puede valer bajo este aspecto mucho más, que la epopeya más clásica y perfecta' [A song, a ballad, a popular tale may, according to this perspective, be of greater value than the most formally perfect epic poem] and, with specific reference to the Spanish Middle Ages, that 'la literatura vulgar debía en aquella época, mejor que en otra ninguna, ser un traslado fiel de los intereses y pasiones que agitaban y conmovían a la sociedad' [the literature of the common people must perforce, in those times more than in any other, have been a true reflection of the ambitions and passions that animated and moved society]: 'Literatura española: Poema del Cid — Crónica del Cid — Romancero del Cid', *Revista de Madrid*, 2nd series, 3 (1840), 306–44 (pp. 306–07, 331). Even the most superficial reading of articles published in that prestigious journal reveals the virtual unanimity of its contributors on such points.

88. As expressed by Gonzalo Morón, *Curso de Historia*, III, 185.

89. *Historia de la civilización española*, I, 258–59.

90. *Historia de la civilización española*, II, 188.

91. *Historia de la civilización española*, II, 210.

92. *Romances*, ed. Cipriano Rivas Cherif, 2 vols (Madrid, 1911–12), I, 24.

93. 'Reflexiones sobre Homero y la tragedia griega: Caracteres distintivos de la literatura antigua y moderna', *El Iris*, 1 (1841), 340–42, 385–88 (p. 388).

94. *El Siglo Pintoresco*, 1 (1845), 164.

95. I reproduce here the following section of Mitjana's article, one that admirably reflects the quintessentially Romantic attractions of the Gothic for nineteenth-century writers:

Las sombras vagas, el crepúsculo melancólico que reinan bajo esas bóvedas elevadas expresan el desfallecimiento del universo oscurecido desde la caída del primer hombre. Un dolor misterioso se apodera del corazón apenas se ha traspasado el umbral de ese noble recinto. Mil pensamientos de temor, de esperanza, de vida, de muerte, se agrupan en el alma, formando con su mezcla indefinible una especie de atmósfera silenciosa que calma, que adormece los sentidos, y al través de la cual se revela envuelto en vagarosa lumbre, el mundo invisible. Un poder secreto nos atrae hacia el punto convergente de las espaciosas naves, allí donde reside velado el Dios redentor del hombre y reparador de la creación, y desde donde emana la virtud plástica que imprime al templo su forma. En sus ejes cruzados se ostenta el símbolo de la eterna salvación, y en su centro, la imagen del Arca, único asilo de las esperanzas del género humano en los días del diluvio y emblema siempre fiel del penoso viaje del hombre sobre las olas de la vida. Las curvas ojivales de los arcos, las agujas que por do quier se lanzan al espacio sin límites, el movimiento de ascensión, de elevación, de cada parte del templo y del templo entero, expresan claramente la aspiración, el vuelo espontáneo de la criatura hacia Dios, su principio y su término. (p. 164).

[The uncertain shadows, the melancholy twilight that reign beneath these soaring vaulted roofs are an expression of the inner weakness of a world darkened by mankind's original sin. A mysterious sorrow grips the heart almost as soon as one steps over the threshold of this noble place. A thousand sensations of fear, hope, life and death, throng the soul, forming in their nameless commingling a kind of balmy silence that quiets and lulls the senses, and in the midst of which the invisible world may be glimpsed in its wavering light. Some secret power draws us to that point where the spacious naves converge, to that point where there resides, beneath a veil, the Saviour of mankind and healer of the created world, to that point whence emanates the virtuous artistic sense that has lent the church its form. In its lines there is set forth before us the symbol of eternal salvation, and at the centre of the cross the image of the Ark, the sole shelter of the hopes of all humanity in the days of the great flood and the timeless faithful emblem of the travails of mankind's journey upon the waves of life. The pointed arches, the needles that everywhere thrust their way into limitless space, the heavenward movement of elevation found in every constituent part of the church and in its whole, express with such clarity the aspiration, the spontaneous flight of every creature towards God, beginning and end of all.]

96. *Obras completas*, ed. by Ricardo Navas Ruiz (Madrid, 1995), I, 651–52.

97. *Obras completas*, ed. by Navas Ruiz, I, 706.

98. *La viña y los surcos*, p. 97.

99. *Obras completas*, ed. by Navas Ruiz, I, 655.

100. *La viña y los surcos*, p. 17.

101. Rubén Benítez, *Bécquer tradicionalista* (Madrid, 1971), pp. 51–52.

102. *Bécquer tradicionalista*, p. 52.

103. *Ruin and Restitution*, p. 76.

104. *Ruin and Restitution*, p. 80.

105. *Bécquer tradicionalista*, pp. 58, 37; Benítez felt that, particularly in the section dealing with San Juan de los Reyes, Donoso Cortés had been the 'modelo de algunas páginas impregnadas de retórica cristiana' [inspiring model of several pages saturated with Christian rhetoric] (p. 35).

106. *Gustavo Adolfo Bécquer. Vida y poesía* (Madrid, 1971), p. 193.

107. *Ensayo histórico*, pp. 421–22.

108. *Ensayo histórico*, pp. 422–23.

109. 'Estudios críticos: Rápida ojeada acerca del rumbo que ha seguido la literatura dramática española en 1847', *Antología Española*, 1 (1848), 97–108 (p. 101).

110. 'Literatura española del siglo XVIII', *Antología Española*, 2 (1848), 53–62 (p. 56).

111. 'En torno al Rivas de los *Romances históricos*', in *La poesía romántica. Actas del VII Congreso del Centro Internacional de Estudios sobre el Romanticismo Hispánico*, ed. by Piero Menarini (Bologna, 2000), pp. 185–91 (pp. 187–88).

112. Cited by Hans Juretschke, 'El problema de los orígenes del romanticismo español', in the *Historia de España Menéndez Pidal. XXXV: La época del romanticismo (1808–1874)*. I: *Orígenes, religión, filosofía, ciencia* (Madrid 1989), pp. 206–07.

113. José María Jover Zamora (ed.), *Historia de España Menéndez Pidal. XXXIV: La era isabelina y el sexenio democrático (1834–1874)* (Madrid, 1981), 'Prólogo', p. xciv.

114. *Historia de España Menéndez Pidal*, XXXIV, pp. xciv–xcv.

115. *Historia crítica del pensamiento español. IV: Liberalismo y romanticismo (1808–1874)* (Madrid, 1984), p. 246.

116. *El romanticismo español: historia y crítica* (Salamanca, 1970), 14.

117. *El Laberinto*, 2 (1845), 369–70, 377–78, 385–90 (p. 390).

118. In the published edition, the passage in full reads as follows:

there is nothing so necessary to the whole improvement, or rather to the whole intellectual existence of a nation, as the possession of a plentiful store of those national recollections and associations, which are lost in a great measure during the dark ages of infant society, but which it forms the great object of the poetical art to perpetuate and adorn. Such national recollections, the noblest inheritance which a people can possess, bestow an advantage which no other riches can supply; for when a people are exalted by their feelings, and ennobled in their own estimation, by the consciousness that they have been illustrious in ages that are gone by — that these recollections have come down to them from a remote and a heroic ancestry — in a word, that they have a *national poetry* of their own, we are willing to acknowledge that their pride is reasonable, and they are raised in our eyes by the same circumstance which gives them elevation in their own. (*Lectures on the History of Literature, Ancient and Modern*, trans. Lockhart, I, 15)

119. 'Romanticismo y revolución', *Estudios de Historia Social*, 36–37 (1986), 345–51; reproduced in *El romanticismo*, ed. by Gies, pp. 320–35 (p. 332).

CHAPTER 2

'Elementary' Historiography:
Spanish Reactions to Guizot

Speaking in a preamble to the course of lectures delivered at the Liceo Artístico y Literario de Madrid in 1841 that, in its published form, became his *Introducción a la historia moderna*, Antonio Gil y Zárate neatly summarized the prevailing Romantic preference for things mediaeval:

> La imaginación se complace hoy día en renovar los recuerdos de la Edad Media. Sus tradiciones, sus costumbres, sus aventuras, sus monumentos tienen para el público un atractivo que no se puede negar. Véanse la literatura y las artes, véanse las novelas, las historias, las poesías de esta época; véanse hasta los almacenes de muebles, por todas partes se encuentra la Edad Media, por todas partes ocupa el pensamiento, recrea el gusto y sirve a satisfacer, ora las necesidades, ora los placeres intelectuales de nuestros contemporáneos.[1]

> [Nowadays the imagination so delights in remembering anew the Middle Ages. Traditions, customs, tales of adventure, historical monuments, all possess for the public an undeniable attraction. Look at literature and the arts, look at the novels, stories, and poems of our day; look even at those places where we purchase our furniture, everywhere we find the Middle Ages, everywhere it occupies our thoughts, satisfies our tastes, and answers as much to the needs as to the intellectual pleasures of our contemporary society.]

At first sight, Gil y Zárate's remarks seem no more than a superficial pleasantry directed at his immediate audience. A closer scrutiny, however, soon begins to yield much wider and far-reaching implications. In fact, this apparently innocuous course of lectures aimed at amusing and instructing Madrid's polite society was to play no insignificant part in fomenting a polemical and ideologically weighted discussion, a crucial debate that was to have at its nucleus opposed views of the essential character of history and of the laws ultimately governing human development.

There are three immediate pointers to be considered here. Firstly, as the full title of the published work with its reference to 'elementos que han entrado a constituir la civilización' [elements that have together come to constitute our civilization] irresistibly suggests, Gil y Zárate was to rely extensively upon the work of the French historian and statesman François Guizot (1787–1874) for his conceptual overview. Secondly, the passage cited is in fact a direct translation from Guizot's lectures on French history delivered at the Sorbonne between 1828 and 1830, published under the title *Histoire de la civilisation en France depuis la chute de l'Empire Romain*.[2] Although he does not specifically acknowledge this particular debt, Gil y Zárate was openly to state in his preamble that among the many works that had aided him in the preparation of his talks, those of Guizot had served as his principal guide; it would be readily evident to those who had read them, he went on, how much he was indebted to the French writer.[3] Just how closely Gil y Zárate relied upon his source text in the example given would not have been immediately perceptible, since Guizot's lectures on the history of France had not then been translated into Spanish; Gil y Zárate, who had spent much of his childhood in Paris, would have read them in the original French. Thirdly, and this is ultimately the most important point, in some of the succeeding lectures Gil y Zárate's reliance upon Guizot might have been rather more apparent to his audience. Here, in dealing with the historical role of the Catholic church, he was closely to paraphrase a number of ideologically controversial sections of the French writer's *Histoire de la civilisation en Europe*, which had already appeared in various Spanish translations. In just a ten-year period, Spanish editions appeared in Madrid (1839, 1840, 1846, and 1847), Barcelona (1839 and 1849) and Cadiz (1839) .Their relative profusion provides an accurate reflection of the considerable — and, as we shall see, controversial — intellectual currency enjoyed by Guizot during the same decade.[4]

The significance of Guizot's work for Spanish writers has yet to be considered at any length by modern criticism. The nearest thing to a full account is provided by Javier Fernández Sebastián, who begins his survey article by stressing the heavy imprint of the historiological approach of the French statesman on a range of Spanish writers of the 1840s, including Gil y Zárate, Eugenio de Tapia, Juan Cortada, and Fermín Gonzalo Morón.[5] Manuel Moreno Alonso has noted the influence of Guizot upon Spanish historians to be 'considerable',[6] and Hans Juretschke has described his presence as significantly underestimated.[7] Andrew Ginger frequently alludes to the importance of Guizot for the articulation of political thought, especially by progressive liberals, but not to the polemical status of his configuration of history nor to the deployment of Guizot's historiographical pattern in those larger general histories of Spain that Romanticism was to produce. Yet the figure of the French historian and statesman was to be central to discussion of the meaning and interpretation of history throughout the 1840s.

It is at this point that Gil y Zárate's course of public lectures at the Liceo, to which I shall return in much greater detail, begins to assume a crucial significance within the Spanish intellectual climate and, more specifically, within the ongoing religious debate. For in the France of the post-Napoleonic Restoration, Guizot's own lectures had been felt to encapsulate a philosophy of history for doctrinaire liberalism, a political movement of which the historian himself was perceived as the intellectual motor. The 'elementary' approach to history adumbrated in the lectures on European civilization contended that cultural advancement was, and always had been in Europe since the fall of Rome, the product of historical interaction. Three civilizing elements — Roman, Germanic, and Christian — had contributed to the gestation of a new European civilization in the wake of the sack of Rome, combining to shape an incipient and still incoherent cultural impulse. As Europe entered the mediaeval period, a process of friction between the opposed groupings of society — throne, Church and nobility, plus, as time passed, populace — had created a permanent state of flux in which alliances regularly changed and in which no one grouping or political influence was allowed to establish enduring domination. This struggle, argued Guizot, had not become a principle of immobility but had proved the indispensable breeding-ground of progress, the most energetic and fertile principle of European civilization.[8] For the French historian, the idea of progress, of development, had been the fundamental idea contained in the very word civilization. In Hayden White's terms, then, Guizot's strategy is a 'Contextualist' one, that represents a 'functional' conception of the meaning or significance of events discerned in the historical field. What happened in that field for the Contextualist historian, as White explains it, 'can be accounted for by the specification of the functional interrelationships existing among the agents and agencies occupying the field at a given time', so that Contextualism suppresses 'abstractive tendencies' and avoids construing events according to 'general teleological principles'; instead, history is driven by 'actual relationships that are presumed to have existed at specific times and places', and the historical account is marked by a 'relative integration of the phenomena discerned in finite provinces of historical occurrence in terms of "trends" or general physiognomies of periods and epochs'.[9]

Crises such as the Reformation or the French Revolution had been marked, argued Guizot, by just such a general idea or principle, and had thus served to impel the inevitable forward movement of history. The French historian viewed the Reformation as a bold process of emancipation of the human mind, without which European civilization could not have experienced the potent advances recorded in recent centuries. As Guizot described it:

> C'est une grande tentative d'affranchissement de la pensée humaine: et, pour appeler les choses pour leur nom, une insurrection de l'esprit humain contre le pouvoir absolu dans l'ordre spirituel. Tel est, selon moi, le véritable caractère, le caractère général et dominant de la réforme.
>
> [This is a great striving towards the emancipation of human thought: and, if we are to describe things in appropriate terms, an insurrection of the human spirit against all absolute power in the spiritual realm. Such is, as I see it, the true nature, the general and prevailing characteristic of the Reformation].[10]

Guizot had elsewhere described the French Revolution as a terrible but legitimate struggle of right against privilege, of legal freedom against arbitrary power. In Ceri Crossley's words: 'It was axiomatic for Guizot that progress exists and is a good. History leads in effect to the triumph of the principles of Enlightenment liberalism'.[11] The Guizot of the 1820s, he observes, espoused the cause of change and employed a rhetoric of movement.[12] Insofar then as Guizot presumed to reveal a *telos* towards which the whole historical process tended — something White regards as indispensable if the Contextualist historian is to arrive at an aggregate or comprehensive view — [13] that over-arching end was a secular one, of human progress.

In the Spanish context, the French historian's committed Protestantism and progressive vision were to make his work unpalatable in the extreme in conservative intellectual circles, and was to elicit a violent reaction among neo-Catholics. On the other hand, the fact that Gil y Zárate was to adhere closely to what were ideologically the most contentious sections of Guizot's lectures argue a more favourable reception of the Frenchman's framework among more liberal writers. As will become apparent in this and in the succeeding chapter, a close examination of historical studies of the period indicates a polemical divide among historians along largely ideological lines. While a number of Spanish writers would side with Guizot's 'elementary' approach, more conservative historians were to adopt an antagonistic historical framework based upon the *Scienza nuova* of the Neapolitan thinker Giambattista Vico (1668–1744). It is a compelling panorama, one which allows the modern historian of ideas to chart the assimilation and integration of conflicting visions of history by opposed ideological camps, each determined to emerge triumphant in an intellectual battle for minds. As we shall see from an analysis of the relevant texts, erudition allied with ingenious explication in an attempt to justify the experience of the contemporary age of transition within a coherent and sequential historical pattern. It is an ideological debate that both assimilates and anticipates elements of a more systematic confrontation between irreconcilable groupings traditionally designated the 'Two Spains'.

Documentary evidence suggests that the last years of the 1830s saw a marked intensification of interest in the philosophy of history as an intellectual discipline; a proliferation of articles in prestigious journals such as the *Revista de Madrid* indicates that it was given a much higher academic profile. Among pieces featuring in this periodical in 1839 was Gervasio Gironella's translation of an article by one Charles du Rozoir under the title 'La historia considerada como ciencia de los hechos'.[14] Among the practitioners of 'la historia politica y moral' [political and moral history] figured the name of Guizot, whose courses on the history of France and on European civilization were hailed as a felicitous combination of erudition and intellectual versatility, at once ingenious and impartial; the French historian, it was concluded, himself a participant member of an 'escuela filosófica y racional' [philosophical and rationalist school], had pioneered a new political science disposed to move forward with the secular world and the institutions of the age, and to exert a formative influence upon new generations willing to countenance that same science and to seek to understand it.[15]

Even in these apparently innocuous comments, the germs of discord are clearly perceptible. Many Catholic intellectuals spurned the idea of modern 'progress' and vilified both the philosophical legacy which their age had inherited and the political changes which it had produced. In many forms of writing, French rationalist philosophy — often designated by the pejorative term 'filosofismo' [philosophizing] — was consistently anathematized as the harbinger of a later wholescale moral collapse and crisis of belief. The ideas of the *philosophes*, described as 'disolventes', or corrosive, on account of their alleged undermining of established values, were regularly charged with bringing about not just the French Revolution but all of the political instability, religious scepticism, and moral uncertainty that had subsequently beset western Europe. As far as conservative literary critics were concerned, they had been ultimately responsible for the balefully immoral spectacle presented by the Romantic dramas of Victor Hugo and Alexandre Dumas, which had enjoyed a short-lived vogue immediately prior to the period under discussion. The prominent Catholic intellectual Alberto Lista, for example, in writing of contemporary literature, would accuse French rationalist philosophy of 'demoliendo poco a poco todas las ilusiones, todas las ideas, todos los sentimientos del corazón humano' [demolishing piece by piece every dream and aspiration, every idea, every feeling contained in the human heart].[16] The neo-Catholic philosopher Jaime Balmes, meanwhile, destined to prove one of Guizot's most trenchant adversaries, referred scathingly to men who believed themselves to be progressive and up-to-date simply because they had swallowed whole the works of the eighteenth century and who consequently saw in society nothing more than material self-interest.[17] The mood of the time meant that Gironella's description of Guizot as belonging to an 'escuela filosófica y racional' would have at once alerted traditionalists to what they might with some consternation have envisaged as a further potential threat to the hegemony of their doctrine. The prospect that Guizot's work might prove a formative influence upon a new generation was to prove repellent to Catholic traditionalists: it was unthinkable that his positive view of the Reformation, and likewise his stipulation that the Church had been merely one of several constituent elements in the development of European civilization rather than that civilization's sole cultural imperative, should achieve the status of received knowledge among younger Spanish intellectuals.

Whatever inimical feelings may already have been aroused in certain circles, the reputation and influence of Guizot became rapidly extended in Spain between 1839 and 1841. Gironella's two-part biographical study of the French statesman, again published in the *Revista de Madrid* in 1839,[18] may have been put together in response to interest awakened by his own earlier piece, but was more probably prompted by the appearance in the same year of separate translations of the *Histoire de la civilisation en Europe* published in Madrid and Barcelona. Each of these Spanish editions carried a translator's preface. The Barcelona translator, one 'H. F. C.' (whom I have thus far been unable to identify) described Guizot's history as one of a select few genuinely enduring works to be produced in a period of rapid socio-political change and transition. He commented: 'El lento y sucesivo desarrollo de todos los elementos que constituyen las sociedades modernas, y que han contribuido a la civilización de los pueblos, está descrito y manifestado con una superioridad y maestría que pasma' [The slow and gradual development of all those elements that constitute modern societies, and which have helped to form the civilization of all peoples, is here described with outstanding skill and with a mastery that is astonishing].[19] An understandable and, one might say, not entirely disinterested proclamation of a work destined, as the translator put it, for immortality. However, a notable caveat is adduced by the translator towards the end of his preface: 'aquí se ve el espíritu de la iglesia, y cuán útiles y benéficos han sido sus efectos en la civilización general, aunque por otra parte al hablar de ella vierte el autor ciertos conceptos y usa a veces cierto lenguaje, el cual no debe extraviarse [sic: printing error for 'extrañarse'?] atendidas sus ideas y opiniones' [here we see the spirit of the church, and how useful and beneficent have been its effects upon civilization in general, although on the other hand the author, in referring to this, professes certain theories and employs at times a kind of language that should not surprise us when we take into account his ideas and opinions].[20] Given the circumstances, overtly negative criticism was unlikely to figure, but the inference is clear: Guizot's historical view of the Church, tainted as the translator saw it by the author's Protestantism, is regarded as a partial, ideologically weighted one, and readers of the Spanish edition are warned against it before they go on to read the substance of the text. More detached observers would naturally not have felt constrained to profess such a circumspect note of disapproval.

The Madrid translator likewise used his preface to introduce readers to Guizot's theory of 'elementos principales' [principal elements], rendered as 'aristocracia, teocracia, democracia, monarquía' [aristocracy, theocracy, democracy, monarchy].[21] This time the translator's stance is even more discreet, although I again incline to the view that this was something largely imposed by circumstances. The translator was José Vicente y Carabantes, an expert in jurisprudence and enthusiastic *literato*, and a regular contributor to popular journals of the time. Carabantes's translation especially seems to have been widely read by Spanish intellectuals, and there is certainly abundant textual evidence to show the rapid penetration of Guizot's framework of ideas during 1840 and 1841.

The former year saw the publication of the first of five general histories of Spain to appear in the course of that decade.[22] The very title of the work is reminiscent of Guizot's published lectures, and it is not long before its author, Eugenio de Tapia, makes explicit one of the dominant influences on his study. In an introductory chapter on Visigothic Spain, he cites admiringly 'Mr. Guizot en su excelente *Historia de la civilización europea*' [M. Guizot in his excellent *History of European Civilization*], and specifically the French historian's assessment of the Fuero Juzgo. The accompanying note informs us that Tapia was not using an edition of the original French but Carabantes's translation of the previous year.[23]

Tapia's history provides many noteworthy instances of the application to Spanish history of Guizot's schema. A particularly good example is found in the section of Volume II dedicated to the Castilian monarchy from 1300 to 1474. Tapia describes the long drawn-out struggle for supremacy between crown and nobility, at a time when the monarchy was not yet firmly established and when the crown consequently lacked the power fully to assert its hold: 'El elemento aristocrático, más poderoso que él, le combate reciamente' [The aristocratic element, more powerful than the former, robustly challenges it].[24] Tapia then re-creates precisely the concept of 'lucha' between contending factions that had so characterized Guizot's historical vision. He later sums up the broader process:

> Los diversos elementos de la sociedad estaban desunidos y discordes; cada uno obraba en dirección distinta, sin encaminarse a un centro común, y he aquí el turbulento estado de la sociedad. Ya desde el tiempo de las Cruzadas se van combinando y centralizando aquellos diversos elementos por varias causas que desenvuelve con maestría Mr. Guizot en su historia de la civilización europea.[25]

> [The diverse elements of society were disunited and in disagreement; each one worked towards a different goal, and shared no common path, and thus the turbulent state of that society. Ever since the time of the Crusades various causes had resulted in the combination and eventual centralization of those diverse elements, as M. Guizot in his history of European civilization has traced with such consummate skill].

To give a clearer indication still of Tapia's reliance on Guizot, it would be worthwhile to cite here two pieces from the Carabantes translation of the *Histoire de la civilisation en Europe* which the Spanish historian was professedly using. Firstly, of the three periods ascribed by Guizot to the development of a civilized Europe, the translator gives the first, culminating in the twelfth century, as 'el de los orígenes y la formación' [that of its origins and of its formative era], as an ordered society took shape out of chaos; the second, lasting into the sixteenth century, as 'un tiempo de ensayo, de tentativa, de vacilación' [an era of trial and error, of hesitation].[26] We are much more immediately aware of Tapia's debt, however, when Carabantes later translates Guizot's comment that the Crusades had 'producido a la vez más libertad individual y más unidad política, e impulsado a la independencia del hombre y a la centralización de la sociedad' [produced at one and the same time greater individual freedom and greater political unity, and driven forward both human independence and political centralization].[27]

Throughout his four-volume history, Tapia acknowledges the seemingly indisputable authority of his French counterpart. Crucially in the present context, he was to cite Guizot on the emancipatory character of the Reformation as a grand insurrection of the human mind against absolute power in the spiritual order.[28] Tapia's own perspective was that the excessive wealth of the Church, the relaxation of ecclesiastical discipline, and the financial and other demands exacted by the papacy, all made desirable 'una grande y prudente reforma' [great and wise reform]. Instead of this, however, and 'conservando la unidad en la creencia del dogma' [with the retention of a unity of doctrine and belief], there had arisen a violent schism that had unhappily flooded Europe with a torrent of blood.[29] This spiritual revolution had, he felt, in common with all political revolutions, exceeded its original brief, yet his view of church reform is far from negative; speaking of the successes of the Reformation, he comments that 'la intolerancia religiosa vencida en Alemania subsistía en los Países Bajos, y sobre todo en España, donde el poder teocrático iba ganando mucho terreno con la terrible autoridad de la inquisición apoyado por el emperador' [religious intolerance, although overcome in Germany, persisted in the Low Countries, and above all in Spain, where theocratic power gained in strength as a result of that terrible authority vested in the Inquisition and bastioned by the Emperor].[30] Tapia indeed seems implicitly to favour the reforms widely made in northern Europe — the phrase 'la intolerancia vencida' leaves us in little doubt —, contrasting them not with the Spanish Counter-Reformation generally but with its most disturbing and notorious manifestation. Of all the allusions made by Tapia to the work of Guizot, and there are many, this measured, relatively positive assessment of the Reformation is the most ideologically significant.

The first two volumes of Tapia's history were reviewed, in the same year in which they had appeared, in an unsigned 'Crítica literaria' published in the mainstream journal *Semanario Pintoresco Español*. The reviewer pointed to the more philosophical approach to history demanded by the new century, specifying a method which sought to explain the causes of events as well as simply to describe their occurrence. Apparently familiar with Guizot's own historical synthesis as formulated in the *Histoire de la civilisation en Europe*, the writer was critical of it on two accounts: firstly, although profound, it was 'diminuta' [excessively small] in its proportions; secondly, and much more significantly, on account of the 'espíritu de nacionalidad' [nationalistic partiality] which dominated the whole and which, according to the reviewer, greatly detracted from that proper objectivity and rigour which ought to inform such judgements. Tapia's own history, the reviewer declared, although more limited in subject matter was nevertheless a work of greater import.[31]

The reference to 'nacionalidad' in the reviewer's criticism is surely of some significance here, and perhaps helps us to explain the tone of some of the remarks. Offended patriotism was at least in part to condition many Spanish judgements of Guizot's work. No better example than that found in another piece from 1840, Diego Coello y Quesada's 'Sobre la dominación en España de los reyes austríacos', one which arguably anticipates the sharp sense of ideological conflict that was shortly to surface in Balmes: when I read the celebrated Guizot, he comments, and particularly those passages dedicated to the civilization of Spain, I could not but hurl from me in a moment of wounded national pride the work of this illustrious writer and 'profundo filósofo de la Francia' [profound philosopher of France].[32] As these comments indicate, and as much of the documentary evidence already examined has tended to suggest, it was impossible for Guizot's more ideologically laden historical judgements to receive truly impartial coverage on account of at least two crucial factors: the religious perspective contained within them, signally in the assessment of Reformation and Counter-Reformation; and the French historian's relatively negative overview of Spain under the House of Habsburg, and more specifically the reign of Philip II. The contentious nature of these verdicts as expressed by a foreign historian, especially by a French historian, were certain to arouse antagonism in an intellectual climate heavily marked by religious retrenchment and virulent francophobia.

Returning now to the lectures by Gil y Zárate published as an *Introducción a la historia moderna* in 1841, it should be possible to appreciate that the determining influence upon the perspective presented in them, Guizot's *Histoire de la civilisation en Europe*, had already become the centre of considerable attention in the Spanish intellectual domain. When we realize the full implications of Gil y Zárate's contribution to the discussion, the emergence of Guizot's work as a keynote for historians assumes much greater clarity. Since Gil y Zárate was likely to have been using at first hand, in the preparation of his lectures, the Carabantes translation relied on by Eugenio de Tapia, it would not be out of place to make some direct textual comparisons between the two in order to illustrate Gil y Zárate's use of Guizot in certain controversial respects.

Firstly, the Spanish writer echoes his French counterpart in perceiving a separation between ecclesiastical hierarchy and people. In Carabantes's words:

> Preciso es decir que el hecho característico, el vicio radical de las relaciones de la Iglesia con los pueblos es la separación de los gobernantes y gobernados, la no influencia de los gobernados sobre su gobierno, y la independencia del clero cristiano respecto de los fieles.

> [It should be said that the most characteristic feature, the weakness at the root of the relationship between the Church and its people is the separation of governors and governed, the lack of any influence upon government by those being governed, and the detachment of the Christian clergy from the faithful.] (II, 53)

The same assessment reappears in Gil y Zárate's text, including the dualistic opposition between 'gobernantes' and 'gobernados' characteristically favoured by Guizot:

> Desde el momento en que se estableció un gobierno en la sociedad cristiana debió suceder lo que naturalmente acontece en todas las sociedades. Los gobernantes se constituyeron en una clase privilegiada y diferente de la de los gobernados.

> [From the moment that government became established in Christian societies, what happened was what inevitably occurs in every society. A privileged governing class was formed, separate and distinct from those other classes that it governed.] (Lección X, 135)

The point is worth underlining in that it accompanies in both texts the view that the Church, from earliest Christian times, had been structured and ordered just like any secular institution (Carabantes, I, 82–83; Gil y Zárate, Lección IX, 106–07) and had thus been set apart from society at large by its independent organization. Traditionalists categorically denied this stress, placing an entirely different emphasis on the concept of church authority, as we find in Balmes and Donoso Cortés. The latter's 1851 *Ensayo sobre el catolicismo, el liberalismo y el socialismo* contains what is evidently a calculated rejoinder, albeit Guizot's name is not mentioned in precisely this context despite figuring large elsewhere in Donoso's treatise. It seems to me preferable to make the relevant citation here in order to convey the impression of direct reply:

> En esta sociedad prodigiosa [la Iglesia] todas las cosas suceden al revés de como pasan en todas las asociaciones humanas. En éstas la distancia puesta entre los que están al pie y los que están en la cumbre de la jerarquía social es tan grande, que los primeros se sienten tentados del espíritu de rebelión, y los segundos caen en la tentación de la tiranía. En la Iglesia las cosas están ordenadas de tal modo, que ni es posible la tiranía ni son posibles las rebeliones. Aquí la dignidad del súbdito es tan grande, que la del prelado está en lo que tiene de común con el súbdito, más bien que en lo especial que tiene como prelado.[33]

> [In this truly marvellous society everything takes place in a way that is entirely different from that of all other forms of human association. In these last-named the distance placed between those who occupy the foot and those who stand at the top of the social hierarchy is so great, that the former come to be tempted by thoughts of rebellion and the latter to be prompted to tyranny. In the Church everything is ordered in such a way as to render equally impossible both tyranny and rebellion. Here, the dignity of the subordinate person being so great, that of the prelate lies in what he has in common with his subject far more than in any special status he might enjoy as prelate.]

Characteristically, Donoso would seek to reinforce the superior nature of the Church as sacred institution, underlining the way in which divine transcends human. Significantly also, within this elevated sphere forms of rebellion are felt — less than convincingly, one is tempted to reflect — to have no place, whilst promptings towards the abuse of power or towards revolt against authority are suggested, metaphorically at least, to be diabolical urges to which secular society alone is subject.

Two salient faults identified by Guizot in detailing what he felt to be the Catholic church's stifling of individual freedoms are rendered, meanwhile, by Carabantes as, firstly, 'la pretensión de transmitir las creencias de arriba a abajo en toda la sociedad religiosa, sin que nadie tuviera derecho de debatirlas por sí propio' [the attempt to relay belief downwards, from top to bottom, in any religious society, so that no person should have any right, on his own account, to subject them to debate], and, as a second such evil principle, what he describes as

> el derecho de coacción que la iglesia se arrogaba: derecho contrario a la naturaleza de la sociedad religiosa, a su origen y a sus máximas primitivas [...]. La pretensión de forzar a creer, si estas dos palabras se pueden poner juntas, o de castigar materialmente la creencia, la persecución de la herejía, es decir, el desprecio de la libertad legítima del pensamiento humano. (II, 31–33)

> [the right to coercive pressure which the church allotted itself: a right that runs contrary to the whole nature of religious society, to its origins and to its original tenets of morality [. ..]. The attempt to enforce belief, if these last two words can ever be placed together, or to persecute or punish, in physical or material terms, any heretical beliefs; that is to say, a contempt for the legitimate human right of freedom of thought.]

Gil y Zárate does not specifically recreate Guizot's characteristic phrasing, but clearly lifts the passage as a whole with all of its implications, commenting:

> La iglesia pretendía transmitir las creencias por los superiores a los inferiores, sin que nadie tuviese facultad para ponerlas en duda ni resistirlas. Además, obligaba a creer, y castigaba con penas corporales la incredulidad, la herejía. Este principio de coacción, tan contrario a la índole de una sociedad en que por el contrario todo debiera ser libertad, todo convencimiento, es el principio más fatal que ha abrigado el cristianismo, y el origen de males y revoluciones sin cuento. (Leccion X, 138)

> [The Church's intention was to transmit belief from those above to those below, without allowing to anyone the opportunity to doubt or to resist. What is more, it forced people to believe, and applied physical punishments against heresy and unbelief. This principle of coercion, so contrary to the nature of a society in which everything ought to be based upon freedom and conviction, is the most fatally flawed principle that Christianity has protected and supported, and has proved the origin of revolutions and ill-events without number.]

Perhaps the most important phrase of all is the last. Gil y Zárate seems to be saying — a traditionalist would certainly have so assumed — that the Catholic church had invited schism and dissent by its prescriptive dogma and unwillingness to admit divergent opinion; in short, that the established ecclesiastical order was to blame for the events of the Reformation, that Protestant rebellion was justified. What is more, the endeavours of the Inquisition to enforce unity of doctrine are severely censured in a barely veiled reference to persecution and torture.

Thirdly, Gil y Zárate repeats Guizot's view that the influence of the Church in political affairs had been a largely negative one, since it had consistently allied itself with despotism. As Carabantes expresses it in his Spanish version of Guizot's lectures:

> grande y saludable influencia en el orden intelectual y moral; influencia más bien perjudicial que útil en el orden político propiamente dicho [...]. La Iglesia sin duda ha invocado con frecuencia los derechos de los pueblos contra el mal gobierno de los soberanos; con frecuencia ha aprobado y aun ha excitado la insurrección; y con frecuencia ha sostenido también cerca de ellos los derechos e intereses de los pueblos. Mas cuando la cuestión de las garantías políticas se ha suscitado entre el

poder y la libertad, y cuando se ha tratado de establecer un sistema de instituciones permanentes que pusiesen verdaderamente la libertad al abrigo de las invasiones del poder, por lo general la Iglesia se ha colocado al lado del despotismo. (II, 79–80, 82)

[A great and salutary influence in the intellectual and moral order; an influence prejudicial rather than useful in the political order proper [...]. The Church has, incontestably, often invoked the rights of peoples against the abuses of government of their sovereigns; it has often approved or even incited rebellion; and it has often championed, in the face of those same sovereigns, the rights and interests of their people. But when the issue of political entitlement has arisen in the form of a contest between authority and liberty, and when any attempt has been made to establish an enduring institutional framework that might genuinely protect liberty from the incursions of authority, the Church has, in the main, positioned itself upon the side of despotism.]

Gil y Zárate is more concise, but this time repeats almost verbatim the crucial phrases as given by Carabantes:

la iglesia ha ejercido una influencia poderosa sobre el orden moral, intelectual y político de la Europa moderna, y esta influencia ha sido mucho más benéfica bajo los dos primeros aspectos que bajo el último [...] a pesar de algunos momentos en que se le ha visto amparar a los débiles contra los poderosos, ser el apoyo de los pueblos, y aun provocar la insurrección, por lo general siempre que se ha tratado de establecer garantías políticas entre el poder y la libertad, la iglesia se ha colocado a favor del despotismo. (Lección X, 143–45)

[The Church has exercised a powerful influence upon the moral, intellectual and political ordering of modern Europe, and this influence has proven far more beneficial under the first two of these headings than under the last [. ..] for despite those occasions on which it has been seen to protect the weak against the powerful, to be the mainstay of peoples, and even to provoke insurrection, every time, generally speaking, that it has come to the establishment of political entitlements between authority on one hand and liberty on the other, the Church has positioned itself in favour of despotism.]

Again we might profitably cite, by way of contrast, the opposing interpretation placed on these issues by Donoso. Describing the Church's role in human affairs, he roundly stated that beneath its most prolific command knowledge had flourished, customs had become more virtuous, laws had been perfected, and every great domestic, political, and social institution had experienced rich and spontaneous forms of natural growth.[34] As the second element in this final assertion implies — and again the sense of his addressing a direct rejoinder to liberal opinion is irresistible — Donoso was virulently to defend the Church against all charges of having allied itself with tyranny:

Ella no ha tenido anatemas sino para los hombres impíos, para los pueblos rebeldes y para los reyes tiranos. Ha defendido la libertad, contra los reyes que aspiraron a convertir la autoridad en tiranía; y la autoridad, contra los pueblos que aspiraron a una emancipación absoluta; y contra todos, los derechos de Dios y la inviolabilidad de sus santos mandamientos.[35]

[She has anathematized only wicked men, rebellious peoples, and tyrannical monarchs. She has defended liberty, against those kings who sought to convert

authority into tyranny; and authority, against those peoples who sought
unrestrained emancipation; and, against all, the rights of God and the inviolability
of his holy commandments].

What readily emerges, as well as the expected degree of missionary zeal, is Donoso's
desire for sacred authority: the concept of emancipation is for him as for Balmes a
dangerously subversive one, connected via its attached adjective with an anarchical
loss of restraint rather than, as for Guizot, with the desirable energies of the human
spirit freeing itself from bondage in the historical working out of the Reformation.
Donoso's text is instead suffused with the idea of divine authority as unquestionable
and human society as inevitably — and Providentially — governed by it.

The appropriations I have been considering are not entirely surprising when we
bear in mind remarks made by Gil y Zárate in the preface to his own published
text, where he confesses that not only the process of editing and printing but also
the original collation of material for the public lectures had been hurried. Barely
having had time to read the most relevant authors, his strategy had been to take
out of each what he considered most opportune, in a rather haphazard process of
citation, imitation and spontaneous personal reflection ('Advertencia').[36] Carabantes's
translation of Guizot would naturally have been a text ready to hand, but not on
this account should Gil y Zárate's use of it be considered any the less deliberate. In
fact, the principal idea underpinning his task is avowedly close to that espoused by
— and later, in a more negative sense, imputed to — Guizot: that of discovering
how historical events and institutions affected the development of individual and
collective freedoms (Lección I, 12). Gil y Zárate, in adopting as his device *la libertad*,
was following in the steps of his French counterpart; as Ceri Crossley puts it, 'For
Guizot it was axiomatic that the meaning of history lay in the growth of individual
freedom'.[37] A signal demonstration of the affinity between the two is the Spanish
writer's description of the Reformation as 'la primera señal de la emancipación de
los pueblos' [the first signal of the emancipation of peoples] (Lección II, 25). As far
as Gil y Zárate was concerned, and here again he is directly though not avowedly
paraphrasing the *Histoire de la civilisation en Europe*:

> Las sectas, las herejías, todo ese partido de la oposición en la Iglesia cristiana, son
> la prueba incontestable de la vida, de la actividad moral que reinaba en ella; vida
> tempestuosa, dolorosa, llena de peligros, de errores, de crímenes; pero noble y
> poderosa, y que ha dado lugar a los más bellos esfuerzos de la inteligencia y de la
> voluntad. (Lección X, 139)

> [Sects, heresies, every party of opposition in the Christian Church, are but
> incontestable proof of the vigour, the active moral life that reigned within it; a
> tempestuous life, and a painful one, full of dangers, errors, vices; but a noble and
> powerful life, one that has given rise to the most splendid efforts of intellect and
> human will.]

Predictably, then, we find in Gil y Zárate's plan a perception of three rival 'poderes'
— aristocracy, democracy, and monarchy — contending for political control in the
Middle Ages, one which extends to a programmatic assessment of their struggle and
its eventual result: 'Con efecto, los reyes después de haberse servido de los pueblos para
abatir a los nobles, adoptaron una política falaz para convertirse en absolutos dueños

de todo' [In effect, the monarchy, having availed itself of the populace in order to defeat the nobility, adopted a fallacious political design aimed at converting itself into unquestioned lord of all] (Lección II, 21–23). He likewise goes on to repeat precisely another of Guizot's fundamental positions, one expressed in the third of the lectures that appeared as the *Histoire de la civilisation en Europe*: namely, that three constituent factors present in Europe at the time of the fall of Rome had, in their later process of interaction, produced modern civilization. Gil y Zárate now viewed these three — the continuing cultural legacy of Roman civilization; the vigour and independence of the Germanic tribes that had overthrown Rome; and the Christian religion, with its stress on spiritual life — exactly as Guizot had done, as diverse elements combining and cohering to make possible cultural advancement (Leccion II, 26–27).

Like Tapia, then, Gil y Zárate has evidently found persuasive both Guizot's abstract pattern of history and several of his specific historical judgements touching upon the Catholic church and the European Reformation that were destined to have notable repercussions. Fernández Sebastián, conscious of both Tapia and Gil y Zárate's assimilation of Guizot's perspective, shrewdly notes that the work of each allows the reader to glimpse an underlying progressive liberal ideology, at a significant remove from the cautious tenets of Spanish *moderantismo*.[38] Not without justification does Hans Juretschke, in informing his readers of Gil y Zárate's *Introducción a la historia moderna*, choose to describe him as a passionate admirer of Guizot.[39] The broad espousal of Guizot's ideas by Tapia and by Gil y Zárate, following on from the appearance of various Spanish editions of the lectures on European history, indicate that the French historian's overview had very rapidly achieved common currency in Spanish intellectual circles, becoming in time what Inman Fox has called the historiographical model of later Spanish liberalism.[40]

Before proceeding to consider rather more adverse reactions to Guizot, it is worthwhile briefly to examine one further major historical study professedly to adopt the French writer's pattern. Juan Cortada's *Historia de España* of 1845 in fact provides the most lyrical testimony to Guizot's influence in the early part of that decade. Discarding, in his prologue, the idea of history as no more than a narrative of battles, a list of names, and a biography of kings, Cortada opts instead for a more philosophically investigative and intellectually satisfying 'exposición de los principios políticos o religiosos que combatían' [exposition of those political or religious principles that were in conflict].[41] If we already suspect at this stage a reliance upon Guizot's method, we are kept waiting only until the next page for confirmation; here the *Histoire de la civilisation en Europe* is described as a classical work that will immortalize its author and be passed on to posterity as a veritable monument to wisdom and instruction. In Guizot's lectures, the Spanish author comments, can be seen the majestic onward march of Europe, the ongoing process of change that had formed its peoples encapsulated in 'los combates de ideas y de principios' [the conflicts of ideas and principles].[42] The same text is then fervently described as a metaphorical compass that had guided him through the wide oceans of historical causation, and as a brilliant guiding light that had afforded him a refuge when he seemed irremediably to have gone astray. In this extensive encomiastic passage, the French historian is then acknowledged as Cortada's great and wise master.[43]

Cortada's overview swiftly reveals Guizot's inspiration in practice. The Spanish historian closely re creates his French counterpart's assessment of the pivotal moment represented in Europe by the fall of Rome. An old world comes to an end and the modern world begins: a new era, which inherits from the Roman Empire a Christian society, a framework of laws, and a distinctive artistic vision, 'elementos que mezclados con los que trajeron los invasores producirán la civilización moderna' [elements which, combined with those furnished by the barbarian invaders, will produce our modern civilization].[44] The Spanish writer's own study is, not surprisingly in view of this introduction, laden with references to 'elementos' or 'fuerzas' relentlessly contending for political mastery in the development of Europe. While Cortada's history cannot be said to be as ideologically contentious as the text that provided its inspiration, he does differ from more conservative historians in certain crucial judgements, such as his description of the Inquisition as 'sarcasmo de la religión de amor predicada por Jesucristo, poderoso auxiliar del despotismo y causa eficaz del atraso de la civilización española' [a parody of the religion of love preached by Christ Jesus, a powerful helpmate of despotism, and an effective cause of the backwardness of Spanish civilization].[45] Likewise his view that the Catholic church had fallen prey to temporal greed and had allied itself with the monarchy in a conspiracy to 'entronizar la ignorancia' [enthrone ignorance].[46] Guizot would undoubtedly have approved of the remark in the editors' prologue that addressed Cortada's method, permeated with a spirit of temperate liberalism according to their appraisal.

Given the enormous prestige enjoyed by Guizot in the early 1840s, a conservative backlash was perhaps inevitable. It may be considered to have begun with another series of lectures, delivered by Fermín Gonzalo Morón in Madrid and Valencia in 1840–41 and published in the capital as the six-volume *Curso de Historia de la civilización de España* that has already figured in my assessment of the mediaeval revival. From what we have hitherto seen, Gonzalo Morón's trenchant opposition to Guizot should come as no surprise. His passionate disavowal of Guizot's perspective in favour of Vico's theory of Providential design will in fact be examined in some depth in the following chapter of this study.[47] Meanwhile, a much sharper sense of conflict can be detected in Balmes's polemical essay *Del Protestantismo comparado con el Catolicismo en sus relaciones con la civilización europea*, the first part of which appeared in 1842. In an early review in the *Revista de España y del Extranjero* — a magazine edited, incidentally, by Gonzalo Morón —, the Bishop of the Canary Islands left his readers in no doubt as to the worth of Balmes's study: at any time such a work would have been commendable and useful, but especially so at the present, when 'el célebre Guizot, aprovechándose de su nombradía en la diplomacia y literatura, ha vertido en su historia general de la civilización europea, los errores más denigrativos a la iglesia católica' [the celebrated Guizot, availing himself of the fame acquired in diplomacy and literature, has poured into his general history of European civilization a series of errors prejudicial in the extreme to the Catholic church].[48] The good bishop, it should be noted, was to maintain his attack in the same magazine in the following year with a blistering 'Ensayo sobre el luteranismo en el gobierno de España en sus relaciones con la iglesia, desde Carlos I hasta la época constitucional', a piece in which 'el calvinista Guizot' [that Calvinist Guizot] would receive further vilification.[49]

Balmes's four-volume essay, published between 1842 and 1844, is described by Antonio Soriano Heredia as one of the most important works of nineteenth-century apologetics and, perhaps more crucially in the present context, as a veritable treatise on the philosophy of history;[50] as Moreno Alonso comments, it allows us to see with considerable clarity Balmes's seemingly unequal struggle against the principal thrust of French liberal historiography.[51] The Spanish writer's essay in fact constituted a systematic rebuttal of Guizot's negative historical judgements concerning the Catholic church; taking the Reformation as a point of departure, the author was to consider the natural question of 'qué es lo que había hecho esta revolución en pro de la causa de la humanidad' [what is it that this revolution has achieved to advance the cause of humanity].[52] An early indication of Balmes's own position is given in the words that immediately follow; unfortunately, he says, this whole issue has been bedevilled by larger errors of perspective, occasioned either by the tendency to judge events in a manner tainted by factional prejudice or, and this comes to be a crucial phrase in many Spanish reactions to Guizot, to do so 'tan sólo por lo que presentaban en su superficie' [only according to what they suggested in their surface appearance]. Thus it is, he goes on, that for certain historians 'los reformadores del siglo XVI contribuyeron al desarrollo de las ciencias, de las artes, de la libertad de los pueblos, y de todo cuanto se encierra en la palabra civilización, y que así dispensaron a las sociedades europeas un señalado beneficio' [the sixteenth-century reformers contributed to the development of science and knowledge, of the arts, of the emancipation of peoples, of everything that is contained in the word civilization, and that they thus bestowed upon European society considerable benefits] (I, 'prólogo').

Guizot is not mentioned by name at this stage, although Balmes, shortly after beginning his study proper, refers to the well-known affirmation of the French historian that 'el Protestantismo no fue otra cosa que un esfuerzo extraordinario en nombre de la libertad, un vuelo atrevido del pensamiento humano' [Protestantism was nothing other than an extraordinary effort in the name of liberty, a daring flight of human thought] (I, 19). The reference is still not attributed, although Guizot is named shortly after when Balmes sums up the French writer's position and alludes once more to the same claim that the Reformation had been 'una insurrección de la inteligencia humana' [a revolutionary act of human intelligence] (I, 36). The reiteration that I have chosen to re-create reflects Balmes's insistence on words that he clearly found profoundly offensive. The Spanish writer, obsessively mindful of his appointed task, keeps this phraseology constantly in his own thoughts and in his reader's view as he strives to overthrow Guizot's developmental framework.

Balmes's own first principle was that 'el principio esencial del Protestantismo es un principio disolvente' [the essential principle of Protestantism is a corrosive principle] (I, 148). The Reformation, he claimed, had engendered no positive and constructive thought, only a negation of existing doctrine; Guizot's view of Protestantism as exemplifying 'l'esprit humain', as a motor of cultural advancement and desirable freedoms, is thus categorically denied (I, 188). Balmes was adamant that only 'el espíritu de los demagogos' [the urges of demagogy] could have moved Guizot to assert that the Roman Catholic church had proved inimical to human liberty and freedom. On the contrary, if the term 'libertad' was understood in its true meaning, then Roman

Catholicism ought to be afforded the boundless gratitude of all humankind: 'ella ha civilizado las naciones que la han profesado; y la civilización es la verdadera libertad' [it has civilized all those nations that have professed it; and civilization is the true name of liberty] (I, 184). Balmes typically underlines the status of 'la religión católica' as the single unifying element in the felicitous development of European civilization, as its sole cultural imperative, thus implicitly denying Guizot's view of diverse elements in a process of flux.[53] His stance is thus uncompromisingly theocentric, one of his specific complaints against Protestantism being that 'la religión cristiana tal como la explicaron los protestantes es una opinión y no más; es un sistema formado de mil partes incoherentes, y que pone el cristianismo al nivel de las escuelas filosóficas' [the Christian religion as explained by Protestants is a mere opinion and no more; it is a system formed of a thousand incoherent parts, and places Christianity on the same level as all other schools of philosophy] (I, 63). As Balmes summarizes, opposing what he saw as Guizot's typically Protestant stress on progress through diversity: 'van ya más de 18 siglos que a la Iglesia se la puede llamar estacionaria en sus dogmas; y esta es una prueba inequívoca de que ella sola está en posesión de la verdad: porque la verdad es invariable por ser una' [for more than eighteen hundred years the Church might have been designated as static in its dogmas; and this is an unequivocal demonstration that she alone is in possession of truth: for truth is invariable in its being singular] (I, 37).[54] In the Spanish writer's mind, the Church had always realized that unity was the source and prerequisite of strength, and consequently had insisted upon that unity in its doctrine: 'para conservar esta unidad era necesaria la sumisión a la autoridad' [in order to preserve that unity, submission to authority was essential] (I, 51–52). If Guizot had propounded a pluralistic rhetoric of movement that might be described as libertarian, then Balmes, we are tempted to reflect, had replied with a rhetoric of unity and stasis that was profoundly authoritarian. Humanity required, he insisted, the indispensable support that authority alone could supply; without this essential source of self-reliance, mankind would simply abandon itself to 'sueños y delirios' [dreaming and delirium] (I, 63). Balmes went on to ask the question: '¿qué beneficio ha hecho el Protestantismo a las sociedades modernas quebrantando la fuerza de la autoridad, única capaz de poner un dique a lamentables extravíos?' [what benefit has Protestantism bestowed upon modern societies in breaking the force of authority, the only force with the capacity to build a dyke against lamentable aberration?] (I, 95).

This section of the text bears out in broad terms Abellán's description of Balmes's more specifically political stance as one of authoritarian conservatism,[55] earlier located by Miguel Artola as extremely close to Absolutism.[56] What we might at least legitimately suspect at this stage is that Balmes's mind was not solely concentrated upon the consequences of the European Reformation. Underlying the immediate textual debate is surely the struggle of nineteenth-century society to come to terms with the profound questioning of established values that had led to, and later stemmed from, the French Revolution. After all, the term 'disolvente' — here used by Balmes to describe the principles of European Protestantism — was normally reserved by Catholic writers for what they regarded as the pernicious and destructive consequences of the French Enlightenment. What is more, Balmes had already accused Guizot of pandering to the proclivities of nineteenth-century opinion. While, we read, unlike the fanatics of radicalism, he had not revealed a wholescale prejudice against religion, he had nonetheless considered it necessary to 'lisonjear el auditorio apellidando libertad' [pander to his audience by invoking the name of liberty] (I, 42): Balmes may or may not have been aware that he could have levelled exactly the same charge against Gil y Zárate, who had included in the first of his historical lectures of the previous year an extensive and lyrically charged encomium of 'la libertad'. Be that as it may, Balmes would claim at a relatively early stage in his essay that Protestantism had ultimately engendered both political fanaticism and religious indifference, even religious scepticism (I, 118). His choice of words in describing Protestant theology makes for an even firmer connection between Reformation and Enlightenment; in addition to the passages cited above, we note the slightly later affirmation that 'La religión cristiana, tal como la conciben los protestantes, es una especie de sistema filosófico más o menos razonable; pues que examinada a fondo pierde el carácter de divina' [The Christian religion as conceived by Protestants is a form of philsophical system that is more or less rational; for when it is subjected to thoroughgoing examination it loses altogether its divine nature] (I, 119). The denigratory references to rationalist philosophical systems that had enthroned humanity and rendered superfluous creator God and Providential design, references peculiarly characteristic of neo-Catholic assessments of events in eighteenth-century France, are here shifted on to a different but related historical target.

Predictably, Balmes goes on to challenge many specific historical judgements found in the *Histoire de la civilisation en Europe*: the allegation that the Church had consistently allied itself with despots; the view that it had for a long period tolerated slavery, and had been dilatory in seeking to abolish it; the accusation that the Society of Jesus had acted clandestinely and subversively in order to stifle important freedoms. On this last point, Balmes cites Guizot's assertion that 'Los jesuitas fueron llamados a luchar contra el curso general de los sucesos, contra el desarrollo de la civilización moderna, contra la libertad del espíritu humano' [The Jesuits were called to fight against the general course of events, against the historical development of modern civilization, against the liberalization of the human mind] (III, 162). The Spanish writer naturally saw things differently, insisting that the Jesuits had not been left behind by intellectual progress but had been at its forefront: 'El espíritu de los siglos es de suyo disolvente, y el instinto de los jesuitas está pertrechado de preservativos contra la disolución' [The spirit of each secular age is in itself corrosive, and the instincts of the Jesuits ever well equipped with preventive treatments against dissolution] (III, 155).[57] It was understandable, he continued, that Protestants and unbelievers had so readily attacked the Society of Jesus, for the Jesuits had been their most potent adversary; but the enemies of religion had encountered in the Jesuits a veritable wall of bronze against which were shattered all attacks against Roman Catholic religion (III, 156). None of the above is remotely surprising. It does seem to me of some significance, however, that Balmes chooses to stress several particular points that Gil y Zárate had earlier appropriated from Guizot's lectures. Unlike his Spanish predecessor, Balmes subjects these matters to discussion not to concur in the French historian's judgements but explicitly in order to disavow them. This is acutely so in the case of the Reformation, and it is here that Balmes's argument is at its most strident.

Firstly, Balmes sees the Reformation not as an expression of human freedom and intellectual inquiry liberating itself from constraint, but as the bringer of discord and division at an historical moment which had promised much. Precisely when potential for the development of European civilization was at its greatest, there resounded in the heart of Germany the voice of the Apostate whose historical role was to 'introducir la discordia en el seno de pueblos hermanos' [bring discord into the bosoms of peoples bound by fraternity] (III, 132); Luther is ultimately labelled no less than an Anti-Christ (III, 147–48). The rise of Protestantism, for Balmes, was intimately related to a loss of historic representational rights and to the growth of Absolutism; if no schism had occurred, then royal power could have been tempered and ancient rights preserved (IV, 120–21). He proceeds to identify two strands of democratic thought: one honourable and moderate, noble and generous; another violent and perverse, one which 'Hermanándose siempre con las pasiones más ruines, se ha presentado como la bandera de cuanto abrigaba la sociedad de más vil y abyecto; reuniendo en torno de sí a todos los hombres turbulentos y malvados, fascinando con engañosas palabras una turba de miserables' [Allying itself always with the most villainous desires, has presented itself as the banner of all that is most vile and abject in society; gathering around it all men given to violent conduct and evil, captivating with its deceitful words a crowd of wretches] (IV, 128–29). As the Spanish writer saw it, 'esta misma democracia inquieta, injusta y turbulenta, que había comprometido el sosiego de Europa en los siglos anteriores al XVI, encontró sus más fervientes patronos en el Protestantismo' [this same unquiet, unjust and violent democracy, which had disturbed the calm of Europe in earlier centuries, was to find in the sixteenth its most fervent sponsors in the ranks of Protestantism] (IV, 131); again the intimate connection in Balmes's mind between Protestant insurrection and more recent scenes that had occurred in revolutionary France is almost unmistakable. In the face of subversive and anti-social ideas, he continued, strong government was the only solution; thus Germany, where Protestantism had incited visions of freedom, had returned to a virtually feudal structuring of society as a reactionary counter-measure (IV, 133). With Protestantism then disseminating all over Europe the seeds of anarchy, there arose 'una necesidad imperiosa, urgente, imprescindible, de centralizar el mando, de fortificar el poder real, de que se obstruyesen todos los conductos por donde pudiesen expresarse principios disolventes, de que se separasen y aislasen todos los elementos que con el contacto y el roce eran susceptibles de inflamarse y de acarrear conflagraciones funestas' [an imperative, urgent and indispensable requirement, to centralize authority, to fortify the power of the monarchy, to block up every conduit by which corrosive principles might be expressed, to separate and isolate all of those elements which through contact and exposure were susceptible to being inflamed and thus prone to fatal conflagration] (IV, 135–36). We cannot but note once more the ubiquitous designation 'principios disolventes' [corrosive principles]; by extension, it is again possible to view Balmes's comments in transferential terms as having a bearing on events in nineteenth-century Spain, signally in the indefatigable attempts by traditionalists to stem the tide of revolutionary ideas that had seemed to threaten the country's borders both during and after the reign of Ferdinand VII.

In the sixteenth-century context, the most salient preventive measure effected in Spain had of course resided in the functions of the Inquisition. Balmes felt that, without such counter-measures as were put into practice by Philip II, the introduction into Spain of Protestantism would have been inevitable. He therefore comments that the Inquisition had never been the instrument of overweening ambition but rather an institution held firm in the face of grave and imminent threat (II, 298). What follows shortly after is breathtaking in its audacity: we can thank the Protestants, declares Balmes, for the severity of the Spanish Inquisition in those times; it was they who had instigated a religious revolution, and, after all, it had always been true that 'toda revolución, o destruye el poder atacado, o le hace más severo y duro' [any revolution either destroys the authority it sets out to attack, or else renders that authority more harsh and severe] (II, 308). As the threat posed by Protestantism receded, he affirms, so did the severity of the Inquisition (II, 320).

Compared with the unequivocal condemnation of the Inquisition expressed by Tapia and Gil y Zárate, and even, as we shall see, by Gonzalo Morón, Balmes's much more retrenched position touches upon the apologist. The cry of 'double standards!' rises in our throats when even the worst excesses of the Holy Office are papered over with exculpatory statements such as 'la religión no puede hacerse responsable de todo lo que se hace en su nombre' [religion cannot be blamed for all of those things that are done in its name] (II, 276) and 'los más horrendos atentados se cometen invocando nombres augustos' [the most horrible crimes are committed in the name of august causes] (II, 276–77), and blithely aphoristic references to 'la doctrina de intolerancia, que con más o menos extensión, es la doctrina de todos los poderes existentes' [the doctrine of intolerance, which to a greater or lesser degree, is the doctrine of every existing authority] (II, 278). Neither are we well disposed to hear that the duty of the intellectual historian is to seek 'veracidad rigurosa en la narración de los hechos, pero guardarse de juzgar por ellos, ni las ideas ni las instituciones dominantes' [strict veracity in the narrative of events, but to guard against judging by those events either prevailing ideas or institutions] (II, 277). For Balmes, however, the Inquisition, established by Queen Isabella in accordance with the desire of her own people and essentially justified in its task, had embraced three distinct periods: the initial prosecution of a struggle against Judaism and Islam, warrantable as the manifestation of an instinct for self-preservation; the subsequent entirely justifiable fight to stem the advances of Protestantism; and, thirdly, the era in which the primary task had been 'a reprimir vicios nefandos, y a cerrar el paso a la filosofía de Voltaire' [to suppress baleful vices, and to bar the way against the philosophy of Voltaire] (II, 280–82). Once more, the intrusion into the debate of the neo-Catholics' favourite *bête noire* seems inevitable.[58]

Given the extraordinary differences between the overview expounded by Guizot and that formulated by Balmes in order to counter it, it is particularly striking that the Spanish writer on many occasions adopts apparently without irony or reserve much of the French historian's characteristic patterning. In describing the social ferment of the Middle Ages, for example, Balmes comes close to repeating Guizot's 'elementary' view of monarchy, nobility, and populace (III, 95–96). In the fourth and last volume of *El Protestantismo comparado con el Catolicismo* the evidence is especially compelling. Detecting in the fifteenth and sixteenth centuries, described as the gestation period of modern European civilization, three political formations — monarquía', 'aristocracia', and 'democracia' — , Balmes affirms that rivalry between them had been the distinctive characteristic of that age (IV, 64). The dominant influence exerted by the first of the three in sixteenth-century Europe is then summarized as follows: 'En Alemania, en Francia, en Inglaterra, en España reinan monarcas poderosos que llenan el mundo con la fama de sus nombres; en su presencia se inclinan humildemente la aristocracia y la democracia' [In Germany, in France, in England and in Spain are powerful reigning monarchs who fill the entire world with their renown; in their presence aristocracy and democracy meekly bow down] (IV, 73). Similarly programmatic is Balmes's subsequent assessment of the qualities and aims of the aristocracy: 'La nobleza no podía compararse con la monarquía ni el clero, ya que no es dable encontrar en ella la expresión de ninguno de los altos principios representados por aquélla y por éste' [We cannot compare the aristocracy with either the monarchy or the clergy, since it contains none of those high principles represented by each of the last two]. The nobility, he felt, benefited from no association with 'grandes necesidades sociales' [great social necessities]; on the contrary, the rights it sought were of a kind designated 'meramente positivo, humano' [purely empirical ones, strictly human] (IV, 78–79). Thus Balmes explicitly concurs in Guizot's prescriptive reference to the alliance between crown and populace in feudal times (IV, 179). On another occasion he adopts Guizot's terms in order to express a conflicting viewpoint, arguing that Protestantism, by undermining the authority of the established church, had disallowed an alliance between populace and clergy and thus ensured the overwhelming victory of monarchy (IV, 141–42).

The key to understanding this apparent contradiction — Balmes's reliance upon a patterning formulated by his ideological adversary — is to be obtained, I would suggest, from a scrutiny of his vocabulary; in the passages cited above, the significant phrases are, firstly, the term 'formas políticas' applied to Guizot's elements of civilization, and, secondly, the description of the motivation and designs of the aristocracy as representing what was 'meramente positivo, humano'.[59] If we call to mind the censorious reference, at the very beginning of Balmes's essay, to historical judgements determined by 'preocupaciones de secta' [factional resentment] and informed only by a consideration of the 'superficie' or surface layer of the past, then it is possible to square the circle. Balmes, as a Catholic traditionalist, regarded Guizot's view of elements of civilization in a process of contention as depicting only the surface of history, even though the assessment of historical events had been gathered into an abstract pattern. As Inman Fox shrewdly comments, although Guizot referred to religion, the arts, literature, and philosophy as component parts of 'la historia interna' [inner history], his survey of French civilization was effectively limited to the study of its laws, its society, and its public morality within the contextual prism of his liberal ideal of progress.[60]

The Spanish writer likewise downplayed the significance of 'el espíritu humano' or the human will as a potent motor of historical development, disavowing the French historian's stress upon 'l'esprit humain' as the most important determining factor in progress. Balmes clearly felt that Guizot had unjustly minimalized the concept of Providence, of divine intervention in human affairs in response to a teleological purpose. Ceri Crossley's well-chosen words are particularly illuminating here: observing that 'in his ordering of the flux of human affairs Guizot generally avoided the language of religion and the sacrilization of history',[61] Crossley reminds us that within the French writer's framework it was human beings who inhabited history and who made it. Guizot held to his belief that salvation and redemption were a matter of individual rather than collective destiny. Although in his mind history displayed a divinely instituted order, he did not seek to present it as God's journey to self-knowledge; while accepting the centrality of religion, Guizot did not 'profess reverence for an unchanging theocratic ideal'.[62] Balmes, on the other hand, was a committed Providentialist. In closing his study, he would lavishly praise Bossuet for having taught mankind to perceive a linkage and a series of phases in historical events which argued for a notion of cause and effect radically different from that later advanced by Guizot.

The tone of much of Balmes's essay reveals the degree of ideological antipathy and personal outrage that had helped to motivate it. However, the words best calculated to aid us in accurately contextualizing and interpreting *El Protestantismo comparado con el Catolicismo* are probably to be found in the fourth volume, where Balmes offers the most important of clues as to the state of the contemporary debate in observing that for many the authority of Guizot will prove decisive, and more so given that

> en algunas de las producciones que han visto la luz pública con pretensiones de filosofía de la historia, se conoce a la legua que el libro de texto de sus autores han sido las obras del escritor francés. (IV, 64)

> [in certain publications that have recently entered the public domain aspiring to the title of philosophy of history, it as plain as a pikestaff that the works of the French writer have served as their authors' textbooks.]

Not only is the tone of resentment that accompanies these words abundantly clear; indirectly, the underlying intention of Balmes's study and the extremity of the arguments contained within it are rendered transparently clear and accountable. Guizot's influence was proving a disquieting intellectual threat to the hegemony of the doctrine Balmes was now setting out to defend. Tapia and Gil y Zárate had both been inclined to accept without serious reservation many of the more contentious — heterodox or openly heretical, as Balmes would have it — judgements made by the French historian, judgements whose wider implications would have appeared yet more unpalatable. The following words taken from the concluding section of Balmes's essay indicate forcefully what was at stake and reveal the direction in which he felt the wider debate had been tending:

> Los profesores de la filosofía de la historia son tal vez los que más se han señalado por su prurito en achacar a la Iglesia el cargo de enemiga de las luces, y de presentar a la falsa Reforma como ilustre defensora de los derechos del entendimiento. (IV, 279)

> [It is university professors of the philosophy of history who have most distinguished themselves by their tendency to depict the Church as an enemy of enlightenment and to represent the sham that was the Reformation as the illustrious defender of the claims of human understanding.]

It was precisely this tendency, now as he saw it worryingly present in the staunchly Catholic territory of Spain, that Balmes was determinedly setting out to countervail.[63] As in the contemporary literary debate that had recently been resolved in favour of the traditionalists, consternation created by the presence of a radical alternative breeds an entrenched reaction exacerbated by an intimate sense of threat. Hence the reactionary writer is forced, in order effectively to repulse that threat, to adopt ideological positions that become increasingly hostile and uncompromising. In fact, as we read Balmes's arguments against Guizot's defence of the Reformation, we become profoundly aware that they are by and large prompted by transferential comparisons with the Spanish writer's own experience of his contemporary age. For, dominating and indeed predicating the religious discourse is the assumption that 'la filosofía incrédula es hija de la reforma' [sceptical philosophy is the Reformation's daughter] (III, 7); Balmes's essay, especially the fourth volume, is therefore ultimately concerned less with an historical assessment of the European Reformation than with his own ideological hostility to the French Enlightenment that he considers to have been the Reformation's rightful heir. Balmes provides the modern reader with a picture, almost unparalleled in its clarity, of the embattled Catholic traditionalist confronting the legacy of philosophical rationalism that he believes to have ushered in both the French Revolution and its nefarious consequences all over Europe. At the same time, that reader becomes increasingly aware of Balmes's conscious rehearsal of many of the prescriptions of reactionary writers of earlier generations, for whom, as Javier Herrero pointedly reminds us, the 'falsa filosofía' of the Enlightenment had its origins in the Protestant Reformation.[64] The endeavours of the forces of Reaction had been indelibly marked, Herrero subsequently comments, by the desire to find a Protestant source for all revolutionary tensions,[65] a phenomenon that was to resurface in Balmes and, as will be made clear, in a very substantial portion of Spanish historiography of the Romantic period in general.

The earlier enthusiastic reception of Guizot's work in Spain had then stirred up a veritable hornet's nest. It is typical of the prevailing tenor of that age that a tolerant and pluralistic historical perspective had eventually to yield to an unswervingly orthodox appraisal of the past. The defeat of radicalism in literature, displaced by a restorative, traditionalist, and Catholic Romanticism founded on Schlegelian principles, together with the potent neo-Catholic revival championed by Balmes and Donoso Cortés, square impressively with the virtually concomitant demise in historiography of Guizot's 'elementary' pattern. The fall of Espartero and the subsequent political hegemony of Narváez in the 1840s provide a further ideological parallel. With hindsight, Balmes's masterstroke was to reformulate the direct historical connection between Reformation and Enlightenment that had so well served the forces of Spanish conservatism after 1789 and, more pointedly, after 1808. It was a period when, as Vicens Vives has pointed out, there was hardly a European intellectual who continued to profess unconditional faith in the ideas of the *Encyclopédie*, or who did not regard them as having been ultimately responsible for the savage historical events of the previous fifty years.[66] Nothing could have been better calculated to discredit Guizot's historical vision than Balmes's affirmation that 'la filosofía incrédula es hija de la reforma'. The growth, in the 1840s, of theories of democratic socialism provided conservative writers with another identifiable target susceptible to authorial manipulation. The hand of men like Balmes and Donoso was likewise undoubtedly strengthened by the events of 1848.

The experience of the European 'Year of Revolution', with Spain's conservative administration able to denounce the latest savage chapter in the unholy history of Progress, proved crucial. Guizot himself had been forced into exile after the revolutionary events of February 1848. The pamphlet *De la Démocratie en France*, written from his refuge in England, vilified democracy, labelling it the destructive passion of modern societies, inimical to all forms of social order. Guizot charged the promoters of the new socialism with reviving the sort of dangerous enthusiasm for things human rather than divine which had characterized the most radical leaders of the French Revolution. Instead of developing historical analyses of recent events, Guizot now explained human conduct in terms of moral evil, validating his judgements by referring to humanity's fallen nature; Christian democratic socialism he regarded as an absurdity, a contradiction in terms. His *Méditations et études morales* (1851), inspired largely by theological concerns, depicted the revolutionary spirit as Satan in human form, at once sceptical and fanatical. Guizot lamented the fact that his contemporaries had not learned from the mistakes of 1789, and felt that only Christianity — Protestant or Catholic — offered a bulwark against the rising revolutionary tide.[67]

In Spain, meanwhile, the year of 1850 would see the completion of Juan Donoso Cortés's combative *Ensayo sobre el catolicismo, el liberalismo y el socialismo*, conceived as a definitive response not just to the philosophy of history formulated by Guizot but, more immediately, to what the Spanish writer saw as the incitement to social disintegration contained in the works of Proudhon. Donoso opted for a position very close to that of Balmes, specifically rejecting the 'elementary' approach of the French historian and attributing to Guizot's history of European civilization the same degree of superficiality earlier imputed to it by his Spanish comrade-in-arms. The tone of Donoso's treatise, however, suggests not a passionate entry into a polemical and as yet undecided intellectual debate, but the confident note of assured victory that produces an apparently magnanimous but ultimately crushing and insidiously ironic tribute to his ideological adversary. This tone is at once perceptible in Donoso's first direct introduction into the debate of the name of Guizot; again it is the perceived superficiality of the French historian's account, the lack of a governing transcendence in his overall plan, that attracts the strongest criticism: there is no sorrier spectacle, proclaims Donoso, than that of a man of brilliant genius bent upon the absurd and impossible task of explaining visible and natural phenomena by purely visible and natural means.[68] Typically Guizot is felt to be guilty, in undertaking such an incongruous task, not of questionable judgement in an area subject to a plurality of interpretations but of transparent deviation from a verifiable truth:

> En este error ha caído un hombre eminentísimo y de grandes excelencias, cuyos escritos es imposible leer sin un respeto profundo, cuyos discursos no se pueden oír sin grande admiración y cuyas prendas personales son superiores todavía a sus escritos, a sus discursos y a sus talentos.
>
> [Into such an error has fallen this most eminent of men, a man of excellent qualities whose works one cannot read without the deepest respect, whose speeches one

cannot hear without the greatest admiration, and whose personal gifts are superior
even to those of his writings, his speeches and his intellectual talents.]

These last phrases, by intensifying the ostensibly pitying note of Donoso's analysis,
consciously or unconsciously serve to heighten the sense of a patronizing or even
contemptuous attitude's being professed by him for the French writer. Thus while
Guizot's analytical sobriety, probing reasoning and harmonious use of language are
highly praised, while he succeeds extraordinarily well in 'ver todo lo visible' [seeing
all that is there to be seen], his intellectual weak spot is, for Donoso, his inability
to perceive what is really important: that is, 'ver de que manera esas cosas visibles
y separadas forman entre sí un conjunto jerárquico y armonioso, animado por una
fuerza invisible' [how these visible and discrete phenomena form themselves into a
harmony and a hierarchy under the pressing influence of an invisible force]. Guizot's
history of European civilization possessed the former — and ultimately superficial
— 'calidad eminente' [eminent quality] but had been bedevilled by the latter — and
much more profound — 'gran defecto' [significant defect]. As Donoso rather cruelly
sums up: 'M. Guizot ha visto todo lo que hay en esa civilización tan compleja como
fecunda: todo, menos la civilización misma' [M. Guizot has seen everything that is
part of that fertile and complex civilization: everything, except that civilization itself].
The French historian, he insisted, had simply missed the heart of the question: within
the Spanish writer's terms, should one seek 'los elementos múltiples y variados' [the
many and varied elements] which together constitute European civilization, then they
are indeed to be found in Guizot's book; should one seek, on the other hand, that
civilization's powerful unifying principle, the vital principle that animates the robust
limbs of its sound corporate and collective identity, it must be sought elsewhere,
for it is not to be found anywhere in that volume. Guizot's 'elementos visibles'
were limited, he indicated in a particularly revealing phrase, to 'la jurisdicción de
los sentidos' [the jurisdiction of the senses]. Yet one of these elements, the Church,
was both 'visible' and 'invisible': Guizot had made the mistake of locating it as an
institution of temporal provenance, bound in time and space, neglecting to consider
it as 'una institución divina' [a God-given institution] possessing 'una inmensa fuerza
sobrenatural' [immense metaphysical force] rather than a mere substance of 'vana
forma' [empty form]. European civilization for Donoso, therefore, is at once unified
and varied: pluralistic on a lower, superficial plane of activity; singular and unitary on
a more elevated transcendent plane. Hence he professes:

> La civilización europea no se llamó germánica, ni romana, ni absolutista, ni
> feudal; se llamó y se llama la civilización católica.
>   El catolicismo no es, pues, solamente, como M. Guizot supone, uno de los
> varios elementos que entraron en la composición de aquella civilización admirable;
> es más que eso, aun mucho más que eso; es la civilización misma.
>   [European civilization was not called Germanic, nor Roman, nor
> Absolutist, nor feudal; it was and still is called Catholic civilization.
>   Catholicism is thus not, as M. Guizot assumes, just one of the various elements
> that went to compose that wonderful civilization; it is more than that, much more
> than that even; it is civilization itself.]

Donoso subsequently restates the desirability of a 'fórmula superior' [superior pattern-

ing] or 'conciliación suprema' [supreme harmony], in fundamental opposition to the French historian, who is dismissed in one final sally: 'M. Guizot ve todo lo que ocupa un instante en el tiempo y un lugar circunscrito en el espacio, y no ve aquello que desborda los espacios y los tiempos' [M. Guizot sees all that lives a single instant in time and occupies a defined spot in space, and fails to see all that entirely overflows time and space].

In retrospect, we can see that Donoso's fire was directed at an already disabled adversary. By the time his *Ensayo* had appeared, Guizot's philosophy of history, one which had threatened to sweep all before it at the beginning of the previous decade, had been effectively discredited. Balmes's mixture of trenchant orthodoxy and insidious transferential comparisons had successfully preyed upon minds susceptible in the extreme to apocalyptically-styled warnings of moral collapse, while the Year of Revolution and the advances of Proudhonian social theories had appeared to prove him right. It should be noted at this point that Guizot himself proved rather more magnanimous in his widely perceived defeat than did his Spanish opponents in proclaiming their ideological victory. In prefacing the sixth French edition of the *Histoire de la civilisation en Europe*, Guizot adopted an attitude towards Balmes and Donoso (both of whom are specifically named) that was eminently respectful and quietly conciliatory.[69] Not so Antonio Ferrer del Río, author of the well-known collection of biographical sketches *Galería de la literatura española* (1846), who in 1851 produced for the periodical *Eco Literario de Europa* a translation with commentary of excerpts from the *Méditations*. The lengthy introductory passage, part of which I cite here, is noteworthy for its summary of the issues at stake, albeit in a spirit of bombastic triumphalism, and for its assimilation of characteristic neo-Catholic vocabulary. As Ferrer del Río affirms:

> Mr. Guizot, el filósofo, el repúblico, el historiador protestante que había logrado llamar la atención del mundo civilizado con los claros frutos de su ingenio, parece despertar al cabo a la luz del catolicismo, y encuentra en ella antorcha salvadora que puede alumbrar los pasos de la humanidad en el caos a que la arrastran los bastardos intereses y los vanos errores del siglo en que vivimos [...] No ha cabido por cierto pequeña parte en esta obra meritoria a los esfuerzos de nuestro compatriota don Juan Donoso Cortés, a quien tributa el mismo Guizot señalados y merecidos elogios.[70]

> [M. Guizot, the philosopher, the republican, the Protestant historian who had attracted the attention of the whole civilized world with the brilliant fruits of his invention, appears at last to have woken to the light of Catholicism, and to have found in her a redemptive flame by which to light the steps of humanity amidst that chaos to which have led us the bastard personal ambitions and the meaningless errors of our present age. [...] No small part, to be sure, has been played in obtaining this most meritorious result by our compatriot Don Juan Donoso Cortés, to whom Guizot himself has dedicated the highest and most well deserved praise.]

For the Spanish commentator, the effective overthrow of Guizot's earlier, more liberal stance 'se muestra a nuestros ojos como el preludio de los no lejanos triunfos que ha de alcanzar la idea católica, por mas que pugnen por contrariarlos y oscurecerlos el genio de la impiedad y la impotente saña del ateísmo' [stands before us as a preface

to those forthcoming triumphs that must surely be realized by the Catholic ideal, for all that the impious genius and the futile raw anger of atheism strive to prevent and obscure them]. Ferrer del Río should have realized that some of these last words were now very firmly part of Guizot's own preferred phraseology.

Broadly speaking, the reaction against Guizot illustrates the predominance of conservative thought in the Spain of the 1840s. As Manuel Moreno Alonso comments, it was an interpretation of the past which was accurately to reflect the ideological emphasis of the historical moment, firmly traditionalist and commitedly anti-liberal.[71] After all, Spain was a country that still went in fear of a violent revolution, and one for which the French Enlightenment continued to represent the bloody route to human catastrophe. The schema propounded by Vico, support for which more fully elucidates the extent and implications of the rejection of Guizot's historical vision, was to provide a much firmer and more reassuring foundation on which to judge the recent past than the theory of human progress adumbrated by the French historian and statesman. In concluding a chapter of his *Ensayo* revealingly entitled 'De la sociedad bajo el imperio de la iglesia catolica', Donoso would forcefully enshrine the commitment to that tradition in which Vico himself stood, to a view of the world as regulated by 'una accion sobrenatural y constante por parte de Dios, el cual gobierna sobrenaturalmente a la sociedad con su providencia, y al hombre con su gracia' [God's constant metaphysical workings, that supply society with a supernatural governance in the form of Providence, and humanity in that of Grace].[72]

Notes to Chapter 2

1. *Introduccion a la historia moderna*, p. 12.
2. The original passage reads as follows:

   Evidemment, l'imagination se plaît aujourd'hui à se reporter vers cette époque. Ses traditions, ses moeurs, ses aventures, ses monuments ont pour le public un attrait qu'on ne saurait méconnaître. On peut interroger [...] ce sujet les lettres et les arts; on peut ouvrir les histoires, les romans, les poésies de notre temps; on peut entrer chez les marchands de meubles, de curiosités: partout en verra le moyen âge exploité, reproduit, occupant la pensée, amusant le goût de cette portion du public que a du temps à donner à ses besoins ou à ses plaisirs intellectuels.

   In the four-volume 1851 edition that I have consulted, the quotation from Vol. III, 214--15.

3. *Introduccion a la historia moderna*, 'Advertencia'.
4. Quite aside from the several Spanish editions of Guizot's major work, I might cite any number of references to the French historian as an obvious authority on a given issue, particularly on the rule of the Visigoths in Spain. Such references are plentiful in the pages of the *Revista de Madrid* from the first published volume in 1838, thus antedating the earliest Spanish translation. José Morales Santisteban, a regular contributor of historical pieces, appealed to the authority of Guizot's *Histoire générale de la civilisation en Europe* on the question of the distribution of population in Spain: 'España cartaginesa y romana', *Revista de Madrid*, 1st series, 1, 349–72 (p. 369). The same author's 'España goda' re-created Guizot's phrasing in declaring that 'En España, como en el resto del imperio romano, todos los elementos políticos estaban enervados y casi extinguidos. La única fuerza social, dotada de vigor y de vida, era el estado eclesiástico' [In Spain, as in the rest of the Roman Empire, all the constituent elements of political life lay exhausted, their life almost extinguished. The only source of social cohesion, possessing vigour and vitality, was the Church]: *Revista de Madrid*, 1st series, 3 (1839), 55–74 (p. 58). Further reference to Guizot would be made in José de Castro y Orozco's article 'Carlos III considerado como reformador', *Revista de Madrid*, 2nd series, 3 (1840), 115–34 (p. 123). Although drawn from relatively obscure sources, such references are of the first importance

in assessing the penetration of Guizot's major historical works and broad conceptual pattern. Perhaps most interesting both as a gauge of Guizot's continuing impact in the 1840s and in its implications for further study are comments professed by none other than Francisco Pi y Margall, writing in the magazine *El Renacimiento* in 1847:

La edad media fue despreciada por los escritores hasta principios de nuestro siglo. La historia sólo nos pintaba sus guerras, su esclavitud y su ignorancia. No había aún reconocido la historia su alta misión: el historiador creía que estudiar la vida de los príncipes era estudiar la vida de los pueblos, y no había aún llegado a sospechar que la civilización moderna fuese resultado de los principios que en aquella época estuvieron en continua lucha. Hoy día han desaparecido ya estas causas. La Europa ha vuelto los ojos a la edad media. Deseoso de sondar las ideas que dominaron en estos doce siglos, ha recogido con avidez sus manuscritos, recorrido los capiteles de sus claustros, examinado las pinturas de sus altares, estudiado con detención sus creencias, sus ceremonias religiosas y civiles, sus costumbres populares, sus muebles, sus trajes, sus objetos más insignificantes. ('Una ojeada a la historia del arte monumental', El Renacimiento, 2 May 1847, p. 58).

[The Middle Ages was, until the beginning of this century, scorned by our writers. History depicted merely its wars, the enslavement of its people, its ignorance. History had not yet acknowledged its elevated mission: for the historian believed that to study the lives of princes was to study the lives of peoples, and had yet even to suspect that modern civilization owed its existence to the principles which in those days found themselves in continual conflict. Nowadays the causes of such misunderstanding have disappeared. Europe has looked again at the Middle Ages. Wishing to gain some apprehension of ideas that prevailed over twelve centuries, it has avidly seized upon their manuscripts, roamed among the topmost stones of their cloisters, examined the artwork of their altars, paid serious attention to their beliefs, to the rituals of their religious and public life, to their popular custom, their furniture, their apparel, their most insignificant objects]

As is readily evident, Pi y Margall both repeats Guizot's essential idea of 'lucha' [struggle] and appears to rely on the same passage from the *Histoire de la civilisation en France* earlier used by Gil y Zárate.

5. Javier Fernández Sebastián, 'La recepción en España de la *Histoire de la civilisation* de Guizot', in *La imagen de Francia en España (1808–1850)* ed. by Jean-René Aymes y Javier Fernández Sebastián (Paris/Bilbao, 1998), pp. 127–49 (p. 127).

6. *La revolución francesa en la historiografía española del siglo XIX* (Seville, 1979), p. 76. Moreno Alonso even goes so far as to indicate that 'Sus ideas hicieron que surgiera en España una polémica controvertida en torno al papel que la iglesia había tenido en la civilización europea' [His ideas aroused in Spain a fierce polemic surrounding the role of the church in European civilization], but supplies no detail. He locates Juan Valera as a figure later opposing Guizot, after Donoso and Balmes in the earlier polemical debate of the 1840s. Of the two last, he remarks: 'No siendo esencialmente historiadores, hacen más bien una filosofía de la historia, reflexiva, crítica, con sentido pragmático y no pocas veces interpretativo' [Not being, strictly speaking, historians, theirs is rather a philosophy of history, contemplative, analytical, pragmatically and not infrequently interpretatively oriented] (p. 172).

7. *Historia de España Menéndez Pidal*, XXXV: I, p. lxix.

8. For an excellent general overview and commentary, see Larry Siedentop's introduction to François Guizot, *The History of Civilization in Europe*, trans. by William Hazlitt (Harmondsworth, 1997), pp. vii–xxxvii; Siedentop describes the work as 'the most intelligent general history of Europe ever written' and one that 'helped to shape the general contours of nineteenth-century European thought'(pp. vii–viii).

9. See *Metahistory*, pp. 17–18.

10. *Histoire générale de la civilisation en Europe depuis la chute de l'Empire Romain jusqu'à la Révolution Française*, 4th edn (Paris, 1840), p. 353.

11. See 'François Guizot and liberal history: the concept of civilisation', in Crossley's *French Historians and Romanticism* (London, 1993), pp. 71–104 (p. 87).

12. *French Historians and Romanticism*, p. 75.

13. See *Metahistory*, p. 19.

14. *Revista de Madrid*, 2nd series, I, 36–66, 222–37.

15. *Revista de Madrid*, 2nd series, I, 225–26, 236.

16. 'Estado actual de la literatura europea', in his *Ensayos literarios y críticos*, ed. by José Joaquín de Mora,

2 vols (Seville, 1844), I, 32.

17. *Obras completas*, VIII, 460.

18. *Revista de Madrid*, 2nd series, 2, 287–311, 383–94.

19. *Historia de la civilización en Europa* (Barcelona, 1839), pp. vi-vii.

20. *Historia de la civilización en Europa*, p. vii.

21. *Historia general de la civilización europea, por M. Guizot, traducida al castellano conforme a su última edición, y anotada por D. J. V. C.*, 3 vols (Madrid, 1839), I, pp. ii-iii.

22. Eugenio de Tapia, *Historia de la civilización española, desde la invasión de los árabes hasta la época presente*, 4 vols (Madrid, 1840).

23. *Historia de la civilización española*, I, 34–36.

24. *Historia de la civilización española*, II, 3.

25. *Historia de la civilización española*, II, 8.

26. *Historia general de la civilización europea*, II, 160–61.

27. *Historia general de la civilización europea*, II, 189.

28. *Historia de la civilización española*, III, 72.

29. *Historia de la civilización española*, III, 73.

30. *Historia de la civilización española*, III, 76.

31. *Semanario Pintoresco Español*, 2nd series, 2 (1840), 355–56 (p. 355).

32. *Revista de Madrid*, 2nd series, 3 (1840), 220–33 (p. 228).

33. *Ensayo sobre el catolicismo, el liberalismo y el socialismo*, ed. by Vila Selma, p. 118.

34. Donoso's chosen metaphor of vegetable growth affords a glimpse of his mature reliance upon Vico, which will be discussed in considerable detail in the following chapter of this study.

35. *Ensayo sobre el catolicismo, el liberalismo y el socialismo*, ed. by Vila Selma, 109–10.

36. There are in fact numerous occasions where the reader suspects Vico to have been one of those authors whom Gil y Zárate had consulted: when he speaks of the 'carácter poético' [poetic character] of the 'primera edad de los hombres' [first age of men] (p. 2); when he alludes to the prevalent energies and instincts of infant societies (p. 4); when he talks of different epochs and the need to perceive 'la ley de generación que existe entre ellas para verlas nacer unas de otras' [the generative law existing among them, causing each to be born of its predecessor] (p. 7). His reliance upon Guizot, however, is much more visibly specific and considerably more ideologically contentious.

37. *French Historians and Romanticism*, p. 89.

38. See 'La recepción en España de la *Histoire de la civilisation* de Guizot', p. 131.

39. *Historia de España Menéndez Pidal*, XXXV, I, 101.

40. *La invención de España*, p. 37.

41. I have used a later edition of Cortada's history, extended to embrace the contemporary age by Gerónimo Borao: *Historia de España, dedicada a la juventud, por D. Juan Cortada, Catedrático y Direcor del Instituto de Barcelona. Adicionada y continuada hasta 1868 por D. Gerónimo Borao, Catedrático y Rector de la Universidad de Zaragoza*, 2 vols (Barcelona, 1872–73). The quotation from Vol. I, 11.

42. *Historia de España*, I, 12--13.

43. *Historia de España*, I, 17.

44. *Historia de España*, I, 32.

45. *Historia de España*, I, 39.

46. *Historia de España*, I, 196.

47. In observing of Guizot that 'el carácter histórico-filosófico de su obra influyó favorablemente en nuestra historiografía' [the historico-philosophical nature of his work exerted a favourable influence upon our own historical writing], Moreno Alonso unaccountably cites Gonzalo Morón alongside Eugenio de Tapia as one of those most positively influenced by the French writer: *La revolución francesa en la historiografía española*, p. 76.

48. 'Juicio crítico del *Protestantismo comparado con el Catolicismo, en sus relaciones con la civilización europea, por el Doctor D. Jaime Balmes, Presbítero', *Revista de España y del Extranjero*, 4 (1842), 80–96, 107–15; the citation from p. 80.

49. *Revista de España y del Extranjero*, 6 (1843), 338–59.

50. 'La filosofía', *Historia de España Menéndez Pidal*, XXXV, I, 331–420 (p. 393).

51. *La revolución francesa en la historiografía española*, p. 174.

52. *El Protestantismo comparado con el Catolicismo en sus relaciones con la civilización europea*, 2nd edn, 4 vols (Barcelona, 1844), I, 'prólogo'. Further references follow in the text.

53. It is worth noting that the declared position of the journal *La Civilización*, in which Balmes had collaborated in the previous year with his friend and ideological ally Joaquín Roca y Cornet, had been, in the words of the latter, that 'la Religión será considerada como el primer elemento civilizador' [Religion shall be considered the principal element of civilization]: *La Civilizacion: revista religiosa, filosófica, política y literaria de Barcelona*, 1 (1841), 16.

54. Balmes had earlier regarded the best weapon against Protestantism to reside in the words of the Bishop of Meaux: 'tú varías, y lo que varía no es la verdad' [You are subject to change, and whatever changes cannot be truth] (I, 10).

55. *Historia crítica del pensamiento español*, IV, 358.

56. *Partidos y programas políticos, 1808–1936* (Madrid, 1975), I, 244; cited by Abellán, *Historia crítica del pensamiento español*, IV, 358.

57. Balmes's choice of words here may have been consciously or unconsciously prompted by the well-known *Preservativo contra la irreligión*, first published in Cadiz in 1812 by Rafael de Vélez, the man described by Javier Herrero as the great theologian of Ferdinand VII; the full title of the work was *Preservativo contra la irreligión; o, Los planes de la filosofía contra la religión y el Estado, realizados por la Francia para subyugar la Europa, seguidos por Napoleón en la conquista de España, y dados a luz por algunos de nuestros sabios en perjuicio de nuestra patria*. Herrero assesses it as

    el primer tratado extenso dedicado a un análisis de la Ilustración, de la Revolución francesa y de las guerras napoleónicas concebidas de forma exclusivamente reaccionaria, es decir, considerados todos esos fenómenos como piezas de una gran conspiración de Satán contra Dios, del mal contra el bien.

    [the first extensive treatise dedicated to an analysis of the Enlightenment, the French revolution and the Napoleonic Wars written from an exclusively reactionary perspective, that is to say in which all of these things are viewed as part of a great satanic conspiracy against God, of evil against good]

    For a full summary, see Herrero, *Los orígenes del pensamiento reaccionario*, 294–316; the citations from p. 294 and p. 300.

58. It may not be inappropriate here to cite other evidence of how debate on this issue was tending. Noteworthy for its heroic tone is the following summary culled from the pages of *El Iris*, referring to a moment when Catholicism appeared to be on the retreat in many parts of Europe:

    Entonces fue cuando Felipe II comenzó a meditar el plan de resistencia que hizo el pensamiento constante de su vida: aprovechándose de aquellos momentos de paz que eran sólo una tregua pasajera, combinó en profundas meditaciones los elementos que debían ser las líneas de defensa contra las ideas de reforma religiosa: alzándose como dique y vallados a su marcha de invasión, la España sostuvo con la pluma y con la espada los antiguos principios del dogma católico: sus fuerzas se consumieron en la lucha, pero el objeto de su amor ha quedado en pie: el catolicismo romano vive en Europa, y a los esfuerzos de su poderoso campeón debe la vida': 'Historia: El príncipe don Carlos de Austria. Artículo 2o. (*El Iris*, 1 (1841), 25)

    [It was at this point that Philip II began to reflect upon a stratagem of resistance that he came to make the constant project of his life: availing himself of those periods of peacetime that were no more than passing truces, he gave coherent form, in the course of his deep meditaton, to what were to be the constituent elements of his lines of defence against religious reform: throwing itself forward, as a defensive wall and pallisade against the invader, Spain held fast with pen and sword to the age-old principles of Cathlic dogma: its forces were worn out in the fight, but the object of their devotion still stands: Roman Catholicism lives and breathes in Europe, and owes its life to the efforts of its powerful champion]

    If such rhetoric surpasses in its hyperbolic lyricism that of Balmes as expressed in the following year, more representative in its condemnation of the Inquisition is the observation of Joaquín Sánchez de Fuentes:

    La Inquisición es la antropofagia política de las naciones que se llamaban civilizadas, y ha sido el elemento que más ha perjudicado el adelanto social, fue la pesadilla de su época en toda Europa. [The Inquisition is the political sarcophagus, the human death, of all those nations that professed themselves civilised, and has become the principle which has wrought most damage upon social porgress, for it was the nightmare of its age throughout Europe] ('Preliminares al estudio del derecho público. Artículo 50.', *Revista de España y del Extranjero*, 9 (1844), 285)

Amador de los Ríos, meanwhile, in a biographical piece on Torquemada written for the magazine *El Laberinto* in 1845, seems to have appreciated both sides of the argument and to have chosen to re-create certain of the phrasing commonly used by Guizot. Stating that, in the time of the Catholic Monarchs, it was not unnatural that 'unidad política' be fortified by 'unidad religiosa', he posed the question:

¿Qué medio podía tenerse por más obvio y sencillo en la época en que se creaban los tribunales, para proteger la libertad civil de todas las clases del Estado, que el de establecer uno, que entendiera exclusivamente en poner al mismo a salvo de los peligros que le amenazaban con una disolución completa?

[To the age that had created courts of law, what means of protecting civil liberty in every part of the State would have appeared more evident, more straightforward, than that of establishing a court whose exclusive allotted task was to preserve that State from the perceived dangers of utter dissolution?]

The Inquisition as guarantor of 'unidad religiosa' thus became a necessity in a country where 'el elemento teocrático había llegado a ser un verdadero principio de gobierno' [the theocratical element had come to be a veritable principle of government]. The Inquisition therefore 'aseguró la unidad religiosa' [made secure religious unity] before ultimately outliving the circumstances that had made it necessary and eventually 'ofreciéndose como un terrible embarazo a la marcha filosófica del espíritu humano' [offering itself as an appalling impediment to the onward forward march of the human spirit]: 'Biografía: Torquemada', *El Laberinto*, 2 (1845), 209–11.

59. I could once more highlight here the choice of 'positivo', a favourite watchword of Spanish traditionalists and consistently used, as a putative antonym of 'espiritual', to denigrate rationalism and materialism.

60. *La invención de España*, p. 37.

61. *French Historians and Romanticism*, pp. 101–02.

62. Crossley, *French Historians and Romanticism*, p. 102.

63. Acutely pertinent in this context are words written by Gabino Tejado, pupil and subsequently ideological ally of Donoso Cortés, in prefacing the posthumous edition of the latter's works in 1854. Tejado makes scathing reference to a

peligroso idealismo, que con el usurpado nombre de *Filosofía de la Historia* ha sido en estos últimos años un magnífico recurso de la perezosa ignorancia, y un arma hábilmente explotada por la malignidad de ciertas escuelas, para obscurecer la verdad y para fundar en sus gratuitas conclusiones histórico-filosóficas todo un sistema de ateísmo político y religioso.

[dangerous idealism which, masquerading under the name of *Philosophy of History*, has become in recent years a marvellous resort of laziness and ignorance, and a weapon skilfully exploited by the wickedness of certain schools of thought with the object of obscuring truth and of founding, in its superfluous historico-philosophical conclusions, an entire system of political and religious atheism]

('Noticia biográfica', in *Obras de don Juan Donoso Cortés, Marqués de Valdegamas* (Madrid, 1891), pp. xix-cx; the citation from p. lxi.)

The new edition, by coincidence or design, appeared in the year of Tejado's own death.

64. *Los orígenes del pensamiento reaccionario*, p. 92.

65. *Los orígenes del pensamiento reaccionario*, p. 94.

66. Cited by José Vila Selma in the introduction to his critical edition of Donoso's *Ensayo*, p. 13.

67. For a fuller commentary see Crossley, *French Historians and Romanticism*, pp. 97–98, on which I have freely drawn.

68. This and the citations that follow are taken from Book I, Chapter VII of the *Ensayo sobre el catolicismo, el liberalismo y el socialismo*, ed. by Vila Selma, pp. 145–48.

69. A lengthy passage from this preface is cited in Spanish by Vila Selma in his edition of Donoso's *Ensayo*, pp. 375–76.

70. 'Meditaciones y estudios morales', por Mr. Guizot', *Eco Literario de Europa*, 2 (1851), 34–49 (p. 34).

71. *Historiografía romántica española*, p. 187.

72. *Ensayo sobre el catolicismo, el liberalismo y el socialismo*, ed. by Vila Selma, p. 120.

CHAPTER 3

'Ideal Eternal History': Vico's Providential Design

When first expounded in Spain, the historical framework adumbrated by Vico does not seem to have been employed as a calculated response to Guizot; the absence, at least at first, of antagonistic references and allusions make the possibility an unlikely one, despite the close coincidence of dates. Nevertheless, the two very different conceptual patterns can be seen, in the mere fact of their co-existence, to offer alternative interpretations of historical development susceptible in the extreme to forms of ideological weighting. Vico's schema would have held obvious and pertinent attractions for more conservative historians and thinkers, who were to apply it to the early nineteenth century both as a putative explanation for the traumas of recent experience and as a desirable antidote to the liberal ideal of progress. Vico's system was thus destined to become the standard-bearer of Spanish opposition to the pattern of ideas informing the *Histoire de la civilisation en Europe*.

Giambattista Vico (1668–1744) had, in his *Scienza nuova*, especially in its third and definitive version of 1744, formulated a theory of historical cycles which provided an interpretation of the past markedly different from that of the Enlightenment. Enlarging upon St Augustine of Hippo's *De civitate Dei* and Bossuet's *Discours sur l'histoire universelle*, the Neapolitan thinker regarded the progress of humankind not as a causal process in purely mechanistic terms but as the pursuit of a collective destiny which God had set before it. As a Catholic teleologist, Vico believed that men responded to mysterious changes in their nature wrought by Providence. He argued for a cyclical pattern of history, eternally repeated, tracing the rise, apogee, and fall of civilizations and contending that each had necessarily to pass through a sequence or *corso* of three distinct eras: an age of gods, an age of heroes, and an age of men. These named phases, as Peter Burke has reminded us, were really no more than a classical commonplace that Vico had found in Herodotus, although the Italian thinker was now to invest them with a new and characteristic meaning.[1] In Vico's plan they represented a much more rigorously defined organic pattern, within which zenith had necessarily to be succeeded by decline and catastrophe before a renewed period of growth could ensue. Vico's sequence represented, in his own words, 'La storia ideale eterna, sopra la quale corron in tempo le storie de tutte le nazioni, ne' loro sorgimento, progressi, stati, decadenze e fini' [Ideal, eternal history, upon the basis of which run the histories of all nations across time, in their birth, development, maturity, decline, and death].[2] Strictly speaking, history was viewed as a spiral rather than as a series of cycles; Vico's theory of *ricorso* meant that history never precisely repeated itself but came to each new prescribed phase in a form differentiated by what had gone before. Summarizing the character of Vico's historicism as a belief in the validity of organic human development and 'in an immaterial soul with its own immanent laws of growth', not subject to mechanical causation but governed by Providence, Isaiah Berlin comments: 'In this sense Vico was a reactionary figure, opposed to the central stream of the Enlightenment'.[3]

Within the schema more recently proposed by Hayden White, meanwhile, Vico's strategy is an 'Organicist' one; the Organicist, as White construes it, 'attempts to depict the particulars discerned in the historical field as components of synthetic processes. At the heart of the Organicist strategy is a metaphysical commitment to the paradigm of the microcosmic-macrocosmic relationship'.[4] This last we can, needless to say and with specificity to nineteenth-century Spain, closely identify with Donoso's stress upon 'acción sobrenatural'. In more general terms, Moreno Alonso detects in Spanish Romantic historiography a tendency to seek the source material of historical events in 'fuerzas internas de carácter religioso o espirituales' [internal forces of a religious or spiritual nature],[5] while Hans Juretschke has noted in his broad contextualization of the Romantic period in Spain that the philosophy of history, a key component of Romantic thought, was rooted in the discourses of theology.[6]

Relevant to the present discussion also is White's contention that the Organicist historian characteristically professes 'the desire to see individual entities as components of processes which aggregate into wholes that are greater than, or qualitatively different from, the sum of their parts';[7] hence Balmes's reference to human structures and institutions as simply the 'superficie', the surface layer of the historical past, and his rejection of what he felt to lack transcendent content. Organicist historians, White continues, will be most closely concerned with the 'integrative processes' underlying and at the same time transcending events, and their accounts 'oriented toward the determination of the *end* or *goal* toward which all the processes found in the historical field are presumed to be tending'. Organicist strategies therefore eschew the search for 'laws' of historical process 'in the sense of universal and invariant causal relationships, after the manner of Newtonian physics'; their principles and ideas only function as causal agents or agencies when they are interpreted as 'manifestations of God's purpose for His creation', so that 'the Organicist makes sense out of the historical process by displaying the integrative nature of the historical process taken as a whole'.[8] It is in precisely these terms that conservative Spanish historians writing in the Romantic period appropriate Vico as an explication of a fundamentally reassuring universe, of a stable and integrated epistemological vision that is profoundly theocentric.

Vico had been revered by Herder, whose own theory of cultural anthropology shared the Italian thinker's organic analogies and application to humanity of metaphors of vegetable growth, and by Goethe, who had regarded the *Scienza nuova* as a work of prophetic insight. The long-neglected masterpiece had not properly resurfaced, however, until 1827, in the form of a French adaptation by the Romantic historian Jules Michelet. Michelet made the point that Vico had been isolated and misunderstood in his own day since he had been born too early, while the English philosopher R.G. Collingwood would much later affirm that the extraordinary merit of Vico's work had only been recognized when, two generations later, German thought had independently reached a point akin to his own.[9] In Spain, Vico's ideas were not popularized until 1838, when Juan Donoso Cortés published in the influential newspaper *El Correo Nacional* a series of articles entitled 'Filosofía de la historia: Juan Bautista Vico',[10] proclaiming in his preamble that the subject of his series of articles was one entirely new to Spain (I, 537).[11] In introducing what was unfamiliar material he allowed himself, before moving on to consider Vico's ideas in detail, two sections aimed at contextualization entitled respectively 'España y la nueva historiografía' and 'Historiografía y filosofía de la historia'. These introductory articles reveal with some clarity Donoso's motivation and aims in popularizing Vico and in hinting at the applicability of his theory of historical phases to nineteenth-century circumstances.

In stating the novelty of his topic in Spain, Donoso lamented in passing the relative paucity of the Spanish philosophical tradition; Luis Vives had endeavoured in vain to sow the seeds of original philosophical inquiry (I, 537), while Jovellanos, an able thinker when it came to matters of government and public administration, had never attempted any thoroughgoing assessment of first principles (I, 538). Having failed to keep abreast of contemporary philosophical and historiographical currents, Donoso felt, 'retrocedemos con acelerado paso a los tiempos de obscuridad y de barbarie' [we are retreating, at an increasing rate, into the times of darkness and barbarism] (I, 539). It is perhaps not coincidental that, in this preliminary section, Donoso should on two occasions use phrasing strongly reminiscent of Vico's own characteristic set of metaphors — the organic analogy of Vives's attempt to 'plantar' [plant] in the 'suelo' [soil] of Spain an original philosophical culture — and terminology — the figurative regression to a state of barbarism mentioned in the lines quoted. The sense of a transferential relationship between the Spanish writer and his subject matter becomes increasingly perceptible in this first article, culminating in Donoso's paraphrase of Vico's assertion that 'Las sociedades nacen, progresan, desfallecen y se extinguen, obedeciendo a ciertas leyes inalterables que presiden a su infancia, a su progreso, a su decadencia y a su muerte' [Societies are born, develop, die, and vanish, in obedience to certain unalterable laws that preside over their infancy, development, decline, and death] (I, 540). A rhetorical question, meanwhile, sees the first appearance in Donoso's text of the theory of Providential design that Vico had himself restated: are the revolutions documented in history, and the several catastrophes charted in its course, merely the products of chance or the inevitable effects of necessary principles, of 'leyes providenciales y eternas' [providential eternal laws] (I, 541)? He effectively makes his own reply in the lines that immediately follow, insisting that historical events should be seen to respond to a higher teleological purpose; if, in the individual or collective historical movement of nations and peoples, wrote Donoso, there cannot be found 'un designio manifiesto de la Providencia' [a manifest providential design], then, quite simply, 'no hay Humanidad; la fatalidad de los antiguos es señora de los hombres y reina de los mundos, no hay filosofía de la Historia' [there is no such thing as Humanity; classical fate holds sway over humankind and all the kingdoms of the world, there is no philosophy of history] (I, 541). In formulating a coherent theory

of history as Providential design, Donoso continues, Bossuet had achieved renown as the last Father of the Church and Vico as a brilliant reformist historian. With Bossuet humanity had discovered 'el nombre de Dios escrito en las páginas de la historia y su providencia dirigiendo ordenadamente por medio de los siglos los pasos de las naciones' [the name of God written in the pages of history, His providence guiding in an orderly fashion the steps of nations along the ages], and the philosophy of history had been born (I, 543).[12] Donoso goes even further in his insistence that the study of the patterns of history must be firmly theocentric, roundly declaring that the philosophy of history itself is impossible without God, for history without divine ordering is no more than chaos (I, 544). The reader of this section of Donoso's text is often acutely conscious of the preference for the sweeping syntheses and ambitious historical patterning identified by José Luis Abellán as particular callsigns of his most important work,[13] while it is equally pertinent to cite Ramón de Campoamor's declaration, in his *Historia crítica de las Cortes reformadoras* of 1845, that 'La historia filosófica es una diosa que amamos todos, pero que el señor Donoso la idolatra' [Philosophical history is a goddess loved by us all, but one truly worshipped by Donoso].[14] One passage clearly called to mind is that which opens Book I, Chapter V of Donoso's *Ensayo sobre el catolicismo, el liberalismo y el socialismo*, where he insists that ignorance of the working out, within the world, of the designs of the Holy Spirit leads to an inability to conceive

> cuál es la causa sobrenatural y secreta de los fenómenos patentes y naturales, cuál es la causa invisible de todo lo visible, cuál es el vínculo que sujeta lo temporal a lo eterno, cuál es el resorte secretísimo de los movimientos del alma; de qué manera obra el Espíritu Santo en el hombre, en la sociedad la Providencia, Dios en la Historia.[15]

> [what is the hidden supernatural cause of visible natural phenomena, what is the unseen cause of all that is seen, what is the link that binds the transient to the eternal, what is the hidden mechanism prompting the movements of the soul; in what way the Holy Spirit works upon humankind, Providence upon society, God upon History].

Predictably, therefore, Donoso is savage in his condemnation of the eighteenth century, an age which he labels 'fanáticamente irreligioso y escéptico' [fanatically irreligious and sceptical]. He summarizes in uncompromisingly robust terms the implications and consequences of eighteenth-century thought: 'destronó a Dios para coronar al hombre, destronó a los reyes para coronar a los súbditos y se sublevó a un tiempo mismo contra la autoridad divina y contra las potestades de la tierra. En este siglo debía ser incomprensible Bossuet, y las sombras de la noche debían caer sobre los anales de la Historia' [it dethroned God with a view to the coronation of humanity, and rebelled at one and the same time against divine authority and against all earthly power. In this age Bossuet must of necessity prove incomprehensible, and the shadows of night fall upon the annals of history] (I, 543). Donoso's words constitute a characteristically ferocious attack upon eighteenth-century France and upon those Enlightenment ideals widely believed to have brought about widespread violent rebellion and a revolutionary bloodbath. Counterbalancing them, however, is a lyrical evocation of Vico as an heroic figure above and apart from the dominant

spirit of his age: while the eighteenth century floundered in 'los abismos de la duda' [the chasms of doubt], wrote Donoso, 'un joven de carácter melancólico y ardiente recorría en sus meditaciones solitarias todo el dominio de las ciencias, y, enriquecido con todo el saber de los tiempos pasados y presentes, echaba los fundamentos de la filosofía de la Historia' [a melancholy and passionate young man would, in his solitary meditations, journey across all the dominions of knowledge, and, enriched with all the wisdom of the ages, past and present, would lay the foundations of the philosophy of history] (I, 544). Out of Vico's known preference for solitude, Donoso creates a sentimental picture loaded with topical symbolism; as I have shown elsewhere, literary criticism of the same period was awash with references to reconstruction on a sure moral foundation away from the gaping chasms of religious scepticism and political uncertainty.[16]

If not rendered absolutely explicit here, Donoso's overview has quite clear impli- cations. It would not seem out of place to state them rather more overtly than the Spanish writer chose to do himself, given that the suggestions in Donoso's text are so transparent. In the first place, the sense of divine reliance, of essential transcendent design, that had informed and underpinned Vico's philosophy of history revealed the Italian thinker, within Donoso's perspective, as an extraordinary luminary in a century that was eventually to be characterized by 'filosofismo', rationalism and unbelief. Without having lived to witness the ultimate consequences of the work of the French *philosophes* nor to see the publication of the *Encyclopédie*, Vico had seemed to anticipate and predict their dire results. By clinging to Vico's theory of cyclical phases, it was possible to see in recent historical events an ordering that was divinely inspired, so that even the baleful spectacle of the previous fifty years could be satisfactorily explained. The French Revolution and the Terror did not call into question the existence of a beneficent God, but revealed humanity to be subject to an eternal and ineluctable law of expiation, which the untold suffering occasioned by revolutionary violence had fearfully exemplified. For, as Donoso clarifies in his pre- sentation of Vico, the Italian thinker had traced a sequential progression of political institutions in each historical cycle, from aristocratic to democratic and, lastly and inevitably, to a state of anarchy. If at this point there appeared no extraordinary leader to replace existing unenforceable law with autocratic control, then there could only be a carnage that represented humanity's expiation for having over-reached itself in its ambition and thus disregarded divine authority: 'El exterminio es un instrumento en la mano de Dios: con él hace que se cumplan las leyes divinas en la sociedad, que ha sacudido el yugo de las leyes humanas' [Annihilation is a weapon in the hand of God: by means of this He ensures that divine laws are kept in a society that has thrown off the yoke of human laws] (I, 568). The crimes which Donoso imputes to eighteenth-century ideals of rationalism and progress square precisely with the kind of scenario evoked in his restatement of the law of expiation as formulated by Bossuet and trenchantly reaffirmed by Vico. The Enlightenment had, as Donoso saw it, sought to usurp the place of God and therefore invited cataclysm on a grand scale. On this point, the Spanish thinker was at one with the conservative Catholic philosopher Joseph De Maistre, who had described the French Revolution in lurid terms as a fearsome act of Providence which might purify humanity and ultimately pave the way for a regenerate Christianity. One of Donoso's closest and oldest friends, the well-known poet and politician Nicomedes-Pastor Díaz, would recall in his unpublished *Cuaderno de autógrafos* that 'yo había vivido mucho con Donoso, y Donoso era una edición de De Maistre con comentarios' [I had lived a great deal in the company of Donoso, and Donoso was an annotated edition of De Maistre].[17] José Vila Selma, who describes Donoso as having been a trenchant Providentialist from an early stage in his intellectual development, cites the celebrated speech delivered at the Colegio de Humanidades, Cáceres, in 1829 and, specifically, Donoso's view that the fall of the Roman Empire had been necessary for society to progress; as Donoso expressed it:

> Cuando las naciones han llegado a este punto de envilecimiento es necesario que una revolución espantosa haga retroceder al hombre al seno de la Naturaleza, para que, purificado de los crímenes que le afeaban, vuelva a seguir la carrera que la providencia le ha marcado.

> [When nations have reached such a degree of debasement, what is necessary is that a fearful revolution return humankind to the bosom of Nature, in order that, purged of the vices which disfigured it, it might return to the path that Providence has assigned to it].[18]

This, as we shall see in the following chapter, is a perspective he was similarly to apply to the revolutionary events occurring in France in 1789 and after.

Within the Spanish tradition, meanwhile, we might establish forceful parallels with the work of the earlier reactionaries, and specifically with the Jesuit priest Lorenzo de Hervás y Panduro's *Causas de la Revolución francesa*. Hervás saw the violence and suffering endured by the French people after 1789 as the effects of divine retribution directed against a perverse nation, Christian in name alone, a nation that, in its degradation, had become an affront to the rest of humanity; in his expansive historical treatise, as Javier Herrero observed, the revolutionary cataclysm had itself become a Providential affirmation of God's love.[19] There are, furthermore, strong connections between Donoso's presentation of his source material here and the apocalyptic emphases of his speeches to the Spanish parliament provoked by the 'Year of Revolution' a decade later, speeches in which, in terms reminiscent of Vico, he announced his willingness to see authority entrusted at such a critical juncture to 'un dictador o césar que tiene una función mediadora y demiúrgica' [a dictator or Caesar possessed of a godlike directing function].[20]

Vico's cyclical theory of history and his espousal of the idea of Providence now allowed traditionalists to view the upheavals that had occurred in 1789 and after as indications that civilization had suffered a relapse into barbarism. The kind of scenario often graphically described by conservative commentators in their depictions of their own age of religious scepticism and rampant materialism forcefully coincide with Vico's own much earlier vision of the catastrophic collapse of the age of men. In Spain, for example, Fray Diego de Cádiz would fulminate in these terms against the last decades of the eighteenth century, describing them, as Javier Herrero puts it, as the end of all things, as the time of the great punishment meted out by God in the form of vengeance against a humanity that had allowed itself to be corrupted by the evil of philosophy.[21] Within Vico's programmatic historical design, a 'second stage of barbarism' arises from an excess of rational speculation and the predominance of technology. In a state of fundamental perversity, money becomes the only value. Imminent dissolution from the age of men to a bestial state is occasioned when a civilization comes to worship a materialist ideology or is in thrall to a science uninformed by conscience. This final degenerate stage in the Italian thinker's process of *corso* precedes a descent into anarchy and is followed by a reawakening of the civilizing cycle in a different and amended form. The dissemination of Vico's sequential pattern would go a long way towards explaining the apocalyptic vision of 'el siglo positivo' [the age of positivism], the widespread revulsion engendered by materialism, and the emphatic call for a regenerate society founded upon spirituality, all of which came to be common currency in the Spain of the 1830s and 1840s. It was time, traditionalists seemed to be arguing, for the historical cycle to begin afresh with a new age of gods fortified by the lessons of previous generations. This application of Vico's plan imposed order upon chaos, stimulated faith and reassurance in a climate of doubt and moral uncertainty, and bastioned the conviction as expressed by Donoso that philosophical inquiry, when based on salutary principles, allowed access to 'inefables placeres aun para los hombres gastados y para las sociedades enervadas' [ineffable pleasures even for an exhausted humanity and for demented societies] (I, 539). As he put it in concluding his series of articles on Vico, the contemporary age was one of renovation, and he looked to society at large to seek solutions in accordance with God's Providential plan; it was time, he insisted, that the nation avert its eyes from the spectacle of wretchedness and misfortune that currently assailed them: 'levantemos nuestro espíritu a la contemplación de las grandes cuestiones históricas y filosóficas, que son como los problemas obscuros que Dios ha arrojado para que los resuelvan los hombres en el seno de las sociedades humanas' [let us elevate our spirits to the contemplation of great historical and philosophical questions, which are like the intricate problems that God has cast before mankind in the bosom of human societies that they might be resolved] (I, 572). Fernández Carvajal is surely correct, therefore, to specify as constants in Donoso's mature thought an intimate connection between the philosophy of history and theology and, subsequently, the revelation of those hidden energies and forces that are at the heart of the former as well as the latter.[22] Abellán, citing this same passage, felt that such a reading effectively locates Donoso within what he designates an ideologically driven Romanticism.[23] Antonio Heredia Soriano's succinct résumé of Donoso's historical outlook likewise provides a clear sense of the perspective that was ultimately to dominate the 1840s debate, a perspective which, as we shall see, is entirely representative of more conservative Romantic historiography: a philosophy of history that has God as its foundation, at its centre, and as its goal, that figures the Church as an exemplary model of social and political organization, that holds to theology as its normative source of knowledge, that views mankind as willing collaborator in a divinely conceived historical pattern, and that prescribes faith as the only secure pathway to and instrument of truth.[24]

Donoso's articles on Vico do seem to have had some considerable impact. Referring to them some seven years later in the literary journal *El Siglo Pintoresco*, Alfredo Adolfo Camus commented on the efficacy of Donoso in ensuring that Spain experience the powerful, irresistible influence that could not but be exerted, even at so late a date, upon historical, political, and literary study by the brilliant legacy of one of the finest minds of the previous age.[25] Camus's remarks are representative of the many eulogistic comments that were to be lavished upon the Neapolitan thinker, and give an idea of the considerable acclaim of which he was now, some one hundred years after his death, the recipient. Camus in fact goes on to describe Vico's death in relative obscurity as the 'Triste pero común destino de los hombres que tienen la desventura de anticiparse al siglo y a la sociedad en que vivieron' [The tragic but all too common destiny of those who are unfortunate enough to be ahead of their own age and of their own society].[26] Crucially also, Camus included in his account an extensive quote from Michelet's free adaptation of the *Scienza nuova*, Book III, an indication that the French historian's work was in active circulation in the Spain of the period.[27] Whether due principally to Donoso's series of articles or to Michelet's French version, the evidence is that the ideas of Vico were widely known and well received in Spain throughout the 1840s.

The first extended application of Vico's ideas in historical scholarship was made by Fermín Gonzalo Morón, a friend and associate of Donoso, in the series of public lectures subsequently published as a *Curso de Historia de la civilización de España*.[28] Of the utmost importance in the present context is that Gonzalo Morón was to employ Vico's patterning in what appears to have been a calculated attempt to challenge and even to discredit the perspective on European history formulated by François Guizot. Adopting the French historian's own characteristic terminology, Gonzalo Morón concurred in the determining presence of 'lucha' in modern history, but insisted that it had not been manifested in a process of friction between opposed groupings indispensable to historical progress; instead, as he saw it, it had involved a tireless human quest for morality and justice in the face of tyranny and aggression. Progress itself was only glorious and swift, he affirmed, when man, conscious of his destiny, was inspired by noble beliefs to undertake heroic deeds (I, 169). Throughout his history, in fact, Gonzalo Morón would opt for the theory of Providential design he traced back through Vico and Bossuet as the true motor of historical development.

The Spanish historian's presentation of Vico, like that earlier made by Donoso, is lyrical in the extreme, while he attributes to the Italian thinker an almost unsurpassable degree of importance in intellectual history. Approvingly citing Vico's theory of historical cycles, he describes it as 'una de las más fecundas y poderosas ideas que haya podido descubrir el genio del hombre' [one of the most fertile and authoritative ideas that human genius has ever discovered]. As he then expresses it:

> El renacimiento de los estudios históricos, la filosofía de la historia, la conciliación y el doble estudio de los hechos y de las teorías, y el examen del mundo moral y político bajo miras vastas y, por decirlo así, universales, todo es debido a la ciencia de Vico. (I, 18)

> [The rebirth of historical study, the philosophy of history, the reconciliation and analytical interaction of theory and fact, and the appraisal of the realms of politics and morality in a wide-ranging and, let us say, all-embracing gaze, all of this is due to the wisdom of Vico.]

Gonzalo Morón saw Vico as the early champion of a salutary reaction against the mechanistic philosophy of Bacon and Descartes (I, 17), a reaction that had culminated in the overthrow of philosophical rationalism. Between them, Vico and Montesquieu had transformed the study of history (I, 19–20). Yet Enlightenment prejudices, he felt, signally in a 'movimiento instintivo y absoluto contra lo pasado' [visceral and unqualified reaction against the past], had stifled true genius: Bossuet had been execrated by uncomprehending atheists, Montesquieu had been misunderstood, and Vico had been lamentably maligned. Again in this respect, Gonzalo Morón is close to Donoso. The former's own passionate involvement in his narrative is obvious as he declares that Vico's life and memory had been made wretched, the object of calumny, that he had been slandered as no more than an obscure, self-contradictory metaphysician (I, 21). However, a felicitous change wrought most famously by Chateaubriand had, he was delighted to say, ushered in a fresh appraisal; idealistic German intellectuals had put an end to the dominant philosophical materialism, thus creating a new and more encouraging scenario. These were circumstances, he felt, that favoured the re-direction of historical study towards the path established by Vico (I, 24).

The overview provided in this introductory section of Gonzalo Morón's history is in every way characteristic of conservative intellectual thought as expressed in 1840s Spain. The Enlightenment is condemned out of hand in transparently pejorative terms and with ill-concealed righteous anger, while the passages dedicated to those writers felt to have championed any form of transcendent philosophy in opposition to rationalism and materialism acquire a sense of almost messianic zeal. Thus Voltaire's study of the Middle Ages is dismissed as superficial, inaccurate, or blatantly false (I, 22), while Chateaubriand's preparation of *Les Martyrs* is lyrically contextualized as a magnificent epic design that had come into being at a time when religion was customarily the object of scorn (I, 23). The latter's historical studies had, felt Gonzalo Morón, lent a new direction to the philosophy of history, 'presentando el cristianismo como el principio civilizador, que regeneró moralmente la humanidad y la salvó del envilecimiento y la corrupción Romana' [representing Christianity as that civilizing principle that had morally regenerated humanity and redeemed it from Roman debasement and corruption] (I, 23); the singularity, in every sense, of the Christian principle as affirmed by the Spanish historian is surely not without significance. Gonzalo Morón was in fact to re-create precisely Chateaubriand's view of the Christian religion as pre-eminent component in the history of European civilization, grounding his account in 'historia moral' and denigrating classical society at virtually every opportunity. Quite apart from specific or even more general judgements, however, it is worthwhile once more to stress the pride of place accorded to Vico in Gonzalo Morón's pattern. Here was a transcendent historical synthesis, an abstract philosophical pattern which allowed the Spanish writer to judge both pagan classical Rome and irreligious eighteenth-century France within an inscrutable Providential design as periods leading inevitably to human catastrophe. The Catholic tradition represented by Bossuet and Vico undoubtedly underpins Gonzalo Morón's assertion that 'el mundo no ha sido regido jamás por una fatalidad ciega, como dieron a entender Voltaire y su escuela. Leyes eternas deciden la suerte de las naciones como la de los particulares' [the world has never been ruled by blind fate, as Voltaire and his school gave us to believe. Eternal laws decide the fortunes of nations and individuals alike] (I, 181). Crucially, then, in the published version of his history, Gonzalo Morón saw fit to include an appendix to the first introductory lecture under the heading 'Ideas de Vico', annotated with references to Michelet's French version of the *Scienza nuova* (I, 65–67). What is more, with the appearance, shortly after the writer's death, of a posthumous volume — more were planned but apparently never published — of *Obras escogidas* edited by his son Ricardo, the prefatory section entitled 'Al público' recalled that in 1841, with his history of Spain, 'acometió mi padre la atrevida y superior empresa de encauzar en nuestra patria los estudios históricos por nuevos y filosóficos senderos' [my father embarked upon the daring and high-minded task of directing historical study in our country into new and philosophical pathways]; Bossuet and Vico, the editor went on, transformed the erudite and literary-minded historian into a thinker and philosopher.[29]

Gonzalo Morón's treatment of Guizot was to be far less encomiastic. The French writer, he felt, had made of historiography 'una ciencia política' [a political science] (I, 25). Although worthy of the greatest respect, 'sólo ha contado en su curso sobre la civilización de Europa los hechos exteriores y políticos, pidiéndoles su razón, y su filosofía; y ha omitido los hechos intelectuales y morales' [in his course of lectures on European civilization he has taken into account only things that are external and political, seeking their logical and philosophical explanation; he has omitted those that are intellectual and moral] (82–83). Yet again the defect of superficiality, incurred by a perceived concern with mere externals, is that imputed to the French writer; the complaint against Guizot, as we saw in the previous chapter, concerns his alleged subordination of moral concerns to more strictly political ones. The second lecture is in fact given over to a résumé of Guizot's position and to what Gonzalo Morón details as its shortcomings. The Spanish historian's priorities were, according to his own assessment, rather different: the progress of humanity needed to be appraised on material, intellectual and moral levels, he affirmed, although stressing that there existed among the three a natural hierarchy; the moral element must always prevail over the intellectual, and the latter over the material (I, 77–78).

What was really at the heart of complaints against Guizot, as readily emerges from a detailed examination of the texts, is a sense of resentment against a perspective that was pluralistic instead of wholeheartedly theocentric. It is not difficult to understand why Gonzalo Morón should have preferred Vico's essentially transcendent synthesis, not least for its insistence upon divine intervention in human affairs. The much more prominent role afforded to Providence accorded, as Gonzalo Morón and numerous other Spanish historians saw it, justifiable pride of place not to affairs of this world but to an unquestionable spiritual authority that clearly intimated and portended the certainty of the next. The emphasis is therefore entirely different from that struck by Guizot; Gonzalo Morón states, in underscoring the role of Bossuet, that the latter had succeeded in 'mostrar en todo los designios de la Providencia, el triunfo y engrandecimiento del Cristianismo' [revealing in everything the designs of Providence, the triumph and the glory of Christianity]. However, he continues, this was by no means entirely to discard things of this world. 'el tipo providencial no destruye en Bossuet lo racional y filosófico de los sucesos' [the Providential pattern does not, in Bossuet, exclude a logical and philosophical assessment of events] (I, 15). Neither, if we are minded to redress the balance, had Guizot neglected the concept of Providential design, but the relative weighting of the two had been profoundly different. Gonzalo Morón is indisputably much closer to the tradition represented by Vico and Bossuet than had been his French counterpart, as is underlined by his assertion that any society in which ambition and self-interest are allowed to prevail over justice and morality offends against the nobility of humankind and violates the august processes of Providence (I, 81).[30] In referring to his own age, Gonzalo Morón, as Donoso had done, seems to appropriate Vico's predictions concerning the imminent collapse of the age of men, drawing attention to 'el pauperismo y la degradación intelectual y moral, resultado necesario a mi modo de ver del apogeo de la industria y del progreso material' [the moral and intellectual impoverishment and degradation that is, to my way of thinking, a necessary consequence of the pre-eminence of industry and material development] (I, 156). Like Donoso, Gonzalo Morón believed that it was a Christian Providence that conferred upon man his sense of moral identity; hence Donoso's blunt observation, in his articles on Vico, that the philosophy of history could only have begun after the implantation of Christianity, and hence also Gonzalo Morón's exclusion of the Roman element from the founding historical components of modern European society. When Donoso himself came to review Gonzalo Morón's published lectures in the pages of the *Revista de Madrid*, he not surprisingly called attention once more to the Providentialist vision adumbrated by St Augustine and much later restated by Bossuet and Vico, in the process describing the latter as Germany's great teacher and the man who had utterly transformed historical study in Europe.[31]

Given its historical reputation as an institution associated with radical or progressive politics, it may, at first sight at least, appear strange that Gonzalo Morón's history should have been based upon a course of lectures delivered over many months at the Madrid Ateneo. However, as Inman Fox tellingly specifies, in its first generation of existence, which he dates from 1835 to 1868, the Ateneo was a fiefdom of the *moderados*, so much so that the *progresista* minister Pedro Gómez de la Serna had created, in 1843, the Chair in Philosophy of History at Madrid's Universidad Central that was to be occupied by Julián Sanz del Río as part and parcel of an express determination to 'neutralizar el predominio doctrinario de los moderados en las cátedras del Ateneo' [neutralize the predominant *moderado* doctrine as expounded by the professors of the Ateneo].[32]

With the publication between 1842 and 1844 of Balmes's *El Protestantismo comparado con el Catolicismo*, meanwhile, came further affirmation of the central role of Providence in historical development. Balmes, in common with numerous other Spanish historians, subscribed to the essential principle of the *Discours sur l'histoire universelle*, a text which, he felt, 'traza con tan sublime maestría el camino seguido por la Providencia' [traces with sublime mastery the course of Providence] (IV, 279–80).[33] As well as using Bossuet's interpretation to argue against Guizot's rather different set of emphases, Balmes also made a number of judgements of recent European history that are avowedly informed by a Providentialist outlook. As he comments in the second volume of his essay:

> en todas las grandes crisis de la sociedad, esa mano misteriosa que rige los destinos
> del universo tiene como en reserva a un hombre extraordinario; llega el momento,

el hombre se presenta, marcha, él mismo no sabe a dónde, pero marcha con paso firme a cumplir el alto destino que el Eterno le ha señalado en la frente. (I, 155)

[at every great crisis of society, that mysterious hand that rules over the destinies of the world has some extraordinary man waiting as it were in reserve; the moment arrives, the man appears, he steps forward, whither he knows not yet himself, but he steps forward with certain tread to fulfil that high destiny that the Eternal one has imprinted upon his brow.]

The specific historical moment at issue here is the aftermath of the French Revolution; the extraordinary genius, needless to say, is Chateaubriand, described with messianic fervour as a holy figure rekindling the flame of faith. Finding everywhere the gory imprint of atheism, but hearing all around the sound of celestial music, the French nobleman had, declared Balmes in the most effusive terms, passionately sung the beauties of religion, revealed its intimate relationship with the natural world and, through divine powers of utterance, vouchsafed to men the mysteries of this golden chain linking earth with Heaven (I, 156–57).[34]

It is not difficult to perceive how serviceable the traditional idea of divine Providence had proved to Catholic writers. It was much more reassuring — and certainly much more expedient — to regard recent turmoil and instability as perplexing but not insoluble problems cast in the way of humanity by an ultimately beneficent God whose purposes necessarily remained inscrutable, rather than as the inevitable human cost incurred in the course of achieving the desirable goals of progress and reform. To men who did not share the aspirations of liberalism, Bossuet and Vico represented a much more comforting and reliable perspective, while the idea of Providence effectively enshrined the philosophy of history as a religious discourse concerned with the exegesis of events occurring within a traditional Christian cosmology. The alternative, it appeared, was to allow the view that the future of humanity remained with men rather than with God, and for Catholic traditionalists it was unthinkable that history should come to be regarded as profane.

It is fair to say, then, that in the 1840s Spanish historiography possessed two distinct and conflicting philosophical overviews upon which to base any interpretation of either the remote or more recent historical past. One, almost entirely indebted to the work of Guizot, was founded upon the development of important human freedoms and implicitly accepted the ideal of progress and the validity of man's aspirations towards perfectibility; the other, grounded in the Catholic tradition of Bossuet and Vico, subordinated human affairs to the workings of Providence within a divinely regulated cosmos in which fallen man must be always conscious not just of his aspirations but also of his necessary insufficiencies. Within this context, the publication, begun in 1850, of the most solid and enduring historical work so far to emerge from nineteenth-century Spain, the *Historia general de España* embarked upon by Modesto Lafuente and concluded by Juan Valera,[35] acquires considerable ideological import as well as its undoubted historiographical significance. While both José María Jover Zamora and, rather more recently, Inman Fox, have justifiably pointed to the singularity of Lafuente's gargantuan project, to its conscious reworking of Mariana and to its postulation of a new and liberal 'general history' that was to prove the yardstick of many modern conceptions of Spanish nationhood,[36] they both neglect to contextualize the great work as pertaining to a pre-existing and clearly signposted nineteenth-century historiographical tradition within Spain. By overemphasizing the originality of Lafuente's history — although one hesitates to say it given the measure, qualitatively as well as quantitatively speaking, of the *Historia general de España* — it is possible to pass over issues of continuity within the ongoing processes of Spanish intellectual history. It is important, I feel, to remember that rather than exclusively a point of departure, as Fox's chosen framework necessarily implies, Lafuente's history is at least in part a culmination, in that it closes a decade which had already seen the publication of four general histories of Spain. While the concept of an innovatory 'historia general' carries with it all of the intellectual weight ascribed to it by both Jover Zamora and Fox as an historical template for a current and future 'invention of Spain', something similar might be said, after all, for the equally ground-breaking one — in the Spanish context — of an 'historia de la civilización' that was at the centre of historiographical concern in the preceding decade. What values constituted the inalienable nucleus of Spanish civilization, as much as what principles defined and determined the general history of Spain, was to be a question that remained at the core of intellectual inquiry in succeeding generations. It seems a pity, therefore, that Jover Zamora should mention in passing only one of those histories published in the 1840s and that Inman Fox should neglect them altogether.

Both Lafuente's initial prologue and the much more substantial 'Discurso preliminar' found in the first volume in fact provide a fertile source of evidence for the arguments already being pursued here. The very beginning of the former, for example, makes reference to the time of political turmoil and moral uncertainty in which Lafuente had begun seriously to study history; long meditation on the past, he states by quoting Thierry, had provided him with an essential sense of 'reposo' [quietude] (I, i), while the certain belief in a Providential design had proved an indispensable vital support. Lafuente then explicitly separates out material from spiritual, seeing a higher guiding principle above and beyond the affairs of men that historical study both contains and reveals. He had begun his task, he recalls, with both 'fe religiosa' [religious faith] and 'fe política' [political faith] in ample measure. The first remained unscathed; however, as he goes on to warn, the second might well have wavered in the face of so many vicissitudes, so much wretchedness among his fellow beings had not history been able to fortify it afresh, 'recordándome a cada paso, por un largo encadenamiento de hechos, que hay un poder más alto que dirige y encamina la marcha de las sociedades' [reminding me at every turn of a vast chain of events that there is a more elevated power that guides and directs the onward path of societies] (I, iv). Lafuente's words, projecting the same sense of 'acción sobrenatural' insisted upon by Donoso Cortés and enshrining the same Providential pattern favoured by the bulk of his predecessors, re-create the idea of regenerationist potential consistently ascribed to history by the Romantic mind. As the same passage continues: 'Titubeaba mi fe en los hombres, pero crecía mi fe en la Providencia' [My faith in men wavered, but my faith in Providence increased]. Given Lafuente's stated view that historical study should seek a teleological purpose in human development and thus concentrate men's minds upon the glorious ends that Providence has in view, it is hardly surprising that he should affirm in concluding his short prologue: 'Acojo gustoso la ley de la Providencia con Vico, y coloco todos los pueblos bajo la guía y el mando de Dios con Bossuet' [I am happy to accept, like Vico, the law of Providence, and, like Bossuet, to place all peoples beneath the guidance and command of God] (I, xxv). In then beginning his 'Discurso preliminar', Lafuente chooses to reiterate his reliance on Providence in professedly refuting the Classical notion of fate, speaking of an elevated principle that some, unable to comprehend, have confused with 'fatalismo'(I, 2). In the same passage the Spanish historian again refers approvingly to both Vico and Bossuet. The mention of Vico is surely not arbitrary or fortuitous, for in Lafuente's assessment of the developmental factors underlying the history of mankind, he depicts individuals and societies as the Italian thinker had done, as organisms which, in their respective spheres of evolution, grow, wither away, die, and are replaced: 'los individuos mueren y se renuevan como las plantas; las familias desaparecen para renovarse también; las sociedades se transforman, y de las ruinas de una sociedad que ha perecido nace y se levanta otra sociedad nueva' [individuals die and are replaced like plants; families disappear and are likewise replaced; societies are transformed, and from the ruins of a society that has perished is born and thrives another that is new] (I, 3). Not only does Lafuente repeat Vico's theory of a discernible cyclical pattern of life, death, and rebirth; his vocabulary is immediately suggestive of the analogies applied to social evolution by Herder.

Common to Vico's schema in the *Scienza nuova* and to later Romantic historicism was the view of historical periods as distinctive wholes: complex yet coherent, characterized by and finding expression in their respective language, imagination and human experience. Lafuente restates this perception, regarding the study of the past as valuable for its assimilation of distinctive expressions of collective human experience at a given time and in a given place (I, 4). He extends this sense of a dynamic organicism to the lives of families and individuals as well as to those of nations and peoples, and firmly underscores the notion of organic interconnection between ages in declaring that 'Lo presente, producto de lo pasado, engendra a su vez lo futuro' [The present, a product of the past, in turn engenders the future] (I, 7). The overview of Spanish history provided in the 'Discurso preliminar' is therefore full of characteristically Romantic judgements, while the sense of patterning consistently detected by Lafuente is clearly informed by Vico.

Firstly, Lafuente's view of mediaeval Spain provides noteworthy reminiscences of the lectures of the Schlegel brothers that had proved so influential in determining the nature of Spanish Romanticism. One of August Wilhelm's more celebrated procla-mations is in fact repeated almost verbatim in Lafuente's assertion that 'Toda Europa fue más o menos caballeresca durante la edad media. Ningún país sin embargo tuvo tantos motivos para serlo como España' [All of Europe was, to a greater or lesser degree, chivalric during the Middle Ages. No country, however, possessed as many reasons for being so as did Spain] (I, 113). At the same time, the notion of sequential phases establishes itself as the Spanish historian's characteristic motif; the age of chivalry he partitions off into successive eras that are respectively 'heroica y guerrera' [warlike and heroic], 'devota y galante' [gallant and devout], and 'extravagante y quijotesca' [quixotic and whimsical]. Once more the suggestion of progression and decline is irresistible.

Characteristically indebted to Vico, meanwhile, is Lafuente's résumé of the Spanish fifteenth century. With the reign of Enrique IV the Trastámara dynasty had, he states, become decadent, and had eventually fallen into degradation and immorality. However, with the accession of the Catholic Monarchs, Spain had witnessed a period of glorious rebirth: 'vamos a asistir al magnífico espectáculo de un pueblo que resucita, que nace a nueva vida, que se levanta, que se organiza, que crece, que adquiere proporciones colosales, que deja pequeños a todos los pueblos del mundo' [we are about to witness the magnificent sight of a people rising again, born into a new life, rising, organizing itself, growing, acquiring massive proportions, leaving behind every other people on the earth] (I, 118). As dissolution is followed by rebirth, and the nation, as a living organism, is regenerated, so the reign of Ferdinand and Isabella assumes the quality of unprecedented cultural efflorescence: 'Todo renace bajo el influjo tutelar de los reyes católicos: letras, artes, comercio, leyes, virtud, religiosidad, gobierno. Es el siglo de oro de Espana' [Under the tutelage of the Catholic Monarchs everything is born anew: literature, the arts, trade, law, personal virtue, religiosity, governance. It is the golden age of Spain] (I, 124). If we are seeking parallels with Vico's plan, however, most striking of all is Lafuente's evocative description of Queen Isabella herself; for here is the appearance, at a specific historical moment, of an extraordinary genius able to divert society from a lapse into barbarism and redirect it towards more noble ends, a phenomenon that the *Scienza nuova* identifies as a potential solution to cultural decline. Balmes had already used the same idea in describing Chateaubriand's emotional reinstatement of Catholicism via a potent appeal to hearts and minds. The terms in which Lafuente writes, however, make the provenance of his own depiction unmistakable:

> Cuando más avocado se podía creer el país a una disolución social, aparece un genio, que sin deber a su primera educación sino la formación de su espíritu a una piedad acendrada, y a la escuela del mundo la reflexión sobre los infortunios que nacen del desorden y de la inmoralidad, acomete la empresa de hacer de un cuerpo cadavérico un cuerpo robusto y brioso, de una nación desconcertada una nación compacta y vigorosa, de un pueblo corrompido un pueblo moralizado, y lleva su obra a próspero término y feliz remate. (I, 122)

> [When a country might be thought to be upon a headlong path to social dissolution, a genius appears, a genius who owes to her formative years no more than a spirit of heightened piety, who has learned in the school of the world only how to reflect upon the calamities that are prompted by immorality and disorder, a genius who undertakes to make a healthy and vigorous body out of what is virtually a corpse, a strong and cohesive nation out of a fragmented one, a morally certain people out of a debased one, and carries her enterprise to a happy and prosperous conclusion.]

Vico's French proponent Jules Michelet had written in strikingly similar terms, in his *Histoire de France*, of the role played by Joan of Arc in reawakening French pride and reshaping the country's destiny. Lafuente now went further in adapting Vico's pattern by locating the reign of the Catholic Monarchs historically as 'la transición de la edad media que se disuelve a la edad moderna que se inaugura' [the transition between a waning Middle Ages and an incipient modern age] (I, 133). The Italian thinker had regarded the European Middle Ages as the historical return or *ricorso* of an 'age of heroes'; the Spanish historian now considered the reign of Isabella and Ferdinand to have ushered in a different historical era, one we can identify with Vico's 'age of men'.

Lafuente reveals in his 'Discurso preliminar' two further salient examples of the cyclical motif. Firstly, he comes to regard the Habsburg dynasty itself as an historical cycle, concluding that, like the earlier line of the Trastámaras, in the space of two hundred years it had passed from a state of the highest vigour to one of utter nullity (I, 182). Secondly, he views the history of Spanish literature also as an extended cycle: it had dawned in the eleventh and twelfth centuries; had become increasingly resplendent in the course of the following three hundred years until it had reached 'pleno día' [the full light of day] in the late sixteenth century; the seventeenth century had ended in 'crepúsculo' [twilight], and night had fallen in the eighteenth century. Lafuente now looked to the nineteenth century as a potential period of regeneration, as a new dawn or 'nuevo resplandor'(I, 164–65).

On the question of literary history, Lafuente's position approximates to that consistently upheld over the previous decades by a series of Romantic critics. He is particularly close to later Romantic criticism in insisting upon the term 'regeneración' to describe the idealistic message of renewal commonly expressed by his own generation in an endeavour to combat the destructive legacy of the previous century. More or less contemporaneous with the preparation and publication of the early volumes of Lafuente's *Historia general* is the recurrent use of the same terminology by literary critics of the mid-century such as Manuel Cañete, who also regularly used metaphors of renewal, of vegetable growth, and of natural cycles to describe larger processes of reconstruction.[37] Cañete regarded Spain's broadly conservative Romanticism, for example, as 'aurora de una regeneración indispensable y fecunda' [the dawning of a fertile and indispensable regeneration], one which 'había de hacer germinar en el suelo removido las semillas de una literatura enriquecida con elementos de duración perdurable' [was destined to prompt the germination, in freshly tilled soil, of the seeds of a literature enriched with elements of durability and strength].[38]

One final note struck in Lafuente's 'Discurso preliminar' that is powerfully reminiscent of Vico is found in his reference to the factional discord that had continued to beset Spanish politics even after the Peace of Vergara that had brought an end to the Carlist War in 1839. The Spanish historian explains the divisions among the triumphant *cristinos* by affirming that 'en las épocas de regeneración parece que el espíritu humano no acierta a vivir en reposo, y busca, si no los tiene, incentivos que le agiten, y nuevas luchas en que gastar el exceso y sobreexcitación de su vitalidad' [in periods of regeneration it would seem that the human spirit is unable to live a life of rest, and seeks out, if it does not already possess them, promptings to action and new struggles in which to expend the nervous surfeit of its own vitality] (I, 275). He thus re-creates Vico's perception of an extraordinary vitality accompanying and defining the early developing phase of a civilizing cycle, an abundance of energy and an insatiable desire for powerful sensation.

Lafuente's reliance upon Vico, it goes without saying, does not necessarily mark him out as a conservative historian; his judgements concerning a number of typically contentious issues leave us in no doubt here. Although he is less than enthusiastic about the Reformation, observing in quite scathing fashion that Martin Luther had acquired a degree of fame and historical status that neither his talents nor his personal virtues had ever merited, and with some optimism states his conviction that in his own age 'la unidad católica se realizará' [Catholic unity will come to be a reality] (I, 144), his view of the role of the Inquisition and of the reign of Philip II are at a far remove from those found, for example, in Balmes. The infamous 'tribunal de sangre' [bloody tribunal] he describes as 'la institución más funesta, la más tenebrosa, la más opresiva de la dignidad y del pensamiento del hombre, y la más contraria al espíritu y al genio del cristianismo' [that darkest and most death-dealing of institutions, most oppressive of human dignity and thought, and most resolutely opposed to the spirit and genius of Christianity] (I, 125). The emperor Charles V is sketched as a foreign prince never really loved by Spaniards despite the glory he had brought to the name of Spain (I, 134–37), while of Philip II he bluntly declares that 'sentimos no sernos posible amarle tanto como le admiramos' [unfortunately we are unable to love him as much as we are in awe of him] (I, 149).[39] Most conclusively, Lafuente proportions to the Cadiz Parliament a degree of commendation and approval that could never have figured in a more conservative account. Identifying and summarizing the core judgements discovered in the *Historia general de España*, Inman Fox remarks upon Lafuente's status as the prototype of the *moderado* historian who is ambiguous with regard to the Habsburgs, concluding that 'Lafuente fue un liberal — aunque un liberal conservador — hasta el meollo' [Lafuente was a liberal — albeit a conservative liberal — to the very core].[40]

While not wishing to dispute such a verdict, I nevertheless find it hard to be persuaded that the construction of a general history of Spain upon the model provided by Guizot extended, as Fox implies, to the monumental historical account supplied by Lafuente. I would instead contend that the latter's extensive use of Vico, like the positive reception accorded the Italian thinker by Donoso Cortés, Gonzalo Morón, and other writers, stemmed ultimately from the *Scienza nuova*'s assertion of the existence of a Providential order behind the apparent chaos of events. Lafuente is in fact unequivocal in his adherence to precisely that sense of sacrilization of history, that belief in an enduring 'poder más alto que dirige y encamina la marcha de las sociedades', that is characteristic of Vico and the Providentialist tradition but, conversely, subordinated to the ideal of progress in the work of Guizot. Equally pertinent here is Lafuente's pointed contrast between a wavering 'fe política' — based, we might reflect, upon an apprehension of external events — and an unswerving 'fe religiosa', or subscription to the idea of a transcendent supernatural order.

If Vico's system came to be seen as offering an effective explanation for recent historical events, showing that, whatever the tribulations of modern Europe, humanity was not directionless or subject to the working out of a blind fate but guided by a divine principle, then it is no more than appropriate that his more enthusiastic admirers should cast him in the role of prophet. The depiction of Vico as a voice crying in the wilderness of eighteenth-century rationalism, religious scepticism, and 'filosofismo' is a natural corollary of the religious discourse imprinted upon the study of history by an unshakable faith in divine Providence. It is also, in a way, a logical extension of the desire to view the mid-nineteenth century as a period of spiritual regeneration after the arid philosophical questioning of the Enlightenment and the many disasters experienced since. Whether or not my interpretation of the evidence is correct, what is beyond dispute is that Spanish historiography during the period in question leaned increasingly heavily on the traditional notion of Providence as a set of eternal laws governing human development. Two examples are especially pertinent in that they are once more reminiscent of Vico. The first is from José de Zaragoza, who marked his admission to the Real Academia de la Historia in 1852 with a *Discurso sobre los sistemas históricos*:

> Es indudable que un principio sublime, una regla dictada por la eterna sabiduría rige los terribles acontecimientos de la historia y decide del nacimiento, prosperidad, decadencia y muerte de los Imperios, de la irrupción y predominio de unas razas, del aniquilamiento de otras, mostrando en todas partes lo deleznable y perecedero de las creaciones del hombre y la vanidad de sus pensamientos. [41]

> [It is beyond dispute that a single sublime principle, a single law dictated by an eternal wisdom presides over the awful events of history and prescribes the birth, prosperity, decline, and death of empires, the rise and pre-eminence of certain races and peoples and the annihilation of others, revealing everywhere the mean and transient nature of the works of man and the hollowness of all his thoughts].

If Vico's characteristic phrasing is present in Zaragoza's text, much of his larger plan underlies the view of history put forward by the Duque de Rivas in his own *Discurso sobre la utilidad e importancia del estudio de la historia*, delivered at the Academia de la Historia in 1853 on the occasion of the nobleman's admission to that same body:

> También en las páginas de la Historia se contempla, se estudia, se comprende cómo la mano invisible de la Providencia encamina al género humano, en sus distintas razas y en todas las regiones del globo, por la misma senda; y dejándolo caminar por ella libremente y según los impulsos del libre albedrío, lo empuja benéfica o lo detiene justiciera, según marcha hacia el fin o retrocede del fin a que lo tiene destinado para sus miras santas e inescrutables. [42]

> [Furthermore, on studying the pages of history one reflects upon and learns from the way in which humankind, in its diverse races and regions of the earth, is directed by the invisible hand of Providence in its journey upon a single path; humanity walks that path freely while, always consonant with the promptings of free will, it is benevolently urged forward or tempered by the restraining hand of justice, according to its progression towards or retreat from that end which Providence, in its holy and inscrutable gaze, has ordained.]

We might fruitfully examine more closely the lexical nucleus of the discourse of Providence expounded not just by Rivas but by all of the writers cited here. It cannot have escaped the attention of the alert reader that for all of these men the language of Providence is a discourse of authority, power, and order; a few salient examples of the phrasing characteristically articulated by them, all previously cited, should be sufficient to make the point. Bossuet had, argued Donoso Cortés, shown the name of God to be writ large in the pages of history, and revealed 'su providencia dirigiendo ordenadamente [...] los pasos de las naciones'; according to Gonzalo Morón, 'el mundo no ha sido regido jamás por una fatalidad ciega [...] Leyes eternas deciden la suerte de las naciones'; Balmes had perceived the actions of a 'mano misteriosa que rige los destinos del universo'; Modesto Lafuente had pointed to 'un poder más alto que dirige y encamina la marcha de las sociedades'; Zaragoza had affirmed that 'una regla dictada por la eterna sabiduría rige los terribles acontecimientos de la historia'; finally, Rivas had declared that the invisible hand of Providence 'encamina al género humano, [...] lo empuja benéfica o lo detiene justiciera'. What each of these texts discloses is the desire for stability and control, the affirmation of divine jurisdiction, in a nutshell the intimate sense of need for a meaningful world order that informs and underpins the majority discourse of Spanish Romantic historiography. What that discourse undoubtedly sought to do was to restore God to what its proponents regarded as His rightful place at the head of the created universe. If the Enlightenment had attempted, in their opinion, to remove the deity in order to enthrone humanity, then it was time to proclaim once more the eternal order of things: fallen man in a transient material life subject to an immortal Creator God who was the source of all enduring authority and power. Previous scales of value had been eroded and undermined, and the whole idea of order and legitimacy needed to be coherently reaffirmed. The 'ideal eternal history' offered by Bossuet and Vico provided both an explanation for the recent past and a reassuring foundation upon which to build for the future; a future, of course, that was envisaged as a godly society conscious of moral discipline and respectful of human institutions rather than an unruly, questioning society easily roused to violence and subversion by inflammatory doctrines and gestures. This essentially conservative response therefore produced what Ceri Crossley has called 'the sacrilization of history';[43] the historian's account acquires a scriptural dimension, and his message for the nineteenth century becomes one of redemption from revolutionary sins. It is also worth recalling that the alternative reading of history adumbrated by Guizot and apparently preferred by some Spanish liberals was predicated upon 'lucha', upon struggle or conflict. If we are minded to see the assertion of Providence as an intimate recourse to order and authority, then it is equally appropriate to stress a further reason for the widespread attacks on Guizot: that is, that the French historian's rhetoric of violent struggle would have been particularly unwelcome in a society that was, it was regularly argued, attempting to recover from the consequences of the most violent revolution of modern times. The argument that progress derived from 'lucha', was, in the circumstances, never likely to succeed, given that recent experience made the connection between the two an unconscionable one for the large majority of Spanish intellectuals.

The resoundingly authoritative — and authoritarian — majority discourse outlined above was to leave its imprint both on accounts of the recent past, as will become apparent in the following chapter of this study, and on more general overviews of the development of the philosophy of history as an intellectual discipline. Belonging to this second category are the two articles written by Facundo Goñy for the prestigious new journal *Revista Española de Ambos Mundos*, which began to be published in 1853 and which was ostensibly modelled upon its much more celebrated Parisian predecessor.[44] The ideals professedly espoused in the magazine's prospectus included political liberalism and progress, while it described its religious affiliation as Catholic and its philosophical stance, perhaps most tellingly, as 'espiritualista'.[45] Goñy's pieces, published under the heading 'De la filosofía de la historia y sus principales escuelas',[46] indicate the considerable influence now exerted by Vico and his supporters on historiography and on the philosophy of history as expounded in mid-nineteenth-century Spain.

Goñy's initial declarations reveal the degree of success achieved by Donoso, Gonzalo Morón, and others in promoting the notion that the philosophy of history had been conceptually impossible prior to the growth of the Christian ideal: 'La filosofía de la historia no existió como ciencia ni fue adivinada siquiera en los tiempos antiguos' [The philosophy of history simply did not exist, nor was it even dreamed of as a branch of knowledge in classical times], he began; instead, he continued, its historical origins were Christian.[47] In common with many of his predecessors, Goñy adopts a rhetoric of transcendence to describe historical processes; after beginning with St Augustine he came to Bossuet, to whom he accorded the singular merit of having been the first truly to understand, in an elevated and all-embracing way, the history of humanity.[48] He then moved on to summarize the reaction against Bossuet's theory of Providence by the disciples of the *Encyclopédie* and signally by Voltaire, who had produced, he put it, a work of little merit in which 'la falta de elevación de miras y la pequeñez de crítica' [the lack of an elevated gaze and the meanness of critical perspective] went hand in hand with an essential ignorance of historical fact.[49] While we do not by now expect to find even the faintest of praise for the author of the *Essai sur les moeurs*, it is nonetheless striking that Goñy's criticism once again centres on a 'falta de *elevación*': the meaning of the journal's 'espiritualista' philosophical stance now seems to acquire somewhat greater clarity.

Dominating Goñy's historical overview was Vico, once more seen as a luminary figure; as the Spanish writer summed up, 'sus especulaciones fueron acogidas con desdén porque se adelantaban demasiado a su época' [his speculations were received with disdain because they were so far ahead of their own age].[50] As he put it in introducing Vico: 'ha pasado con razón por el fundador de la ciencia histórica, y sus escritos ocupan un alto lugar entre las más notables producciones del entendimiento humano' [he has, with good reason, been seen as the founding father of the science of history, and his writings occupy an eminent place among the most noteworthy products of human understanding].[51] Goñy felt Vico to be entirely original, even if his system ultimately represented, and here we find a startling and apparently discordant phrase in the context of these articles, 'un fatalismo repugnante por su espíritu antiprogresivo' [a fatalism that is repugnant to us due to its anti-progressive spirit].[52]

It is at this point, as I see it, that the modern reader detects what seems to be Goñy's intimate dilemma. As a nineteenth-century liberal, he instinctively rebelled against Vico's ineluctable historical pattern governed by Providence, a pattern that was commitedly theocentric and which apparently minimalized the ability of humanity to control its own destiny. He had likewise, it is worth stating, tempered his praise of Bossuet's vision of history by describing it as one adumbrated with excessive rigidity and burdened by an exaggerated first principle, and would go on to state his disagreement with Herder's perception of humanity as no more than the outward sign of a Providential creating spirit.[53] Clearly, Goñy felt unable to share any programmatic theory of human destiny, yet he still regarded Bossuet, Vico, and Herder as the great triumvirate of thinkers who had dedicated their efforts to the philosophy of history

in the seventeenth and eighteenth centuries, as men who had transcended the
limitations, the 'prisma demasiado estrecho' [excessively narrow prism], of Voltaire and
the Enlightenment. Furthermore, Goñy's ultimate condemnation of Vico's philosophy
of history as 'un fatalismo repugnante' simply does not square with his enthusiastic
exposition of its major premises. The solution, it seems to me, is that for Goñy, as
for so many other Spanish commentators of the same period, Vico's belief in the
certain collapse of an 'age of men' had proved an uncannily accurate anticipation in
its own time of events occurring later in the eighteenth century; in short, Vico was
felt prophetically to have forecast the revolutionary tumult of 1789 and after. The
crucial indicators are to be found in Goñy's summary of the descent into barbarism
as formulated within Vico's pattern, for he describes it in terms that exactly re-create
contemporary Spanish depictions of the worst excesses of the French Revolution. All
of the vocabulary characteristic of such depictions is present in Goñy's observation
that, at the end of the age of men,

> sucedió que el progreso social e intelectual destruyó los símbolos y las creencias,
> y aflojó los vínculos que unían a los hombres entre sí; la sociedad quedó sin base
> ni fundamentos morales, principió a reinar el individualismo, y los pueblos se
> disolvieron volviendo a dispersarse y a caer en la brutalidad primitiva.

> [it came to pass that social and intellectual progress destroyed the symbols and
> beliefs, and loosened the essential connections, that bound humankind together;
> society was left without a moral foundation, individualism came to reign over all,
> and entire peoples were fragmented, rent apart and left to fall once more into
> primitive forms of brutality].

Superimposed upon Vico in this passage is, I would contend, a nineteenth-century
judgement of the effects of the Terror. The same impression is redoubled when Goñy
goes on to affirm that

> cuando una sociedad ha llegado a este último período, infaliblemente se cor-
> romperá: porque se han roto los vínculos que la mantenían unida, porque la razón
> individual ha echado por tierra las creencias comunes, porque no queda en el
> hombre otro resorte que el deseo de riquezas y de goces materiales.

> [when once a society has arrived at this last stage, it will inevitably fall apart:
> because all of those connections that have made it united have been broken,
> because individual reason has razed to the ground communal beliefs, because
> there is left to mankind no other recourse except the desire for wealth and
> material pleasures].[54]

What I am suggesting then is that Goñy, in common with numerous other Spanish
writers, transposes onto his account of Vico a nineteenth-century awareness of actual
historical events; events which had taken place after the Italian thinker's death but
which his writings had seemed to predict. In other words, Goñy's account, like many
others of the same period, presents us with a classic case of historical transference.
The feeling is reinforced when we take into account the content of Goñy's course of
lectures delivered at the Madrid Ateneo in 1847 and published in the following year
as a *Tratado de las relaciones internacionales de España*. Here the Spanish writer examines
both the internal organization of Spain and its relations with the rest of Europe, much
of the focus being upon the reordering of his own nation and of the continent in

general in the wake of the French Revolution and the Napoleonic Wars. Goñy's essay is perhaps most remarkable, however, for the way in which it apparently seeks an accommodation between Vico's Providential outlook and Guizot's theory of progress through conflict.

The world is always moving forward, Goñy states at the outset; profound historical change and violent catastrophe have continually seen rich and powerful societies emerge and flourish only to be swept in their turn from the surface of the globe in response to 'leyes generales y eternas' [general and eternal laws], but, even as whole peoples disappear and historical institutions are consigned to oblivion, 'los principios, las ideas, las conquistas hechas por el espíritu de la humanidad que son a los pueblos lo que el alma a los individuos, sobreviven a las más hondas sacudidas, y se transmiten de pueblo en pueblo y de generación en generación' [the principles, the ideas, the great feats of the human spirit which are to peoples what the soul is to individuals, will survive the most profound commotions and will be transmitted from people to people and from generation to generation].[55] We discover, then, in close alignment, Vico's transcendent theory of phases and Guizot's articulation of the workings of 'l'esprit humain'. They are subsequently applied directly to the course of events that had affected modern Europe, whose end-dates in this context, are, we suspect, 1789 and 1848. The entire continent, affirms Goñy, found itself in one of those 'grandes crisis orgánicas de que apenas nos ofrece ejemplo la historia' [great organic crises of which history itself offers us but few examples], one in which 'un mundo nuevo tiene que constituirse sobre los escombros y ruinas de otro que acaba' [a new world must be constructed out of the debris and ruins of another that is ended].[56] The imagery and metaphors of the *Scienza nuova* are undeniably present, but once more merge with those of the *Histoire de la civilisation en Europe* in the following description:

> La Europa, pues, experimenta una descomposición rápida y completa en su organización política, y está destinada a constituirse de nuevo cuando hayan cesado las hondas revoluciones que hoy la trabajan, cuando haya terminado la lucha de los encontrados elementos que hoy se chocan y se combaten en su seno.

> [Europe, then, has experienced a rapid and utter dissolution of its political organization, and is destined to be constructed afresh when once the far-reaching revolutions that today beset it have come to an end, when once has ceased the struggle between those opposing elements that today meet in combat at its very heart].[57]

Goñy then clings to much of Guizot's phraseology and wider vision, for all that much of his commentary intimates not just his application of Vico but also his Catholic commitment; it should immediately be apparent, meanwhile, just how forcefully the vocabulary found here coincides with that later used to explain Vico's philosophy of history in Goñy's journal articles. With a train of events that proclaimed 'con toda la exageración del fanatismo el principio de libertad' [with all the exaggeration that belongs to fanaticism the spirit of liberty], he stated, France had been 'agitada por el vértigo revolucionario' [hurled around in the revolutionary maelstrom].[58] The history of the Spanish monarchy he subsequently traced through 'las épocas de su desarrollo, grandeza y decadencia' [the ages of its development, grandeur, and decline].[59] Society required shared scales of value, intimate connections whose severance could only be catastrophic; hence 'cuando un principio común deja de vivificar a los pueblos, sus vínculos de unión se relajan, y desaparece la fuerza de la asociación. Por eso no ha hecho nada grande ninguna sociedad escéptica y descreída' [when a single common principle no longer enlivens peoples, the connections that bind them together are slackened, and the power of association is lost. For this reason, a sceptical and disbelieving society has never accomplished anything that is great].[60] In the case of Spain, he then argued, 'el principio religioso fue la base y el cimiento de nuestra unidad nacional y el que ha impreso su carácter propio a la sociedad española' [the religious principle was the foundation and the mortar of our national unity and the principle that has lent a distinctive character to Spanish society], so that 'la nación española ha sido una nación esencialmente católica' [the Spanish nation has been an essentially Catholic nation] in all of its historical phases of 'nacimiento' [birth], 'colosal desarrollo' [colossal expansion] and, in the period of Catholicism's own 'decadencia' [decline] in Europe, 'postración y debilidad' [exhaustion and infirmity].[61]

Not just here but, more suggestively, in Goñy's later articles on the philosophy of history, is disclosed, I would argue, a dilemma that is very much that of nineteenth-century liberalism: the desire to trust in the perfectibility of humanity worryingly called into question by a consciousness of the bloodbath and the political tyranny that political radicalism had produced. As articulated by Susan Kirkpatrick, an entire generation of Spanish liberalism identified itself with ideals of progress, social dynamism, and individual liberty, as a generation disposed to reappraise received ideas in a spirit of critical analysis; at the same time, however, it felt profound consternation at the spectacle of human ambition, materialism, and cynicism that were rife within it, and at the open divisions and gaping wounds of a new society.[62] Liberalism's determination to come to terms with the reality and with the philosophical legacy of the Revolution, to preserve and legitimize the genuine improvements it was felt to have wrought, had then to contend with the reactionary pressures of an age which looked back upon events in revolutionary France as a terrible moral aberration. In conservative minds the Revolution was no more than a nightmare, a fearful act of depravity whose influence must be entirely extirpated. Goñy then, desiring to subscribe to an ideal of human progress, finds it unconscionable personally to adhere to Vico's larger perspective, but is drawn in spite of himself to Vico's schema as a putative explanation for the troubled history of Europe between 1789 and 1848. He therefore profoundly resents Vico, whose 'antiprogresivo' account is in conflict with the professed aims of the liberal project; it is surely for this reason that Goñy uses a term such as 'repugnante' to describe a philosophy of history that he otherwise admires for its intellectual originality and enduring cultural significance. At the same time the transferential relationship evidenced by his text — between, on the one hand, his restatement of the premises of the *Scienza nuova*, and, on the other, a vocabulary that signposts his own generation's retrospective appraisal of revolutionary terror — renders transparent his intimate difficulties.

Vico, we might then conclude, had been adapted to the professed needs of a different age, and his philosophy of history applied to events taking place long after his death. Goñy's texts provide a signal example of Moreno Alonso's felicitously alliterative assertion of the emergence of history as 'verdadera protagonista de las preocupaciones presentes' [the true protagonist of current concerns].[63] There was, it goes without saying, a latent ideological strategy underpinning what Gonzalo Morón chose rather disingenuously to call the social mission of the philosophy of history;[64] the ideological positioning that would ultimately dominate Spanish Romantic historiography in fact contains, as Moreno Alonso indicates, a clear sense of dogmatic conservatism.[65] If my interpretation of Goñy's commentary seems unduly adventurous, then Spanish depictions of revolutionary France, along with further material to be examined in the next chapter, will clarify matters to a far greater degree. As we are about to see, Spanish historians' accounts of the recent past were almost without exception grounded in traditional theories of Providence; their assessments of modern history allow us to perceive the further implications of Spanish responses to Vico, particularly in the rhetoric of catastrophe and renewal that was to be at their core. If Vico was commonly considered to have been a prophetic figure ahead of his own time, it was because nineteenth-century Spanish historians detected remarkable confirmation of his theory of phases in recent European history.

Notes to Chapter 3

1. See Burke's helpful exposition and commentary in his *Vico*, Past Masters Series (Oxford, 1985), pp. 54–64.
2. Cited by Isaiah Berlin, *Vico and Herder: Two Studies in the History of Ideas* (London, 1980), p. 64n.
3. *Vico and Herder*, p. 72.
4. *Metahistory*, p. 15.
5. See *Historiografía romántica española*, pp. 125–26.
6. *Historia de España Menéndez Pidal*, XXXV: I, 'Prólogo', p. lxix.
7. *Metahistory*, p. 15.
8. *Metahistory*, p. 16.
9. *The Idea of History* (Oxford, 1946), p. 71.
10. Reproduced in *Obras completas de don Juan Donoso Cortés, Marqués de Valdegamas*, ed. by Hans Juretschke, 2 vols (Madrid, 1946), I, 537–72. References follow in the text.
11. If my own surmise is correct, this was not strictly true: see my *Spanish Romantic Literary Theory and Criticism*, pp. 115–16. As Ramón Ceñal has noted, however, originality was anyway not the principal merit of these articles. The pieces should always be valued, he put it, for having been the channel by which Vico came to be noticed in Spain, and his importance as the foremost pioneer of the philosophy of history to be properly acknowledged, and at a time when Vico, in his principal designated role, had been only very recently discovered and was still relatively little known, even in more sophisticated cultural circles. ('J. B. Vico y Juan Donoso Cortés', *Pensamiento*, 24 (1968), 351–73 (p. 355). See also the same author's 'La filosofía de la historia de Donoso Cortés', *Revista de Filosofía*, 11 (1952), 91–113.
12. Bossuet received considerable attention in Spain during the Romantic period, and Spanish versions of the *Discours sur l'histoire universelle* appeared in Paris (1834) and Madrid (1842).
13. See Abellán's *Historia crítica del pensamiento español*, IV, 333.
14. Cited by Andrew Ginger, *Political Revolution and Literary Experiment*, p. 53; as Ginger indicates, Campoamor goes on to satirize Donoso's self-indulgent immersion in a romantic past.
15. *Ensayo sobre el catolicismo, el liberalismo y el socialismo*, ed. by Vila Selma, p. 125.
16. See my *Spanish Romantic Literary Theory and Criticism*, pp. 115–20, 135–46.
17. The two men had met at Quintana's *tertulia* in 1832; see Enrique Chao Espina's biography *Pastor Díaz dentro del romanticismo*, *Revista de Filología Española*, 46 (1949), p. 36.
18. See the *Ensayo sobre el catolicismo, el liberalismo y el socialismo*, ed. by Vila Selma, p. 40.
19. *Los orígenes del pensamiento reaccionario*, p. 163; Herrero cites from the two-volume Madrid edition of

1807, the full title of which was *Causas de la Revolución de Francia, en el año de 1789, y medios de que se han valido para efectuarla los enemigos de la religión y el estado*.

20. Words chosen by José Luis Abellán in his summary of Donoso's position: see *Historia crítica del pensamiento español*, IV, 336.

21. *Los orígenes del pensamiento reaccionario*, p. 143.

22. R. Fernández Carvajal, 'El pensamiento español en el siglo XIX', in *Historia general de las literaturas hispánicas* (Barcelona, 1969), V, 207.

23. *Historia crítica del pensamiento español*, IV, 335.

24. *Historia de España Menéndez Pidal*, XXXV: I, 395.

25. 'Homero y la Ciencia Nueva', *El Siglo Pintoresco*, I (1845), 49–54 (p. 49): author's italics.

26. *El Siglo Pintoresco*, I, 50.

27. *El Siglo Pintoresco*, I, 51–52.

28. *Curso de Historia de la civilización de España, lecciones pronunciadas en el Liceo de Valencia y en el Ateneo de Madrid en los cursos de 1840 y 1841 por el profesor de historia en ambos establecimientos literarios*, 6 vols (Madrid, 1841–46). References to Gonzalo Morón's history follow in the text. The course of lectures was to be eulogized, in the pages of the magazine *El Iris*, by Pedro Sabater, who positively gushed his approval:

   No hay en Valencia quien no recuerde con placer aquella época gloriosa para su Liceo, en la que, colocado al frente de una de sus cátedras el brillante joven D. Fermín Gonzalo Morón, pronunciaba desde ella sus elocuentes lecciones sobre la historia de España, arrancando entusiasmados aplausos a una escogida y numerosa concurrencia. (*Curso de Historia de la civilización de España*, por D. Fermín Gonzalo Morón', *El Iris*, 2 (1841), 22.

   [There is not a person in the whole of Valencia who does not recall with pleasure the period of glory of its Liceo, in which the brilliant young scholar Don Fermín Gonzalo Morón occupied one of its professorial chairs, from which he pronounced his series of eloquent lectures on the history of Spain, drawing enthusiastic applause from a large and select audience]

   This was, perhaps not coincidentally, an almost immediate prelude to Gonzalo Morón's extensive series of articles entitled 'Examen filosófico del teatro español' and published in the same journal.

29. Fermín Gonzalo Morón, *Obras escogidas* (Madrid, 1875), 'Al público'. Among the works whose publication was planned but apparently never realized was one that I have been unable to consult, tantalizingly in the present context entitled *El cristianismo y el filosofismo*.

30. In a review of Tocqueville's study of North-American democracy published in the first volume of the *Revista de España y del Extranjero*, a journal of which he was editor, Gonzalo Morón reveals even more explicitly the influence of Vico upon his thinking, asserting that 'un país llegado al apogeo de la civilización material, pero sin creencias morales, ofrece la humanidad automatizada y envilecida, un cuadro desagradable y repugnante, y los síntomas de una disolución social' [a nation which has in material terms reached the apex of its civilization but which lacks moral values, presents a most disagreeable and repulsive picture of a mechanical and degraded humanity, and betrays all the symptoms of social dissolution]: *Revista de España y del Extranjero*, 1 (1842), p. 82.

31. See Donoso's *Obras*, I, 931–46 (p. 934). For Juretschke, the contact between the two was of not inconsiderable importance, since both Donoso Cortés and Gonzalo Morón represented in Spanish intellectual circles a preference for the new discipline of philosophy of history: see *Historia de España Menéndez Pidal*, XXXV: I, 82.

32. *La invención de España*, pp. 29–30.

33. The meaning of history as adumbrated by Balmes is very evidently a Providentialist one; the entirety of his writing in the areas of sociology, philosophy and religion is characterized by that fact (*La revolución francesa en la historiografía española*, p. 173). He goes on to cite a remark that links Balmes closely with one of the key metaphors of this Providential vision: 'se da demasiada importancia a los hechos que flotan en la superficie de la sociedad, y se dejan los que suceden más allá en el fondo' [too much importance is given to those things that float upon the surface of society, while those that dwell below, in its depths, are neglected]: *Obras*, I, 169; see *La revolución francesa en la historiografía española*, p. 175.

34. This passage had not been penned for *El Protestantismo comparado con el Catolicismo*, but instead formed part of a much earlier unpublished piece entitled 'Apuntes sobre Chateaubriand', certainly written by 1838; see my *Spanish Romantic Literary Theory and Criticism*, pp. 121–22.

35. *Historia general de España, desde los tiempos más remotos hasta nuestros días*, 30 vols (Madrid, 1850–67). References follow in the text.

36. See José María Jover Zamora, *Historia de España Menéndez Pidal*, XXXIV, pp. lxxxiv-lxxxv; Inman Fox, *La invención de España*, pp. 39–40.

37. See my *Spanish Romantic Literary Theory and Criticism*, pp. 177–79.

38. 'Crítica literaria: del neo-culteranismo en la poesía española. Zorrilla y su escuela', *Revista de Ciencias, Literatura y Artes*, 1 (1855), 34–46 (p. 36).

39. Jover Zamora highlights precisely these features, illuminatingly relating them to Lafuente's 'trayectoria política e ideológica' [political and ideological trajectory]: 'a member of parliament for the Progressive party in the liberal government of 1854-1856, he distinguished himself for his championing of the cause of Roman Catholic unity; he criticised religious freedom and criticised the Inquisition, but defended Philip II': *Historia de España Menéndez Pidal*, XXXIV, p. lxxxiv.

40. *La invención de España*, p. 40.

41. *Discursos leídos en la Real Academia de la Historia el día 12 de abril de 1852 con motivo de la admisión de D. José de Zaragoza* (Madrid, 1852), p. 16.

42. *Discurso del Excmo Señor Duque de Rivas sobre la utilidad e importancia del estudio de la Historia, y sobre el acierto con que le promueve la Academia, in Discursos leídos en las sesiones públicas que para dar posesión de plazas de número ha celebrado desde 1852 la Real Academia de la Historia* (Madrid, 1858), pp. 247–57 (p. 249).

43. *French Historians and Romanticism*, p. 102.

44. Referring to the journal, Juretschke comments: 'En las páginas de la revista predomina el interés por la filosofía de la historia' [Prevalent in the pages of this journal is an interest in the philosophy of history]: *Historia de España Menéndez Pidal*, XXXV: I, 61.

45. *Revista Española de Ambos Mundos*, 1 (1853), p. vii.

46. *Revista Española de Ambos Mundos*, 1, 613–25 and 2 (1854), 93–106.

47. *Revista Española de Ambos Mundos*, 1, 613–15.

48. *Revista Española de Ambos Mundos*, 1, 617.

49. *Revista Española de Ambos Mundos*, 1, 618.

50. *Revista Española de Ambos Mundos*, 1, 93.

51. *Revista Española de Ambos Mundos*, 1, 619.

52. *Revista Española de Ambos Mundos*, 1, 624.

53. *Revista Española de Ambos Mundos*, 1, 617–18 and 2, 94. As Hayden White puts it, Herder could not entertain the idea of randomness as an ultimate reality: 'He insisted — for religious or metaphysical reasons — that this field of happening [the historical process] has an ontologically prior and spiritually superior ground or purpose, a purpose which assured *him* of the ultimate unity, integration, and harmonization of the parts in the whole': *Metahistory*, p. 70.

54. *Revista Española de Ambos Mundos*, 1, 624.

55. Facundo Goñi [sic], *Tratado de las relaciones internacionales de España: lecciones pronunciadas en el Ateneo de Madrid* (Madrid, 1848), p. 11.

56. *Tratado de las relaciones internacionales de España*, pp. 25–26.

57. *Tratado de las relaciones internacionales de España*, p. 49.

58. *Tratado de las relaciones internacionales de España*, p. 42.

59. *Tratado de las relaciones internacionales de España*, p. 53.

60. *Tratado de las relaciones internacionales de España*, p. 55.

61. *Tratado de las relaciones internacionales de España*, p. 56.

62. *Larra: el laberinto inextricable de un romántico liberal* (Madrid, 1977), p. 175.

63. *Historiografía romántica española*, p. 60.

64. The phrase formed one of the sub-headings of the first section of his *Curso de Historia de la civilización de España*, I, 7.

65. *Historiografía romántica española*, p. 187.

CHAPTER 4

Exorcizing the Revolutionary Demon

Spanish writers of the Romantic period were remarkably consistent in their explanation of the events of the previous one hundred years. The broad framework of their narrative of recent European history reveals an interpretation that was, on the surface at least, one of cause and effect: the cause, a philosophical ethic that had privileged human reason and spurned God and the Church; the inevitable effect, revolutionary cataclysm. At the same time, however, all of the greater and more far-reaching processes of thought and response, all of the fundamental expressions of human experience developing and occurring since the mid-eighteenth century, were felt to be contained within a higher and inscrutable teleological purpose. The discourse of history was therefore once more to bear a religious imprint, testifying to an intimate reliance upon divine authority, and it was again to reveal the hallmarks of Vico's theory of organic phases, characterized in this case by an ubiquitous rhetoric of catastrophe and renewal. The overview shared by most Spanish commentators was basically this: that the rationalism and irreligion of the French *philosophes* had brought about a human cataclysm of unprecedented proportions; that the French Revolution had been an infernal crucible of horror and devastation; that humanity had thus been castigated for its moral aberrations; and that, in order to further the process of reconstruction, it was essential that the present generation eradicate the remaining pernicious effects of revolutionary radicalism and religious scepticism and seek to promote in their stead a renewed sense of spirituality.

The crucible of revolution provided, then, for the subsequent Romantic narrative of journey into darkness and magnificent rebirth figured by Andrew Ginger; in omitting all reference to Vico and thus excluding from consideration any application of his cyclical theory of history, however, the modern critic is able to perceive neither the informing structures of that narrative nor the ideological promptings of many of its forms of expression.[1] As Donoso Cortés was to sum up: 'La revolución francesa debía ser lógicamente el sangriento comentario y el término providencial de la emancipación humana, como también el último de sus extravíos' [The French Revolution had logically to be the bloody commentary and the providential end result of human emancipation, and likewise its ultimate aberration].[2] Even the adverb 'lógicamente', apparently quite casually employed, speaks volumes for the way in which Spanish historiography was to inscribe events occurring in eighteenth-century France within a systematized pattern. In its assessment of the recent past, Spanish Romantic historiography is then profoundly reactionary, and re-creates without significant changes of emphasis the 'mito fundamental' or founding myth, as Javier Herrero describes it, that had characterized the earlier trenchantly conservative treatises of men like Zeballos, Forner, Hervás y Panduro, Fray Diego de Cádiz, and the 'Filósofo Rancio'.[3] Manuel Moreno Alonso, underlining the essential antagonisms that inform this vision of recent history, comments that in the face of those conceptions of historical process belonging to and generated by the French Revolution, Romantic historiography would prove to be of a diametrically opposite nature.[4]

A detailed examination of Spanish journals reveals an obsessive degree of weight given to the perceived heinous crimes of the French Enlightenment. Many of the more unrestrained attacks upon philosophical rationalism, materialism and political radicalism are to be found in articles which are seemingly entirely irrelevant to eighteenth-century France. Similarly, it would seem that European history of the previous century had been concentrated upon one nation and, more specifically still, upon the cultural and political effects of one prevalent framework of ideas.[5] The tone of a large number of pieces would be one of resentment and outrage, and reactionary sentiments against any contemporary form of radicalism were to be insistently and bluntly expressed. Within the current climate of opinion, the following summary given by Francisco Martínez de la Rosa in the *Revista de Madrid* in 1841 is, if representative in its verdict, remarkably moderate in its tone. As he expresses it:

> Hubo una nación, enriquecida largos años con los tesoros de las ciencias y de las artes, excelente entre todos por su civilización y cultura, y cuyos filósofos, como desde una cátedra, predicaban a todos los pueblos de la tierra sus principios y sus doctrinas. Vejeces y antiguallas apellidaron la Religión y el culto: socavaron los altares, antes de derribarlos; y excitaron a las naciones a sacudir juntamente el yugo de la superstición y de la tiranía.

> [There once was a nation, which for many long years the treasures of art and science had rendered prosperous, pre-eminent among all others on account of its culture and civilization, whose philosophers, as if from a university seat, preached to all peoples of the world their principles and their doctrines. They referred to religion and to the worship of God as old wives' tales and pieces of old junk: they dug away beneath the altars before overturning them; and they inflamed all the nations with a desire to shake off together the twin yoke of superstition and tyranny.][6]

Martínez de la Rosa contents himself, in the main, with recounting what seems to have been intended as an instructive and salutary tale warning of the potent dangers of human self-aggrandizement, and with undermining the premises of the French Enlightenment by recourse to irony, signally in his choice of vocabulary and metaphor. His extended appraisal of the revolutionary events in France, given in the sprawling historical account compiled between 1823 and 1851 and published as *El espíritu del siglo* — intended, its author stresses in the initial 'Advertencia', as a *'curso de política aplicado a los sucesos contemporáneos'* [course in applied politics in the light of recent events] — is similarly dispassionate when compared to most other contemporary analyses; the Revolution, he here stated in introducing his subject and in anticipating for us some of the keynote terms that will characterize this and the following chapter, 'no debe considerarse como el trastorno de un gobierno y la perturbación de un Estado, sino como el anuncio de una *crisis social*, común a todas las naciones europeas, y cuyo influjo ha de sentirse de una en otra generación' [should not be judged the disruption of a specific government and the upheaval of a single state, so much as the declaration of a *social crisis*, common to all the nations of Europe, and whose effects must needs be felt from one generation to the next].[7] Rather than its mere lack of passionate rhetoric and, concomitantly, its rational scrutiny of the political detail of events, what really sets Martínez de la Rosa's historical essay apart from those of the majority of his contemporaries is the absence within it of any over-arching metaphysical parameters: the ineluctable progress of the Revolution is at no stage seen as the working out of a Providential design, as an explication of human actions as ultimately governed by some teleological purpose. His analysis is founded on the human rather than on the divine, and, like Guizot's famous historical synthesis of the 1820s, resists the sacrilization of history. I suspect that it was precisely the absence of a discernible programmatic overview of events that led Joaquín Francisco Pacheco to observe of the work that it lacked any 'sistema completo' [thoroughgoing systematic approach].[8]

There is ample circumstantial evidence for the influence of Guizot upon *El espíritu del siglo*, confirming Ginger's contention that the entire work is 'a resonant synthesis of ideas from the corresponding French school of Doctrinaire thought':[9] the Spanish writer's text is positively littered with references to the determining 'principios' and contending 'elementos' of monarchy, nobility, Church, and populace. Within Martínez de la Rosa's terms, the principal motive force of historical change was the 'Spirit of the Age' itself, reminiscent of Hazlitt but not without similarities with Guizot's 'l'esprit humain'. Those who sought to stand against such a tide were inevitably to be swept aside by it: the Spanish writer regarded Louis XVI, for example, as having sown the seeds of discord among the armed forces, and ultimately as having cast his people into the arms of the revolutionaries, by seeking to countermand the spirit of the age in late eighteenth-century France.[10] This did not, of course, prevent Martínez de la Rosa from condemning, in the same section of his work and in much more representative fashion, the 'espíritu de impiedad que distinguió al siglo décimoctavo' [the distinctive impious spirit of the eighteenth century] , nor did it affect his outright rejection of the revolutionary Constitution of 1791 as a document which 'ha contribuido a extraviar a otras naciones, que la han tomado malamente por guía, yendo en busca de la libertad' [has tended to lead astray those other nations that have mistakenly sought it as a guide in their quest for liberty].[11]

When it came to assessing revolutionary events in eighteenth-century France, meanwhile, other commentators were less subtle and infinitely more strident. The same rhetoric of destruction that inevitably accompanied accounts of the motivation and consequences of the French Enlightenment tended to be used with considerably greater fury. One piece taken from the Catholic weekly *El Reflejo*, published in Madrid in 1843, makes in essence the same point as Martínez de la Rosa; what distinguishes the later piece is the degree of execration it expresses. As the writer, one M. V. y Almazón, saw it, 'El filosofismo fue como el clarín de guerra que anunciaba la revolución en todas partes' [This philosophizing was like a call to battle that heralded revolution everywhere], as an embattled Christianity saw its sacred truths subjected to the clinical analysis of 'la razón extraviada' [reason gone awry]. The charge made against the overweening arrogance of eighteenth-century rationalism is typical: 'el filósofo que había comenzado por denunciar los abusos, creciendo en su orgullo quiso llegar hasta Dios, y por no confesar su pequeñez le negó desoyendo a su conciencia' [the philosopher, who had begun by denouncing abuses, as his pride grew sought to usurp the place of God, and, rather than admit to his own meanness and deaf to his own conscience, denied God]. Public morality, he continued, inseparable from the Christian ideal, had perished; in its stead 'proclamaron los filósofos a la razón vencedora, y colocáronla sobre un trono sostenido por la inmoralidad y la anarquía' [the philosophers proclaimed the triumph of reason and placed her upon a throne supported by immorality and anarchy].[12]

Deserving of notice here is the presence of the pejorative term 'filosofismo', an essential component in conservative vocabulary and one regularly used by even the most respected voices in Spanish intellectual circles in order to denigrate the achievements of eighteenth-century France. It had been much earlier employed by Juan Pablo Forner, who, in disparaging sham intellectuals of that century who had proclaimed themselves philosophers more out of a hollow desire for individuality than out of a love of truth and a wish to teach that truth,[13] had bemoaned what he called the 'afectado filosofismo de los modernos' [affected philosophizing of modern men].[14] The term was now consistently applied to the French *philosophes*, earlier labelled by Forner a 'secta libre' [free sect] whose doctrine was in essence 'una independencia desenfrenada que atropellaba los vínculos más fuertes de las sociedades civiles' [an untrammelled independence that rode roughshod over the most potent binding values of civil society]. As he put it, they had been 'Empeñados en destruir la religión por sus fundamentos, y siendo éstos incontrastables, se valieron sofísticamente de los abusos de la religión para arruinarla' [Bent upon the destruction of the very foundations of religion, and, finding these unshakable, availed themselves of a series of sophistries by which to abuse religion and eventually to consign it to ruin].[15] Giovanni Allegra therefore comments with reference to Forner, and with some justification, that in his work may be found all of the embryonic features of nineteenth-century Spanish traditionalist thought.[16] The term 'filosofismo' was in effect regularly used in the 1830s by the influential figure of Alberto Lista, and by the 1840s was common currency; Diego Coello y Quesada, for example, disparagingly referred to 'el principio individualista creado por el filosofismo del siglo XVIII' [the individualist principle created by eighteenth-century philosophizing].[17] Confirmation of the meaning it had acquired is found in José Amador de los Ríos's inaugural speech opening the academic year at the University of Madrid in 1850, where we read that 'negando a Dios, para negar después la humanidad, osó el filosofismo del pasado siglo trastornar todas las verdades, derramando en los corazones la amarga ponzoña de la duda' [denying God and denying afterwards humanity, the philosophizing of the previous century dared to pervert all our truths, pouring into all our hearts the bitter poison of doubt].[18] One particularly startling example of its usage is provided by Gabino Tejado, former pupil and ideological ally of Donoso Cortés, who managed to include in an article entitled 'Poesía popular' a fulminating wholesale attack on the eighteenth century and all of its works.[19] In what purported to be an historical résumé of the popular verse tradition we encounter a blistering condemnation of that entire age, described as a 'monstruo gigantesco de filosofismo y de incredulidad, que dejó, al expirar en los brazos de la Convención, el funesto legado de cimientos destruidos, que pugna por reconstruir el presente siglo, medio ahogado entre el polvo de las ruinas' [colossal monster of philosophizing and unbelief, which, when it expired in the arms of the Constitution, left as its deathly legacy those wrecked foundations that our own century, half stifled by the dust of the ruins, now strives to reconstruct]. Tejado sketches out the age as an infernal outrage against the principles of Throne and Altar, as a 'Terrible emplazamiento de la monarquía ante los verdugos, de la religión ante las bacanales' [The monarchy horribly consigned to die by execution, and religion at the hands of orgiastic hedonism], and ends by invoking the shade of Voltaire: 'si el filósofo de Ferney hubiera levantado por un momento del sepulcro la cabeza encanecida, al contemplar sus hechuras, se hubiera vuelto a encerrar en su tumba huyendo avergonzado de Robespierre y Marat' [if the philosopher of Ferney had lifted for one moment his grey head from the grave, he would, at this spectacle of his own making, have locked himself back in his tomb in shameful flight from Robespierre and Marat].[20]

To view the Terror as did Tejado, as a logical extension of the conclusions of Voltaire, whose village retreat at Ferney became the 'cultivated garden' of his practical philosophy and a refuge from idealism and metaphysics, was a characteristic expression of nineteenth-century conservatism. Unlike numerous other writers, Tejado does not go so far as to suggest that violent revolution had been part of Voltaire's conscious plan. At the same time, however, it is typical of the period that only the smallest concessions were made to the registering of possible improvements and advances that the Enlightenment might have been felt to have wrought; in Almazón's article, as in Forner's earlier study, the recognition that the *philosophes* had initially sought to denounce contemporary abuses is the only note to sound less than entirely negative and condemnatory. Similarly, a lecture by José de la Revilla given at the Ateneo in Madrid and reported in the *Semanario Pintoresco Español* referred to a 'manía filosófica, noble en su origen, pero perjudicial en sus efectos, porque aspiraba nada menos que a trastornar los fundamentos sociales, destruyendo la fe y las creencias de los pueblos' [philosophical mania, of noble origins but prejudicial in its effects, for it sought no less than to disturb the foundations of society by destroying faith and belief among all peoples].[21] The same complaint, untempered this time by any acknowledgement of laudable intentions, was to inform Joaquín Roca y Cornet's substantial and suggestively titled *Ensayo crítico sobre las lecturas de la época en la parte filosófica y social* of 1847. For Roca, eighteenth-century philosophy looked down with contempt upon any sign of religious faith; polarized positions are in fact the order of the day, as he imputes to the *philosophes* an incapacity for any kind of discernment: 'A los ojos de la filosofía enciclopedista, la fe, lejos de ser una necesidad de la inteligencia humana era más bien su aniquilamiento, no habiendo medio entre el idiotismo de la creencia y las luces de la filosofía' [In the eyes of those philosophers of the *Encyclopédie*, faith, far from being necessary to human intelligence represented the annihilation of intelligence, there being no middle path between the idiocy of belief and the light of truth of philosophy]. These self-proclaimed 'reformadores del espíritu' [spiritual reformers], he went on, had brought into the intellectual domain a form of savage fanaticism similar to that which marked out the Jacobins in the world of politics.[22] There is a further explicit connection in the passage that follows: 'Este jacobinismo intelectual debía producir una reacción análoga a la que provocó el terrorismo. Los Jacobinos políticos habían empleado un estraño medio para hacerse vitorear como promotores de la dicha del espíritu humano, y era cubrir su patria de sangre y de ruinas' [This intellectual Jacobinism necessarily prompted a reaction akin to that produced by the Terror. The political Jacobins had employed a very strange means of making themselves appear champions of human happiness, their means being to cover their country in blood and ruins].[23] The principal aim of the French thinkers, according to the vast majority of Spanish commentators, had been precisely this: the calculated destruction of existing scales of value. As Almazón observed: 'nace el filosofismo; sublevan al pueblo sus predicaciones, y perecen a un tiempo la religión, el trono, la nobleza, todo lo que constituía la vieja sociedad minada' [philosophizing is born; its preaching causes the people to rebel, and religion, the monarchy, the aristocracy, everything that went to make up the old society, now undermined, perishes together].[24] His allegation that materialism had destroyed all human hopes and illusions, abandoning mankind to the abyss, approximates closely to Lista's own earlier charge that the *philosophes* had been guilty of 'demoliendo poco a poco todas las ilusiones, todas las ideas, todos los sentimientos del corazón humano' [demolishing, step by step, every aspiration, every idea, every kind of feeling in the human heart].[25]

This broad-brush approach to intellectual history made ideological invective the salient characteristic of commentaries on the French Enlightenment. Balmes, for example, challenged the idea that anything positive or constructive could have come out of eighteenth-century France. Since so much thought was being dedicated to the beneficent effects of philosophy upon civilization, he ventured, let us ask ourselves the following question: 'qué ha hecho la revolución de Francia, esa hija predilecta de la filosofía, de la inteligencia abandonada a sí misma, sin moral, sin religión, sin ningún enlace con las tradiciones antiguas' [what has been accomplished by the French Revolution, that favourite daughter of philosophy, of intelligence given over to self-abandon, bereft of morality, bereft of religion, bereft of any connection with our old traditions].[26] Elsewhere, the same writer emphasized that France before 1789 had long felt the influence of what he designated the school of Voltaire, which he likened to some nefarious constellation of ideas come to unleash upon humankind a pestilential atmosphere of turbulence and disease.[27] The ideals of the previous century were regularly and uncompromisingly caricatured in programmatic summaries; Gervasio Gironella, in a biographical piece on Metternich published in the *Revista de Madrid*, made the following thumbnail sketch of intellectual currents prevailing at the time of the Austrian statesman's arrival at the University of Strasbourg in 1788: 'profesábanse entonces de lleno las ideas del siglo XVIII; era el tiempo de la filosofía de Voltaire, de Helvetio, de Rousseau, de aquel vacío sensualismo que arrojaba las cabezas de los jóvenes a agitaciones efervescientes' [at that time the ideas of the eighteenth century were being proclaimed in full flow; it was the age of the philosophy of Voltaire, of Helvetius, of Rousseau, of that empty sensualism that hurled young minds into seething agitation].[28] Even in the weightiest historical studies, descriptions of the previous age read more like the typical oratorical periods of a prosecuting counsel than the considered appraisal of an impartial historian. Fermín Gonzalo Morón, writing in his *Ensayo sobre las sociedades antiguas y modernas* of 1844, placed an angrily derisive interpretation upon the changing thought-patterns evidenced by the eighteenth century, referring to the Enlightenment's proclamation of 'la soberanía y casi infalibilidad de la razón humana' [the sovereignty, the nigh infallibility of human reason] and to its evaluation of mankind as simply 'resultado de sus sensaciones materiales' [the end result of its own material sensations]. Such was their aberration, he concluded, that they presented to the world as some splendid discovery their contention that a human being was merely 'un ser tan perecedero y miserable, como el reptil, que se arrastra penosamente sobre el suelo' [a being as transitory and loathsome as the reptile that painfully drags itself along the ground].[29] Immediately evident is the expression of disdain, which in fact permeates the whole of this passage and which seems to have influenced the lexical choices and value judgements it contains. Thus sovereignty, for traditionalists the divinely ordained power vested in the monarch, and infallibility, belonging to God's supreme representative on earth, had been removed from their hitherto transcendent sphere and delivered instead into the purely temporal hands of human reason, as Gonzalo Morón clearly intimates. Beguiled as he saw it into fatal error, humanity had emerged, within the earth-bound perspective of the Enlightenment, as no better than the accursed serpent condemned to crawl upon its belly.[30] Beyond the rhetoric, however, lies the sense of revulsion for the ultimate consequences of rationalist philosophy, a sense of revulsion that characterizes both Catholic responses to the Enlightenment and, it should be said, cultural production generally in early nineteenth-century Spain. There is, then, a fundamental process of continuity between the vision of those writers cited here and the majority perspective obtaining in 1808, when, as Manuel Moreno Alonso notes, the vast majority of Spaniards regarded the fearful revolutionary upheavals suffered by France as the fruits of that human error that had been preached by the new philosophers, and of their impiety; the entire country, he observes, was pervaded by a rampant terror of contagion by Europe's contemporary diseases, identified as secularization, laicism, and philosophical analysis.[31]

Gonzalo Morón, meanwhile, would summarize, in the same study and in somewhat greater detail, the salient features of Enlightenment thought, its aspirations and its implications. I believe it is worthwhile to cite the following extensive passage in full, since it encapsulates, arguably better than any other text of comparable length, the attitude towards the Enlightenment then prevalent among Spanish intellectuals:

> La filosofía del siglo XVIII es muy digna de severa reprobación, cuando se consideran sus doctrinas como un sistema capaz de dirigir a la sociedad y al hombre; empero sus teorías fueron por desgracia muy hábilmente escogidas para trastornar el antiguo edificio social. Todas ellas se encaminaron a arrancar del hombre las ideas religiosas, morales y de orden público, y a materializarle, resultando de aquí un gran impulso en favor de los intereses y de las pasiones populares. Comenzóse por desacreditar y negar la verdad del cristianismo, por considerar como una preocupación hija de los hábitos los sentimientos de deber, atribuyéronse a la autoridad todos los males y calamidades sociales, sostúvose que los papas y los reyes, el altar y el trono desde tiempos muy antiguos se habían puesto de acuerdo para oprimir y tiranizar la humanidad; propagáronse

mil errores y falsas ideas sobre la supuesta libertad de las repúblicas antiguas y la independencia del hombre en su figurado estado natural, y para completar y dar un carácter científico a este sistema destructor, los ideólogos y fisiólogos negaron la inmortalidad del alma, y no vieron en el hombre sino necesidades físicas y sensaciones materiales, origen único de sus ideas, y razón determinante de todos los actos de su voluntad. Jamás, desde las extravagancias de los filósofos griegos, se habían proclamado tantos errores, sostenídose tantas mentiras, ni creado un sistema más falso. Empero había en él unidad, estaba admirablemente calculado para minar las antiguas instituciones, y sus dos carácteres distintivos, como he dicho ya, eran declarar al hombre absoluto señor, arrancando de él todas las creencias religiosas y morales, y materializarle.[32]

[Eighteenth-century philosophy merits the most severe censure, when once its doctrines are considered as a system capable of directing society and humankind; for its theories were, unfortunately, very skilfully chosen as a means of undermining the former social edifice. The end of each and every one was to tear away from humanity its religious, moral and civic values, and to turn it into a group of purely material beings, and thus came powerful promptings towards self-interest and vulgar passions. It all began with moves to discredit and deny the truth of Christianity, by making feelings of personal obligation appear the mere promptings of habit, and then every wickedness and social disaster was attributed to vested authority, it being argued that popes and kings, throne and altar had since times of old colluded together to oppress and tyrannize humanity; a thousand errors and falsehoods were bandied about concerning the supposed freedoms of the ancient republics and the independent life of man in what was denoted his natural state, and then, to put the finishing touches to this destructive system and provide it with scientific credentials, these ideologues and physiologists denied the immortality of the soul, and saw in mankind no more than physical necessities and material sensations, the exclusive sources of his ideas and the determining rationale behind his every voluntary act. Never, since the whimsies of Greek philosophy, had there been proclaimed so many errors, had there been propounded so many lies, had there been created a more fallacious system of thought. Yet it possessed a unity, it was admirably calculated to destroy the foundations of the former institutions, and its two distinctive features, as I have said, were to declare mankind lord of all, taking away from him all of his religious and moral values, and to turn him into a purely material being.]

In general terms, then, the traditionalist response to Enlightenment ideals of progress and reform is a discourse that might aptly be described as Manichaean.[33] The recurring antagonisms are manifold yet coherent, and centred on identifiable polarities of outlook and intimate being: spiritual and material; faith and reason; religious and profane; divine reliance and human self-sufficiency; in short, traditional Good and revolutionary Evil. On the side of Good are ranged order and authority, throne and altar — Gonzalo Morón himself uses the phrase — the ennobling qualities of faith and the personal self-discipline of Christian morality; hostile to these are the opposing forces of popular radicalism, material ambition and self-interest, science and reason: in a word, secularism. It goes without saying, therefore, that secularism in all of its forms is within these same terms a falsehood, a moral aberration, a human error that seeks to deny the transcendent truth of religion. As will become abundantly clear in the course of this chapter, Spanish commentators, when they did not go so far as to label Enlightenment ideals 'mentiras' or 'errores', used words that underscored their perception of the Age of Reason as an aberration: thus 'trastornar' and 'extraviar' , together with their respective derivatives, were commonplace choices and particularly apt within a historical discourse that sought to articulate fixed moral categories. According to the same polarities, the Ancien Régime represented order and stability, while revolutionary thoughts and deeds stood for chaos. In Gonzalo Morón's view of the French Enlightenment:

> el carácter esencial de la misma era negativo. Léanse todos sus libros, reúnanse todas sus teorías; no hay una doctrina organizadora, no hay un sistema de gobierno, no hay más que invectivas contra lo pasado, ideas disolventes, errores crasísimos sobre el hombre y las sociedades.

> [the whole character of the same was negative. Read its books, collect together all of its theories; there is no coherent doctrine, there is no system of government, there is no more than a series of invectives against the past, a set of corrosive ideas, a bundle of the most blatant lies about man and society].[34]

Another keynote term here, it goes without saying, is 'ideas disolventes' : consistently part of the widespread allegation that the Enlightenment had eroded existing previously reliable scales of value without replacing them with viable and enduring new ones.

Not only does Gonzalo Morón provide a particularly clear insight into the terms of reference within which accounts of the recent past were commonly cast. His text is also a synthesis of the historical discourse of which it forms a part: a synthesis, that is, of prevalent choices of rhetoric, metaphor, and terminology. His description of the Enlightenment as a 'sistema destructor' eroding the foundations upon which society was traditionally based, as much as his allusion to the distortions to which the term 'libertad' had been subject, his view of the *philosophes* as the perpetrators of an impious fraud, or his interpretation of eighteenth-century intellectual history as the working out of an insidious conspiracy, are all entirely representative. In this sense Gonzalo Morón's commentary both crystallizes the set of attitudes at the core of the Catholic response to the Enlightenment and exemplifies that response's preferred mode of expression. Meanwhile, the lack of transcendent historical scrutiny consistently imputed not just to the Enlightenment but also to Guizot's liberal historiographical model here acquires a further and ultimately more far-reaching dimension. As far as Catholic historians were concerned, an exclusive concern with externals, with material realities, necessarily stemmed from a perception of humanity itself as bereft of spiritual purpose or even of spiritual aspirations, as dependent upon 'necesidades físicas y sensaciones materiales' , while a concomitant neglect, in the pages of history, of human society's 'creencias religiosas y morales' was felt to imply, ultimately, an adherence to a school of thought that had effectively discarded them.

This same passage, and this seems to me crucial if we are thoroughly to contextualize the visceral reaction against Enlightenment thought of which Gonzalo Morón's tirade forms a part, leads us directly back to an earlier generation of reactionary figures. Fray Fernando de Zeballos, for example, like Gonzalo Morón almost seventy years later, had conceived of the *Ilustración* [the Enlightenment] or 'falsa filosofía' [false philosophy] as a sinister conspiracy whose aim was universal destruction.[35] In describing the origins of Deism, he had used precisely the same metaphor of the demolition of an existing

edifice so commonly found in historical writing of the 1840s: the emblem of the
Deists, Zeballos asserted, depicted a church whose vaulted roof was being attacked by
Martin Luther, whose walls were being bludgeoned by Calvin, and whose foundations
were being destroyed by Gregorio Pauli, founding champion of the new sect.[36]
Likewise, Gonzalo Morón's caustic and distorting references to the Enlightenment
stress upon humanity's 'estado natural', or natural state, had numerous precedents in
Spanish reactionary thought, which relentlessly asserted that, in Javier Herrero's words,
the goal of philosophy was to allow man to satisfy his most bestial urges. Hervás y
Panduro, the latter observes, was typical in regarding eighteenth-century aspirations
towards *libertad* as no more than the unrestrained indulgence of 'las pasiones animales'
[animal passions] and as the destruction of moral conscience, constituting nothing less
than 'la transformación del hombre en fiera' [the transformation of man into a wild
animal].[37] For Manuel Moreno Alonso, Hervás was himself the physical victim of
the impious character of his age, whose effects he predicted and lived to see become
reality in 1789.[38] Not without justification, then, does Dalmacio Negro Pavón tell us
that Hervás furnished later traditionalists with an entire arsenal of weaponry.[39]

Such was the prevailing tenor of the historical discussion that a writer of the stature
of Balmes could detect, in the machinations of eighteenth-century philosophy, a
satanic plot that would not be entirely out of place in modern pulp fiction. In a series
of articles published in 1841 in *La Civilización*, a magazine which he himself edited in
conjunction with his ideological ally Joaquín Roca y Cornet, he attributed to French
intellectuals the following motivation and aims, casting his terms in the first person
plural and between quotation marks for added dramatic effect:

> ataquemos al gobierno e involucremos con él a todas las instituciones antiguas;
> halaguemos empero a la sociedad, y constituyéndonos órgano de todas las pasiones,
> eco de todas las quejas, defensores de todos los intereses no satisfechos, reuniremos
> en torno nuestro una falange poderosa, que nos servirá por ahora de escudo para
> defendernos, y luego de ariete para derribar todo lo existente.

> [let us attack the government and, with it, all traditional institutions; but let
> us at the same time heap much flattery upon society, and make ourselves the
> instrument of all its passions, the echo of all its complaints, the defenders of all its
> unsatisfied ambitions, let us gather around us a powerful phalanx that will serve
> first as our shield and defence and then as the battering ram with which we shall
> bludgeon to the ground all that presently exists].[40]

These, he insisted, had been the true thought-processes, the veritable deeds of a
perverted intelligence; in this way had the ground been prepared for the terrible
Revolution. Many of the distinctive trappings, we might be tempted to say, of a
sensation-novel, much of the typically overwrought and inflammatory language and
depiction of a *novela por entregas* had been transposed on to a piece of supposed
intellectual history. If we have any historical sense, we do expect to encounter in such
pieces a particular form of rhetoric, a distinctive way of describing and interpreting
cultural history, but we are surely not prepared for the literary extravagance of
Balmes's summary. On this issue at least, Revuelta González's affirmation that Balmes
was little given to rhetoric and rarely gave himself over to frenetic bursts of feeling is
called into question.[41]

The above example, although a particularly acute one, is not by any means unrepresentative of a body of opinion that resolutely refused to come to terms intellectually with Enlightenment thought; instead, the latter is simply disparaged wholesale, while conspiracy theories abound. Again found in *El Reflejo* is a commentary by V. M. Flórez on the alleged historical misrepresentations to which Enlightenment writers resorted in order to further their nefarious purposes; Flórez in effect imputes to the *philosophes* a machiavellian design that constituted, in his words, nothing less than a great historical conspiracy. He then sums up the strategy of 'la escuela filosófica' [the philosophical school], which, hurling itself upon past ages 'desfiguraron toda su fisonomía, disfrazándola en villano y ridículo traje' [disfigured them entirely, arraying them in a rough and ludicrous disguise]. The *philosophes*, he went on, had poured such quantity of sarcasm upon the Church — upon its sacraments and mysteries as well as upon its institutions — as to render it contemptible in the eyes of many.[42]

What we are naturally led to conclude, therefore, is that not only had the French Enlightenment proved erroneous in its judgements — complaints against the historical prejudices, for example, of Voltaire, prejudices usually ascribed to his irreligious views, have already been detailed — but the writers who professed those judgements had also proved to be guilty of shamelessly calculating insincerity. Deliberate falsification of history was a charge regularly made against the *philosophes*, and most especially against Voltaire. José de Zaragoza spoke for many Spanish intellectuals of his generation — many, it is tempting to add, unaware of the log present in their own eye — when he denounced an historiographical method consisting of a predetermined manipulation of events in accordance with a given writer's own ideological preferences; tortured logic and selective reference thus came to be the literary strategies by which an attempt was made to 'anublar la luz clara de la historia, y dar en tierra con las ideas y creencias religiosas, y más adelante con todo el edificio social' [cloud the clear light of history, and raze religious values and beliefs to the ground along with, in time, the entire social edifice].[43] Consequently, a false history and a false philosophy founded upon 'la base deleznable de la mentira' [the despicable foundation of lies] came to replace historical objectivity. No single work exemplified the tendency, in his opinion, better than Voltaire's *Essai sur les moeurs*, which, rather than an historical study ought to be considered, asserted Zaragoza, 'una gran calumnia contra el cristianismo, referida por el más ingenioso de los calumniadores' [a great calumny against Christianity written by a man with incomparable genius for calumny].[44] For the Spanish writer, Enlightenment historiography was itself part of a larger conspiracy that would ultimately produce the movement's great 'practical philosophers': such was the ironic title he allotted to Marat and Robespierre, in tracing a logical sequence between *philosophes* and Terror. The summary is worth reproducing in full as a salient example of the prevailing attitude towards Enlightenment historiography:

> Durante el siglo XVIII se escribía la historia para demostrar que casi todos los males que habían afligido a la humanidad, provenían de la religión, del sacerdocio o del fanatismo, palabras sinónimas y sacramentales. Con la historia se probaba una tesis impía, o se elevaba a principios incontestables las opiniones dominantes. Las inspiraciones de lo bello, de lo grande, era preciso ir a buscarlas en la antigüedad pagana; allí sólo residían los más nobles sentimientos que enaltecen a la especie humana, el amor de la patria, el heroísmo, las virtudes sublimes, la abnegación

individual, la libertad, la pureza de las costumbres. La religión de Cristo sólo había engendrado ignorancia, barbarie y corrupción. El influjo de esta secta de historiadores filósofos fue incontrastable e inmenso; sus efectos desastrosos los llora todavía el mundo. Consecuencias, si bien no legítimas, naturales de tamaña aberración, eran producir la conmoción violenta de lo existente, la vacilación de las creencias religiosas, la desvirtuación de las costumbres públicas y privadas de los pueblos; y todo este trabajo intelectual de la secta filosófica vino a condensarse en Marat y Robespierre, verdaderos y lógicos filósofos prácticos producidos por aquella escuela.[45]

[During the eighteenth century people wrote history in order to show that virtually every evil that had afflicted humanity stemmed from religion, from its priesthood or from its fanaticism, those synonymous and sacred terms. With such history one might prove some impious thesis or else raise to the status of incontrovertible principle the opinions of the moment. If we were to be inspired by beauty and grandeur, we should seek them in pagan antiquity; there alone might be found the most noble sentiments to have elevated humankind, its love for country, its heroism, its most sublime virtues, its instances of individual self-sacrifice, its freedoms, its unblemished way of life. The religion of Christ had merely engendered ignorance, barbarism, and corruption. The influence of this sect of philosopher historians was as incontrovertible as it was immense; its calamitous effects are still to be lamented by the entire world. Some consequences, which while hardly the lawful children were certainly the natural offspring of such aberration, were the violent disturbance of everything that lived, the vacillations of religious faith, the corruption of public life and private morality among all peoples; and the entire intellectual enterprise of this philosophical sect that would crystallize in the form of Marat and Robespierre, truly and logically the twin practical philosophers which that school was to produce.]

Zaragoza's complaint that the French Enlightenment had heaped 'la mentira y la calumnia' [falsehood and calumny] upon the glorious history of Spain's overseas expansion and empire was also a representative point of view.[46] For example, the noted poet and literary critic Enrique Gil y Carrasco, writing in his friend Espronceda's journal *El Pensamiento* in 1841, had inculpated those philosophers of the last century, who with a curious sense of satisfaction, as he put it, had taken great pleasure in turning the Spanish empire into a bloody and savage tyranny with only devastation and annihilation as its systematic processes.[47] Offended patriotism here clearly allied with the instinctive antipathy felt against the French Enlightenment by the nineteenth-century Catholic mind. Far surpassing this accusation, however, was the commonly expressed view, transparent in Zaragoza's text and explicitly declared in many others, that the Enlightenment itself had not represented genuine if misdirected human endeavour but a diabolical plan calculated to produce a revolutionary Armageddon. It is therefore not surprising that, when it came to depicting the French Revolution, many writers abandoned themselves entirely to morbid evocations of lurid human depravity. After all, if the Revolution was the culmination of a satanic plot hatched by warped and demented subversives, then to describe it in all of its awfulness would be a challenge to the most active reactionary imagination. Perhaps the most impressive attempt of its kind was that provided for readers of the first issue of the prestigious new journal the *Revista de Madrid* in 1838. It came from the pen of none other than Juan Donoso Cortés, and forsook any sense of reality in favour of scenes of nightmare and the rhetoric of apocalypse, amply justifying Revuelta González's detection of a preference, in Donoso's writing, for a rhetoric seething with fantastic and phantasmagorical images and internal connections.[48] Readers familiar with Donoso's literary criticism may at once be put in mind of certain passages contained in his review of Pacheco's *Alfredo*, or else in his condemnation of violent excess in the theatre, upon reading the following extraordinary evocation of the 1793 revolutionary government:

> la libertad era el numen que se agitaba en los pechos de los monstruos en sus tenebrosas orgías: el numen que revelándose contra la obra de Dios sepultó al mundo moral en las tinieblas de la noche: el numen despiadado y siniestro que levantó del polvo a las masas populares, que las convidó a un festín en donde para aplacar su sed las ofreció en copas de oro sangre humana, en un metal que deslumbra un veneno que enloquece: el numen después de que enloquizas, las dijo. — Ni hay Dios, ni hay reyes: el trono del cielo y los tronos de la tierra están vacíos — y que diciendo así colocó sobre sus sienes las espléndidas diademas de entrambas majestades.[49]

> [liberty was the guiding spirit that stirred the hearts of these monsters in their orgiastic darkness: a guiding spirit which, revealing itself against the work of God, buried the moral world in the shades of night: a merciless and macabre guiding spirit that raised the masses out of the dust, invited them to a banquet where they were offered human blood in golden goblets to slake their thirst, in dazzling metal a poison to turn their minds: a guiding spirit that told them, when once they were demented: 'There is no God, there are no kings and queens: the throne of heaven, like all the thrones on the earth, sits empty', and after saying such words the spirit placed upon the brow of each of them the splendid crowns of both kinds of majesty.]

Donoso then continues, in more temperate and aphoristic mood, by observing that France at the time of the Revolution had been the only nation in the world to dethrone God in order to enthrone humanity;[50] in other words, he tells us what the final part of the nightmare vision cited above is intended to represent. This seems to me crucial, since it allows us to account for many of the extravagant choices made by Donoso in constructing the earlier sequence. Firstly, and least specifically, much of the imagery suggests Revelation, the End of All Things, a horrible parody of the vision vouchsafed to St John the Divine.[51] The choice of the language of apocalypse is important since it reveals the prevailing attitude among nineteenth-century Spanish writers towards revolutionary France; the end of civilization as traditionally conceived, social dissolution and a descent into barbarism and inhumanity, a human catastrophe effectively closing the age of men. I use the last phrase deliberately because it seems to me that all of the portrayals of convulsion and destruction found in Spanish accounts of eighteenth-century France correspond, albeit in a febrile and hyperbolic way, to the pattern earlier adumbrated by Vico: a particular form of civilization had run its course, had become overly reflexive rather than virile and energetic, had become prone to the abuses of scientific analysis and rational questioning, had forsaken its moral conscience, and had thus fallen into a vortex of irreversible decline leading inevitably to cataclysm. In the article already cited, for example, Donoso himself referred to 'las teorías desorganizadoras' [the theories of disorganization] of the revolutionaries, theories that had signified, as he put it, a world on fire, Europe in conflagration. In the same passage he summed up the Revolution as 'el retroceso indefinido hacia la primitiva confusión de las sociedades humanas, el desheredamiento de sus gloriosas conquistas, y por término de su carrera la conquista tal vez de su primitiva barbarie' [a limitless withdrawal into the primitive chaos of human societies, a loss of the glorious conquests that heritage had provided, and, as the end point of the journey, the conquest perhaps of an earlier primitive barbarism].[52] Andrew Ginger, who writes elegantly and persuasively of much of Donoso's output and who is professedly aware of those 'eschatological notions so often deployed of the Revolution' by Spanish Romantic writers,[53] neglects even to mention Vico, which is all the more startling when he describes Donoso's depiction of 'the violent death of earlier society as a vast, bloody sacrifice necessary to expiate its sins prior to the magnificence of re-birth over the ruins'.[54] As we shall see, historical interpretations of the aftermath of the Terror were to be informed by a rhetoric of reorganization and renewal, of reconstruction, deriving principally from Vico's schema; the social edifice had been destroyed, its very foundations eroded by 'filosofismo', and society had effectively to be rebuilt on solid and enduring bases. Donoso once again exemplifies the tendency in concluding his article, pointing to a 'movimiento de regeneración que entre nosotros se observa' [regenerative movement which may be seen amongst us],[55] while the same metaphor is glimpsed in the passage from Tejado that I cited earlier, where we read of a 'funesto legado de cimientos destruidos, que pugna por reconstruir el presente siglo' [deathly legacy of wrecked foundations that our own century now strives to reconstruct].[56]

Secondly, if the reference to a 'copa de oro' and the accompanying phrase 'en un metal que deslumbra un veneno que enloquece' puts us in mind of Cervantes and 'all that glisters' — the golden chalice offered by the merciless and macabre spirit in orgiastic celebration contains not the sacrament of spiritual life in the divine blood of Christ but the blood of human sacrifice — then it is surely not coincidental. One of the charges most often levelled against the *philosophes* during the period in question was that they had turned men's minds with seductive theories whose intimate reality belied their external appearance.[57] An extended use of precisely this analogy was made by Diego Medrano, writing in the *Revista de Madrid* in 1842: eighteenth-century thinkers, he averred, believed that they had discovered the philosopher's stone, 'extendiendo ideas nuevas o ataviadas de nuevo, cuyos vestidos deslumbradores al principio y empapados en sangre después, se han deteriorado en seguida y convertido por último en miserables harapos' [propounding new ideas, or ideas arrayed in gaudy new clothes, dazzling at first and afterwards drenched in blood, clothes that have swiftly worn away and eventually become the meanest rags].[58] Javier de León Bendicho, in the same journal in the previous year, had likewise referred to the seductive phrases of materialist philosophers as siren voices which had captivated undiscerning minds,[59] while Leopoldo Augusto de Cueto, in describing the historical moment of the Cadiz Parliament, commented: 'los derechos del hombre y otras palabras de difícil inteligencia alucinan el entendimiento de los más ilustrados, y el dogma de la soberanía nacional, mal comprendido […] es acogido […] como una ilusión seductora' [the rights of man and other barely intelligible words turned the minds of the most knowledgeable, and the dogma of popular sovereignty, misunderstood at that, […] is received […] like some seductive vision].[60] Roca y Cornet, meanwhile, also had recourse to the metaphor of dazzled eyes in reconstructing the consequences of rationalist thought, commenting: 'Las doctrinas deslumbradoras del último siglo preocupaban los ánimos; creyóse desde entonces en teorías absurdas, en utopías impracticables' [The dazzling doctrines of last century occupied all minds; from that point on people believed in the most ludicrous theories, in the most impracticable and utopian of schemes].[61] Crucially, the same accusation was to be aimed at theories of democratic socialism; Sabino de Armeda's 'Breves reflexiones sobre el socialismo', appearing in *El Laberinto* in 1845, transposes the analogy onto the contemporary situation, warning that those pseudo-philanthropists who peddle their subversive wares of social perfectibility, concealing their deadly poison beneath a cloak of false Christian charity, are simply inciting the people to the delirium of a fresh social revolution.[62] Alberto Gil Novales is just one of many modern historians to highlight the presence, within Spain, of the disproportionately giddy fear of the French Revolution first and of socialism later.[63]

Thirdly, Donoso exposes what he saw as the jaundiced associations that the term 'libertad' had acquired in the France of 1793. This interpretation of liberty he opposes, in terms immediately reminiscent of Edmund Burke, to his preferred understanding of freedom as underpinned by and reliant upon order, to 'la libertad que necesitan los individuos, el del poder, que es la necesidad imperiosa de todas las sociedades' [the kind of liberty that individuals require, that belonging to authority, which is imperatively necessary to any and every society].[64] If Donoso's consideration of the French Revolution and its aftermath owes much to Vico's theory of historical phases, then the related idea of Providence as a discourse of order and authority is likewise present in the same piece: it is Providence, he asserted, that allows humanity to regenerate itself after the trauma of violent revolution. Society in such moments, he claims, 'se rejuvenece y fecunda' [grows young and fertile once more], while he is adamant that 'este fenómeno no será explicado jamás por la razón humana sino por la Providencia: con las revoluciones y sin Dios, yo no comprendo ni la humanidad ni la historia' [this is a phenomenon that can never be explained by human reason but by Providence alone: with revolutions and without God, neither humanity nor history make any sense to me whatever].[65]

Finally, as I have intimated, there is a discernible connection in terms of rhetoric between the passage originally cited, evoking the carnage of the French Revolution, and other areas of Donoso's writing. In reviewing his friend Joaquín Francisco Pacheco's drama *Alfredo* in 1835, he had fulminated against those who, ignorant of the true nature of Romanticism, claimed to follow its banner while profaning its heaven-sent gift of inspiration. The muse of certain literary practitioners he likened to a murderous, dagger-wielding phantom clad in rags, whose blaspheming mouth thirsted for blood, whose feet trod only on corpses and mire, and whose forehead was branded with the words 'incest' and 'profanity'.[66] The image is immediately recognizable as one derived from the depiction of the whore of Babylon in chapter seventeen of the book of Revelation. What is more, the prose of St John the Divine discloses a further possible link with the lurid passage already cited, for the woman is described as 'decked with gold and precious stones and pearls, having a golden cup in her hand full of abominations and filthiness of her fornication'. Just as tellingly in the present context, the woman is said to represent the depraved city that 'reigneth over the kings of the earth', while this part of Revelation makes continued reference to a cup containing the fierceness of the wrath of God. All of these images help to explain Donoso's eschatological portrayal in his own visionary sequence.

In 1838, meanwhile — the same year in which his nightmare vision of the Terror appeared in the *Revista de Madrid* — Donoso insisted that the world of some contemporary dramatists represented 'un horrible desierto sin vegetación y sin verdura; en medio de su soledad se levanta un cadalso, y al pie de ese cadalso suele haber un verdugo que amenaza y una víctima que gime' [a ghastly wilderness devoid of vegetation and of any green growth; in the midst of this fastness there is erected a scaffold, and at the foot of that scaffold is customarily found a menacing executioner and a groaning victim].[67] Here, I would contend, is clear evidence of an intimate connection in the minds of Spanish writers between, on the one hand, the bloody revolution ultimately spawned by Enlightenment rationalist philosophy, and, on the other, the vision of social disintegration and moral collapse which radical Romantic drama, chiefly imported from France, seemed to those same writers to portend. We might profitably cite on this point comments made by José Escobar with specific reference to Alberto Lista's articles on French Romantic drama published in *La Estrella* in January 1834; although Lista was censuring French Romantic drama, writes Escobar, what he was really attacking was that country's Revolution: in his condemnation of a literature produced by the dehumanization of society, he was providing an ethical, and therefore ideological, response, to a specific historico-social question.[68] The scaffold or 'cadalso', as both regular feature of the wilder dramas of the 1830s and potent emblematic image of the earlier Terror, provides the essential link. This transparent connection between revolutionary cataclysm and later literary radicalism goes a long way towards explaining the wholesale febrile rejection of French and French-inspired Romantic drama by a large body of Spanish critical opinion. The nihilistic vision such works appeared to contain — and we have only to remember the outrage of Larra in his condemnation of Dumas's *Antony* to be conscious of how broadly based that rejection came to be — did not exist solely in the realms of imaginative hypothesis; if Larra felt Dumas's drama to signify 'la *desorganización social*, personificada en *Antony*, literaria y filosóficamente' [the *social disorganization* personified in *Antony*, both literarily and philosophically speaking],[69] then for very many Spanish intellectuals the stark recollection of events in recent French history made the sense of menace the plays seemed to convey all the more immediate. French Romanticism, as Philip Silver succinctly observes, emerged as 'politically and literarily threatening'.[70]

Donoso, meanwhile, was to carry the same graphically macabre rhetoric into much of his political commentary. An article entitled 'La religión, la libertad, la inteligencia', published in *El porvenir* in 1837, blamed *progresista* machinations for much of the contemporary political instability. As Donoso furiously asked: '¿quién, decidnos, ha concitado las borrascas, quién acelera nuestra disolución, quién causa nuestra agonía, quién cava nuestro sepulcro, quién prepara los negros atavíos de nuestros tristes funerales?' [who, tell us, has called up the tempests, who is bringing us ever more swiftly to dissolution, who is the cause of our death-throes, who is digging our grave, who is making the ghastly preparations for our funeral ceremonies?]. The answer, if predictable, is most revealing in its associations, and anticipates the tenor of much of the material to be considered in the following chapter of this study; for Donoso attributed responsibility for the current turbulent atmosphere to 'el partido imbécil que continúa entre nosotros la obra de los antiguos revolucionarios, sin alcanzar su poder, sin tener su inteligencia, y que sólo parece a tan enormes gigantes en que proclama la libertad y es ateo' [that party of imbeciles that is continuing in our midst the work of the former revolutionaries, but lacking their power, lacking their intelligence, and is akin to such colossal figures only in that it proclaims the slogan 'liberty' and is atheist].[71] In 1843, writing in the pages of the *Revista de Madrid* of the regency of María Cristina, he effectively renewed the charge, demanding 'Execración, en fin, para aquellos hombres apartados de la mano de Dios que con voz de libertad han levantado a las turbas, y han encendido sus pasiones, y las han desencadenado sobre las víctimas indefensas, y han pedido después a la iniquidad victoriosa el precio de su sangre' [Execration, then, be upon those men who have abandoned God and who with the shout of 'liberty!' have stirred up the masses, have inflamed their passions, have unleashed those passions upon defenceless victims, and have afterwards begged of victorious iniquity the price of their lives in blood].[72] All of which squares with his rather more specifically directed assertion that it was indispensable to 'traer a la memoria de un pueblo demente que el árbol de la democracia no robará sus jugos al árbol de la monarquía y que los pueblos descansarán todavía por largo tiempo al abrigo de su sombra' [remind a demented people that the tree of democracy shall not steal its sap from the tree of monarchy, and that nations and peoples shall rest a great while longer in the shelter of the latter].[73]

If we are minded to pursue the same connections still further, then we encounter in the *Ensayo sobre el catolicismo, el liberalismo y el socialismo* another comparable piece of rhetoric, initiated by Donoso's fulminating declaration that he knows of nothing under the sun more vile and despicable than that part of the human race that has removed itself from Catholic teaching. At the very bottom of the heap — or, conversely, at the very peak of 'vileza' and 'degradación' — are, we note, 'las muchedumbres engañadas por los sofistas y oprimidas por los tiranos' [the masses who have been deceived by sophists and oppressed by tyrants] — while Donoso identifies two specific historical moments in which he felt such repugnant events to have occurred; these are, predictably, imperial Rome and revolutionary France: the paganism of the ancient world he regarded as having lurched from abyss to abyss, from sophistry to sophistry, until it had eventually fallen into the hands of Caligula, described as a ghastly monster in human form, with irrational desires and bestial urges; modern paganism, meanwhile, 'comienza por adorarse a sí propio en una prostituta, para derribarse a los pies de Marat, el tirano cínico y sangriento, y a los de Robespierre, encarnación suprema de la vanidad humana con sus instintos inexorables y feroces' [began by worshipping itself in the person of a prostitute, to throw itself after at the feet of Marat, the cynical and bloody tyrant, and at those of Robespierre, the superlative personification of human vanity in his pitiless animal instincts].[74]

Donoso's favoured rhetoric, then, allows us to see fundamental affinities, within his perspective, between the ghastly reign of Caligula, the merciless days of the Terror, the literary nightmares of Alexandre Dumas and the political maelstrom inhabited by Spanish *progresistas*. All are characterized by moral debasement, the indulgence of primitive passions and lurid depravity; the essential materialism of the Classical world, the illusory promises of Enlightenment rationalist philosophy, the nihilistic outlook of Romantic radicalism and the perverse rabble-rousing of contemporary political extremists, all lacking in the spiritual values that Donoso was so desperate to inculcate and which he felt to reside exclusively in the Catholic tradition. By the time that the *Ensayo* was being written, however, Proudhon's theories of democratic socialism had become the latest historical adversary, as evidenced by Donoso's denunciation of the French political thinker's system as — ironically — an aberrant modern 'maniqueísmo', one which resided in the affirmation 'que Dios es el mal, que el hombre es el bien, que el poder humano y el divino son dos poderes rivales y que el único deber del hombre es vencer a Dios, enemigo del hombre' [that God is evil, that man is good, that human and divine authority are rivals and that man's only duty is to vanquish God, who is his enemy];[75] there is therefore an irresistible parallel with Donoso's castigation of the Enlightenment for having supplanted God and enthroned humanity in His place. A close comparison is also afforded with Donoso's later, equally caustic, summary of the thought-processes of 'la escuela liberal' — 'que no hay otro mal sino el que está en las instituciones políticas que hemos heredado de los tiempos, y que el supremo bien consiste en echar por el suelo estas instituciones' [that there is no evil other than that to be found in the political institutions that we have inherited from past times, and that the greatest good consists of razing those institutions to the ground][76] and with his similar encapsulation of the premises of the 'escuela racionalista' [rationalist school], during the course of whose transitory reign, he declares, 'el principio disolvente de la discusión ha dado al traste con el buen sentido de los pueblos' [the corrosive principle of that debate has rid nations and peoples of all common sense].[77] All of these citations serve to show how integrated and how consistent is Donoso's core set of concepts, and how his ideological discourse is suffused with the motifs found in the work of the earlier Spanish reactionaries, motifs that were vigorously recycled as the contemporary situation required.

In historical studies as in literary criticism, however, nightmare visions and dire warnings were commonly counterpointed by effusive descriptions of regenerationist impulses, both in the sphere of aesthetics and within society at large. Prominent in such perceptions, perhaps inevitably so since in his life and work the two appeared to be intimately conjoined, was Chateaubriand. As we saw in the previous chapter, his designated Providential role was that of an extraordinary genius sent to rekindle faith and encourage spiritual regeneration in a society rent asunder by atheism, revolutionary tumult, and the carnage of the Terror. As Gonzalo Morón saw it in his general history of Spain, the illustrious French nobleman, whose very name was to be uttered only with the utmost veneration and respect, had raised a precious monument to Christianity, while the beneficial effects of his inspired work had been transparently clear: 'su brillante y poderosa musa ha sabido despertar a la sociedad de la indiferencia y del marasmo mortal, en que el ateísmo la sumiera' [his brilliant and potent muse has been able to rouse society from that state of indifference and that moral quagmire in which atheism had submerged it].[78] The same degree of lyricism and the same Providential purpose were accorded to Chateaubriand in other surveys of recent history. For example, Antonio Ferrer del Río's biographical piece written for *El Laberinto* in 1844 contextualizes the appearance of *Le Génie du christianisme* in terms of heroic grandeur, in a style that is one of florid intensity:

> Olvidado el culto, por tierra los altares, demolidos los templos, es una especie de recreo pasearse entre sus santas ruinas. Blanco el cristianismo del escarnio y de la befa [...] se ha extinguido la antorcha de la fe en el fondo de los corazones: de la privación de los consuelos religiosos en tan prolijos años de adversidades proviene la necesidad de esos mismos consuelos. Oprimidos los espíritus bajo el enorme peso de la duda, espantados del ateísmo y de sus consecuencias, flotan vacilantes en pos de un faro que les guíe, de un puerto que les albergue, y puerto y faro hallan a la vez en aquel precioso libro.[79]

> [With worship neglected, with altars levelled to the ground, with churches demolished, strolling amidst the sacred ruins became a form of pastime. Religion itself was the object of mockery and scorn [...] the light of faith had been extinguished in the depths of hearts: being deprived of the consolations of religion during so many years of adversity made those same consolations so very necessary. Our spirits, oppressed by such an enormous weight of doubt, and instilled with fear by atheism and all its consequences, were floating aimlessly in search of a guiding light, in search of a sheltering harbour, and they found both together in that one precious book.]

Ferrer del Río might well have been familiar with the French nobleman's own retrospective contextualization; in the preface written for the 1828 edition, Chateaubriand had stated: 'Ce fut donc, pour ainsi dire, au milieu des débris de nos temples que je publiai le *Génie du Christianisme*, pour rappeler dans ses temples les pompes du culte et les serviteurs des autels'.[80] The Spanish writer's lavishly poetic narrative, meanwhile, through its extraordinary mixture of metaphors, reproduces many of the most commonly found elements of the broader historiographical discourse: the references to revolutionary iconoclasm, emblematized by the scattered ruins of altars in churches razed to the ground; religious scepticism as an intolerable burden oppressing hearts and minds; the fear and disorientation of an age desperate to rediscover a sense of values and purpose re-created in images of storm-tossed humanity seeking spiritual shelter. José Vicente y Carabantes had written in similar terms in *El Arpa del Creyente* in 1842,[81] while Rafael María Baralt, again in a piece of literary biography that appeared this time in the popular magazine *El Siglo Pintoresco*, affirmed that Chateaubriand had done more than produce a book of outstanding lyrical beauty; he had created if not a formal manual then at least a source-book for men like Bonald, De Maistre, Fraissinous, and Lamennais, who, he continued, in their common rejection of eighteenth-century ideas, 'trabajaron con él en pro de la grande obra de la regeneración filosófica' [laboured with him in the grand cause of philosophical regeneration].[82] José María Quadrado, meanwhile, coincided so forcefully and so exactly with Ferrer del Río in describing the opportune appearance of *Le Génie du christianisme* that one of the two passages must certainly have prompted the other. Quadrado summed up the genius of Chateaubriand as a herald of peace, faith, and lyricism at a time when common moral ties had been sundered, when our susceptibility to beauty had been sullied by contact with the twin contagion of incredulity and egoism; the French writer had, like the dove in the wake of the great flood, he went on, brought back an olive branch to a devastated world and had intimately reconnected Europe's religious and literary traditions.[83] Implicit in Quadrado's text, as in so many other contemporary accounts, is the view of the Revolution and Terror as the castigation of humanity, as the working out of an ineluctable law of expiation comparable to the scriptural narrative of the flooding of the earth, another example of how so much historical writing of the period in question is rooted in religious fundamentalism; Chateaubriand's own position in *Le Génie du christianisme* was, after all, predicated upon the view that the *Encyclopédie* had been nothing less than a modern Tower of Babel constructed of science and reason.[84] The point is reinforced as Quadrado then specifies the beneficent impact of Chateaubriand's work on the glories of Christianity, his lexical choices again recalling antediluvian sin and subsequent reparation in references to a world shaken by the great tempest.[85] Quadrado, identified by Hans Juretschke as belonging to an influential group of conservative Catholic writers that included men of the stature of Pedro José Pidal, Gervasio Gironella, the Marqués de Viluma, Joaquín Roca y Cornet, and Pablo Piferrer, was to take up arms against the entire rationalist experience of the Revolution from a Romantic standpoint, one grounded in history and tradition.[86] This was, needless to say, a stance widely adopted, and one which I have elsewhere examined in considerable detail. On this point, Juretschke himself cites a piece by a very young Pedro de Madrazo published in the Romantic journal *No me olvides* in 1837. Madrazo here affirmed that the first generation of French Romantics 'se levantaron contra las obras de los filósofos revolucionarios del siglo XVIII' [rose up against the works of the revolutionary eighteenth-century philosophers] by employing 'el recuerdo del feudalismo, la cristiandad, la leyenda, la balada y la catedral gótica' [the memory of feudalism, Christianity, legend, the ballad, and the gothic cathedral].[87]

In reading Spanish assessments of events in France, we are then markedly aware of the frame in which those events are almost inevitably cast: the Enlightenment as a nefarious plot with, in the form of the Revolution, the most catastrophic consequences, and the abject depravity of the Terror as a return to primitive chaos out of which the Catholic revival provides a spiritual civilizing principle of renewal. Humanity, it was felt, had severed its relationship with Creator God and thus invited the self-inflicted carnage represented by the events of 1789 and after, and only a consciousness of human insufficiency and necessary reparation could return society to more enduring and stable bases, bases provided by spiritually motivated reconstruction and a deference to organization and authority both temporal and divine. As Juretschke shrewdly underlines, the quest for spiritual experience that was so firmly to characterize Romanticism in Spain was a process of deep-seated yearning bastioned by an awareness of the French revolutionary phenomenon of 1789. Contextualizing this profoundly felt and obsessively expressed commitment, Juretschke felt the conscious aim of the Romantics had been effectively to supersede an intellectually weak and inadequate philosophy which had, in the course of the Enlightenment, sought to abuse Newtonian physics with a view to holding all of humanity in thrall.[88]

The degree of emotional involvement commonly found in this rhetoric of history indicates not just instinctive ideological antipathy to Enlightenment ideals and a lyrically expressed personal affinity with the perceived messianic 'mission' of Chateaubriand. The sense of paranoia that accompanied depictions of eighteenth-century history as conspiracy and the Revolution as apocalypse stemmed ultimately from primitive fear: the spectre of violent social revolution not on the other side of the Pyrenees but within Spain itself. As the same writers who had lambasted the tendencies of the previous age themselves confessed, the Revolution might be over but its effects had been far from erased; Quadrado, writing in 1844, acknowledged as much in remarking that 'En nuestros temores siempre tenemos vuelta la vista a la Francia de 1793' [Our fears always lead us to look back over our shoulder to the France of 1793].[89] Balmes, meanwhile, openly acknowledged that in the early part of the nineteenth century the doctrines of the previous age had taken up firm residence in some of Spain's most brilliant minds; these doctrines had not become deeply rooted within Spain but had nevertheless, he put it, prompted considerable bloodshed, so that even after thirty years of disasters and upheavals the future outlook for the country was such that one could barely contemplate it without stepping back in terror.[90]

Such comments, not for the first time in this chapter, make for an irresistible linkage between the period of the 1840s and those early years of the nineteenth century in which the revolutionary threat was undoubtedly more immediate. Moreno Alonso observes, with reference to the historical events of 1808, that institutional religion had since the Middle Ages provided Christian Europe with its best guarantees of stability; the collapse of such stability in moments of crisis —and he specifies here the Reformation, the wars of religion and the French Revolution— had given rise to an exorbitant fear, on the part of those who still found essential reassurance in the structures and provisions of an earlier time, of a nebulous and precarious future.[91] Balmes, meanwhile, was writing in 1841, and, as we shall see later, the 'regency' of Espartero proved to be the stuff of nightmare in many conservative minds. Almazón, it should be noted, in an article already cited, repeated Balmes's view almost exactly in acknowledging that 'Aquel siglo ha pasado; pero sus consecuencias aún pesan sobre el nuestro. Aquel siglo ya ha pasado; pero en él se consumó una revolución grande, completa, general, espantosa' [That age has passed; but its consequences still press upon our own. That age has now passed; but in it there took place an immense, entire, thoroughgoing, and fearful revolution]; what is more, its insidious legacy remained: 'la revolución pasó como la tempestad, pero quedan sus estragos y las doctrinas que sembró, y que sólo el tiempo y continuados esfuerzos podrán borrar' [the revolution passed away like a great storm, but its ravages remain, like the doctrines it has sown, which only time and indefatigable effort can hope to erase].[92]

Those brilliant minds of the Spanish intelligentsia to whom Balmes referred, meanwhile, and among whom the evil doctrines spawned by the French Enlightenment were perceived freely to have circulated and even to have thrived, were, it hardly needs to be stated, the liberals of the Peninsular War and signally the *doceañistas*, the proponents of the Cadiz Constitution of 1812. As Javier Herrero puts it, for Fray Diego de Cádiz and his contemporaries 'la maldad del siglo' [the evils of the secular age] had reached a culminating point in the deeds of the French revolutionaries; for his successors writing some twenty years later, the apex of modern depravity resided in the actions of the Cadiz liberals.[93] Readings of nineteenth-century Spanish history will be seen to indicate that the connection established by Herrero may be pointedly extended, in unexpected ways and to a hitherto unsuspected degree, one further generation, into the decade of the 1840s. This is, of course, implicitly to deny the very different connection between the ideals of the Cadiz radicals and the essential nature of Spanish Romanticism that has underpinned so many studies published in the last thirty years and that has until recently provided a substantial degree of critical consensus. As I argued in my assessment of Spanish Romantic literary theory and criticism, there are in fact strong grounds for questioning such a perspective. I believe that the source material to be examined in the latter part of this study will reveal, within even broader intellectual parameters, how precarious and illusory is that assumption and how it can be seen conclusively to be belied by the weight of the historical evidence.

Notes to Chapter 4

1. See Ginger, *Political Revolution and Literary Experiment*, pp. 15–23, 30.
2. *Obras*, I, 775; cited by Moreno Alonso, *La revolución francesa en la historiografía española*, p. 187.
3. Herrero details the pervasive reactionary myth as follows:

> El mito fundamental, a cuyo alrededor se agrupa la constelación de imágenes que forman el argumento principal contra la Ilustración, es el de la existencia de una conspiración universal de las fuerzas del Mal contra el Bien. Esas fuerzas, cuyo último origen es Satán, se organizan en el siglo XVIII en una triple conspiración: la conspiración de los filósofos, que, adorando la Razón, la utilizan para destruir la Fe y de esta forma entregarse al inmundo libertinaje, que es su verdadero fin; la conspiración de los jansenistas, que se proponen llevar el satánico ideal de libertad a la Iglesia misma y disminuir mediante reformas el poder absoluto de la monarquía romana (no olvidemos que el pontífice era entonces uno de los reyes europeos); finalmente la conspiración masónica, que se propone la ejecución práctica de los perversos principios de razón, derechos humanos y libertad; es más, los masones han comenzado a realizar en sus logias una sociedad en la que se borran las clases sociales, atacando así el orden natural querido por Dios. Esas tres conspiraciones se reunieron a fines del siglo XVIII y se propusieron la destrucción de la civilización europea, mediante una revolución universal que comenzó en Francia en 1789. Los movimientos liberales, las democracias parlamentarias, no son sino los medios de que Satán se vale para realizar tan diabólica empresa. (*Los orígenes del pensamiento reaccionario*, pp. 23–24.

> [The fundamental myth, around which cluster a constellation of images that collectively form the substance of the argument against the Enlightenment, concerns an all-encompassing conspiracy of Evil against Good. The forces of evil, which originate in Satan himself, are in the eighteenth century organized into a triple-headed conspiracy: that of the philosophers, who venerate Reason and use it as a means of destroying Faith, in the process abandoning themselves to the most dehumanized licentiousness which is their true goal; that of the Jansenists, who take it upon themselves to carry this satanic ideal of freedom into the Church itself and, by means of reforms, diminish the absolute power of the Vatican (and let us not forget that in those days the Pope was counted among the monarchs of Europe); finally, that of the freemasons, which aimed at the practical exercising of all those perverse principles of reason, human rights and freedom; what is more, the masons have begun to bring to form, in their lodges, a society in which class distinctions are erased, thus undermining the natural order beloved of God These three conspiracies merge at the end of the eighteenth century and together undertake the destruction of European civilization, by way of a total revolution begun in France in 1789. Movements of political liberalism, parliamentary democracy, are simply the means employed by Satan to fulfil his devilish enterprise.]

4. *Historiografía romántica española*, p. 123.

5. Moreno Alonso regards this obsession with the French Revolution as having been prompted by the 'actuaciones revolucionarias' of Spain's own recent history, making events that had occurred in the neighbouring country a 'punto obligado de referencia': *La revolución francesa en la historiografía española*, 45.

6. 'El sentimiento religioso', *Revista de Madrid*, 3rd series, 2 (1841), 313–22 (pp. 318–19).

7. *Obras*, ed. by Seco Serrano, V, 55.

8. *D. Francisco Martínez de la Rosa* (Madrid, 1843), p. 69.

9. *Political Revolution and Literary Experiment*, p. 15.

10. *Obras*, ed. by Seco Serrano, V, 108.

11. *Obras*, ed. by Seco Serrano, V, 113, 136.

12. 'La sociedad actual', *El Reflejo* (1843), 145–-46 (p. 145).

13. *Reflexiones sobre el modo de escribir la historia de España* (Madrid, 1816), p. 52.

14. *Reflexiones sobre el modo de escribir la historia de España*, 65–66.

15. *Reflexiones sobre el modo de escribir la historia de España*, pp. 50–52. Herrero details two specific moments in Forner's evolving definition of the term 'filosofía'. The first, belonging to the *Discursos filosóficos sobre el hombre*, published in 1787 and therefore prior to the revolutionary upheavals occurring in France, he designates 'una de las más triviales y pedestres formulaciones del dogma reaccionario de que la filosofía significa el triunfo del animal en el hombre' [one of the most trivializing and simplistic formulations of reactionary dogma, in which philosophy figures as the triumph of the bestial instinct in man]. The second, reproduced from the *Discurso sobre el espíritu patriótico* of 1794, is much more virulent, and sees Forner savage the term wholesale as 'horrendo fruto de una sofistería audaz que sólo ha sabido inspirar ruina, destrucción, destrozos, mortandades, rapiñas, sacrilegios, proscripciones, rabia, ferocidad, cual jamás se ha visto en los anales de la locura humana' [the horrible fruits of the most audacious sophistry, one which has brought only ruin, destruction, pillage, death, rapine, sacrilege, persecution, animal rage, brutality, of a kind never before seen in all the annals of human madness]. See *Los orígenes del pensamiento reaccionario*, pp. 122–24.

16. *La viña y los surcos*, p. 55. Allegra here regards Forner, along with Capmany and Jovellanos, as one of the 'representantes de mayor relieve de la cultura antiiluminista' [most prominent representative figures of anti-Enlightenment culture].

17. *Revista de Madrid*, 2nd series, 3 (1840), 222.

18. *Oración pronunciada en la solemne apertura*, pp. 6–7.

19. Tejado (1819–91) was to publish an historical novel, *Víctimas y verdugos*, that re-created in typically graphic fashion the horrors and bloodshed of the French Revolution and the Terror. He would later edit a five-volume collection of Donoso's work, with an extensive biographical introduction. Abellán describes Tejado's outlook as 'inseparable de Donoso Cortés', locating him ideologically 'en la doctrina tradicionalista de la última época donosiana' [within the traditionalist thinking of Donoso's final phase]: *Historia crítica del pensamiento español*, IV, 332n.

20. *El Laberinto*, 2 (1845), 135.

21. *Semanario Pintoresco Español*, 2nd series, 1 (1839), 156.

22. *Ensayo crítico sobre las lecturas de la época en la parte filosófica y social*, 2 vols (Barcelona, 1847), I, 282.

23. *Ensayo crítico sobre las lecturas de la época*, I, 283.

24. *El Reflejo* (1843), p. 145.

25. *Ensayos literarios y críticos*, I, 32. A much more lavish expression of the same basic view can be found in an article by José Ferrer y Subirana appearing in *La Civilización* in 1842:

> Con esa filosofía se deshojan las ilusiones, el entusiasmo se apaga, se endurece y seca el corazón. Con ella son incompatibles las santas inspiraciones, y los arranques sublimes del alma. Como que es fría, no conoce los ardores del celo: como que es material y está avezada a reptar por el suelo, no conoce el vuelo ni los transportes del espíritu: como que es estrecha y mezquina, no conoce el hervor de las pasiones que se derraman por el estado: como que es individual y egoísta, no comprende los ímpetus del desprendimiento, y el dulcísimo encanto de las humanas simpatías. (*La Civilización*, II (1842), 63–64)

> [With this philosophy illusions are stripped bare, enthusiasm is snuffed out, the heart is hardened and withered. Sacred aspirations are incompatible with it, as are the sublime impulses of the soul. Its coldness makes it unfit to feel the feverish heat of desire; its material nature disposes it to crawl like a reptile upon the ground, for it knows neither the soaring elevation nor the transports of the

spirit: its narrow meanness makes it oblivious to the inspiring passions that spill over upon the public stage: its anarchic egoism is uncomprehending of the urges of selflessness and those sweetest charms of human sympathy]

Ferrer y Subirana translated and edited a collection of essays by Bonald as *Observaciones religiosas, morales, sociales, políticas, históricas y literarias* (Barcelona, 1842); we might note also the appearance in Madrid in 1871 of the *Pensamientos religiosos, filosóficos y políticos de Bonald, traducidos por la redacción de la revista 'Altar y Trono'*.

26. 'La civilización. Artículo 2', La Civilización, 1 (1841), 49–59 (p. 58).

27. Obras, VI, 39; cited by Moreno Alonso, *La revolución francesa en la historiografía española*, p. 175.

28. 'Biografía contemporánea: Metternich (Príncipe de)', Revista de Madrid, 2nd series, 2 (1839), 97–116 (p. 98). Gironella, who was successively editor of both the Revista de Madrid and the Semanario Pintoresco Español, signed the piece, as was his custom, 'G. G.'.

29. *Ensayo sobre las sociedades antiguas y modernas y sobre los gobiernos representativos. Por Don Fermín Gonzalo Morón, Profesor del Ateneo y autor de la Historia de la Civilización de España* (Madrid, 1844), p. 60.

30. This was of course a commonplace in earlier reactionary writing. As Abellán reminds us, Antonio José Rodríguez had concluded in his *El Philoteo* that 'la esencia de la Ilustración es la liberación del animal contra el yugo de la fe' [the essence of the Enlightenment resides in the unshackling of the animal from the yoke of faith], while Francisco Alvarado, the *Filósofo Rancio*, had contended that rationalist philosophy itself demonstrably consisted of a desire to 'justificar y promover las pasiones todas que nos son comunes con las bestias, y en que frecuentemente las exceden nuestros vergonzosos abusos' [justify and advertise those passions that we have in common with the beasts, which beasts we frequently outdo in our wild and shameless excesses]: see *Historia crítica del pensamiento español*, IV, 156, 174.

31. *La generación española de 1808*, pp. 29–30.

32. *Ensayo sobre las sociedades antiguas y modernas*, pp. 68–69.

33. With reference to earlier reactionary thought as expressed in Spain, the point is amply documented. In contextualizing the ideological position of Menéndez y Pelayo, for example, Antonio Santoveña Setién summarises thus:

La cosmovisión católica así planteada se caracterizaba por una argumentación dualista y maniquea en la que liberalismo y catolicismo aparecían como posiciones contrapuestas. Frente a la estima de las ideas liberales como una creación de Satanás y, por ende, encarnación teórica del error, el caos y las tinieblas, es decir, del Mal, se oponía el Bien, concretado en la doctrina católica que, por haber emanado de Dios, era símbolo de verdad. (*Marcelino Menéndez Pelayo: revisión crítico-biográfica de un pensador católico* (Santander, 1994), p. 21)

[The Catholic vision of the world here presented was characterized by a dualistic and manichaean argumentative structure in which liberalism and catholicism appear as the opposed points of view. Against an appraisal of liberal ideas as the creation of the devil, and, in consequence, the theoretical manifestation of human error, chaos and darkness, or, put simply, Evil, was ranged Good as specified in Catholic doctrine, which, since it emanated from God, was a symbol of truth.]

As Abellán points out, the 'enfrentamiento maniqueo [...] entre los representantes del Bien y del Mal' [manichaean confrontation [...] between the representatives of Good and Evil] [a vast movement in ideas] found in the work of men like Fray Fernando de Zeballos became 'un vasto movimiento de ideas': *Historia crítica del pensamiento español*, IV, 154–55. The prevalence of this perspective within Romantic thought, however, has not hitherto been seriously considered.

34. *Ensayo sobre las sociedades antiguas y modernas*, 87.

35. In dedicating to Campomanes his six-volume work published in Madrid in 1775–76 entitled *La falsa filosofía; o, el ateísmo, deísmo, materialismo y demás nuevas sectas convencidas de crimen de Estado contra los soberanos y sus regalías, contra los magistrados y potestades legítimas*, Zeballos insisted that 'además de la impiedad y de la irreligión que dicha filosofía predica va a revolver el orden público, a derribar a los soberanos y a disipar a los magistrados y gobiernos establecidos' [quite aside from the impiety and irreligion disseminated by the said philosophy, it is set to place public order in a state of upheaval, remove sovereign monarchs from their thrones, and to dissipate the rule of law and established forms of government]. As he went on, expressing violent consternation at the dissemination of their ideas

in France and abroad: 'ascienden de las podridas lagunas de sus corazones vapores pestíferos que se esparcen por la atmósfera común que todos respiran, ya en libelos y folletos que llevan el aire del tiempo, ya en palabras que vuelan de sus malos coloquios' [there rises up from the fetid stagnant water of their hearts the most pestilential vapours, which then permeate the air breathed by us all, whether in the pamphlets and propaganda that bear the stamp of their passing age, or in the words which flow from their evil converse]; cited by Herrero, *Los orígenes del pensamiento reaccionario*, p. 92.

36. See Herrero, *Los orígenes del pensamiento reaccionario*, pp. 94, 160.

37. See Herrero, *Los orígenes del pensamiento reaccionario*, p. 96.

38. *La revolución francesa en la historiografía española del siglo XIX*, p. 120.

39. *Historia de España Menéndez Pidal*, XXXV: I, 557.

40. *La Civilización*, 1, pp. 56–57.

41. 'Religión y formas de religiosidad', in *Historia de España Menéndez Pidal*, XXXV: I, 215–333 (p. 221).

42. 'Estudios históricos: sociedad pagana', *El Reflejo* (1843), 84–86 (p. 84).

43. *Discursos leídos en la Real Academia de la Historia*, pp. 11–12.

44. *Discursos leídos en la Real Academia de la Historia*, p. 12. There is no evidence to suggest that in Spain 'certain of the philosophes, and most notably Voltaire, continued to exercise a profound influence during the period of Romanticism', as Hayden White affirms with reference to the broader European context: see *Metahistory*, p. 47.

45. *Discursos leídos en la Real Academia de la Historia*, pp. 12–13.

46. *Discursos leídos en la Real Academia de la Historia*, p. 14.

47. *El Pensamiento* (1841), pp. 78–79. In the same article, a review of an historical work by Martín Fernández de Navarrete, Enrique Gil singled out for criticism Voltaire, 'que no sabía o no quería elevarse al principio de una inteligencia suprema' [who was either unable or unwilling to elevate his mind to the contemplation of a supreme intelligence] and who had thus, the Spanish writer felt, been unable to comprehend 'la idea de la Providencia' [the idea of Providence] (pp. 77–78).

48. *Historia de España Menéndez Pidal*, XXXV: I, 221.

49. 'España desde 1834. Artículo I: Consideraciones generales', *Revista de Madrid*, 1 (1838), 3–19 (p. 12).

50. *Revista de Madrid*, 1, p. 13.

51. Moreno Alonso, though he does not specify, refers to Donoso's detection, in post-revolutionary France, of 'un condenable espíritu pagano, que surge de la libertad revolucionaria, esencialmente anticatólica' [a damnable pagan spirit, proceeding from revolutionary freedom, one which was in essence anti-Catholic]: *La revolución francesa en la historiografía española*, p. 187. The passage cited exemplifies this perfectly. At the same time, I find that Moreno Alonso, in this assessment, rather overestimates Donoso's favourable evaluation of the ends of the French Revolution as initially conceived, as an emancipation of humanity and banner of civilization. Once one is aware of Donoso's depiction of the Terror, it becomes difficult to profess, with the same degree of lyricism bestowed by the modern historian, that the nineteenth-century writer 'siente una gran admiración por la revolución francesa, sobre todo por su sublimidad y magnificencia, a la que rinde tributo de especial admiración' [felt a great admiration for the French Revolution, above all for its sublimity and magnificence, to which qualities he dedicates a special tribute] (p. 187).

52. *Revista de Madrid*, 1, p. 7. It is illuminating to compare Donoso's rhetorical emphases and essential motifs with others voiced much earlier in the first volume of *La falsa filosofía* by Fray Fernando de Zeballos, for whom, in the later eighteenth century,

se estrecha demasiado el número de los verdaderos cristianos, inclinándose naciones enteras a caer en la antigua barbarie del gentilismo. Quien hoy considere atentamente el teatro del mundo y le comparare con su imagen sacada de los siglos pasados, verá si hay bastante fundamento para temer, sin adivinar, que está próximo a manifestarse el hombre de pecado. (Cited by Herrero, *Los orígenes del pensamiento reaccionario*, p. 97)

[the number of true Christians is shrinking excessively, entire nations being inclined to relapse into the age-old barbarism of the gentiles. Anyone who carefully considers today the theatre of the world and compares it with how it looked in past ages, will see whether or not there is any reason to fear, without the gift of foresight, the imminent appearance of the anti-Christ]

This apocalyptic 'hombre de pecado' is for Zeballos, as Herrero notes, none other than 'el ilustrado'.

53. *Political Revolution and Literary Experiment*, p. 21.

54. *Political Revolution and Literary Experiment*, p. 30. The connection seemingly cannot be missed, for Ginger immediately afterwards cites comments from Donoso's *Lecciones de derecho político*: 'Entonces la Providencia borra a ese pueblo del libro de la vida, borra a esa sociedad del libro de las sociedades […] sale del seno de sus escombros magnífica y resplandeciente, como renace de sus cenizas el fénix' [It is at this point that Providence erases such a people from the book of life, wipes the name of that society from the annals of societies […] it rises magnificently resplendent from the rubble just as the phoenix rises from its own ashes] (*Obras*, I, 328). Later, in his otherwise discerning assessment of Donoso's *Discurso de apertura en Cáceres* of 1829, Ginger writes of imagery in which 'the eighteenth century is compared with the Day of Judgement', and summarizes Donoso's view that in that age 'The terrible culmination occurs in the Revolution and gives way to the new era'(p. 144), but without at any stage referring to the patterning of the *Scienza nuova*. The absence of Vico in Ginger's study does seem to me a most unfortunate omission.

55. *Revista de Madrid*, 1, p. 18.

56. It is worth bearing in mind here Abellán's comments regarding traditionalist responses to the French Revolution:

Los reaccionarios españoles resaltan las violencias revolucionarias como prueba de que sus advertencias estaban justificadas; ahora nadie puede dudar ya que la razón conduce a la anarquía, la ilustración a la subversión y la tolerancia a la impiedad. La necesidad de luchar contra las ideas enciclopédicas se identifica así con la necesidad de salvar a España del caos revolucionario. (*Historia crítica del pensamiento español*, IV, 158)

[The Spanish reactionaries highlight revolutionary violence as proof that their own cautions were justified; it was now impossible to doubt that reason led to anarchy, the Enlightenment to subversion, religious tolerance to impiety. The need to combat the ideas of the *Encyclopédie* is thus identified with the need to save Spain from revolutionary chaos]

57. If we call to mind the suggestion of a transferential relationship between Enlightenment and Reformation evidenced so powerfully in Balmes, then we should not be surprised by Pedro Benito Golmayo's comparable re-creation of the effects of Protestantism: 'introduce principios erróneos, que bajo una belleza aparente y engañosa ocultan un veneno mortal, principios, que llevan consigo el germen de la anarquía, y para cuyo sostenimiento fue necesario levantar ejércitos y cadalsos, que inundasen la Europa de sangre' [it introduces error-laden principles which, beneath their deceptive appearance of beauty conceal a mortal poison, principles which contain within themselves the seeds of anarchy, and for the upholding of which it was necessary to enlist armies and erect scaffolds that have bathed all of Europe in blood]: 'La reforma protestante', *Revista de Madrid*, 3rd series, 1 (1841), 468–93, 2 (1841), 161–83 (p. 162), 3 (1842), 196–223.

58. 'Del progreso', *Revista de Madrid*, 3rd series, 3 (1842), 461–79 (p. 462).

59. 'Consideraciones sobre la religión católica y el protestantismo', *Revista de Madrid*, 3rd series, 1 (1841), 317–42 (p. 318). This was yet another phrase commonly employed by the forces of reaction; the Spanish translator of Nonnotte — extremely influential in his day, as Herrero shows — described the voices of Voltaire and his followers as 'mortal y encantadora voz de las sirenas de nuestros días' [the deadly enchanting voices of the sirens of our own age], as the expression of a 'funesta confederación': see *Los orígenes del pensamiento reaccionario*, pp. 35–45 (p. 42).

60. Cueto's comments belong to a biographical piece on the Conde de Toreno, commissioned by Nicomedes-Pastor Díaz for the *Galería de españoles célebres contemporáneos* of 1842, that was later to preface the Rivadeneyra edition of Toreno's *Historia del levantamiento, guerra y revolución de España*, Biblioteca de Autores Españoles, 64 (Madrid, 1872); the citation from p. xiii.

61. *Ensayo crítico sobre las lecturas de la época*, I, pp. v–vi. The entire introduction is an explicit exhortation to a generation of Spaniards to discard the corrosive thought-patterns of the *philosophes* and to return to the tried and trusted formulae of past times; in this appeal addressed to 'la juventud española', Roca professes:

Las tradiciones que habéis heredado de vuestros mayores, al paso que recuerdan días de gloria, son fecundas en el porvenir. En vano un soplo de frenética intolerancia derribó monumentos para que olvidaseis lo pasado. Vuestra sed ardiente de saber para mejor juzgar lo busca entre las ruinas, y lo halla en las páginas de la historia. (p. ii).

[The traditions you have inherited from your forebears, at the same time as they recall days of glory are rich in future prospect. It was in vain that a frenetic burst of intolerance overturned historical monuments in an attempt to make you forget the past. Your passionate thirst for knowledge with which to judge for yourselves is seeking that past among the ruins, and is finding it in the pages of history.]

Once more, the choice of imagery is familiar, as equally in Roca's subsequent reference to 'esta desazón universal que corroe lentamente el corazón de las sociedades modernas' [this ubiquitous disquiet that is gnawing away at the hearts of modern societies] (p. iii). Also typical is the affirmation that 'en el orden providencial del mundo la luz de la verdad nacía más brillante de las aberraciones del pensamiento, así como los desfogues de la tormenta tornan el aire más puro' [in the Providential ordering of the world the light of truth shone most brilliantly after the aberrations of human thought, and so also the venting of the storm serves to render the air more pure] (p. vi).

62. *El Laberinto*, 2, 351.
63. 'Las contradicciones de la revolución burguesa', in *La revolución burguesa en España* (Madrid, 1985), pp. 45–58.
64. *Revista de Madrid*, 1, 7. Flórez, writing in *El Reflejo*, was similarly to protest against the distortion to which he felt the term 'libertad' had been subjected in Revolutionary France. As he puts it:

En el siglo pasado se nos fatigó con la pretendida libertad de los tiempos antiguos; no se la concebía sino cubierta de un gorro frigio, y bajo de un nombre romano bien sonoro. Paradoja fue esta de una nación delirante, conducida al abismo por desenfrenados demagogos, que aplicaban los principios filosóficos. ('Estudios históricos: principio de la sociedad cristiana', *El Reflejo* (1843), p. 92.)

[Last century we were taxed with the supposed freedoms of classical times; that freedom could only be conceived of as wearing a phrygian cap, and bearing a sonorous Roman name. Such was the paradox of a nation in delirium, led to the brink of the abyss by demagogues who knew no restraint in their application of the principles of philosophy.]

65. *Revista de Madrid*, 1, 5.
66. *Obras*, I, 172–73.
67. *Obras*, I, 406; see my *Spanish Romantic Literary Theory and Criticism*, pp. 81–82.
68. 'Romanticismo y revolución', in *El romanticismo*, ed. by Gies, p. 326.
69. *Obras*, II, 248.
70. *Ruin and Restitution*, p. 12.
71. *Obras*, I, 378.
72. *Obras*, I, 809.
73. *Obras*, I, 775.
74. *Ensayo sobre el catolicismo, el liberalismo y el socialismo*, ed. by Vila Selma, pp. 129–30.
75. *Ensayo*, ed. by Vila Selma, pp. 172–73.
76. *Ensayo*, ed. by Vila Selma, p. 232.
77. *Ensayo*, ed. by Vila Selma, p. 244.
78. *Historia*, II, 55.
79. 'Biografía: Chateaubriand', *El Laberinto*, 1 (1843–44), 295–98 (p. 296).
80. Cited by Benítez, *Bécquer tradicionalista*, p. 61.
81. 'Literatura religiosa', *El Arpa del Creyente*, 2, 9–10; reproduced in José Simón Díaz, *El Arpa del Creyente (Madrid, 1842)*, CIPP, 7 (Madrid, 1947), pp. 3–5 (p. 4). See also my *Spanish Romantic Literary Theory and Criticism*, pp. 124–25.
82. 'Estudios literarios: Chateaubriand y sus obras', *El Siglo Pintoresco*, 3 (1847), 121–27 (p. 124); in *Obras literarias publicadas e inéditas de Rafael María Baralt*, ed. by Guillermo Díaz-Plaja, Biblioteca de Autores Españoles, 204 (Madrid, 1967), pp. 127–36 (p. 131). Baralt was elected to the chair left vacant in the Real Academia Española on the death of Donoso Cortés in 1853. On taking up his place in the Academia, he made a speech dedicated to the work of Donoso and specifically to the famous *Ensayo*; he summed up the latter's position with the words 'El bien, finalmente, no es posible sino por medio de la acción sobrenatural de la Providencia, ni es dado concebir el progreso más que como resultado necesario de la sumisión pasiva y absoluta del elemento humano al elemento

divino, y no de otra manera' [Good, in sum, is not attainable other than through the supernatural workings of Providence, neither can we conceive of progress other than as the necessary result of humanity's absolute yielding of itself before the divine, and by no other means]: Rafael María Baralt, *Discurso de recepción pronunciado en la Real Academia Española*, in *Obras literarias*, pp. 107–27 (p. 109). In concluding his oration, Baralt himself declared, in broad terms and via an extended metaphor relevant both in the context of the present study and in that of nineteenth-century Spanish history generally: 'La tradición […] es nervio al par que nobleza de las naciones; porque, al modo que una fortaleza murada y guarnecida, mantiene el orden interior, conserva el legítimo dominio e impide que poderes extraños, violentos e invasores penetren de sobresalto y mano poderosa en el país' [Tradition [...] is the sinew and the true nobility of nations, in the same way that a walled and garrisoned fortress is able to maintain order within its bounds, defend legitimate authority and prevent any violent and aggressive external power from entering its lands either by stealth or by force of arms]. Nonetheless, this progressive liberal pursued with something of a caution: 'el culto intolerante y fanático de lo pasado, encerrado en el espíritu y la acción del pueblo en un círculo de ideas y de movimientos estrechísimo, termina siempre por envilecerle y degradarle. Lo pasado es la semilla, no el fruto del árbol de la ciencia' [any intolerant or fanatical veneration of the past, which confines the spirit and the acts of a people within a narrowly reductive sphere of ideas and workings, must eventually degrade and and enslave that people. The past is the seed, not the fruit, of the tree of knowledge] (p. 126). Baralt's preference for 'La sensata tradición que nada legítimo excluye, la tradición liberal y generosa que únicamente rechaza lo que perturba y desconcierta' [That sensible kind of tradition which never excludes what is lawful, that generous and liberal tradition that rejects only what is disturbing and damaging to concord] amounts, as Guillermo Díaz-Plaja indicates, a moderating revision of Donoso's declared position: see Baralt, Obras literarias, 'Estudio crítico', pp. lxiv–lxv.

83. Reproduced as part of the introduction to the Austral edition of *El último abencerraje. Atala. René* (Madrid, 1944), p. 5.

84. Allegra makes much the same point with reference to the rather earlier reaction of Jovellanos:

La Revolución francesa era para Jovellanos, como para los martinistas y los místicos de la Restauración, un castigo de Dios, cuyo desencadenamiento titánico y cuyo derramamiento de sangre podría resultar, por reacción, algo saludable para el género humano corrompido y ensoberbecido por las filosofías. (*La viña y los surcos*, p. 63)

[For Jovellanos, as for the Martinists and for the mystic writers of the Restoration, the French Revolution was a punishment administered by God, the titanic course and the bloodshed of which might ultimately bring about some good, in the form of a salutary reaction, for a humankind rendered corrupt and vain by philosophy]

Allegra goes on to cite Jovellanos's ode dedicated to Vargas Ponce, which invokes a tireless struggle against the 'feroz quimera' [ferocious chimera] of the Revolution, its 'bandera tricolor impía' [impious tricolour], its 'dogmas y cruentos ritos' [savage dogmas and rituals], its 'leyes y moral nefanda' [death-dealing laws and morals] and its 'infanda deleznable gloria' [infamous and despicable glories] (p. 64).

86. *El último abencerraje. Atala. René*, pp. 13–14.

87. *Historia de España Menéndez Pidal*, XXXV: I, 155–56. Abellán characterizes Quadrado (1819–96) as 'historiador y apologista católico, que siguió las directrices tradicionalistas de Donoso Cortés' [historian and Catholic apologist, who followed the traditionalist lines drawn by Donoso Cortés]: *Historia crítica del pensamiento español*, IV, 354n. Quadrado would in later life produce a two-volume *Discurso sobre la historia universal* (Barcelona, 1880) avowedly modelled on Bossuet and a work lavishly praised by Menéndez Pelayo in contradistinction to the historical studies of Voltaire — whose method, according to Don Marcelino was to 'hacer la historia por epigramas' [write history in epigrams] — and Guizot — who had preferred instead to 'descoyuntar los hechos en el potro de un inflexible mecanismo doctrinario' [dislocate every part of fact upon the rack of some inflexible doctrinal machine]; cited by Juretschke, *Historia de España Menéndez Pidal*, XXXV: I, 163.

88. See *Historia de España Menéndez Pidal*, XXXV: I, 130–31.

89. *Historia de España Menéndez Pidal*, XXXV: I, p. xx, p. xxiii.

90. From an essay much later included in Quadrado's *Ensayos religiosos, políticos y literarios* (1893); cited by Juretschke, *Historia de España Menéndez Pidal*, XXXV: I, 156.

91. *La Civilización*, 1 (1841), 54.
92. *La generación española de 1808*, p. 69.
93. *El Reflejo* (1843), p. 146.
94. *Los orígenes del pensamiento reaccionario*, p. 143.

CHAPTER 5

Reading Spain's Recent Past

What we have thus far seen is that Spanish writers of the Romantic period were to concur, in the main, with the historical judgement of the Enlightenment voiced by Friedrich Schlegel, a figure who had by the 1840s acquired some considerable reputation within Spain as an eminent representative of German philosophy, described by Almazón as 'tan luminosa como cristiana' [as brilliant as it is Christian].[1] In his 1812 Vienna lectures, the German theorist had roundly declared: 'It is indeed difficult to compute how much evil, both in opinion and in action, was produced by the doctrines of natural right, and the statesmanship of reason, in the last half of the eighteenth century'.[2] Despite, however, the panegyrical attention regularly devoted to Chateaubriand and other Catholic thinkers, the influence of these powerful and allegedly evil adversaries — political radicalism, religious scepticism, and an all-encompassing materialism — had not been, and seemingly could not be, eradicated. Overviews of the contemporary age, therefore, typically contain a profound awareness of their historical legacy. Gabino Tejado writing in *El Laberinto* in 1845, pointed to the ominous philosophical consequences produced by an historical age of transition:

> Por una parte el espíritu del análisis agitando convulsivamente sus alas de hielo, escudriñando los secretos más íntimos del corazón humano, y pretendiendo clasificar con una precisión anatómica las concepciones más ideales de la mente, y las ilusiones más misteriosas de la inocencia y del genio. -Por otra parte un escepticismo repugnante y estéril, que todo lo excluye, que todo lo falsifica, y que no escarmentando en fin al ver que a cada instante tiene que desmentirse a sí mismo, parece que se propone negar la humanidad, y desmentir la Providencia.[3]

> [On the one hand the spirit of analysis whirling its icy wings, looking deep into the most intimate secrets of the human heart and striving to categorize, with anatomical precision, the most idealistic conceptions of the mind and the most mysterious yearnings of genius and innocence. On the other a repellent and sterile scepticism, suppressing and falsifying all it finds, undaunted even on finding that it must contradict itself at every step, and set, it would seem, upon the denial of all humanity and the rejection of all Providence.]

Tejado's words are representatively — and, once more, graphically — macabre in their personification of 'el análisis' as some all-seeing, darkly malignant and ineluctable angel of death. Irresistibly, if indirectly, we infer it to stand as a ghastly emblem of the historical consequences of characteristic Enlightenment preferences for human reason and scientific inquiry. Irresistibly also, his sonorous phrases can be seen to portend the same catastrophic collapse of civilization as traditionally conceived, of the values and aspirations that constituted humanity's principal forms of intimate reliance, that we have so frequently encountered in historical writing of the period. Rather unnervingly, they include in their imagistic framework what was in subsequent decades to become the salient metaphor of literary Naturalism, whose task as appointed by Emile Zola was unflinchingly to dissect its contemporary society. Certain other equally suggestive lexical choices, however, are much more akin to the decade in which Tejado was writing: the sense of chaotic disruption implied in the use of derivatives of 'agitar' and 'convulso'; 'excluir', to intimate religious scepticism's marginalisation or banishment of those core values commonly felt to underpin a harmoniously structured cosmological vision where God was firmly in His heaven and all was consequently right with the world; the employment of 'repugnante', reinforcing the feeling that what we are reading is at least partly a defence mechanism prompted by instinctive revulsion and profound disquiet; 'falsificar' and 'desmentir', carrying a strenuous note of moral superiority directed against a system that nightmarishly threatened Tejado's perceived good order, whose own singularity and ultimate authority he and his ideological allies regarded as unquestionable. Enlightenment scepticism prompts, then, a modern historical recasting of the fundamental scriptural accounts of Fall and even of Apocalypse. Especially telling, in its position at the end of this passage, is the reference to Providence. As we saw in the previous chapter, human reliance upon a Providential design or teleological purpose as confirmation of a transcendent and beneficent supernatural order was at the very core of Spanish Romantic historiography. Providence provided a rationale, a degree of accountability, one of those 'ideales' without which nineteenth-century society would appear spiritually destitute. In a separate piece, Tejado again lamented 'esa falta de idealismo tan notable en estos tiempos, que ha dado lugar a que nuestro siglo se califique a sí propio con el dictado de *positivo*' [the lack of idealism that is so evident at the present moment, and which has led our century to designate itself an age of *positivism*].[4] This last term, as elsewhere in Spanish intellectual history of the period, is employed in a markedly negative sense, as a destructive keynote that, in its wider implications, paradoxically denies its own etymology; hence the almost inevitable sarcasm which accompanied its use.[5]

Some further examples of this sort of writing quickly confirm just how typical were both Tejado's uncompromising stance and his chosen framework of imagery. Sabino de Armeda made essentially the same judgement, again in *El Laberinto* and just a few months later, employing the familiar rhetoric of destruction in references to a crumbling social edifice and relentless political strife, and coming to regard scepticism as the only abiding principle of the contemporary age. This itself he viewed as material proof that 'hemos mamado con la leche el materialismo, triste herencia que nos legó el siglo pasado' [with our mothers' milk we have imbibed that materialism that is the sorry legacy bequeathed to us by the century before ours].[6] Meanwhile, in his journal *Revista de España y del Extranjero*, Fermín Gonzalo Morón railed against the tendency towards the kind of egoism, destructive personal ambition, pride, and sham erudition 'que han legado a la Francia el enciclopedismo y su revolución' [bequeathed to France by its *Encyclopédie* and its Revolution]. According to his diagnosis, the state of contemporary France, in thrall to an odious materialism, was symptomatic of Enlightenment disease and provided Spaniards with a salutary lesson in the consequences and future prospects of eighteenth-century philosophy; any society founded on such principles, he insisted, 'no tiene bases sólidas ni estables' [has no sound and enduring foundations]. Gonzalo Morón's prescription for his own nation comes as no surprise: a necessary change of direction, involving a forswearing of 'las doctrinas del siglo pasado' [the doctrines of last century] and the preparation of a 'nueva reorganización social' [new social reorganization]; without such remedies, his generation would bequeath as its legacy to the next a catalogue of immorality, disorder, and upheaval in the wake of the series of calamities, disasters, and misfortunes that had embittered recent experience.[7] Classically structured in its rhetoric, oratorical in its characteristic tripartite expression and roundly alliterative, his words are clearly intended to intensify to the utmost degree this fresh sense of apocalyptic antagonism between catastrophe and reconstruction, between what it might not be entirely inappropriate, given the semantic field and linguistic register of the piece, to label New Jerusalem and Armageddon. Markedly different in tone but remarkably similar in diagnosis and prescription are comments made by Alberto Lista, who asserted that the current generation, formed in the aftermath of the 'errores e ilusiones' [errors and illusions] of the French Revolution and heedless of reliable moral truths, needed to be succeeded by one whose entire formation resided in the religious principle; as he summed up: 'Instituciones morales son las que hacen falta en Europa, no políticas' [What Europe needs are moral institutions, not political ones].[8] Lista's sobriety of expression does not in itself render his message any the less trenchant. Armeda's antidote, meanwhile, was a comparable one, predicated also upon a fundamental distinction between spiritual and material or 'fondo y forma': the canker currently devouring society, as he put it, 'no se cura con remedios empíricas ni con revoluciones y trastornos, se cura moralizándola' [cannot be cured empirically nor by revolution and upheaval, what it needs is a moral cure]. What had to be avoided at all costs, he insisted, was any imitation of the reckless prescriptions of 'los filósofos del siglo pasado' [the philosophers of last century], whose vanity and arrogance had led to their believing themselves to be self-sufficient and all of the values bequeathed to them by the past to be redundant.[9]

Crucially, all of the above passages communicate a profound sense of historicity in their metaphorical insistence upon a legacy transmitted from one generation to the next, stressing a necessary interdependence and interconnection between ages. The organicity of such a vision — bastioned by the continued references to society as a collective body beset by disease and requiring therapeutic treatment — led, nevertheless, to an uncomplicated and reductive practical application of this historical sense in relation to these writers' own immediate past, present and future. It is as such an extreme example of what Hayden White describes as an effort, on the part of nineteenth-century historical thought, to 'search for adequate grounds for belief in progress and optimism in the *full awareness* of the failure of eighteenth-century historical thinkers to provide those grounds'.[10] For the aim was clear: to eradicate the pernicious effects of the Revolution by re-instituting the Christian ideal as civilizing principle. As the secretary of the Ateneo, Fernando Alvarez, put it in a speech reported in the *Revista de Madrid*, modern society must choke off 'las negras semillas de duda, de impiedad, de subversión y de discordia arrojadas por algunos hombres eminentes de la última mitad del siglo XVIII' [the evil seeds of doubt, impiety, subversion, and discord scattered around by certain great men of the second half of the eighteenth century]; it was now indispensable, he continued, to retrace the steps that had been taken along the false path of materialism and to seek shelter once more in religion, the only philosophical truth.[11] Balmes too was of a like mind, affirming that Catholicism represented 'el más fecundo elemento de regeneración que se abriga en la nación española' [the most fertile regenerative element that is cherished by the Spanish nation].[12] Donoso Cortés, characteristically revealing the location of his text within the tradition represented by St Augustine, Bossuet, and Vico, was insistent that modern society had been led in a most destructive direction, 'a la deificación de la materia y a la negación absoluta, radical, de la providencia y de la gracia' [to the deification of matter and the radical, unconditional rejection of Providence and Grace], and that the sorry spectacle of contemporary human insufficiencies — characteristically expressed as 'extravíos' and 'errores' — stemmed directly from a 'negación del sobrenaturalismo católico' [rejection of Catholic metaphysics] that required to be reversed; as he subsequently stated in uncompromising terms, and via the employment of the single most emblematic metaphor encountered in this corpus of writing:

> la acción sobrenatural y constante de Dios sobre la sociedad y sobre el hombre es el anchísimo y seguro fundamento en que se asienta todo el edificio de la doctrina católica, de tal manera que, quitado ese fundamento, todo ese gran edificio en que se mueven anchamente las generaciones humanas viene abajo a igualarse con la tierra.

> [the constant supernatural workings of God upon men and upon society is the immeasurably broad and secure foundation upon which all Catholic doctrine rests, so that if this foundation were to be removed, all of that great edifice within which generations of humankind have freely moved shall come tumbling to the very ground.][13]

As a final example, the young Manuel Cañete, in one of his earliest published pieces, summed up what was necessary in particularly succinct terms:

> El escepticismo, esa gangrena que nos ha legado como un fatal presente la filosofía de la pasada centuria, produce por cada bien muchos males de grandísima consideración; ¿por qué, pues, no hemos de sepultarlo en la tumba misma en que reposa Voltaire y los de su escuela?

> [Scepticism, that gangrenous thing bequeathed to us like some deathly tribute by the philosophy of last century, for every good work it does spawns many and considerable evils; why, then, should we not inter it in the same tomb where Voltaire and all of his followers are laid to rest?] [14]

Yet if the remedy seemed obvious, it was equally clear, as Cañete's evident frustration reveals, that the historical consequences of the Enlightenment could not simply be wished away. There are many texts, several already cited, that bear eloquent testimony to the intense uncertainty and disorientation felt by a large number of intellectuals. As Dalmacio Negro Pavón has noted, a close examination of nineteenth-century Spanish thought quickly reveals the degree of profound consternation felt by successive generations.[15] In a turbulent period of critical yet unpredictable historical events, it

is not entirely surprising that a number of relevant texts evince abrupt and violent changes of mood: typically from the description of a luridly apocalyptic general panorama to the passionately optimistic reporting of a salutary reaction instigated by the devastating lessons of the recent past. Javier de León Bendicho, writing in the *Revista de Madrid* in 1842, provides a particularly clear illustration; his 'oscuro cuadro' [dark picture] represents a society beset by moral disintegration where 'crímenes atroces' [horrible crimes] abound, and where the present generation has been tainted by the woeful legacy of the previous age: as he puts it, 'nutrida en la satánica escuela de la rebelión' [nourished in the satanic school of rebellion]. Again in apparent frustration he confesses himself bewildered that 'los hombres de orden' [men of order] should not appeal directly to religious sentiment in an effort to lend some cohesion to a society that was in danger of fragmenting.[16] The section that immediately follows, however, is in direct contrast to that preceding it; León Bendicho goes on to detect, to his gratification, 'una revolución prodigiosa a favor de las buenas doctrinas' [a prodigious revolution in faour of sound doctrine] vigorously active within Spain. The tone is now entirely different:

> aunque en nuestro país no faltan por desgracia espíritus estacionarios que, apóstoles de la intolerancia del siglo XVIII, pretenden ser la rémora de la especie humana en una época de reorganización social; lo cierto es, que ésta existe apoyada en las purísimas máximas del catolicismo: que las teorías materialistas se desprecian, como que entre los hombres ilustrados aun las ciencias físicas aspiran a catolizarse; y que en vez del odioso lema 'Ecrassez l'infame' con que el Patriarca de Ferney deslustró su genio, todos ven en la religión de J. C. la fuente de los progresos intelectuales del género humano.[17]

> [although our country still houses, regrettably, a few backwoodsmen who continue to preach the eighteenth-century doctrine of intolerance, and who thus hinder humanity at a time of social reorganization, what is certain is that such a reorganization is with us, founded on the purest Catholic teaching, and that materialist ideas are now treated with scorn, for among the wise even the physical sciences are now a part of those Catholic aspirations. For instead of that execrable slogan 'Ecrassez l'infame' with which the Patriarch of Ferney chose to sully his own genius, all now see in the religion of Christ the source of humankind's entire intellectual progress.]

Voltaire, the ubiquitous *bête noire* of Spanish Catholic intellectuals, is once more invoked — his denigratory epithet for the Church included — for the purposes of execration, and the rhetorical transformation is complete: imminent catastrophe gives way to spiritual renewal. Gonzalo Morón, himself not averse to dire warnings of approaching cataclysm, coincided with León Bendicho in an article published in the same year. The nineteenth century, he felt, had seen a renewed dedication to the mission of social reorganization involving ideas opposed to those of the previous age: such a mission was being accomplished, he commented, 'por medio de los estudios históricos, y el movimiento intelectual, que ellos han creado' [by means of historical study, and the intellectual movement it had created]. As he continues, in the most suggestive terms: 'este gran trabajo es el acontecimiento moral más importante de esta época; es la preparación de todos los materiales de reorganización; es la inauguración de una nueva fase para la humanidad; es por último la reparación de las injusticias

pasadas' [this great enterprise constitutes the most significant moral event of our age; it constitutes the preparation of all the necessary resources for reorganization; it constitutes the inauguration of a new phase in human history; and, finally, it constitutes the reparation of past injustice].[18]

Gonzalo Morón in effect draws together a number of the threads closely interwoven in the present study. Firstly, he insists that the historical role of the nineteenth century is one of renewal and reconstruction after the self-inflicted human catastrophe that the Enlightenment had occasioned: this point of view, as we have seen, was that which broadly prevailed during the period in question. Secondly, the man who had spoken so admiringly of Vico in his lectures on Spanish history that were first delivered and published in the previous year has evidently applied the Italian thinker's pattern to recent historical events: the phrase 'reorganización social' — one consistently favoured by Gonzalo Morón — and the accompanying classification of his own age as 'una nueva fase para la humanidad' make for an irresistible linkage between the two. Thirdly, and perhaps most importantly, a sense of the most potent motivating factor behind not just Gonzalo Morón's historical discourse but that of Spanish Romantic historiography in general is provided by the association of 'los estudios históricos' and 'el movimiento intelectual' with 'la reparación de las injusticias pasadas'.[19] If the Enlightenment, as so many Spanish commentators saw it, had falsified history for its own nefarious purposes, then that was a wrong which had now to be righted.

The implications here are legion, and serve to confirm several of the historiographical trends already identified: a fresh rewriting of European history, privileging not the democratic institutions of Greece nor the republicanism of the ancient world, whose ill-fated imitation had proved the ruin of society in the previous century, but rather the noble spiritual ideals of mediaeval times that might once again elevate men's minds and lead modern society in a positive direction; the denial of the Enlightenment assertion that throne and altar had been instruments of obscurantism and tyranny, together with the reinstatement of monarchy and organized religion as the enduring bases upon which Spanish society had always been founded and upon which it should now continue to function; an historical assessment of political institutions that underscored order rather than freedom as the principal guarantor of civilized society and thus disparaged recent aspirations towards democracy as a desirable goal; a providentialist interpretation of the past in which perfectibility was an inalienable gift of Grace and inaccessible to human reason.

All of these judgements are therefore brought to bear upon recent events in Europe, in a calculated attempt to overturn the prescriptions of the French Enlightenment and to neutralize their residual influence upon the contemporary situation. Thus José María Pallarés, for example, writing in the *Revista de Madrid*, identified religious faith as society's most potent developmental principle, claiming that for whole civilizations, just as for individuals, faith could never long be discarded since it represented a civilization's whole moral existence; by faith alone might a civilization regain its energy and strength, and if faith were temporarily extinguished then it would soon rise afresh in human hearts and seek new sources of sustenance. Eighteenth-century 'filosofismo', he insisted, contained no vital solutions for contemporary society; that society must instead benefit from the lessons to be learned from a patient study of past history.[20]

One of the salient historical miscalculations of the *philosophes*, it was commonly felt, had lain in their ill-conceived attempt to re-institute in modern Europe the political and intellectual framework of Classical times. As José Morales Santisteban expressed it, again in the *Revista de Madrid*, eighteenth-century French philosophers heedlessly adopted the perspective of Greek and Roman writers and deduced from them a set of general principles; this became 'un cuerpo completo de doctrina sencillo, deslumbrador, pero completamente inaplicable a las sociedades modernas' [a complete doctrinal system, a simple but dazzling one, one entirely inapplicable to modern societies]. We note once more the choice of 'deslumbrador' to designate the superficial attractions but practical inapplicability of these ideas. If in that same period in which 'las ideas democráticas bullían en las cabezas de los hombres' [democratic ideas were swarming in the minds of men], the author went on, society had rejected them, was it not the very height of extravagance to attempt to reproduce them in the present day, when they had been 'ya analizadas, ya desacreditadas, ya reprobadas por la razón y por la experiencia' [thoroughly analysed, thoroughly discredited, thoroughly condemned on the grounds of both reason and experience]?[21] If democracy, an anachronism in modern times, had been effectively discredited thanks to the baleful consequences it had produced in France, why should it continue to be pursued by Spanish *progresistas* as some kind of transcendent political end? Thus ran the argument. Gonzalo Morón referred to 'la ambición, las pasiones bajas, el deseo de goces materiales, la desaparición de las grandes virtudes y de las almas apasionadas, el egoísmo, y cierta medianía intelectual, producto de la democracia' [personal ambition, base instincts, the desire for worldly pleasures, the extinction of great virtues and exalted souls, egoism, and a certain intellectual mediocrity that democracy inevitably produces] and was as exasperated as much as repelled by continuing efforts to promote radical political change. In the name of democracy, he asserted, it was intended to construct society upon the principle of 'la igualdad más lata y absurda' [the most absurdly sweeping notion of equality], under the auspices of a 'soberanía de número' [sovereignty of the many] to destroy all of those values that had underpinned past ages, and to erect upon the site of this destruction 'el reinado del pueblo en el interés de las clases bajas y proletarias' [the kingdom of the common people in the interests of the lower classes and the proletariat].[22] The familiar rhetoric of destruction is then once more brought into play, as democracy is linked with the collapse of traditional values; more telling, however, given the contemporary ideological terms adopted in this piece, is the transposition of 'pueblo' from its customary status of imaginative subject to the hitherto less frequent but subsequently, within the nineteenth century and after, received status of political subject: from its ultimately reassuring role of historical guarantor for *Volksgeist* and embodiment of *casticismo* to a profoundly disturbing one — as far as the writers considered here were concerned — of focus for ideological radicalism. As José Escobar shrewdly observes, veneration of 'the people' comes to an abrupt end once the term acquires a social reality and once there is a demand for political rights, and gives way to a fear of 'the power of the people'.[23] Gonzalo Morón, we might say, was uncomfortably conscious of what Inman Fox describes as a new socio-political reality in which *el pueblo* came to be a pro-active political subject,[24] a perception that was wildly at odds with the essentially nostalgic conservative

Romantic picture of 'the people' as collective imaginative construct organically transmitting a stable cultural legacy. He nonetheless continued in similarly trenchant mood, professing such a radical perception to be 'injusta, subversiva de todas las ideas de orden y de moral, origen de los desastres y calamidades más terribles, y la única que es capaz de paralizar los progresos europeos, y barbarizar la sociedad' [unjust, subversive of every idea of morality and order, the origin of the most fearful calamities and disasters, and the only way of bringing progress to a halt all over Europe and returning society to barbarism.][25] In fact many of the principal keywords already highlighted as determining the character of this historical discourse are present: democratic ideas are a subversion of order, a recipe for catastrophe, a harbinger of returning barbarism. For Gonzalo Morón's was far from being a solitary voice, however extraordinary the fever pitch of his rhetoric. Philip Silver remarks, for example, of the much more moderate Alberto Lista's response to the 'revolutionary situation' of Spain in the wake of the Peninsular War: 'here what was needed was a political system that avoided the mistakes in France. According to Lista all attempts to render monarchy and democracy compatible must be resisted', while 'any participation by the "pueblo" would only lead to a Republic and to anarchy'.[26]

Having relieved himself of his feelings of outrage, however, Gonzalo Morón strikes a much more confident note in asserting that in Europe democracy was a mere novelty, one that could never really take root without precipitating 'la disolución social' [social dissolution]. What had sustained the continent across history had been religion, monarchy, and certain shared principles of honour and personal integrity; such values were still essential if Europe were to retain foundations that were firm and enduring.[27] Again the ubiquitous terms — social dissolution on one side of the ideological divide contrasted with the solid foundations represented by the other — that have proved the hallmark of the body of writing examined here. One incalculably important difference, nevertheless, is that Gonzalo Morón is not now writing of historical aberrations that he felt had occurred in France between fifty and one hundred years previously; he is directly concerned with the immediate present, specifically with the shaping of contemporary Spanish society. Not surprisingly, such perceptions of the essential components of Spanish culture reveal no grey areas, no difficult shading. As José Ferrer y Subirana expressed it, for example, at the core of Spanish society had always lain two constitutive elements, Throne and Altar, around which was to be found all that was elevated and glorious 'así en los días de su infancia, como en la época de su mayor virilidad y encumbramiento, lo mismo cuando la nación apenas constaba de dos palmos de tierra, como cuando guardaba la corona de dos mundos' [as much in the days of its infancy as in the period of its greatest maturity and splendour, when the nation consisted of a sparse few acres of land as when it wore the twin crowns of the old world and the new]. Given their pre-eminence throughout the infancy and maturity of Spain's distinctive national culture there was no reason, to replace or dilute their authority; just the opposite: true patriots, he affirmed, wish to maintain the power of the throne and defend the unity and vigour of Catholicism.[28] Anything else would be not just unpatriotic but an abdication of responsibility.

Part and parcel of this defence of 'altar y trono' was a reading of nineteenth-century national history accommodated to their reinstatement, one which minimalized the role of *libertad* as historical keynote and underscored instead the instinctively heroic and inspirational qualities of monarchy and religion. The traditionalist discourse as applied to recent Spanish history is therefore committed to an account of the Peninsular War that privileged 'por Dios y por el Rey' [for God and King], subordinating in the process the centrality of the ideal of liberty within the national rising. Balmes, writing in 1842 during the hegemony of Espartero, sets out the case with what he deems a timely reminder; the cry of 'Rey y Religión', he professed, echoed across the entire Peninsula as a general battle cry inextricably linked to 'el noble sentimiento de la independencia de la patria' [that noble desire for the independence of our homeland] in the hearts of virtually all Spaniards.[29]

Balmes was directly refuting Joaquín Francisco Pacheco's view that *religión* and *libertad* had been allied and complementary forces each indispensable to eventual victory. The first volume of Pacheco's *Historia de la regencia de la reina Cristina* had been published in the previous year, and in it we find a balanced appraisal of the events of 1808–14 best encapsulated in the passage to which Balmes was to make such a scathing reply: 'tres fueron las grandes ideas que ajitaron a la nación española en aquella memorable lucha, tres los principios de su resistencia desesperada; el Rey, la Religión, la Libertad' [the great ideas that stirred the Spanish nation to that memorable struggle were three, three things inspired their desperate resistance; King, Religion, Liberty]. The first two Pacheco describes as respected objects of Spaniards' veneration for many centuries, things which had been founding components of their nation state; the third, he asserted, was 'la idea moderna, el principio del siglo presente' [a modern conception, the principle underpinning our own age] that had, inevitably, been born and nurtured in the historical struggle. Without monarchy and religion, he concluded, the rising against the French could never have taken place; without the idea of liberty, Spanish resistance could never have endured and prospered.[30]

It was against this last contention specifically that Balmes now railed. He categorically denied the contribution to the struggle of the idea of liberty as conceived in 1812 — the date is of course significant; instead, he held, it had hampered the patriotic cause, being a source of discord that could well have led to unmitigated disaster.[31] We are reminded, therefore, that one of the historical 'past injustices' as far as conservative commentators were concerned, one of the false interpretations requiring correction, was the view that the Peninsular War had resulted in the triumph of Spanish liberalism. As Balmes continues, in what we might describe as an historical airbrushing:

> Y si en 1808 nada se vio en España de movimiento liberal, si las ideas liberales no asomaban siquiera en nuestro horizonte, si los motivos del alzamiento fueron el Rey y la Religión, ¿cómo puede sostenerse que fuese la libertad una condición necesaria del desarrollo del alzamiento, y ayuda indispensable sin la que las ideas monárquicas y religiosas no hubieran sostenido la guerra en 1812?

> [And if there was no such thing as a liberal movement in Spain in 1808, if such ideas had not even appeared on our horizon, if the inspiring principles of the rising were God and King, how on earth can it be argued that liberty was a prerequisite of the rising's good fortunes and an indispensable source of aid without which monarchy and religion could not have carried on the war in 1812?][32]

We have only to set Balmes's words directly against Pacheco's verdict to appreciate the nature of the dispute; the latter saw it thus:

> El movimiento liberal no hubiera levantado a España en 1808; las ideas monárquicas y relijiosas no hubieran sostenido la guerra en 1812, si otros principios, si otras esperanzas no hubiesen nacido en su ayuda.

> [The liberal movement could not have inspired Spain to rise up in 1808; monarchy and religion could not have carried on the war in 1812 if other principles, other hopes had not come to their aid].[33]

It must be stressed that even a writer as staunchly conservative as Balmes should have found the majority of Pacheco's account entirely unexceptionable. There are early references, for example, to the supplanting of the great tradition of Lope de Vega by an imposed French taste exemplified by the precepts of Boileau (the metaphor Pacheco chooses, perhaps by unconscious association, is 'destronar' [dethrone]). Pacheco then alludes to the appearance within Spain of the works of 'todos los filósofos y publicistas de la escuela revolucionaria' [all those philosophers and public figures of the revolutionary school], including Voltaire, Helvetius, and Rousseau, hardly a glowing reference to the French writers. The spirit of such writings, and of enlightened circles at the Spanish court, he regards as separated by a considerable gulf from the instinctive sentiments of the Spanish people. Adherent to long-standing traditions, 'El español encerraba en una misma fe, proclamaba en una misma fórmula, la confesión de Dios y la adoración del Rey; y ni la filosofía, ni el republicanismo de unos pocos, extranjeros más bien que nacionales por su educación y por sus ideas, eran aun suficientes a conmover la gran masa popular' [For Spaniards, belief in God and love of the King were contained and expressed in a single formula; neither the philosophy nor the republicanism of a few, foreigners rather than Spanish nationals in terms of their education and ideas, were enough to shake the great mass of the people]. As Pacheco continued: 'La verdad es que el contajio extranjero, el contajio liberal y filosófico, se hallaba poco extendido, y no era amenazante todavía' [The fact is that foreign contagion, liberal and philosophical contagion, was not then widespread, and still posed little threat].[34] He even went on to regard the Cadiz liberals as 'empapados en la filosofía francesa del siglo que acababa de pasar' [steeped in the French philosophy of the century that had just come to an end], and viewed the 1812 Constitution as containing 'el germen de lucha y de destrucción' [the seeds of conflict and destruction],[35] sentiments that will acquire larger significance later in the present chapter. What seems most to have offended Balmes, particularly under the radical liberal régime of the Duque de la Victoria ——who had himself replaced or 'destronado' Queen María Cristina as Regent, was the idea that liberalism had become the defining spirit of the contemporary age; hence the apoplectic reaction.

It is hardly surprising that, given the many ideologically motivated internal conflicts occurring in Spain after 1814, historical interpretations of the war against Napoleon should have been the subject of intellectual feuding. Indeed even in recent times we find markedly divergent emphases in accounts of the popular rising against the French. Giovanni Allegra, for example, goes a long way towards recreating both the substance and the ideological implications of Balmes's interpretation. He describes a calculated stratagem effected by the liberals of the Cadiz Parliament and designed to marginalize what he calls the true protagonists of the struggle against France; as a means to their ultimate end, the pursuit of their revolutionary policies, they strived, he states, to associate liberalism with victory and to exclude those traditionalists who had fought for the old Absolutist order.[36] Negro Pavón, meanwhile, in contextualizing with rather greater sobriety the political perspective of 1808, stresses that nationalism in Spain had always been based upon religion rather than state due to the weak configuration of the latter in mediaeval times.[37] As he puts it, religious belief had proved the only effective common tie, especially in the presence of a political adversary that was a threat to the sovereign integrity of the nation as well as to its professed religion.[38] Napoleon himself, he comments, was depicted in Spain, as in other parts of Europe and often by French propaganda, as defender of Jacobinism; the principal cause, he felt, of the perceived incompatibility of liberalism with the Spanish tradition.[39] This last judgement, it must be acknowledged, sits more than comfortably with the evidence I have been considering here. Suggestive also is Negro Pavón's observation that it was the traditionalists who had discovered the transcendent significance of 'el pueblo, cuyo *Volksgeist* es la religión' [the people, whose *Volksgeist* is their religion],[40] especially pertinent in the broader context of the evolution of Romantic ideas in Spain. Javier Herrero, expanding upon his assessment of Capmany's *Centinela contra franceses*, makes essentially the same point; in appeals to nationalist sentiment, he observes, the common denominator was the identification of the Roman Catholic religion with true patriotism, while things French or indeed anything foreign was characterized by impiety or outright atheism. Counterpointing these, the Spanish people was figured as one chosen by God as a bastion against the ravages of heresy.[41] Capmany himself saw the struggle with the forces of Napoleon as a war more holy than had been the Crusades, as he expressed it in the *Centinela*, thus formulating what Herrero calls the essential thrust of future conservative interpretation.[42] How potently influential that interpretation was to become is suggested by so many of the accounts written thirty or forty years later.

An emphasis more commonly found in, roughly speaking, the last thirty years, however, has been that defended by ideologically committed commentators such as Aranguren, Díez del Corral, Abellán, and Martínez Torrón. For Abellán, nothing could be further from reality than any interpretation of the Peninsular War as some reactionary and xenophobic patriotic event; the struggle had been founded, he insisted, upon the country's desire to free itself from its past more so than upon resistance against a foreign aggressor.[43] Martínez Torrón, in his study of the historical origins of Spanish Romanticism, waxes rather more lyrical, affirming that the Peninsular War constituted the bursting forth of a liberal Romantic revolution[44] and reiterating the claim at every subsequent opportunity, always insistent that the conflict had been a totally romantic war, with all the essential features of a revolution.[45] Within this tenaciously argued framework, then, it was a period in which Quintana had been the champion of the first liberal generation of Spanish Romantics, the highpoint of a distinctively Spanish Romanticism whose political fruits would be the revolutionary events of 1808 and after, culminating in the Cadiz Constitution of 1812.[46] Just how polarized are even late twentieth-century accounts of the Peninsular War becomes most startlingly evident when we juxtapose this view with that of Allegra, who roundly asserts that we are not dealing with a war of independence in the sense preferred by liberals but with a war against the kind of revolutionary aspirations and reforms then represented by France.[47] For the Italian critic, the rising against the French at once acquired all the essential characteristics of a religious war.[48]

This is certainly neither the time nor the place extensively to rehearse such familiar — and conflicting — interpretations, although it should be noted how sharply the reading offered by Abellán and Martínez Torrón — like that of Díez del Corral, for whom the 1808 rising had been a rising against the monarchical ideal, or that of Miguel Artola, who insisted that while Spaniards went into war against the French they were at the same time pronouncing, in deeds as well as words, the obsolescence of the Ancien Régime — differs from the perspective adduced by writers of the 1840s. It might be worth reminding ourselves at this stage that the Conde de Toreno, one of the most radical reformers of the Cadiz Parliament and in later years a continued apologist for even its most controversial legislation, describes thus, in his *Historia del levantamiento, guerra y revolución de España*, the patriotic rising of May 1808:

> aquellos nobles y elevados sentimientos, que engendraron en el siglo XVI tantos portentos de valor y tantas y tan inauditas hazañas, estaban adormecidos, pero no apagados en los pechos españoles, y al dulce nombre de patria, a la voz de su rey cautivo, de su religión amenazada, de sus costumbres holladas y escarnecidas, se despertaron ahora con viva y recobrada fuerza.

> [those exalted noble sentiments, which in the sixteenth century had given rise to such portentous gallantry and such unprecedented feats of arms, lay dormant, but not extinguished, in Spanish hearts. At the sweet name of their country, and at the call of their captive king, their endangered religion, and their maligned and downtrodden way of life, those sentiments were roused again with forceful and renewed intensity].[49]

It is very much, I suspect, with this passage in mind, that Leopoldo Augusto de Cueto, unsympathetic towards Toreno's ideological positions, declared the most edifying feature of the latter's famous account to reside in 'la demostración de que no hay poder tan robusto y encumbrado que pueda hollar impunemente las creencias, los hábitos, los intereses y el orgullo de un pueblo' [its demonstration that no power, however strong and self-confident, can tread underfoot with impunity the beliefs, customs, interests and pride of a whole people].[50] Even Blanco White, who felt only revulsion for any kind of blind patriotism or religious fanaticism, averred that resistance to the French had arisen chiefly from 'an inveterate attachment to the religious system whence our present degradation takes source';[51] Blanco felt that 'Religion, or, if you please, superstition, is so intimately blended with the whole system of public and domestic life in Spain' that the entire population fell into the categories of 'bigots' and 'dissemblers'.[52] It was thus that he professed, in the pages of *El Español*, that one of the salient errors of Spanish liberals had been to believe that 'de repente se trastornan las ideas arrraigadas de un país' [a country's most deeply rooted ideas can suddenly be utterly changed].[53]

If it may be felt imprudent to impose a committedly liberal modern reading upon the entirety of those events occurring between 1808 and 1814, then the same should be said of the conjunction between political liberalism and literary Romanticism that such a reading almost inevitably projects and contains. Both Abellán and Martínez Torrón eventually find it necessary to counterpoint their association of *romántico* with *liberal* with a recognition of the collective weight of the traditionalist interpretation prevalent during a great part of the nineteenth century. Although he privileges the perspective of the Cadiz liberals, Abellán acknowledges that alongside them one must place the traditionalists, for whom the people had risen in favour of *casticismo* and the Absolutist system and against every form of foreign interference; there was, he observes, a bit of everything, especially of this last, and only by recognizing such can we understand the nineteenth-century manifestation of an enduring conflict between the 'Two Spains'.[54] Martínez Torrón, in similar fashion — and while pointedly clinging to the dictum 'imposible disociar liberalismo y romanticismo' [it is impossible to dissociate liberalism and Romanticism][55] that he feels to be exemplified by what he calls 'authentic' Romanticism rather than by 'la espúrea rama reaccionaria de sus orígenes' [the spurious reactionary version found in its origins],[56] concedes that what followed was the triumph of a *moderado* version represented by Martínez de la Rosa and, later still, that of a traditionalist one headed by Zorrilla, phenomena which he feels to have been in accordance with the ideological tendencies of their respective moment.[57] There is, it goes without saying, a degree of self-contradiction here, given that Martínez Torrón's thesis is precisely that Spanish Romanticism's historical origins lay in radical or even revolutionary liberalism rather than in political conservatism; the problem, I would contend, resides in his reductive definition of an uniquely 'authentic' Romanticism as a generalized worldview commensurate with revolutionary political impulses that would find their expression in liberal thought, a definition that wilfully excludes Spanish Romanticism's majority intellectual expression.

Conversely, Allegra, it should be noted, disparages what he calls Hugo's simplistic but nonetheless influential equivalence of *le romantisme* with *le libéralisme*,[58] one which, historically speaking and in the nineteenth century at least, did not enjoy good fortune in Spain. His account reveals instead a sympathetic practical employment of that understanding of 'Romantic' that came to be predominant in the Spain of the period; in comments likewise applicable to the historical moment of the Peninsular War, he affirms the presence of a Romantic bedrock immune to Enlightenment cynicism towards everything sacred and reinforced by a militant religious zeal.[59] Allegra's scrutiny of the evidence is conducted, in effect, from a fundamentally Schlegelian standpoint, with all of that standpoint's traditionalist connotations; it is as committed an account, in ideological terms, as those provided by Abellán and Martínez Torrón, although it betrays a very different affiliation. The kind of 'historical sense' projected by Allegra, however, does at least avoid the sort of anachronistic labelling placed upon events by an incautious application of historically incongruous terminology. A crucial case in point is his reminder to the modern reader that, at the beginning of the nineteenth century, Spain was not a nation in the modern sense of the term but a collectivity unified principally by a sense of belonging to a single faith.[60] This understanding of 'pueblo' — as a collective imaginative subject rather than as a proletariat containing an element of political solidarity — is much more consonant with the thought-patterns of the age and much more calculated to provide us with a genuine apprehension of the processes of intellectual history.

What is beyond dispute, at least, is that Romantic commentators of the 1840s as much as modern readers — and, as will become more fully apparent in the following chapter, men like Balmes and Gonzalo Morón subscribed wholeheartedly to many Romantic prescriptions in broad areas of aesthetics, historical writing, and religious ideas — were offered two essentially divergent interpretations of the events of 1808– 14: that bequeathed to them by reactionaries like Fray Diego de Cádiz, Vélez, and Hervás y Panduro; and, on the other hand, the much more radical and fundamentally revolutionary assessments of men such as Toreno, Quintana, and Blanco White. As Allegra states, these opposed interpretations represented the cohering, in early nineteenth-century Spain, of two opposing conceptions of life and the world and of human history, conflicting visions that were destined to breed within Spain a sharper confrontation on all levels than virtually anywhere else in Europe.[61] Rarely, in effect, do we find a balanced and level-headed scrutiny of the sort provided by Francisco Martínez de la Rosa, renowned for his attachment to a *via media*. In his essay 'La revolución actual de España', written in the course of the conflict itself and transparently intended as a justification of the Cadiz Parliament and the moderation of many of its counsels, Martínez de la Rosa, like Quintana, regarded the rising as a necessary and desirable aspiration to civil and political freedom on the part of a populace that had been effectively enslaved for the previous three hundred years. At the same time, nonetheless, he drew attention to Spanish society in its lower echelons as 'apegada a los antiguos usos' [attached to old ways] and 'amante de sus reyes y de la religión santa de sus padres' [devoted to its kings and queens and to the holy religion of its forebears].[62]

This kind of temperate analysis was, needless to say, the exception rather than the rule. Abellán cites, on the liberal side of the divide, the letters written by Quintana to Lord Holland in 1852, very late in his life but entirely characteristic of their author's unswerving political commitment, and reproduces the following eloquent passage in which Quintana vehemently rejects the notion that an instinctive attachment to monarchy and religion had been the exclusive or primary motivation behind Spanish resistance to Napoleon:

> el azote funesto que este desdichado país tenía sobre sí le enseñaba en lecciones de dolor y de sangre su deber para lo futuro. Así es que la idea de reformar nuestras instituciones políticas y civiles no fue ni podía ser efecto del acaloramiento de unas pocas cabezas exaltadas, ni tampoco conspiración criminal de un partido de facciosos.

> [the death-dealing scourge that this wretched country brought upon itself had taught it, in bloody and painful lessons, what were its future obligations. Consequently, the idea of reforming our civil and political institutions did not nor ever could have come from the frenzied actions of a few hotheads, nor else from the criminal conspiracy of a particular seditious party.][63]

Well documented also are the intimate difficulties posed by the hostilities for José María Blanco y Crespo, who fervently espoused *afrancesado* ideals of liberty, progress, and reform, but could not support their being imposed upon his countrymen by force of arms. Although dedicated to the patriotic struggle, Blanco, as Abellán comments, had clearly identified the war with revolution:[64] in the *Letters from Spain*, for example,

Blanco would praise in the inhabitants of Seville 'the wonderful effort by which, in spite of their passive habit of submission, they had ventured to dare both the authority of their rulers, and the approaching bayonets of the French'.[65]

A generation later, however, it was to be the traditionalist account that prevailed. Quintana's concluding words perhaps intimate this in conveying an inevitable degree of frustration or even resentment, while we might also cite the introductory section of Miguel Agustín Príncipe's 1844 history *Guerra de la Independencia*: after making reference to 'el magnífico cuadro de nuestra santa insurrección' [the magnificent canvas of our sacred rebellion], the author asks the question: '¿Por qué la voz de libertad política, lanzada casi al mismo tiempo que el grito de independencia nacional, halló menos eco que ésta en los corazones de algunos?' [Why should the call of political freedom, made at almost exactly the same time as the call of national independence, have found so much weaker an echo in the hearts of some?][66] Instrumental in this respect, we are tempted to conclude, had been the kind of broad-brush vilification that has been a feature of the material considered here. As Allegra points out, the very term *afrancesado* came to mean not so much a friend of France and a political collaborator as a friend of that country's whole Enlightenment culture, and consequently implied an advocate of the *Encyclopédie* and a supporter of violent revolution; Vélez, like many others, had warned of an attempt to continue the *disolvente* practical tendencies of the French in the pronouncements of the Cadiz Parliament, making many liberal policies necessarily unpopular in the prevailing circumstances of French occupation.[67] Abellán, who concurs in this view albeit with what is readily perceptible as a different ideological emphasis, observes that the term *afrancesado* had been insidiously manipulated; the followers of Absolutism had distorted its meaning, lumping together *doceañistas* and *josefinos* (adherents of Napoleon's brother Joseph as king of Spain) as equally inspired by French revolutionary doctrine.[68] The same fundamental connection was to resurface with similar intentions later in the century; deserving of notice in this context is the link as restated by Balmes between the motivations of Spanish liberals and the reforming ideals of the Enlightenment, ideals that the Catholic historiographical discourse so passionately decried. The spirit of liberty was not dangerous, argued Balmes, solely in that it had threatened discord among Spanish patriots; it laboured under a further misfortune: namely, that many of its supporters professed their unqualified acclamation of 'los principios religiosos y sociales de la escuela filosófica del siglo décimoctavo' [the religious and social principles of the eighteenth-century philosophical movement].[69]

Here we are on far less contentious ground. Aranguren, for example, has observed that independence and revolution were mutually sustaining concepts lived and professed in conjunction by the Cadiz liberals,[70] while Heredia Soriano would detect in the beginnings of Spanish liberalism influences of diverse origin but having in common the characteristic features of Enlightenment thought.[71] As Martínez Torrón summarizes, Spanish liberalism had striven, since the war against the French, to effect a complete overhaul of Spain based upon the revolutionary principle of the sovereignty of the people.[72] Ideological opponents of the *doceañistas* certainly saw it that way: for Fray Diego de Cádiz, the Spanish liberals of 1808 were the direct heirs of the French revolutionaries, and Rafael de Vélez was to include the radicals of the Cadiz Parliament in the typically satanic conspiracy detailed in his *Preservativo contra la irreligión*.[73] In the same way, Miguel de Lardizábal, one of the five members of the Council of Regency during the Peninsular War, concluded that anti-monarchist agitation came principally from followers of the *philosophes* in the Cadiz Parliament,[74] while the president of that Council, Pedro Quevedo y Quintana, would liken the Cortes de Cádiz to the revolutionary Assembly constituted in France some twenty years earlier.[75] It is worth recalling also that the royal decree of July 1814 that revoked the earlier abolition of the Spanish Inquisition by the Cadiz Parliament, intended to 'remediar el mal que habían hecho a la religión católica las tropas extranjeras heterodoxas' [remedy the evil wrought upon the Catholic religion by heretical foreign troops], held that the '*Cortes generales extraordinarias*' celebrated in the besieged city had followed one of the principal measures of Bonaparte himself; the assembly had put an end to the powers of the Holy Office, continued the document, 'pretextando su incompatibilidad con la Constitución de Cádiz' [using as a pretext its alleged incompatibility with the Cadiz Constitution].[76]

We are dealing with, in Heredia Soriano's words, a common front that was 'político-filosófico-religioso' and whose aim was to prevent the successful introduction into Spain of any revolutionary philosophy.[77] It was an easy step, as Herrero puts it, from hatred of France to hatred of everything French; the tendency was thus to identify Enlightenment ideas and democratic liberalism with all that was French, to label the Spanish liberals as enemy agents, as traitors to their country and in the pay of Napoleon, and to view the newly-designated liberals of Cadiz as the personification of those appalling heresies that were the Enlightenment and *afrancesado* thought.[78] Menéndez Pelayo, after all, in referring to the conflict later in the century, was bluntly to state that the Peninsular War, as well as a struggle for Spanish independence, had been nothing less than a 'guerra de religión contra las ideas del siglo XVIII difundidas por las legiones napoleónicas' [religious war against those eighteenth-century ideas disseminated by the Napoleonic forces]; the great cultural historian crushingly labelled Argüelles and Toreno 'los enciclopedistas a la moda' [the *Encyclopédie*'s men of fashion].[79] Revuelta González starkly reminds us of the polarizing effects of the war with France, seen by guerrilla priests as a critical choice between faith and revolutionary liberty, between Christ and the Constitution.[80] He further cites José Vidal's *Origen de los errores revolucionarios de Europa y su remedio*, published posthumously in 1827 and which articulates a Manichaean distinction between hostile camps that we can label 'goodies' (royalists) and 'baddies' (constitutionalists and atheists).[81]

What modern analyses do not necessarily convey, however, whatever their own possible ideological leanings, is precisely the sense of immediacy contained in the much earlier interpretations that I am examining here. When Balmes sought to drive home his point in the pages of the Madrid journal *El Pensamiento de la Nación*, specifying this time the motivation and aims of the constitutionalist liberal rising headed by General Riego in 1820, the urgency of his own self-appointed task in the face of a perceived heinous threat is readily evident: 'A impulsos del ardor revolucionario renació el espíritu propagandista de la escuela enciclopédica, y las ideas contrarias a la Religión de los españoles se esparcieron por todos los puntos del reino' [At the urging of revolutionary passion the propagandist spirit of the *Encyclopédie* came back to life, and ideas contrary to the religion of Spaniards were spread all over our kingdom].[82] This, for me, is the heart of the matter. As I suggested earlier, fulminating attacks against Enlightenment conspiracy and revolutionary bloodbath were not fuelled exclusively by righteous anger. A much more potent catalyst was the feeling that the same kind of dangerous radicalism had been imported into Spain, had flourished among the liberal patriots during the recent war against France — signally in the Cadiz Parliament and specifically in the Constitution of 1812–, and had triumphed in the shape of the Espartero régime. As far as traditionalists were concerned, the years since the death of Ferdinand VII had seen the same kind of attacks against organized religion, the same democratic ferment, the same displacement of monarchy as principle of government that had brought France to chaos and barbarism.[83] Carlos Seco Serrano powerfully elucidates just how such a view of things would have crystallized in conservative minds; the liberal administrations of Toreno and Mendizábal, he comments, seemed to traditionalists to embody the final push in the offensive being mounted by revolutionary atheism.[84] The administration in power since 1840 now portended the same direct route to catastrophe in nineteenth-century Spain; in that year, Seco Serrano observes, revolution took to the streets in the form of premeditated rioting orchestrated by the *progresistas*, with the result that the elected government found itself at the mercy of the revolutionary Madrid Junta.[85]

At the time, Gonzalo Morón had made this connection even more forcefully than Balmes. While his overview of the Peninsular War was essentially the same, borne out by his verdict that 'la independencia, la monarquía y la religión fueron los resortes prodigiosos que movieron instintivamente a nuestro pueblo a una de las más desesperadas y heroicas luchas, de que nos hacen memoria los anales del mundo' [national independence, monarchy, and religion prodigiously inspired in our people an instinctive reaction, moving them to one of the most desperate and heroic struggles chronicled in the history of the world],[86] he opted for a still closer association between events occurring in France and Spain. If the former country had experienced an historical decline from the century of the Sun King to the horrors and convulsions of the Revolution, the latter had fallen from past glories to a state of things where, in the hands of a 'revolución raquítica' [ramshackle revolution] for which there was neither precedent nor historical justification other than in the lack of knowledge and foresight on the part of a few weak-willed men, it had sunk into a nadir of chaos and structural instability.[87] This, we immediately note, is precisely the depiction of events so fiercely resented by Quintana.

Gonzalo Morón, as much as Balmes, was actuated by the conviction that monarchy and religion were an inalienable part of national culture, and that democratic or republican principles were as out of place in 1840s Spain as they had been in eighteenth-century France. The latter himself sounded this note of profound conviction in the article already cited, stressing that the majority of Spaniards remained attached to ideas, customs, and preferences that were their heritage of many centuries; as a consequence, he went on, 'consérvase adicta a la religión; y no han bastado a apartarla de ella todos los esfuerzos de la impiedad, y todos los sacudimientos que la han trabajado por espacio de 30 años' [they remain devoted to their religion, and all the impious efforts, all the commotions that have plagued them for the last thrity years, have been unable to separate them from it].[88] Gonzalo Morón, meanwhile, in a piece of high *casticista* rhetoric, appealed to legislators to refrain from adulterating the principles held dear by the Spanish people: respect religion and monarchy, awaken the national pride and integrity that is at the core of every Spaniard, he proclaimed.[89] If this degree of respect were not forthcoming, then he forecasted devastation on a grand scale, accusing radicals of being ignorant both of the true state of their own country and of the means that would prove requisite for the triumph of their doctrine; if they were intent, he continued, upon destroying not just the outward form of institutions but also the belief-system that underpinned them, if they remained in thrall to 'ideas que no son Españolas' [ideas that are not Spanish], then their very memory would be accursed, their deeds anathema to generations yet to be born. In truly apocalyptic terms, he envisaged that after bloodshed and discord, after illusory promises of progress and reform, they would merely have nurtured religious scepticism, destroyed popular faith, 'aniquilado la nacionalidad española' [utterly destroyed Spanish nationhood], and demeaned all of those noble moral qualities that had brought the nation admiration and renown across the course of history.[90]

What we see here once more is the clearest example of historical transference; Gonzalo Morón has taken the emblematic nucleus of Catholic accounts of eighteenth-century French history — from the proposals of the *philosophes* right through to the Revolution and the Terror — and transposed them onto his own nightmare predictions of the consequences of unbridled radicalism in 1840s Spain. The fraudulent promises of progress and improvement, the arbitrary destruction of society's foundations, the debilitating erosion of faith, and the inevitable headlong descent into a maelstrom of slaughter, were all set to be repeated as one group of delirious subversives — the supporters of Espartero — imitated the historical ravings and demented actions of another — the *philosophes* — with the same horrible consequences. All of the violent rhetoric, all of the apoplectic accusations, indeed all of the favourite metaphors of bloodshed and destruction are set rampaging forward, with characteristically evangelical zeal, against the *progresistas*. For Gonzalo Morón regarded the unreconstructed radicals of the Cadiz Parliament, the men behind the 1812 Constitution, as primarily responsible for inflaming and destabilizing Spanish politics a whole generation later; in a period which promised regeneration, he declared, 'siguen con imperturbable serenidad, salvo honrosas excepciones, en sus errores y extravíos tan fecundos en males, y dirigen y encienden las pasiones políticas' [with a few honourable exceptions they carry on, imperturbable in their serenity, set upon those errors and misconceptions of theirs that are so prolifically evil, and they inflame and manipulate political passions].[91]

Contrary to what we are often led to believe, trenchant criticism of the Cadiz Constitution and of those who continued to espouse it as a workable solution to Spain's continuing ills was not confined to ultramontane conservatives. As Negro Pavón has wisely noted in commenting on Hermosilla's three-volume *Historia del jacobinismo* of 1823, this prominent *afrancesado* emerges as a critic of the Cadiz charter; now, however, it was the Jacobins of the 1820–23 constitutional parliament who were the object of his attack.[92] Of Martínez de la Rosa the same modern critic observes that his utopian tendencies were increasingly mitigated by contact with Romantic traditionalism, to the extent that in elaborating the Estatuto Real, the political charter of 1834, he had renounced the Constitution of 1812 as dangerous as well as impracticable.[93] Martínez de la Rosa in fact commented of the 1812 Constitution in his *Bosquejo histórico de la política de España* that it was 'punto menos que imposible regir con aquel código una antigua y vasta monarquía' [hardly less than impossible to govern a vast and ancient monarchy by means of that charter].[94] The *moderados* in general viewed the 1812 Constitution as the product of a particular and distinctive historical moment, exaggerated in its provisions and unsuited to the requirements of the contemporary situation, and considered the *progresistas* and their aspirations to be out of step with circumstances. As Leopoldo Augusto de Cueto saw it in qualifying his praise of Toreno's historical account:

> con la experiencia de los trastornos y convulsiones originadas por la aplicación de tales doctrinas, convenía que el historiador hubiese dicho que a la par con el espíritu reformista, que iba tomando cuerpo y enseñoreándose de la situación, nacían también males de curación larga y difícil: la discordia, la insubordinación social, la indiferencia religiosa.

> [in light of the commotions and upheavals experienced as a result of the application of such doctrines, a historian might profitably have commented that, alongside the reformist spirit that gradually took shape and acquired command of the situation, so also there developed ills that even with time would be difficult to cure: civil strife, social insubordination, religious indifference.][95]

Nicomedes-Pastor Díaz summed up this widely held opinion in surveying the political scene in 1841. Across Europe, he commented, the new century had opted for monarchy as first principle of order and freedom and had once again sought guidance and direction in religious ideals; yet Spain had still to suffer the delusions of 'los hombres de 1812, anacronismos vivos del siglo, estacionarios en la tendencia y en la marcha de su espíritu, enemigos del poder, enemigos del trono, enemigos de la religión y enemigos de todas las instituciones que dan fuerza, enlace y cohesión al cuerpo político y social' [the men of 1812, the walking anachronisms of our age, their sterility of spirit present in both inclination and decision, enemies of authority, enemies of the throne, enemies of religion, and enemies of all those institutions that lend energy, internal strength and cohesion to our society and body politic].[96] A new and more moderate generation, he claimed, had now raised a solemn and vigorous protest against what he designated 'rancias preocupaciones revolucionarias' [outdated revolutionary concerns], 'teorías trastornadoras' [head-turning theories], 'exageraciones democráticas' [democratic whimsies], 'ojeriza antimonárquica' [anti-monarchical obsessions], and, finally, 'el fanatismo irreligioso de nuestros decrépitos jacobinos' [the fanatical irreligion of our decrepit Jacobins].[97] As just one more example, the widely respected figure of Andrés Borrego, as Negro Pavón comments, conceived of *doceañismo* as a form of Jacobinism; he cites Borrego's own remarks that the prevalent tenets of the Cadiz Parliament, the principles that had animated Spanish liberalism in 1812, were of a militant revolutionary order, while the sense of *desengaño* subsequently felt in Europe generally and in Spain in particular had been as universal as it had been complete.[98] We necessarily conclude, therefore, that when León Bendicho, in an article cited much earlier in this chapter, savagely attacked an undesignated group of 'espíritus estacionarios' that he labelled unreconstructed 'apóstoles de la intolerancia del siglo XVIII' [apostles of eighteenth-century intolerance], he could only have been referring to those surviving unrepentant *doceañistas*.[99]

Whether the linkage was instinctive, a process of natural association, or — as so often seems the case — calculated, a crudely effective political weapon preying upon fear and trepidation, one thing seems in little doubt: present-day Spanish radicals, as much as the *doceañistas*, were being tarred with the same brush that had painted so black the thoughts and actions of the French Enlightenment. In tarnishing the historical reputation of the *philosophes*, Catholic commentators were sullying also the pretensions of the *progresistas* towards institutional reform and democratization. After the fall of Espartero in 1843, it was of course considerably easier to write out of contemporary history the 'achievements' of the *progresista* faction. Antonio Ferrer del Río, saluting the declaration of Queen Isabella's coming of age, denied that political radicalism had been one of the grand causes inspiring the *cristinos* in the Carlist War. Don Carlos, he asserted, had been defeated by 'la Providencia y la fortuna' [Providence and fortune].[100] Radicalism, a pernicious aberration, had not reared its ugly head, insisted Ferrer del Río, until the recent war had ended: the throne of Isabella II had emerged unscathed from civil war; it had not hitherto been threatened by 'el oleaje revolucionario, que en su tremendo empuje había arrollado instituciones antiguas y destruido clases poderosas' [the revolutionary tide which, in its tremendous swell had demolished alike ancient institutions and powerful social classes]. The honourable struggle against the usurper had been undertaken in the name of the just cause, under the banner of the legitimate monarch, a cause dear to the hearts of Spaniards because it represented their intimate tradition; as Ferrer del Río saw it, the Spanish people's proverbial veneration of their ruler had weighed more heavily in the balance than the unhinged ideas and unrestrained raw passions of the radicals.[101] Radical liberalism is yet again viewed as an expression of man's baser instincts, like Enlightenment philosophy — condemned in exactly the same terms — a collapse of desirable moral responsibility and restraint.

So much of the writing with which I have been dealing here, perhaps more specifically its intimacies of outlook or, if we are semiologically minded, what we might call its essential structures, may be considered the manifestation, in intel-lectual terms, of what came to be the salient overtly ideological characteristics of the 'década moderada' whose course was plotted by General Narváez. As Abellán asserts, the dominant thrust of the period was its aspiration towards unification and centralization;[102] while José María Jover remarks that, as one of its priorities, Spanish *moderantismo* consolidated and indeed regarded as its sacred goal the successful construction of a centralized and unitary Spanish state.[103] Even more recently, Inman Fox has emphasized the commitment of the *moderados* to a uniform and rigorously centralized Spain.[104] As Martínez de la Rosa put it much nearer the time, the nation could breathe more easily, weary of political instability and desirous of peace, and was well disposed to trust in better fortunes when once had been restored 'los principios conservadores, más propios para hermanar la libertad y el orden en una vasta monarquía' [those conservative principles better equipped to reconcile freedom and order in a vast monarchy].[105] The premise may be pointedly extended into areas other than that of politics: of relevance in the present context is Seco Serrano's comment that Narváez opted for consensus solutions founded upon a traditionalist conception of historical continuity,[106] while equally pertinent is Antonio Heredia Soriano's observation that, in a campaign especially potent from 1844 due to its close association with established centres of power, traditionalists sought by every means at their disposal, to countervail the revolutionary enterprise of Spanish liberalism, seeking instead the restoration of an integratory Catholic vision of life, knowledge, and experience.[107] Some of the salient features of the historical writing considered here even evidence parallels with the premises of the authoritarian grouping led by the Marqués de Viluma; one of the faction's spokesmen, Santiago Tejada, deplored the lamentable situation, as he put it, of those peoples in whose countries, like Spain, ancient institutions had been wantonly destroyed, in a passion, by false revolutionary theories recklessly applied, and railed against the inspiration, within nineteenth-century constitutional change, of 'principios anárquicos y disolventes' [principles of anarchy and dissolution].[108] Evident also should be the link with the prescriptions of Spanish neo-Catholicism as headed, more than a decade later, by Cándido Nocedal; one of the defining elements of Nocedal's ideology was, as Begoña Urigüen González observes, the forceful connection between liberalism and revolution: it was followers of Donoso Cortés, among whom might be numbered Nocedal himself, who would reaffirm the causal link between liberalism and social revolution.[109]

Meanwhile, if we are minded to carry the same thread of discussion further into the nineteenth century, then the position of Menéndez Pelayo in his *Historia de los heterodoxos españoles* can be seen as one further stage in an increasingly developmental sequence. After all, Don Marcelino himself trenchantly categorized the eighteenth century as 'el más perverso y amotinado contra Dios que hay en la historia' [the most perverse and ungodly age in the chronicles of history].[110] Indeed, like many of his predecessors writing in the 1840s, Menéndez Pelayo communicates to his reader a potent sense of ideological commitment to the reparation of past injustice. Referring to the works of the religious reactionaries active at the turn of the century, he was adamant that 'La resistencia española contra el enciclopedismo y la filosofía del siglo XVIII debe escribirse largamente' [Spanish resistance against the *Encyclopédie* and eighteenth-century philosophy merits extensive treatment], however unlikely their vindication at an historical moment ideologically hostile to their achievement.[111] Don Marcelino saw it as a moment when, instead, 'La revolución triunfante ha divinizado a sus ídolos y enaltecido a cuantos le prepararon fácil camino' [The revolution has created its own idols and raised on high all those who smoothed its path]. His subsequent observations, as well as being ideologically revealing in themselves, provide the modern reader with an acute sense of the processes of continuity operative within nineteenth-century conservative thought:

> Quien busque ciencia seria en la España del siglo XVIII, tiene que buscarla en esos frailes ramplones y olvidados. Más vigor de pensamiento, más clara comprensión de los problemas sociales, más lógica amartilladora e irresistible hay en cualquiera de las cartas del Filósofo Rancio, [...] que en todas las discusiones de las Constituyentes de Cádiz, o en los raquíticos tratados de ideología y derecho público [...] con que nutrió su espíritu la primera generación revolucionaria española.[112]

[Anyone seeking real erudition in eighteenth-century Spain should look for it in the forgotten figures of these unsophisticated monks. In the letters of the *Filósofo Rancio* there is a greater intellectual vigour, a clearer understanding of social problems, a weightier and more irresistible logic than in all the proceedings of the Cadiz Parliament and all the ramshackle treatises of ideology and common law that were to nourish the spirits of the first generation of Spanish revolutionaries.]

What these words make transparently clear, in the light of the extensive body of evidence assessed here, is a direct line of descent from the reactionaries praised by Menéndez Pelayo on through the traditionalist opponents of the Cadiz radicals to the work of the majority of historians writing in the Romantic period and eventually to the intellectual positions of Don Marcelino himself. José María Jover has recently illustrated the great cultural historian's formulation, with reference to the events surrounding the creation and precarious existence of the First Spanish Republic in 1873, of a dialectical vision of the history of Spain in which the prevalent antagonisms are those between federal and centripetal government, between 'revolución' and 'catolicismo'. Citing the 1882 epilogue to the final volume of the *Historia de los heterodoxos españoles*, Jover underlines the enduring influence of Menéndez Pelayo's appraisal of the First Republic, an imagistic pattern that he designates the crystallization of a myth and that effectively constitutes one of the two essential polarities of outlook upon which his entire philosophy of Spanish history was based. Especially noteworthy in the present context is the degree of consonance with the earlier conservative Romantic perception of revolutionary chaos: Don Marcelino refers to 'tiempos de desolación apocalíptica' [times of apocalyptic desolation], to the 'anárquica independencia' [anarchical independence] of some regions, to battles in the streets, to the drunken pillaging committed by an army that 'profanaba los templos con horribles orgías' [profaned churches in horrible orgies]; a time when, he states, 'la Iglesia española proseguía su calvario' [the Spanish Church trod its path to Calvary].[113] There are obvious parallels, then, with the dominant Romantic view of the excesses of the French Revolution, signally in terms of framing, imagery, and metaphor.

Nor, as we might be led to believe, was the political and broader ideological climate consistently inimical to the earlier reactionaries and their trenchantly conservative perspective on historical events. Balmes, writing in 1844 shortly after the establishment of the new régime under Narváez, could afford to sound much more optimistic than two years previously. He credited with the improved state of affairs then as he saw it brightening the horizon, not government but the natural homogeneity of a God-fearing nation together with the beneficent influence of 'el espíritu dominante en Europa, que ya se avergüenza de profesar las doctrinas de los filósofos del siglo pasado' [the prevalent mood in Europe, which is now ashamed of having professed the doctrines of last century's philosophers].[114] As Heredia Soriano succinctly observes, the traditionalist grouping of which Balmes formed an important part was to make an essential contribution to Spanish intellectual life of the 'década moderada' and one intimately attuned to the prevailing historical current; after 1844 especially, he notes, when the prevailing socio-political climate was in his favour, Balmes undertook the significant task of cultural reorientation and reorganization along strictly Catholic lines, attaining in the process a series of intellectual, pedagogoical and literary heights that had remained long unconquered by Spanish traditionalist thought.[115] Iris Zavala, meanwhile, comments that, in the wake of the Napoleonic invasion, there existed not the remotest possibility that the propositions of the French *philosophes* be employed in the construction of a new Spanish national identity to underpin the emerging bourgeois state, for they could not be countenanced without a thoroughgoing apprehension of the revolutionary excesses they had been felt directly to prompt.[116]

The expression of fear and concern naturally did not disappear as if by magic with the changed balance of political power, which after all could not be relied upon to last. Dire warnings against materialism and religious scepticism, what Fernán Caballero labelled the 'máximas impías y disolventes' [teachings of impiety and dissolution] of the *philosophes*,[117] continued to be voiced, but it is fair to say that the emphasis during the 'década moderada' was firmly on renewal. Salvador Costanzo, writing in the *Semanario Pintoresco Español* in 1844, was able to claim in optimistic mood that the tendency to incredulity that had possessed itself of the French philosophers and spread like a contagion across Europe had yielded to 'el cristianismo con toda su pureza y con la importancia de las sublimes verdades que inculca' [Christianity in all of its purity and in all of the weight of the sublime truths that it teaches], which now — as evidence, it would seem, of reparation, and as a natural form of restoration — shone out bright like the sun after a passing storm. This he felt to be true in all forms of intellectual endeavour, delighting in the proclamation that

> Un profundo convencimiento de estas doctrinas, contrarias en verdad a las de la escuela materialista del pasado siglo, ha presidido después en los escritos de nuestros filósofos contemporáneos, e igualmente inspiró a los poetas de nuestra edad, los cuales nunca perdieron de vista en sus cantos las augustas verdades de una religión a la cual han acudido para formar los argumentos de sus composiciones acabando así de desterrar los restos de la mitología que había estado tan en voga entre los poetas del siglo pasado.[118]

> [A profound conviction of the truth of this doctrine, truly contrary to that of the materialist school of last century, has since been prevalent in the writings of our current philosophers, and has likewise inspired the poets of our own time, who never did lose sight of the august truths of a religion to which they have now come in search of material for their work, finally consummating the banishment of the remnants of mythology that had been so in vogue among poets of the previous century.]

The linkage established in these words is important. Costanzo was just one of many writers demonstrating a fundamental connection between Romantic historiography and national literary history. Those who had, as Philip Silver puts it, refurbished Spain's dominant historithemes, were expounding a set of would-be national values that went beyond the socio-political;[119] they were equally to effect the selection and formulation of a new national literary canon and an overview of Spanish literary history strikingly different from that which had obtained before the appearance on the scene of men like Böhl von Faber and Agustín Durán.[120] Thus Fernando Garrido, writing in 1868, was to see the historical origins of Spanish neo-Catholicism as cohering in the accommodation, from 1843, of a European conservative Romanticism with a dominant political *moderantismo*.[121] For Sánchez Llama, the conjunction is emblematizd by Donoso Cortés in the address marking his admission to the Real

Academia Española in 1848, a speech that marks the clearest impact of Schlegelian Romantic historicism and of neo-Catholicism in Spain's cultural institutions.[122] Just as, then, the spiritual revival of the nineteenth century was commonly considered an effectual antidote to the irreligion of the eighteenth, returning to society its traditional certainties, so Romanticism was widely regarded as a constructive and invigorating transformation in aesthetics, reinstating the valuable *casticista* ideals which neo-Classicism had spurned or neglected. As we shall see in the next chapter, literary history as conceived by the Romantic mind provides further evidence of the broad philosophical intentions underlying the Spanish historiographical discourse.

Notes to Chapter 5

1. *El Reflejo* (1843), p. 146.
2. *Lectures on the History of Literature*, trans. by Lockhart, II, 173.
3. 'Poesía popular', *El Laberinto*, 2 (1845), 134–36 (p. 134).
4. *El Laberinto*, 2, 214.
5. See my *Spanish Romantic Literary Theory and Criticism*, pp. 143–44.
6. In this brief piece, entitled 'Breves reflexiones sobre el socialismo', Armeda wrote:

    La sociedad actual está herida de muerte; la sociedad actual es un edificio que se arruina, porque arruinados yacen sus cimientos: ese violento desasosiego, esas fuertes sacudidas que a cada paso atruenan nuestros oídos, esa encarnizada lucha de encontrados principios y encontradas ideas que combaten entre sí por adquirirse el dominio de una sociedad que carece de creencias, y cuyo único principio es, por decirlo así, el escepticismo, nos lo prueban hasta la evidencia. (*El Laberinto*, 2, 351–52)

    [Modern-day society is mortally wounded, it is a building that is falling into ruin, because its very mortar has crumbled to dust: this violent disquiet, this wild agitation which assails our ears at every step we take, this merciless struggle between opposed ideas and principles that contend for mastery of a society bereft of values and whose only abiding principle is, in a nutshell, scepticism, is evident proof.]

7. 'Noticia de varias obras inglesas publicadas en este siglo sobre los árabes. Estado actual en Europa y en España de la literatura árabe. Deberes del gobierno español sobre la enseñanza de las lenguas orientales, protección de sus profesores y traducción de manuscritos árabes', *Revista de España y del Extranjero*, 1 (1842), 28–36 (pp. 30–31). In an earlier review of Tocqueville, published in the same volume of the journal, Gonzalo Morón had similarly decried 'la bastarda dirección de las ambiciones individuales y de los intereses materiales' [the ill-born aims of individual ambition and material self-interest]: *Revista de España y del Extranjero*, 1, p. 18.
8. Cited by Negro Pavón, *Historia de España Menéndez Pidal*, XXXV: I, 573.
9. *El Laberinto*, 2, p. 351.
10. *Metahistory*, p. 48; author's italics.
11. 'Memoria leída por el Secretario del Ateneo Científico y Literario de Madrid el día 29 de diciembre de 1842', *Revista de Madrid*, 3rd series, 4 (1842), pp. 89, 93.
12. 'La religiosidad de la nación española', *La Civilización*, 2 (1842), 193–213 (p. 193).
13. *Ensayo sobre el catolicismo, el liberalismo y el socialismo*, ed. by Vila Selma, pp. 140–41.
14. 'Crítica literaria: Estado actual de la poesía lírica en España. Artículo 2º.', *Revista de Europa* (1846), 163–78 (p. 166).
15. *Historia de España Menéndez Pidal*, XXXV:: I, 535.
16. 'Instituciones monásticas', *Revista de Madrid*, 3rd series, 4 (1842), 5–24 (pp. 21–22).
17. *Revista de Madrid*, 3rd series, 4, p. 22.
18. *Revista de España y del Extranjero*, 1 (1842), p. 31.
19. Gabino Tejado wrote along these same lines in *El Laberinto* in 1845, claiming that it was essential to

    combatir con la pintura fiel de la verdad histórica, una porción de preocupaciones arraigadas en nuestras masas por la fuerza de la revolución, que desnaturalizando sus recuerdos, confundiendo sus tradiciones de lo pasado con sus pasiones presentes, les hacen mirar como odioso todo lo que no se acomoda a éstas, y anatematizar con la más buena fe del mundo ya sus glorias más preciadas, ya los principios más luminosos.

[combat, with the faithful tincture of historical truth, a portion of concerns that have taken hold among the people at large due to the revolutionary tumult, concerns which have distorted their collective memory, leading them to confuse past traditions with present-day passions, and have tended to make them consider odious all that does not pander to the latter and pour hatred, in all possible good faith, upon their most precious past glories and most enlightening steadfast principles]

Tejado decried specifically among radical intellectuals 'ese ciego amor a todo lo que nuevamente ha sido, y cuya mala inteligencia pervierte no pocas veces su juicio y su corazón' [that blind faith in all that has most recently been, the imperfect knowledge of which has not infrequently perverted their hearts and minds] (*El Laberinto*, 2, pp. 214–15).

20. 'Sobre la imparcialidad y divergencia histórica', *Revista de Madrid*, 3rd series, I (1841), 436–52 (p. 438).
21. 'Carácter distintivo de la sociedad antigua y moderna', *Revista de Madrid*, I (1838), 201–19 (pp. 216–18).
22. 'Examen de los bienes y males producidos por la democracia. Reseña y juicio de la obra *De la democracia en América* por Mr. Alexis Tocqueville. Instituciones políticas, gobierno y costumbres de los Estados-Unidos', *Revista de España y del Extranjero*, I (1842), 17–28, 71–91 (p. 72).
23. 'Romanticismo y revolución', in *El romanticismo*, ed. by Gies, p. 329.
24. *La invención de España*, p. 36.
25. *Revista de España y del Extranjero*, I, p. 80.
26. *Ruin and Restitution*, p. 15. Silver is here himself drawing on Antonio Elorza's *La modernización política en España, Ensayos de historia del pensamiento político* (Madrid, 1990), p. 157.
27. *Revista de España y del Extranjero*, I, p. 87.
28. 'De la nacionalidad', *La Civilización*, 2 (1842), 61–72 (pp. 71–72).
29. 'La religiosidad de la nación española', *La Civilización*, 2, 193–213 (p. 204).
30. Joaquín Francisco Pacheco, *Historia de la regencia de la reina Cristina* (Madrid, 1841), I, 64–65; this was the only volume of the planned three-volume study to appear.
31. *La Civilización*, 2, p. 206.
32. *La Civilización*, 2, p. 207.
33. *Historia de la regencia de la reina Cristina*, pp. 65–66.
34. *Historia de la regencia de la reina Cristina*, pp. 22–23.
35. *Historia de la regencia de la reina Cristina*, pp. 68, 70–71.
36. *La viña y los surcos*, pp. 36–37.
37. As Geoffrey Best states: 'The State did not matter much to the mass of the people. They knew it mainly through its conscription to army and navy service and its collection of taxes, which inclined them to dislike it. Their religion and monarchy mattered enormously, in connection with some apprehension of Spain's (passing) greatness in the world and a common culture which included, among other things, a great deal of national pride': *War and Society in Revolutionary Europe 1770–1870*, new edition (Stroud, 1998), p. 169. For Best, 'the Spanish people's war' had proved 'the most original, the most sustained, and the most effective of its kind' (p. 180). He underlines the centrality of religion within the conflict by observing of the struggle against Napoleon: 'Some Juntas were chaired by bishops or priests. Priests, monks and friars were prominent everywhere. Thus "the people" in an unusually literal sense began it' (p. 171).
38. *Historia de España Menéndez Pidal*, XXXV: I, 535.
39. *Historia de España Menéndez Pidal*, XXXV: I, 556–57.
40. *Historia de España Menéndez Pidal*, XXXV: I, 556.
41. *Los orígenes del pensamiento reaccionario*, pp. 226–27.
42. *Los orígenes del pensamiento reaccionario*, p. 247.
43. *Historia crítica del pensamiento español*, IV, 17.
44. *El alba del romanticismo español*, p. 12.
45. *El alba del romanticismo español*, p. 130.
46. *El alba del romanticismo español*, p. 111.

47. *La viña y los surcos*, p. 40.
48. *La viña y los surcos*, p. 17.
49. *Historia del levantamiento*, p. 56.
50. *Historia del levantamiento*, p. li.
51. *Letters from Spain, by Don Leucadio Doblado* (London, 1822), pp. 441–42.
52. *Letters from Spain*, pp. 7–8.
53. Cited by Manuel Moreno Alonso, *Blanco White: la obsesión de España* (Seville, 1998), p. 170.
54. *Historia crítica del pensamiento español*, IV, 17.
55. *El alba del romanticismo español*, p. 178.
56. *El alba del romanticismo español*, p. 153.
57. *El alba del romanticismo español*, p. 113.
58. *La viña y los surcos*, pp. 148–49.
59. *La viña y los surcos*, p. 17.
60. *La viña y los surcos*, p. 40.
61. *La viña y los surcos*, p. 29.
62. *Obras*, ed. by Seco Serrano, IV, 375.
63. See *Historia crítica del pensamiento español*, IV, 69.
64. See *Historia crítica del pensamiento español*, IV, 79.
65. *Letters from Spain*, p. 441.
66. *Guerra de la Independencia*, 3 vols (Madrid, 1844), I, 2. The frontispiece of Vol. I carried an epigraph from Quintana: 'No ha sido en el gran día/ El altar de la patria alzado en vano/ Por vuestra mano fuerte:/ Juradlo; ella os lo manda: ¡ANTES LA MUERTE/ QUE CONSENTIR JAMAS NINGUN TIRANO!' [The altar of the nation has not been raised, upon the great day and by your powerful hand, in vain: swear it; that altar commands you: BETTER DEAD THAN TO EVER APPEASE A TYRANT!].
67. *La viña y los surcos*, p. 41.
68. *Historia crítica del pensamiento español*, IV, 120.
69. *La Civilización*, 2, pp. 207–08.
70. *Moral y sociedad: la moral social española en el siglo XIX* (Madrid, 1966), p. 46.
71. *Historia de España Menéndez Pidal*, XXXV: I, 341
72. *Ideología y literatura en Alberto Lista* (Seville, 1993), pp. 28–29.
73. As Abellán notes, Vélez saw the struggle against the Napoleonic forces as 'una guerra de religión contra filósofos y liberales' [a religious war against philosophers and liberals]: *Historia crítica del pensamiento español*, IV, 171. In his three-volume *Apología del Altar y el Trono; o, Historia de las reformas hechas en España en tiempo de las llamadas Cortes, e impugnación de algunas doctrinas publicadas en la Constitución, diarios, y otros escritos contra la religión y el estado* of 1818, Vélez would implicitly link the provisions of the 1812 Constitution with the 'corrosive' effects of Enlightenment doctrine, pronouncing:

    La constitución habla del rey, pero ella respira por todas sus páginas un republicanismo sin igual. La constitución intenta regenerar la España; mas todos sus artículos tiran a su destrucción. La constitución se dirigirá a consolidar el Estado; pero, en realidad, sus leyes todas lo disuelven, lo arruinan. (Cited by Negro Pavón, *Historia de España Menéndez Pidal*, XXXV: I, 562).

    [The constitution speaks of the king, yet each one of its pages breathes an unequalled spirit of republicanism. The constitution is intended to regenerate Spain; but every one of its articles tends towards its destruction. The constitution is aimed at the consolidation of the State; but, in reality, each and every one of its laws debilitate and ruin it]
74. See Negro Pavón, *Historia de España Menéndez Pidal*, XXXV: I, 560.
75. See Abellán, *Historia crítica del pensamiento español*, IV, 165–66.
76. Cited by Moreno Alonso, *La generación española de 1808*, p. 90.
77. *Historia de España Menéndez Pidal*, XXXV: I, 343.
78. *Los orígenes del pensamiento reaccionario español*, pp. 222, 272.
79. *Historia de los heterodoxos españoles*, VI, 9, 70–71; the second comment cited by Moreno Alonso, *La generación española de 1808*, p. 89. Toreno's biographer, Leopoldo Augusto de Cueto, detected in his subject's first celebrated speech in the Cadiz Parliament 'pensamientos visiblemente inspirados por el *Contrato social*, que eran los que, halagando las pasiones y los oídos, y no sometidos al examen de

la razón, corrían entonces con mejor fortuna' [thoughts evidently inspired by the Social Contract were those which, flattering ears and passions and never subjected to the scrutiny of reason, were then in most happy circulation]; Toreno, he felt, had been victim of a 'contagio común' [common contagion]: *Historia del levantamiento*, p. xv. Cueto excused Toreno's use of such inflammatory language on the grounds of immaturity and inexperience, but described his speech on the question of the second article of the 1812 Constitution, concerning the relationship between monarch and representative government, as 'especioso' [specious], as one founded upon 'ideas teóricas, plausibles en la apariencia, pero en el uso engañosas' [theories plausible in appearance but deceptive once applied] (p. xviii). In the latter part of his biographical study he openly rebuked the liberal statesman and historian of the Peninsular War for producing little more than an 'apología' of the actions of the Cadiz radicals (p. liii).

80. See *Historia de España Menéndez Pidal*, XXXV: I, 220. The citation from an anonymous sermon published in Gerona in 1822.

81. *Historia de España Menéndez Pidal*, XXXV: I, 564.

82. *El Pensamiento de la Nación*, (6 March 1844).

83. One could detail any number of Catholic denunciations of Mendizábal's legislation expropriating ecclesiastical assets and effectively closing down monasteries and convents. Even in the more stable political climate of 1852 Canga Argüelles, on taking up his seat in the Real Academia de la Historia, looked back with some considerable rancour to what he saw as the pillaging of sacred institutions by rabble:

Los institutos monásticos han sido despiadadamente hostilizados por la revolución, sin perdonarse medio de hacerlos desaparecer del cuadro de los elementos civilizadores. La revolución pronunció inexorable una sentencia de exterminio, y viéronse desaparecer instantáneamente, entre los locos aplausos de la muchedumbre, aquellas instituciones que, en sus primitivos tiempos, salvaron a la Europa de la barbarie.

[The monastic institutions have been mercilessly attacked by the revolution, which has used every possible means of removing them from among the constituent elements of our civilization. The revolution pronounced its inexorable death sentence upon them, and instantaneously there were seen to vanish, to the wild applause of the masses, those institutions which in its earliest times, saved all of Europe from barbarism.]

(Y Discurso del Excmo. Señor D. Felipe Canga Argüelles sobre la influencia de los institutos religiosos en los adelantos de la Historia', *Discursos leídos en las sesiones públicas que para dar posesión de plazas de número ha celebrado desde 1852 la Real Academia de la Historia* (Madrid, 1858), 45–63 (p. 47)).

84. *Obras de D. Francisco Martínez de la Rosa*, 'Estudio preliminar', I, p. lxxxi. Cueto described Toreno's appointment of Mendizábal as finance minister as one of the politician's 'más reparables errores' [most notable errors]; the elections that ushered in Mendizábal's own subsequent administration he felt to have taken place 'bajo el influjo revolucionario' [under revolutionary influence]: *Historia del levantamiento*, pp. xlii-xliv. Cueto went on to view the political events of 1840 as a titanic struggle between the heroic efforts of 'los conservadores' and the anarchic tactics of 'el partido revolucionario' (pp. xlvi-xlvii).

85. *Obras de D. Francisco Martínez de la Rosa*, I, p. lxxxiv.

86. 'Reseña política de España. Artículo 12°', *Revista de España y del Extranjero*, 2 (1842), 241–53 (p. 244).

87. 'Reseña política de España. Artículo 15°', *Revista de España y del Extranjero*, 3 (1842), 97–107 (p. 97).

88. *La Civilización*, 2, p. 212.

89. *Revista de España y del Extranjero*, 2, p. 245.

90. *Revista de España y del Extranjero*, 2, p. 245.

91. 'Movimiento intelectual de España: la Restauración, revista católica', *Revista de España y del Extranjero*, 6 (1843), 36–39 (36).

92. *Historia de España Menéndez Pidal*, XXXV: I, 572.

93. *Historia de España Menéndez Pidal*, XXXV: I, 583–85. The Estatuto Real was, for Raymond Carr, a 'conservative constitutional settlement' in marked contrast to that of 1812: see *Spain 1808–1939* (Oxford, 1966), p. 157. Vicente Llorens would describe it as an 'especie de carta otorgada que

sustituyó a la Constitución de 1812, mitigando considerablemente su radicalismo democrático' [aristocratically bestowed charter, which, in replacing the 1812 Constitution, considerably diluted its democratic radicalism]: *El romanticismo español* (Madrid, 1979), p. 231. Donald Schurlknight forges persuasive connections between Martínez de la Rosa's political enterprise and his Romantic drama *La conjuración de Venecia*, underscoring the imprint of conservatism upon the text: see '*La conjuración de Venecia* as/in Context', *Revista de Estudios Hispánicos*, 32 (1998), 537–55.

94. *Obras*, ed. bySeco Serrano, VIII, 336.

95. *Historia del levantamiento*, p. liii.

96. 'La situación política de 1841', *Obras*, II, 35. Díaz was by no means a reactionary figure: his political affiliation lay with Joaquín Francisco Pacheco in the *puritano* faction of his party, described by Jover Zamora as 'situada a la izquierda y preocupada por hacer del moderado un régimen liberal, consecuente y moderno' [located on the left of the party and determined to make the moderado régime a liberal, modern and consequential one]: *Historia de España Menéndez Pidal*, XXXIV, 380. Juan Cortada, meanwhile, would use the same term 'anacronismo' in his general history of Spain, in underlining that the 1812 Constitution would have been an inappropriate blueprint for the government of the country in the later political climate of the 1830s and 1840s: see Cortada's *Historia de España*, II, 193.

97. *Obras*, II, 36.

98. See *Historia de España Menéndez Pidal*, XXXV: I, 613.

99. It is interesting, within this context, that one of the works chosen for inclusion in Eugenio de Ochoa's *Apuntes para una biblioteca de escritores españoles contemporáneos en prosa y verso*, published in two volumes in Paris in 1840, was Vicente Arnao's *Opinión de un jurisconsulto español sobre la constitución de Cádiz de 1812*, originally written in Valencia in 1813. The excerpt, hardly by coincidence, contains the following virulent condemnation of the legislation:

Pobre España! El vulgo tendrá por una temporada la satisfacción de ver subir y bajar al solio sus iguales o sus desiguales; pero muy luego no verá el mismo en ellos sino tiranos efímeros que se suceden hasta acabar con la ley misma que los elevó y con el estado, en medio de las atroces convulsiones de la anarquía. […] Tal es el término a que por mil caminos será conducida la nación española, si llegara a adoptarse la constitución proyectada en Cádiz. […] su fruto no puede ser otro sino el eventual y siempre atroz, que las convulsiones de una masa de hombres sin lazo social arrojan de sí, después de mil horrores y calamidades. […] ¿Y ha habido quien se atreva a presentra a la moderna Europa, a la Europa a costa de mil males ilustrada, semejantes delirios para servir de constitución a una nación tan principal como la española?(I, 73)

[Poor Spain! The common people shall for a time have the satisfaction of seeing their equals and unequals rise and fall; but they shall very soon come to perceive them as no more than passing tyrants who fast succeed one another until the very law that brought them to power is at an end, and with it the state itself, amidst the horrible convulsions of anarchy [...] Such is the end to which a thousand roads lead the Spanish nation, if it were once to adopt the constitution drawn up in Cadiz. [...] Its fruits cannot be other than that eternally terrible eventuality, the detritus left behind by a multitude lacking in all social ties after it has experienced a thousand horrors and calamities. [...] And is there a single person who dares to present to modern Europe, to a Europe that has learned the lesons of a thousand infamous deeds, such a set of delirious ravings as the constitution of a nation as eminent as Spain?]

100. Cortada wrote in similar terms of the ending of the Carlist War with the Peace of Vergara, affirming that 'El extraño término de esa lucha fue indudablemente traído por la Providencia, que por caminos tan desviados e imprevistos pone fin a los acontecimientos humanos, cuando los hombres les vaticinan todavía duración muy larga' [The curious outcome of that struggle was undoubtedly the work of Providence, which, in its indirect and unpredictable ways brings all human enterprises to a conclusion, even when men can see no end in sight]: *Historia de España*, II, 176–77.

101. 'Bosquejo histórico. Minoría de Isabel II: declaración de su mayor edad', *El Laberinto*, 1 (1843–1844), 38–40 (p. 39).

102. *Historia crítica del pensamiento español*, IV, 20.

103. *La civilización española a mediados del siglo XIX* (Madrid, 1992), pp. 168–69.

104. *La invención de España*, p. 39.

105. *Obras* , ed. bySeco Serrano,VIII, 390.

106. *Obras de D. Francisco Martínez de la Rosa*, I, p. xci.

107. *Historia de España Menéndez Pidal*, XXXV: I, 391.

108. Cited by Jover Zamora, *Historia de España Menéndez Pidal*, XXXIV, 389.

109. *Origen y desarrollo de la derecha española*, p. 276.

110. *Historia de los heterodoxos españoles*,VI, 9–10.

111. Antonio Santoveña Setién contextualizes the diverse forms of expression of this 'pensamiento antirrevolucionario español' [counter-revolutionary Spanish thought], united in their 'resistencia a la expansión de las ideas revolucionarias y al nuevo orden que éstas patrocinaban' [resistance against the spread of revolutionary ideas and the new order sponsored by these ideas], insofar as they provided antecedents for the work of Don Marcelino; he subsequently goes so far as to assert that 'el deseo de contribuir a combatir, en la medida de sus posibilidades, el avance de las ideas revolucionarias empujó a Menéndez Pelayo a ejercer de historiador' [it was the desire to contribute everything that he could to the struggle against the onward march of revolutionary ideas that led Menéndez Pelayo to become a historian]: see *Marcelino Menéndez Pelayo: revisión crítico-biográfica*, pp. 19–20, 94.

112. *Historia de los heterodoxos españoles*,V, 362–63.

113. 'La cristalización del mito', *Romanticismo y realismo. Primer suplemento*, ed. by Zavala, 93–96 (p. 93). The text reproduced here is taken from Jover's *Realidad y mito de la Primera República. Del "Gran Miedo" meridional a la utopía de Galdós* (Madrid, 1991), pp. 87–91.

114. *El Pensamiento de la Nación*, 6 March 1844. As Seco Serrano noted in recapturing the ideological climate of the day, and consciously or unconsciously adopting one of the preferred images of the time: 'El desquite de las viejas monarquías es un hecho, porque todo el mundo cree estar de vuelta de los gastados cantos de sirena de la Revolución' [The revenge of the old monarquies became a reality, since the whole world believed itself to have turned the tide against the worn-out siren voices of Revolution]: *Obras de D. Francisco Martínez de la Rosa*, 'Estudio preliminar', I, p. xxix.

115. *Historia de España Menéndez Pidal*, XXXV: I, 391.

116. *Romanticismo y realismo. Primer suplemento*, p. 31.

117. In the historical novel *La familia de Alvareda*, set at the time of the French occupation: *Obras*, I, 159. See on this point my *Spanish Romantic Literary Theory and Criticism*, pp. 164–65.

118. 'De las reformas que experimentó la poesía italiana después de mediado el siglo pasado, y de las poesías de Alejandro Manzoni', *Semanario Pintoresco Español*, 3rd series, 2 (1844), 389–91, 394–95 (p. 394).

119. *Ruin and Restitution*, p. 126.

120. For a thoroughgoing critical account of the formation of this 'canon isabelino', see Íñigo Sánchez Llama, *Galería de escritoras isabelinas: la prensa periódica entre 1833 y 1895* (Madrid, 2000).

121. Fernando Garrido, *Historia del reinado del último Borbón de España* (Barcelona, 1868–69), II, 476; cited by Sánchez Llama, *Galería de escritoras isabelinas*, p.82.

122. *Galería de escritoras isabelinas*, pp. 88–89. She further cites the 'canonization' of Fernán Caballero by Eugenio de Ochoa (in 1849) and the Duque de Rivas (in 1856), two writers who, she contends, 'comparten en el período isabelino los valores del neocatolicismo y el historicismo romántico schlegeliano' [share, in the reign of Isabel, the values of neo-Catholicism and Schlegelian historical Romanticism] (p. 97).

CHAPTER 6

Ideology and Aesthetics:
The Uses of Literary History

One of the most pervasive expressions of Romantic ideas in Spain in the first half of the nineteenth century was the employment of the organicist perspective on the development of human civilization formulated by Herder — viewed by Rene Wellek as 'the fountainhead of universal literary history' — [1] and more systematically applied to the history of European literature by August Wilhelm and Friedrich Schlegel. In my study of the reception of Romantic aesthetics in Spain, I underlined in some considerable detail that the prevalent interpretation of literary Romanticism among Spanish writers and critics was one derived from Schlegelian formulae. First advanced in the country by Böhl von Faber and later informing the perspectives on the history of Spanish literature adduced by Ramón López Soler, Agustín Durán, and other commentators of the 1820s, the same interpretation proved resurgent after the years of intense critical controversy between 1834 and 1837, and went on to dominate Spanish literary criticism of the 1840s. The idea of literature as a profound expression of national identity and as a mirror in which a society's intimate thought-patterns are reflected, as the most reliable indicator of the collective imaginative hypothesis of a people living within a particular time and place, represented a conscious trans-formational break with the universalizing prescriptions of neo-Classicism. Romantic historicism therefore acquired from its origins considerable ideological momentum as a theory of cultural nationalism. Herder himself had encouraged Germans to ignore the inroads made by foreign — principally French — cultural influences and to revisit instead the unspoilt native sources of the Middle Ages and the sixteenth century. The brothers Schlegel, meanwhile, emphasized the independent cultural achievement of Spain in the Middle Ages and in the *Siglo de Oro*, and were instrumental in inspiring the rediscovery, in the nineteenth century, of a literary tradition which the neo-Classical age was felt unjustly to have neglected. Crucial to the present argument, however, is the use of the Schlegelian framework by *casticista* writers eager to underscore the ideals of monarchy and religion that they felt to constitute the inalienable nucleus of Spanish culture. In this way, the exposition of literary history in the Romantic mode became a further means of combating neo-Classical, and by extension Enlightenment, heresy. The history of literature, like other areas of historiographical enquiry, thus acquired a potent and trenchantly expressed ideological dimension.

There are any number of assertions of the basic historicist perspective to be culled from literary criticism of the period, although we require no more than a representative sample immediately to familiarize us with the discussion as it occurred. For example, an anonymous reviewer writing on the development of Spanish theatre in the magazine *El Reflejo* in 1843 observed that dramatic art had always and of necessity been 'la expresión del pensamiento, el retrato de las costumbres, y el barómetro de la ilustración de los pueblos' [the expression of a people's thought, a portrait of its way of life and a barometer of its intellectual progress].[2] José María Pallarés had written similarly of historical narratives in an article published in the *Revista de Madrid* in 1841, regarding them as a representative insight into the society that had produced them, into that society's belief-system, values and cultural preferences, and as a faithful representation of collective moral life in a given period, concluding that 'En efecto: la literatura es la expresión de la sociedad' [In effect, literature is the expression of its society]. Mediaeval texts, he went on, and singularly the *romances*, contained in abundance marvellous deeds of arms, gallantry, honour, and nobility; whatever the degree of incredulity these might at first sight awaken in the present age, he was insistent that they represented 'un fiel traslado del espíritu de aquellos tiempos' [a faithful communication of the spirit of that age] without which the nineteenth-century mind should be unable accurately to judge nor fully to understand its true meaning.[3] In the same year, Joaquín Roca y Cornet would require that literary works be judged not just by their intrinsic aesthetic or intellectual merits but, more importantly, 'por la relación que tienen con la marcha intelectual o moral de la sociedad' [by their relationship to the moral or intellectual development of that society].[4]

All of these extracts, selected from innumerable similar comments made in Spain in the course of several decades, are of course no more than restatements of what had come to be seen as axiomatic: the historicist formula, most specifically Bonald's celebrated proclamation that 'La littérature est l'expression de la société' together with Larra's equally well known assertion that 'la literatura es la expresión, el termómetro verdadero del estado de civilización de un pueblo' [literature is the expression, the true thermometer of a given people's civilization],[5] had quite simply acquired the status of received truth.[6] Not surprisingly then, José Amador de los Ríos, in opening the academic year at the Universidad Central, Madrid, in 1850, would repeat almost precisely Larra's metaphor in declaring that literature, just like the other arts, represented 'el barómetro más seguro de la civilización y cultura de los pueblos' [the most reliable barometer of any people's civilization and culture].[7] Angel Fernández de los Ríos, meanwhile, writing in the magazine *El Siglo Pintoresco*, preferred the metaphor of the mirror used by the Schlegels to commend the intimate relationship between Golden-Age society and Calderonian drama as that society's intimate expression; literature not as the mirror of an eternal and unchanging Nature but as 'el espejo en que se reproduce fielmente la fisonomía intelectual de los pueblos' [the mirror in which is reflected the intellectual physiognomy of peoples], a developmental phenomenon subject to historical change.[8] Accordingly, Salvador Costanzo amongst others was led to remark that if the literature of a people were to be the most energetic and faithful expression of that people's political, religious, and social structures, it inevitably followed that one could not attempt to write a literary history without delving sympathetically into historical customs and cultural inclinations and without taking due account of 'la constitución política y religiosa de los pueblos' [the political and religious constitution of peoples].[9]

This reference to distinctive political and religious institutions provides, indirectly at least, a pointer to the way in which the tenets of Romantic historicism were frequently employed. In the ongoing literary debate of the 1830s, one of the most influential contributions had been made by Alberto Lista, a respected moderate in both literary preferences and ideological outlook, who had lent his support to Schlegelian or 'historical' Romanticism in a cluster of important articles appearing mainly in the second half of the decade. Lista's insistence that the origins of Romanticism lay in 'la ruina de la religión gentílica y la abolición del gobierno republicano' [the collapse of pagan religion and the abolition of republican government],[10] together with his overview of literary history in which the term figured in what he regarded as its only acceptable sense — 'entendiendo por romántico lo perteneciente a la literatura cristiana y monárquica, propia de nuestra civilización actual' [understanding by the term 'Romantic' everything pertaining to that Christian and monarchical literature peculiar to our modern-day civilization],[11] provided further influential backing for A. W. Schlegel's historically-based pattern. The same might be said of Antonio Gil y Zárate's judgements as expressed in his ambitious *Manual de literatura*, the first volumes of which appeared in 1842 and contained as an essential definition the assertion that 'es romántica la [literatura] que nació en la edad media como producto de la nueva civilización que brotó y se arraigó en Europa después de la caída del imperio romano' [Romantic literature is that which came into being in the Middle Ages as a product of the new civilization that sprouted and took root in Europe after the fall of the Roman Empire].[12] Once more, I might adduce here any number of further similar comments made in the course of the three or four decades immediately following the war with France.

In the last decade of the twentieth century, roughly speaking, modern criticism came to recognize, perhaps more openly than hitherto, that Schlegelian Romantic historicism constituted the majority understanding of Romanticism within Spain. D. L. Shaw, for example, markedly unsympathetic towards such traditionalist positions — and indeed towards my own earlier study, nonetheless accepted the prevalence, quantitatively at least, of the formulae deriving from Herder and the Schlegels, acknowledging that those Spanish critics adopting their characteristic perspective were always in a very large majority; this at least, he averred, admitted of no doubt.[13] What most closely occupies us here, however, is the explicit linkage between literary and political spheres commonly encountered in this body of writing, the implications of which I was unable fully to explore in my earlier study. It should be noted, for example, that both Lista and Gil y Zárate, as A. W. Schlegel had done, viewed monarchy and religion as the contemporaneous institutional components that accompanied and informed the production of Romantic literature in modern societies. Lista went further in stressing that the essential features of Romantic art could only come into being after the historical collapse of republican forms of government. The clear intimation here in terms of contemporary institutional debate was that Romanticism and republicanism, or Romanticism and democracy, were antithetical historical phenomena and thus mutually incompatible. Little wonder then that arch-conservatives and defenders of throne and altar, such as Juan Donoso Cortés, Jaime Balmes, Fermín Gonzalo Morón, and Gabino Tejado, were loud in their acclamation of historical Romanticism as a literary creed and of A. W. Schlegel as a visionary figure who had revised the false perspectives of eighteenth-century neo-Classicism. Writing in *El Iris* in 1841, Gonzalo Morón lauded 'el mérito distinguido del *Curso de literatura dramática* del alemán Schlegel, que ha abierto a la crítica literaria una dirección más vasta y filosófica que la seguida anteriormente' [the special merits of the German writer Schlegel's *Course on Dramatic Literature*, which has opened up to literary criticism a broader and more philosophical direction than that it had earlier followed], and acknowledged his own debt to the 'doctrinas' [doctrines] of the German theorist.[14] The piece from which this passage is taken, a two-part consideration of early Spanish theatre, had been preceded, in the same magazine, by Gonzalo Morón's fifteen-part 'Examen filosófico del teatro español', in which Schlegelian Romantic judgements and perspectives predominated.

Three years earlier Donoso Cortés, in a series of articles entitled 'El clasicismo y el romanticismo' and published in *El Correo Nacional*, had underlined the view that Romanticism had first been established in the cultural climate of the Middle Ages and had been characterized by a 'culto del espíritu' [devout preference for the spiritual] derived from the overwhelming historical changes wrought by the Christian faith; as a consequence, Donoso affirmed, modern literature, like modern society, was especially concerned with things of the spirit. Balmes, meanwhile, in his 1842 essay 'De la originalidad', would profess a typically Schlegelian Romantic historicism in declaring that a literary school whose inspiration was derived from pagan mythology was entirely unsuited to contemporary times. The Christian religion, he commented, had been the salient distinguishing factor between the respective literatures of the Classical and modern worlds, while he praised Chateaubriand for having shown how futile was the imitation of Classical authors by modern writers.[15] Hans Juretschke therefore shrewdly comments that Balmes's piece reproduces in essence the entire Romantic aesthetic, even more bluntly asserting that 'En su credo artístico, Balmes es romántico' [In terms of his artistic creed, Balmes is a Romantic].[16] Tejado, beginning his career as literary critic in 1845, concisely summarized the familiar Schlegelian distinction between Classical and Romantic in remarking that each represented 'un orden distinto de cosas, que señalan dos literaturas distintas de dos épocas diversas' [a distinct order of things, signposted by two very different literatures belonging to discrete historical periods].[17] Finally, the young Manuel Cañete, writing in 1846 in the *Revista de Europa*, stressed that the German thinkers who had been the founding fathers of Romanticism had succeeded in their efforts to 'rejuvenecer los sistemas literarios del globo' [reinvigorate the literary systems of the world at large].[18]

None of this should be particularly surprising, despite the misleading association of Spanish Romanticism with political liberalism that has been writ large in so many studies of the period. As José Luis Varela has shown, the rather different association of neo-Classicism with republicanism represented a constant in conservative thought. Varela indicated that, in order to make an accurate reading of nineteenth-century textual evidence, we must appreciate the context in which key terms were used: for the reactionary writer, republicanism signified nothing less than anarchy and revolutionary subversion; likewise neo-Classicism was the doctrine of a pro-French faction, a faction guided by a materialistic outlook that had already led to a revolutionary bloodbath whose shock-waves were still acutely felt throughout Europe.[19] The initial ideological thrust of European Romanticism had been markedly conservative, so much so that José Joaquín de Mora had famously proclaimed in 1820 that 'El liberalismo es en la escala de las opiniones políticas lo que el gusto clásico es en la de las literarias' [Liberalism in the field of political opinion corresponds to classical taste in literature].[20] To those Spanish Catholics striving effectively to combat the philosophical legacy of the French Enlightenment, the Christian and monarchical bases of Schlegelian Romanticism offered an alternative reading of literary history and a strategy for the direction of contemporary literature especially calculated to rebuff all of the intellectual positions associated with eighteenth-century France, whether these be republicanism, a democratic constitution, or neo-Classical taste. The opportunity to invigorate Spanish thought and creative production via a *casticista* appeal to past national traditions represented a natural counter-offensive, one in which historical Romanticism had a prominent role to play. Gonzalo Morón himself made the point in remarkably explicit terms, affirming that the dominant thrust of contemporary literature tended not just towards a restitution to the Middle Ages of a true sense of its worth, but also, and these next words are crucial, to extract from a true estimate of the mediaeval achievement 'bases de reorganización y de gobierno, que neutralicen los principios disolventes de las sociedades modernas' [foundations of reorganization and government that might neutralize those principles tending to dissolution in modern societies].[21]

The reappearance of the familiar phrase 'principios disolventes' at once alerts us to the specific ideological agenda underpinning Gonzalo Morón's ostensibly literary task. It intimates also the calculated ideological strategies in which the essential components of Schlegelian Romantic historicism — in this case the underscoring of the heightened spirituality of mediaeval culture — now regularly figured. In this context we immediately recall Nicomedes-Pastor Díaz's well-known assertion regarding the poetic inspiration of the young José Zorrilla: 'su pluma no pudo menos de hacer contrastar lo que hay de mezquino, glacial y ridículo en la época actual, con lo que tienen de magnífico, solemne y sublime los recuerdos de los tiempos caballerescos y religiosos' [his pen could not but contrast the meanness, absurdity, and cold impersonality of our contemporary age with the magnificence, solemnity, and sublimity of those times of chivalry and religion].[22] At the same time, Gonzalo Morón's phrasing stands comparison with other representative pieces of critical writing. Here we may cite the profound disquiet elicited by the first performance in Spain of one of Dumas *père*'s most notorious plays, prompting Larra's disavowal of 'la *desorganización social*, personificada en *Antony*, literaria y filosóficamente' [the *social disorganization* personified in *Antony*, in both literary and philosophical terms],[23] and likewise the consternation felt by an anonymous reviewer writing for the *Eco del Comercio* on realizing that 'el pensamiento dominante en este drama es eminentemente antisocial, si vemos en él preconizado el adulterio y completamente hollados todos los principios conservadores de la moral y de la sociedad' [the dominant emphasis in this play is highly anti-social, for we see in it a glorification of adultery, while all those principles that safeguard morality and society are simply trodden underfoot].[24] Díaz's expansive piece 'Del movimiento literario en España en 1837' had reassuringly noted, just as Gonzalo Morón's later article was to do, that humankind's instinctive apprehension of beauty had not been definitively lost and that, indeed, 'detrás de la aparente disolución que nos circunda, los primeros albores de la reorganización y de la vida social despuntan sobre el horizonte' [beyond the spectacle of dissolution that hems us in on every side, the first rays of a new dawn, one of reorganization and stable social life, begin to glow upon the horizon].[25] An essentially conservative historical Romanticism, then, was to be the chosen means of countervailing the spectre of social disintegration raised by both literary and ideological radicalism.

The literary argument, and by extension the consideration of literary history, was in fact to reveal the same degree of polarization already encountered in broader historical overviews; the Manichaean distinction between spiritual ennobling and rationalistic profanity, the concomitant rhetoric of destruction and renewal, the preferred phrasing alternating between the enervating threat of utter 'disolución' and the optimistic perception of a regenerative dawn, all find similar expression here. Within this dualistic framework, both the creative production of past ages and contemporary forms of literary Romanticism are systematically ascribed their inevitable part: while the mediaeval period and the Golden Age are honoured as examples of historical reality and imaginative hypothesis in a process of intimate cultural correlation, the eighteenth century is — characteristically — seen as a period of rupture, as a time when artistic production lost its spontaneity of expression and its organic connection with the collective imagination, with consequences as disastrous in the field of literary history as the catastrophic end result of the Enlightenment had proved in the broader cultural and political spheres. Responses to Romanticism reveal a similar fissure: historical Romanticism is warmly commended for its recreation of the same imaginative sympathies and qualities of spiritual elevation that had so ennobled the literary Middle Ages and *Siglo de Oro*; Romantic radicalism, conversely, is viewed as a corrupted literary form possessing all of the perversities and prompting all of the delinquencies of the Enlightenment rationalism to which it owed its descent.

If this reading of events, one that the present chapter will seek to reinforce, flies in the face of much modern criticism, then I hope that the far-reaching interconnections we can subsequently establish between literary history and other forms of Spanish Romantic historiography will convincingly make the case in favour of my hypothesis. Modern-day commentators who have superimposed personal, ideologically informed interpretations of what constitutes 'authentic' Romanticism on to the reality of nineteenth-century events and on to the scrutiny of nineteenth-century thought-patterns, in some cases without the benefit of a thoroughgoing knowledge of many of the relevant texts, have done a grave disservice to Spanish intellectual history. For what the decade of the 1840s represents is neither the defeat or 'betrayal' of Romanticism nor an anti-Romantic reaction; as a detailed examination of commentaries on literary history produced by that decade will show, what really characterized those years was an interpretation of the national literary past precisely — and, in the main, consciously — in accord with Schlegelian formulae, together with an exhortation

— or, in some cases, stipulation — that contemporary Spanish literature continue to be commensurate with Schlegelian projections of Romanticism as the expression in art of chivalry, monarchy, and the Christian ideal. Literary radicalism, chiefly imported from France and occurring principally in the theatre, was decried not just for its *criticismo* but also on the grounds that it was an aberration, a misrepresentation of what was then almost universally regarded as genuine Romanticism. As Shaw has recently noted, rectifying his earlier proclamations on the same issue, the writers he designates 'románticos subversivos' formed no more than a small minority and provoked a violent reaction among the more traditionally inclined.[26]

One fundamental characteristic of the vision of literary history produced by this majority Spanish Romanticism was that it accorded a new pride of place to the Middle Ages in the development of Western culture, and not just to learned forms of literature and the other arts but particularly also to the popular verse tradition. In the case of Spain, this meant the revival of the mediaeval *romancero* as a treasure-house of the country's most intimate cultural heritage, one that depicted with peculiar and unerring accuracy the distinctive customs and thought-patterns of its age, essentially different from those of Classical antiquity. José de la Revilla, in a wide-ranging piece, concisely expressed this typically Romantic premise in affirming that creative literature in the Middle Ages necessarily had recourse to a way of life and outlook on the world different from those of previous ages, for it possessed, 'por cimiento de su civilización renovada, otra religión, otro culto, otra tendencia, distintas de las que imperaban en el ánimo de los antiguos dominadores de la tierra' [as the mortar of its revitalized civilization, a new religion, a new form of worship, a new set of inclinations, all very different from those that had governed the minds of the former rulers of the world].[27] Gonzalo Morón likewise felt that the extensive narrative poems of the Spanish Middle Ages reflected the religious, warlike, and chivalric spirit that had characterized the period, and indicated that the *romances*, which he calls 'el género más nacional de poesía que hemos tenido' [the most truly national poetic genre that we have produced], like so many other texts of the Middle Ages and *Siglo de Oro*, successfully lent creative expression to everything that most potently, energetically and intimately represented Spanish history and Spanish ways of life. At the same time he praised the work of Agustín Durán and the latter's 'recto criterio' [sound judgement].[28] Gabino Tejado would describe the *romance* as the spontaneous poetic expression of its age, an 'eco verdadero' [true echo] of the times in which it had originated,[29] while an anonymous review of Gil y Zárate's *Manual de literatura* enthusiastically cited the encomiastic Schlegelian assessment of the Spanish *romancero*, affirming that the national popular verse tradition contained those intrinsic qualities demanded by Spain's distinctive civilization. These defining qualities, specified as faith, honour, and gallantry, had lent mediaeval Spanish literature its peculiar physiognomy; consequently, and these are the crucial phrases, 'era religiosa y caballeresca y una verdadera representación de la sociedad española' [it was devoutly religious and chivalric, and a true representation of Spanish society].[30] Amador de los Ríos, finally, was to proclaim that Spain's mediaeval art faithfully depicted Christian society in all of its vigorous natural instincts and, in the process, 'reveló las creencias con la pureza que recibían del dogma' [revealed popular beliefs in all the purity they acquired from doctrine]; as a result, he concluded, this art, coarse and unsophisticated but spontaneous and alive, 'se muestra en armonía con la sociedad' [is evidently in harmony with its society].[31] All of these citations indicate not just the prevalence of the basic historicist outlook, but also an understanding of what German Romantic theory saw as an intimate and affective correlation, a profoundly seated harmony, between a given society and its imaginative expression. Amador, in underscoring the 'pureza' contained in mediaeval Spanish society's pattern of belief and projected in its creative literature, came close to repeating Friedrich Schlegel's contention that in Spain's national literary tradition 'There is nothing which can degrade thought, corrupt feeling or estrange virtue. Every where there breathes the same spirit of honour, principle, and faith'.[32]

Precisely the same intimate harmony between literature and society was the keynote in contemporary historical judgements of the Spanish Golden Age, while the defining characteristics of both nation and literary production were perceived as constant. As Salvador Bermúdez de Castro argued in an influential article published in *El Iris* in 1841, Golden-Age drama accurately reflected 'todas las pasiones, todos los sentimientos, todas las costumbres de la nación' [all of the nation's passions, all of its intimate feelings, its entire way of life]; as such it was a 'mágico espejo de la verdadera poesía' [magical mirror of true poetry] in profound affinity with the popular mind. He saw the theatre of the *Siglo de Oro*, then, as the expression in literature of the Spanish *Volksgeist*: 'El honor, la religión y la galantería eran los caracteres distintivos de la sociedad española: el honor, la religión y la galantería son los ejes eternos de los antiguos dramas' [Honour, faith, and gallantry were the distinctive features of Spanish society: honour, faith, and gallantry are the eternal pivots upon which the old dramas turn].[33] Gonzalo Morón, writing in the same magazine in the same year, in affirming that Spaniards had seen in Golden-Age drama a dynamic and varied living picture of their way of life, their nationhood and their glories,[34] was in fact closely paraphrasing Friedrich Schlegel; for the German theorist: 'As the Spanish monarchy was, down to the middle of the seventeenth century, the greatest and the most splendid in Europe, and as the national spirit of the Spaniards was the most developed, so the stage of Madrid, the living mirror of Spanish life, was the first which arrived at its period of glory'.[35] An anonymous article published in *El Reflejo* in 1843 reiterated too that Golden-Age plays had been 'en armonía con la índole, gustos y sentimientos del público' [in harmony with the inclinations, tastes, and intimate feelings of their public]; as such they were a true expression of Spanish society and 'el verdadero drama nacional' [an authentic national theatre],[36] while José de la Revilla, writing in the magazine *Museo de las Familias* in the same year, explained the success of Golden-Age drama by describing it as 'original, nacional y popular' [original, national, and popular].[37] Gabino Tejado, we should note, would continue to echo this view well into the second half of the century, contending that the drama of the Golden Age had been nothing more and nothing less than a true reflection of those ideas and affective ties that constituted 'el fondo, el espíritu vital de nuestra antigua España' [the bedrock, the vital spirit of our Spain of old], a noble Spain he described as 'ascética, guerrera, pundonorosa, gigante, romancesca' [self-denying, warlike, honourable, colossal, romantic] that had been vividly depicted upon the sweeping canvas of its national theatre.[38] Crucially, Tejado intimates an ideological adherence to this perspective in proclaiming Golden-Age drama to represent a 'triunfo permanente del espíritu sobre la materia' [permanent triumph of spirit over matter]; as he continued: 'los intereses puramente mundanales, los que llamamos intereses positivos en estos tiempos de materia y de prosa, apenas tienen espacio ni lugar en nuestra literatura' [wordly interests, those that we label with the term Positivism in this materialistic and prosaic age, hardly find the smallest space in our literature].[39] The religious note present in many such commentaries was something pertaining to the Schlegelian texts themselves, for Friedrich had described Calderón as 'In every situation and circumstance, [...] of all dramatic poets, the most Christian, and for that very reason the most romantic'.[40] Menéndez Pelayo, in his *Historia de las ideas estéticas*, would see shortcomings in the German cultural historian's overview that he attributed to a limited knowledge of the original texts, particularly a lack of familiarity with Tirso and Moreto, yet both Tejado and Amador de los Ríos expressed no such caveat; Amador, in praising Gil y Zárate's *Manual de literatura*, cited from it the important passage distinguishing A. W. Schlegel's judgement of Calderón from that of Sismondi: the great German writer had viewed him 'desde las alturas de la más elevada poesía y le coloca en el punto culminante del romanticismo' [from the heights of the most exalted poetry, and places him at the culminating point of Romanticism], while the Swiss historian had regarded him 'a través de la prosaica manera de los dramáticos franceses, y además en la parte religiosa con todas las prevenciones de un protestante contra la comunión católica' [through the prosaic prism of the French dramatists, and, what is more, from a religious point of view with all the typical prejudices felt by a Protestant against the Catholic communion].[41]

Resentment against the Swiss writer is transparently clear both in Gil y Zárate's text and in Amador's own subsequent work; a resentment fuelled no doubt by Sismondi's refusal to countenance the idealistic vision of the Spanish Golden Age enshrined in Schlegelian theory and later prevalent in the writings of the Spanish Romantics. For in his *De la Littérature du Midi de l'Europe*, first published in 1813, Sismondi had crushingly — and ironically, in the context — viewed Calderón as 'l'homme de son siècle, l'homme de la misérable époque de Philippe IV' [a man of his age, that wretched age of Philip IV], his work a potent illustration of the state of corruption and decadence into which Spanish culture and society had by then sunk.[42] In Gil y Zárate's historical account, as in that of Amador some twenty years later, there looms large a feeling of disgust both for the neo-Classical preferences of France and, more broadly, for the lack of spiritual elevation perceived in that country's cultural models. Amador felt that Sismondi had been unable to penetrate the founding principles of Spanish civilization since he had been hampered by an 'espíritu de secta' [religious bias] that had rendered him ignorant of all sense of elevation; instead Amador saw the Swiss writer as tainted by the prescriptions of the French Enlightenment — blinded by 'el genio de la incredulidad' [the spirit of incredulity] that had conditioned his intellectual formation — and as thus incapable of appreciating the very different belief-system of Spaniards as reflected in their literature.[43] That Sismondi's judgement be viewed as the inevitable result of Protestant prejudice is typical of the period. What more strikingly emerges from these texts, perhaps, is the degree of orthodoxy — and I use the term precisely on account of its religious connotations — that the idealistic vision of the Spanish Golden Age propounded by the German theorists of historical Romanticism had now acquired.

Within the same framework, Spanish literature and ideas of the eighteenth century were felt to have been unnaturally coerced into following alien neo-Classical precepts that had destroyed their hitherto unquestionable authenticity as a faithful imaginative recreation of national culture. As is often the case when we come to study literary history and literary criticism of the years from 1840, we realize that the way had been most effectively prepared by Agustín Durán: in his famous *Discurso* of 1828, Durán had referred to the burying, in the eighteenth century, of Spain's distinctive creative genius 'bajo las ruinas de su magnífico templo' [beneath the ruins of its magnificent basilica] and its attempted replacement by 'un edificio pobre, mezquino y caduco, fundado sobre arena movediza, y extraño a los hábitos, costumbres, creencia y modo social de existir de sus compatriotas' [a mean, shabby and rotten building, founded upon shifting sand, and alien to the customs, habits, beliefs, and entire social existence of its compatriots]; he attributed this act of literary vandalism to 'los esfuerzos de los críticos del siglo pasado y presente, y el partido antinacional' [the efforts of critics of the last century and this one, and of the anti-national party].[44] As Amador de los Ríos was to see it, some thirty years later, those Spanish writers subscribing to the agenda of the newly-installed — and French! — Philip V seemed to have believed that literature had nothing in common 'ni con las creencias, ni con los sentimientos, ni con las costumbres' [with either our beliefs, intimate feelings, or way of life]. This crass misjudgement or 'error lamentable', perhaps admissible at the time of the Renaissance given the spontaneous enthusiasm that the recovery of the models of Classical antiquity had then provoked, had been catastrophically repeated in the eighteenth century, 'cuando el filosofismo del pasado [siglo] rompía todas las trabas de la autoridad' [when last century's philosophizing was breaking all bounds of authority]; the Enlightenment preference for Classical models he regarded as 'una aberración más en medio de tantas aberraciones como estaba el mundo presenciando' [just one more aberration among the countless aberrations the world was then witnessing].[45]

The ideological note here is clear, as is the aggrieved patriotism of José de la Revilla on reflecting that, under the Bourbon dynasty, all of those vices affecting the French nation and its royal court had been re-created in Spain in miniature, making Spaniards no more than mere echoes of that country's own very different inspiration; Spain had therefore inevitably been bound by the conventions, historical customs, taste and, ultimately, by the literature of a foreign nation, and had suffered the 'yugo tiránico' [tyrannical yoke] of Reason, which had stifled imaginative expression.[46] Javier de Burgos referred in like manner to a 'servidumbre francesa' [slavery to the French] that had informed Spanish culture under Philip V.[47] Manuel Moreno López, writing in the *Revista de España y del Extranjero*, was just as blunt in his assessment. As he put it, the extinction of the House of Austria and the accession of Philip V of Bourbon, had radically and abruptly changed Spanish intellectual life, taste, and customs; from that moment on, he gloomily synthesized, everything became French: our customs, our language, even our thoughts.[48] Gabino Tejado likewise referred to a period when a new French dynasty had imported into Spain the beliefs, social customs and literary doctrines of the court of Louis XIV;[49] in continuing his assessment of the eighteenth century, he labelled it a 'siglo "filósofo-mano"' [age of philosophical mania].[50] Some eight years later, in 1853, he scathingly remarked upon the gift of 'postración literaria' [literary lethargy] bestowed upon Spain by the 'siglo de los enciclopedistas' [age of the *Encyclopédie*]; it had resulted in a sham restoration permeated with 'todos los miasmas volterianos' [all of Voltaire's noxious emanations], one modelled upon a literature that was not just foreign but imaginatively alien to Spain.[51] As his historical summary concluded: 'contra la antigua piedad católica de nuestros padres, tuvimos nuestro poco de filosofismo volteriano' [in contrast with the devout Catholicism of our ancestors, we did acquire a small amount of Voltaire-style philosophizing].[52]

Common to all of the above pieces is their representation of the imposition of neo-Classical taste as an artificial and discordant severing of the hitherto harmonious relationship between a people and its imaginative expression. This predominant note is, once more, fundamentally Schlegelian. Both August Wilhelm and Friedrich's re-evaluation of Golden-Age theatre had been accompanied by an historical assessment of Spain's eighteenth-century literature as a period of decline after the glorious achievement of the previous century. The cause of this decadence, they felt, lay firmly in the principle of imitation, by which, to cite Giovanni Allegra's analysis, a fathomless abyss separated critical judgement from popular preference.[53] Thus according to Enrique Gil y Carrasco, if the arts were broadly understood to be faithful barometers — and he too uses the key phrase — of their historical age, the succession to the Spanish throne of a prince of the royal house of France had, not surprisingly, led to the replacement of an original and spontaneous native dramatic tradition by one of cold and prescriptive imitation; the unnatural imposition of French taste had meant that literature effectively ceased to be 'la expresión moral de la sociedad' [the moral expression of society].[54] Mesonero Romanos, writing in the *Semanario Pintoresco Español* in 1842, meanwhile, lamented the fanatical idolatry bestowed upon the literary precepts of Aristotle, Horace, and Boileau, which had led eighteenth-century writers unjustly to censure Spain's own 'grandes ingenios' [great geniuses] of the previous century; the Golden-Age dramatists, he insisted, had raised their national theatre to incomparable heights in their own time, while the elder Moratín had conversely produced a series of plays, impeccably neo-Classical in construction and vision but 'todas perfectamente soporíferas' [all perfectly calculated to send one to sleep].[55] Alcalá Galiano concurred in this judgement in condemning both Montiano and the elder Moratín, while he described Cadalso's *Sancho García* as a less than mediocre composition, one that had carried the spirit of imitation to the length of reproducing the heroic couplets of French drama, 'cuyo martilleo es insufrible a oídos españoles' [whose monotonous hammerblows are insufferable to Spanish ears].[56] The same writer would elsewhere declare in no uncertain terms that eighteenth-century Spanish literature was not just an imitation of French neo-Classicism but a poor copy of the literary output of the France of Louis XIV, which he described as entirely disfigured.[57] The Spanish *restauradores*, he subsequently affirmed, in the course of their laudable desire to correct the many deficiencies of early eighteenth-century literary style, 'despojaron el estilo de lo que tenía de espontáneo y español castizo' [stripped our style of everything that was spontaneous and truly Spanish].[58]

These last words effectively crystallize the issue. Whereas the Age of Reason had disparaged Spain's national cultural tradition, the changed perspectives ushered in by Romantic literary theory reinstated the native Spanish models of the Middle Ages and Golden Age by championing them as a pure and authentic representation of the country's imaginative identity. It was, significantly, this historicist understanding and interpretation of Romanticism that was to underpin the large majority of critical judgements during the period under discussion. Diego Coello y Quesada, writing in the popular *Semanario Pintoresco Español* in 1840, recreated with a lavish use of rhetoric the process of transformation from Enlightenment neo-Classicism to the Romanticism of the contemporary age; first his explanation for the aesthetic preferences of Enlightenment France:

> El pueblo que quiso hacer la gran parodia de Atenas y de Roma, el pueblo que en su sed de libertad, en su anhelo de igualdad mentida había arrancado la corona de la frente de sus reyes para levantar sobre ella a los nuevos tribunos, no podía menos de aceptar con entusiasmo los dramas de Voltaire, dramas en que los acentos de libertad, de gloria, se escuchaban, dramas en que los recuerdos de la antigua Grecia y de la augusta Roma se encontraban juntos

> [that people who endeavoured to create a great parody of Athens and Rome, that people who in their thirst for liberty, in their striving for false equality, had snatched the crown from the brow of their king and elevated in his place the new tribunes, could not but receive with enthusiasm the dramas of Voltaire, plays in which the tones of glorious liberty could be heard, plays in which memories of ancient Greece and the august days of Rome were combined].[59]

In his sweeping tones, as in so many similar evocations detailed in the previous chapter of this study, it is the extirpation of kingly power that emblematizes the political ideology of the Enlightenment, itself disparaged wholesale as a 'gran parodia' founded on a concept of 'igualdad mentida': the label of lamentable moral aberration firmly imprinted upon it by traditionalist historiography. At the same time, meanwhile, we are reminded of how, in the eyes of Spanish Romanticism, the inspiration of neo-Classical models was an integral component in the Enlightenment project, both aesthetically and ideologically speaking: neo-Classicism and republicanism hand in hand.[60] In opposition to this internally consistent and unitary cultural model, in Coello y Quesada's highly lyrical prose, emerged 'otra bandera apoyada en las tradiciones de los siglos, en los poéticos recuerdos de la edad media. Y esa enseña debió levantarse en Alemania, allí donde cada ruina de los desnudos castillos es un recuerdo, allí donde todo ofrece al alma la memoria de esos siglos pasados ya' [another different banner based upon centuries-old traditions, upon poetic memories of the Middle Ages. And that standard had necessarily to be unfurled in Germany, where every naked castle ruin is in itself a memory, where all that one finds proffers to the soul a reminder of ages past]. Romanticism therefore represented for him another internally coherent but intrinsically different world-view, one which recreated in aesthetic terms the spiritual elevation and dynamic certainties of the Middle Ages and one directly inspired by the conscious and ennobling memory of the sublimity of the Christian past. Its mission, as Coello y Quesada saw it, lay in a form of transcendent enabling process: a process in which the continuity of the mediaeval tradition be effectively re-established after the forced interregnum represented by the Enlightenment: 'Esta y no otra fue la misión del romanticismo, misión por cierto grande y gloriosa, y triunfó, sí, y la Francia humilló su altiva frente, y ella, la patria de Voltaire y Helvecio admitió la literatura de Shakespeare y Calderón' [Such and none other was the mission of Romanticism, a great and glorious mission to be sure, and it did indeed triumph, and France bowed its proud head, and France, the homeland of Voltaire and Helvetius received within it the literature of Shakespeare and Calderón].[61] Coello y Quesada therefore rejected the slur that Romanticism somehow represented immorality and depravity.

As I have shown elsewhere, most accusations of this type were anyway quite specifically directed, their target the dramas of Hugo and Dumas and the handful of Spanish imitations they had inspired in the 1830s. Gonzalo Morón, in typical fashion, railed vehemently against the wilder dramas of that decade, describing them as 'una literatura corrompida, parto bastardo de la filosofía anárquica del siglo XVIII' [a corrupted literature, the bastard birth of anarchic eighteenth-century philosophy],[62] while subscribing enthusiastically, as we have seen, to the tenets of Schlegelian or historical Romanticism. Eugenio de Tapia fulminated in similarly strong terms against 'las monstruosidades del género absurdo que con el mismo nombre [romanticismo], *malamente aplicado*, ha invadido la literatura moderna' [the monstrosities of that absurd genre which with the same name of Romanticism, *mistakenly applied*, has invaded our modern literature].[63] His view of the issue was perfectly straightforward: Spain already possessed 'una poesía lírica y dramática del género romántico' [a lyrical and dramatic poetry of the Romantic genre] of extraordinary beauty; why then the desire to 'propagar en España una secta de espúrio romanticismo, de extranjeros delirios, de monstruosidades y crímenes inauditos' [cultivate within Spain a spurious Romantic sect, one of foreign depravities, monstrosities, and unprecedented criminality]? Surely it was preferable to follow in the glorious steps of Spain's own most distinguished writers. Literary innovation he applauded, so long as it respect 'la moral, el decoro, la gallardía y el castizo lenguaje de nuestros antepasados' [the morality, decorum, gallantry, and true-blooded Spanish language of our forebears].[64] Tapia pulled no punches in expressing his disgust that works like *Angelo*, *Antony*, *La Torre de Nesle* 'y otros tan abominables como ellos' [and others as abominable as they] could be commonly designated 'Romantic'.[65] Revilla's position seems to have been informed by the same basic distinction between conflicting interpretations of Romanticism, as is revealed by his proud observation that Spanish theatre 'felizmente ha comenzado a cerrar los pasos a las inspiraciones sensuales de Dumas, y abiértolas al espiritualismo, en cuyo seno existe la sublimidad de la poesía' [has, fortunately, begun to close its doors against the sensualist inspiring models of Dumas, and has opened them to that spirituality in whose bosom throbs the true poetic sublime].[66] Typically, the drama of Dumas is perceived not as genuinely Romantic but as a by-product of eighteenth-century sensualist philosophy; as expressed in the regular 'Revista de la quincena' in the literary magazine *El Pensamiento*, 'Dumas pertenece por su moral a esa ruidosa escuela literaria que acompañó en Francia a la última revolución [...] revistiendo el escepticismo del siglo pasado' [In terms of morality, Dumas belongs to that rowdy literary movement that emerged in France alongside its recent revolution [...] bearing all the trappings of the scepticism of last century].[67] We cannot but note the insistent connection between the Romantic radicalism of the 1830s and the religious scepticism originating in the French Enlightenment and at large since the eighteenth century. Equally prominent, however, is the perceived antagonism between the 'extranjeros delirios' of this 'secta de espúrio romanticismo' and the moral superiority of a truly Romantic and *castizo* Spanish tradition.

Such was the ferocity of this concerted attack on Romantic radicalism that by 1840 José María Quadrado was prompted to attempt to strike a more temperate note. Writing in the *Semanario Pintoresco Español*, he felt obliged to qualify the analogy between 'los principios disolventes y anárquicos del siglo XVIII' [the eighteenth-century principles of anarchy and dissolution] and the anarchical literature of his own age, or, as he put it, 'entre los horrores de los jacobinos y los horrores de los románticos' [between the horrors of the Jacobins and the horrors of the Romantics]. He himself condemned as loudly as anyone else 'ese cúmulo de absurdos morales y literarios que no sabemos por qué ha de llamarse romanticismo' [that heap of moral and literary absurdity that, one knows not why, has to be called Romanticism]. As far as he was concerned, however, the question of definition had been admirably resolved by Lista, whom he credited with having guaranteed 'la caída de esta moda, a cuya sombra el mal gusto y la inmoralidad empezaban a cundir terriblemente' [the fall from favour of this passing fashion, beneath whose auspices bad taste and immorality were beginning to spread most terrifyingly].[68]

The move away from this temporary vogue towards the instinctive spirituality of the Golden-Age tradition, identified by Revilla as a more reassuring tendency towards a coherent literary movement, was very much in keeping with contemporary interpretations of Romanticism. We can regard in the same light the words of an unnamed commentator eulogizing in the pages of the *Semanario Pintoresco Español* Mariano Roca de Togores's 1837 drama *Doña María de Molina*. The reviewer welcomed the fact that modern Spanish theatre, in the hands of a select band of young writers, was taking on 'aquel carácter original, filosófico y profundo que conviene al gusto del país' [that original, philosophical and intellectually profound character that is in accord with national taste]. Spanish dramatists had momentarily given their public to fear that the national stage might follow the 'funestos ejemplos' [fateful examples] offered by France. However, belonging to a different society, dedicated to studying its true nature and needs and mindful of the cultural and social differences that separated Spain from its neighbour across the Pyrenees, they had written for a more impartial and thoughtful audience, one that still believed that 'la moralidad es la primera prenda de los obras del ingenio' [morality is the principal gift of works of genius]. Spanish dramatists were therefore now availing themselves of a 'justa libertad literaria' [true literary freedom] and finding sublime models in Spain's own Golden-Age drama; writing accordingly, they were being loudly applauded by popular audiences who saw in these works 'la expresión de sus ideas, de su civilización y de su poesía' [the expression of their own ideas, their own civilization, their own poetry].[69] As a later review in the same volume of the *Semanario Pintoresco* indicated, radical dramas — in this case Gil y Zárate's notorious *Carlos II el hechizado* — might be dismissed as no more than conscious imitations of extravagant French originals, of a type written with the aim of rivalling the most extravagant productions of Hugo and Dumas;[70] another influential critic, Salvador Bermúdez de Castro, trenchantly labelled such plays 'insulsas imitaciones de groseros originales' [insipid imitations of unpalatable originals].[71] As the reviewer of García Gutiérrez's *El paje* expressed it, again in the same volume of the *Semanario Pintoresco*, literary critics devoutly wished contemporary dramatists to 'aprovechar de lo favorable de la nueva escuela, sin incurrir en los errores de sus modelos' [take from the new school what is beneficial without falling into the same errors as their inspiring models]; to give free rein to the imagination 'sin abandonar empero la verdadera filosofía; la filosofía de la virtud' [without discarding, nonetheless, the true philosophy, that is the philosophy of virtue].[72]

Charges of moral criminality levelled against Romanticism by its enemies were therefore, in most cases, refuted; as an anonymous reviewer in the *Semanario Pintoresco* saw it, this was a marginal question prompted only by the fact that certain writers 'guiados por varios estímulos más o menos criminales, han explayado sus principios antisociales bajo la forma de moda' [guided by various more or less criminal stimuli, have propounded their anti-social principles in a fashionable guise].[73] The common view was thus that the name of Romanticism had been unnaturally distorted out of its true meaning by the nefarious shock-tactics of a handful of plays. Coello y Quesada, in the article already cited, would affirm that 'Acaso en ninguna nación el romanticismo (y ya hemos dicho lo que por esta palabra tantas veces parodiada entendemos) pudo hallar tan favorable acogida que en España, en la nación que tenía a un Calderón, a un Lope de Vega, y a un Moreto' [Perhaps in no other nation could Romanticism (and we have alrady stated what we understand by this word that is so often parodied) find such a favourable reception as in Spain, the nation that produced men like Calderón, Lope de Vega, and Moreto]; for what are the works of our great dramatists, he continued, if not 'bellísimos, magníficos poemas donde el amor, la religión, el honor, todos los sentimientos elevados y caballerescos se encuentran por do quier' [the most beautiful and magnificent poems, in which love, faith, honour, every elevated and chivalric sentiment can everywhere be found].[74] What is particularly striking about not just this passage but many similar ones of the same period is their revelation of the extraordinary resilience, within Spain, of the basic Schlegelian definition. Coello y Quesada, like the majority of his contemporaries, continues to expound the essential formula found in the Schlegels' Vienna lectures *after* events of the 1830s, signally in the theatre, might have led to a redefining of Romanticism or at least to the questioning of the previous working definition. That the reiteration of what was a fundamentally reassuring interpretation of the term owed much to extra-literary considerations is probably beyond dispute, but this does not alter the basic fact of its broad restatement. Leonardo Romero underlines this rejection of the pessimistic inclinations of French Romantic theatre in the work of Lista, Donoso, Quadrado, and others, all of whom subscribe, nonetheless, to the basic prescriptions of historical Romanticism.[75]

Coello y Quesada is equally representative in his prescriptions for Spanish theatre: Romantic drama had, he declared in continuing his treatment of the same theme, come to Spain in the guise of a long-lost son in unfamiliar attire; let it retain those noble and elevated feelings found in Golden-Age theatre, but let it be less narrative and more overtly philosophical, let it be 'crítico y pensador' [scrutinizing and thoughtful] in keeping with the demands of the nineteenth century.[76] Bermúdez de Castro insisted in similar terms that 'libertar al drama antiguo de todo cuanto es incompatible con nuestras nuevas costumbres, es la gran obra que puede regenerar el teatro enlazando los vástagos del porvenir con los troncos y las tradiciones de los pasados tiempos' [to free the old drama of all that is incompatible with our changed way of life, that is the great enterprise that can regenerate the theatre, binding the new shoots of the future to the trunks of past traditions];[77] these last words intimate the profoundly conservative idea of organic connection between present and past underlying the critical discourse. Writing later that year in the same magazine under his pen-name of 'Lúculo', Bermúdez was to hail Gil y Zárate's *Un monarca y su privado* as a felicitous mixture of 'el género español y el género romántico' [the Spanish and the Romantic] and as a noteworthy change of style from the concessions to passing fashion that the same author had allowed himself to follow in *Carlos II el hechizado*.[78] We encounter, then, the prevailing distinction between 'good' and 'bad' forms of Romanticism that so acutely defines the historical moment. As expressed in an article significantly headed 'Reforma teatral' and published in the *Revista de Teatros* in 1841, the temporarily fashionable French Romantic drama was treated as a foreign import conceived by minds 'más exaltadas y facticias que las nuestras' [more extreme and factitious than our own]; as such it could not take root, the reviewer wrote, in a country where Romantic works had been born centuries before in a drastically different form. It had been replaced by a necessary and manifest transformation in which Spanish dramatists were producing a new version of the old *comedia* 'adecuada a nuestros gustos, a nuestras exigencias, y a nuestras circunstancias' [well suited to our tastes, our needs and our current situation];[79] the references to alien, subversive forms of cultural expression incompatible with Spain's own collective imagination, as much as the emphatic repetition of the possessives based on 'nuestro', forcefully indicate once again the *casticista* provenance of the critical account. Mesonero Romanos clearly documents prevailing changes in the theatre, commenting a year later that Spanish drama was returning to the model of the *comedia* and 'apartándose de la exageración y los horrores' [stepping away from wild exaggeration and horrors]. He recognized the leading role played by, among others, Gil y Zárate and Zorrilla, and placed the latter within a conscious revival of the school of Rojas and Calderón.[80]

A young generation of Spanish writers had then, as Agustín Durán read it, been no more than briefly 'deslumbrados por el Romanticismo malo' [bedazzled by a wicked form of Romanticism]; subsequently, and having duly studied 'la poesía nacional' [our national poetry], they had chosen to follow instead 'el camino trazado por la buena crítica' [the path laid down by sound criticism], producing in the process 'obras que honran la presente generación' [works which honour the current generation].[81] José Escobar has accordingly noted that for Durán an idealized vision of 'el pueblo', a Spanish version of the German *Volksgeist* imaginatively anchored in Golden-Age theatre, represented a safeguard for a *casticismo* that had been threatened by Romantic radicalism.[82] Philip Silver, meanwhile, observes that 'historical Romantics' were moved to define themselves with references to a 'good' Romanticism and in reaction to the version imported from France.[83] Where I differ with this analysis is in the question of degree: Silver sees such moments as the only occasions when a protean and extremely broad-based 'community of thought', professed by an ever larger *moderado* sector, committed itself to any kind of firm definition; while concurring in his perception of historical Romanticism within Spain as a widespread 'current of opinion, a strategy of legitimation, a general ambience',[84] as should now be abundantly clear I detect within that intellectual community perhaps a greater degree of coherence and a more specific intentionality of purpose, and certainly a more transparent employment of its own chosen terminology. These issues aside, it should not surprise us, given the popularity of Durán's basic point of view, to find Fermín Gonzalo Morón noting that, in contrast with the previous age, 'La filosofía de este siglo ha descubierto, que su misión ha sido, y es más noble y elevada, como que tiene por objeto satisfacer las necesidades morales de los pueblos' [Philosophy has in our time discovered that its mission has been and remains more noble and more elevated, that it has as its object that of satisfying the moral necessities of nations].[85] Moral necessities, it went without saying, that were objectively verifiable, and precisely determined by an orthodox and homogeneous native tradition: in a nutshell, the essential *casticismo* of conservative historical Romanticism. What we have, then, is what Pérez-Bustamante Mourier defines as the perception, in a stylized but stereotypical form, of what differentiates a people, a process culminating in a *casticista* outlook that is constructed from within, a sympathetic and positive but self-satisfied and manipulative attempt at an integrative vision.[86]

In order fully to illustrate the argument I have been developing in this chapter, I feel it worthwhile at this point to examine the broad application of the framework of ideas considered here in one significant and representative text: Amador de los Ríos's introduction to his *Historia crítica de la literatura española*, the first volume of which was published in 1861. This practical exposition of all of the major tenets of Romantic historicism renders transparently clear the ideological uses of literary history in mid-nineteenth-century Spain.

In common with the previous generation of Romantic critics, for example, Amador laments the imposition, in the reign of Philip V, of an alien and unnatural set of artistic prescriptions. Whilst acknowledging the abject state of Spanish literature at the time of the Bourbon succession, he denounces the dogmatic and monolithic adoption of 'el más reprensible exclusivismo' [the most reprehensible exclusivism] (pp. xli–xlii) actively encouraged by the new royal court among the intelligentsia in an attempt to restore artistic standards. Ignacio de Luzán, he felt, had condemned out of hand the glories of the national literary past simply because they had not observed to the letter prescriptive neo-Classical formulae; Luzán seemed to him to have been ashamed of his compatriots, imputing to them the crime, as Amador sarcastically puts it, of flouting a set of artistic rules 'que no podía convenir a las costumbres ni a las creencias del pueblo castellano' [incongruent with the customs and beliefs of the people of Spain], and this within a popular verse tradition habitually free from such prescriptive dogma (p. xliii). The really telling phrase here is surely the one I have cited in the original; more damning than the autocratic imposition of arbitrary precepts had been, in Amador's eyes, the determination to inflict upon a nation a set of aesthetic models and standards alien to its cultural heritage, a proceeding which, unsurprisingly in his view, 'llegaba al cabo con su exclusivismo y su intolerancia a irritar el sentimiento nacional' [came eventually, as a result of its exclusivism and intolerance, to offend patriotic feeling] (p. xliv). Thus Vicente García de la Huerta, in the *Teatro español* of 1785, had set out to prove to 'la muchedumbre imitadora' [the rabble of imitators] that such nationalistic feeling was a perfectly justified and respectable position; Huerta's text is described by Amador as a 'formidable máquina de guerra, levantada contra los galicistas' [formidable engine of war deployed against the gallicists] (p. liv), despite its undoubted exaggerations. The same defence of national culture wins Tomás Antonio Sánchez considerable acclaim, for he had, according to Amador, popularized after a period of lamentable abandonment and neglect some venerable monuments of Castilian culture, in the process throwing to the ground a set of erudite but alien and obsessive concerns nurtured by factional exclusivism; the texts published by Sánchez are themselves described by Amador in terms immediately reminiscent of Herder and the Schlegels as 'testimonios muy provechosos para el conocimiento de los usos y costumbres de la edad media' [valuable sources of evidence contributing to our knowledge of the customs and way of life of the Middle Ages] (p. lvii).

In the same section of his introduction, Amador reveals even more clearly the ideological direction of his study, for while his accusation that 'Lograban los partidarios de la escuela galo-clásica a fuerza de sarcasmos y denuestos desacreditar las producciones del teatro español' [The supporters of the gallo-Classical faction, by means of their endless sarcasm and mockery, succeeded in discrediting Spanish theatre] is an assertion entirely representative of the period in its tone and argument, the real cause of much of the venom contained in his text is shown in the following comment that 'habíanse también los partidarios del arte clásico postrado de rodillas ante el espíritu enciclopédico' [the followers of Classicism had, moreover, gone down on their knees before the moving spirit of the *Encyclopédie*]. Once more, neo-Classical taste and perceived Enlightenment sedition are intimately connected. Amador, meanwhile, teases out the rather obvious irony residing in the fact that 'los que negando toda autoridad y rompiendo toda tradición, proclamaban en absoluto el libre examen, levantaron en medio de sus exagerados principios fanáticos altares a un arte y a una literatura que representaban una civilización, muerta había muchos siglos' [those who rejected all authority and broke with every tradition, and trumpeted aloud the value of free and independent inquiry, in the midst of their extreme principles raised an altar to the art and literature of a civilization that had died many centuries before]. As we suspect, his view of the Enlightenment generally is very much that of Spain's conservative Romanticism, as his broad-brush evocation illustrates: 'todo lo había invadido aquel espíritu trastornador, para quien nada significaba el respeto de las generaciones pasadas, haciendo en consecuencia estériles o frustráneas las saludables enseñanzas de la historia' [there had invaded everything that perverse spirit in whose eyes the respect of generations past stood for nothing, a spirit which consequently rendered the salutary lessons of history fruitless and futile] (pp. lxiv–lxv). Indeed so close is the connection that Amador, like numerous other Catholic commentators, stigmatizes the entire age as having been inspired by 'el genio de la incredulidad, que parecía presidir los destinos del siglo XVIII' [that spirit of incredulity which seemed to direct eighteenth-century destiny] (p. lxv). Such had been the philosophical tendencies of that age, and such the intolerance of the factions which had sought a place within them, he went on, that the writing of a history of Spanish literature would have been an impossible task.

Amador's view of his own age as one struggling to overcome the legacy of the previous century, as an age of renewal after the man-made catastrophe that had preceded it, also squares impressively with the tenor of broader historical studies; as he saw it the nineteenth century had no option but to take up the legacy bequeathed it: 'triste herencia por cierto, si hubieran venido a punto de realizarse todos los sueños de las sectas filosóficas, abortadas por el enciclopedismo' [a sorry legacy to be sure, if all the dreams of those philosophical sects spawned by the *Encyclopédie* had ever come to fruition]. However, since humanity never suffered in vain even the most painful disasters and tribulations, his own age had begun to reconstruct 'lo derribado sin razón ni ley' [what had been senselessly and lawlessly demolished] (p. lxvi). Implicit within Amador's account is again the sense of a Providential design, of a working out of events according to a predisposed divine pattern. Again like cultural historians, moreover, Amador detects the residual influence of the baleful thought-patterns of the eighteenth century in the early decades of his own: he regrets, for example, that Moratín, in his *Orígenes del teatro español*, had not shed 'aquel espíritu de escuela, que debía esterilizar aún por algún tiempo las más esquisitas investigaciones de la erudición' [that spirit of faction, which would go on poisoning the ground of the finest investigative research for several years to come] (p. lxviii); Hermosilla he regards as 'dominado de reprensible exclusivismo' [dominated by a reprehensible exclusivism], his textbook of rhetoric *Arte de hablar en prosa y en verso* a lamentable example to set before nineteenth-century students (p. lxviii). Finally, in mentioning Martínez de la Rosa's 1827 *Poética*, he feels that the author's undoubted talent simply accentuated the feeling of regret that he had not been able to cast off entirely the prescriptive neo-Classicism of his youth and align himself foursquare behind the new 'movimiento filosófico que tomaba a su vista la crítica literaria' [that new philosophical movement that literary criticism was adopting before his very eyes] (p. lxxii).[87]

Amador's view of Martínez de la Rosa's text sharply contrasts, for example, with that recently adduced by Martínez Torrón, who sees the *Poética* as a work of transition, a bridge towards Romanticism, declaring that in Martínez de la Rosa's commentary the new Romantic aesthetic was clearly present, even though that commentary derives principally from neo-Classical sources. The divergence of interpretation stems directly from the fact that Martínez Torrón's thesis sets aside more or less completely the question of literary form as a factor in the definition of 'Romantic'. To discard such a question, of course, is to fly in the face of the entire nineteenth-century context — when the issue of the definition of Romanticism inevitably *did* contain a formal question — and thus to distance onself unduly from the historical reality. Martínez Torrón contends that if a given writer *feels* as a Romantic would, even though he express those feelings in neo-Classical forms, then that writer is essentially a Romantic; to our own day such an assertion is hardly outlandish, but it is so fundamentally at odds with the nineteenth-century Spanish mind that to use such a premise in an attempt sympathetically to understand the intellectual workings of that century is surely misguided.

The shift in critical attitudes to which Amador refers is in fact evidenced for him by the 'saludable doctrina' [salutary doctrine] disseminated by Lista (p. lxix), which had produced, as far as Amador was concerned, an incalculably beneficial effect on

Spanish literature and literary ideas. A commendable change of perspective on the national literary past meant that the Spanish *comedia* was finally being recognized as an imaginative communication of 'las costumbres y las creencias de aquel gran pueblo que había sujetado a su triunfante carro el cuello de dos mundos' [the customs and beliefs of that great people that had yoked to its triumphal chariot two worlds]; Calderón, he continued, was a 'llama viva' [living flame] whose work faithfully reflected Spain's entire civilization (p. lxxi). The Schlegelian provenance of the whole is, as on many occasions, inescapable. Not surprisingly, then, Agustín Durán, who like Lista had turned his mind to the sources of genuine Spanish art, as Amador expressed it, had sought there 'la ley superior de su existencia' [the transcendent principle of its existence] (p. lxxiii). He had produced, according to Amador, the crowning achievement of his generation in the field of literary study, while his work had led to many younger men's grouping themselves around 'la bandera de la tolerancia' [the banner of tolerance], their task being to 'restituir al pueblo español el sentimiento de su nacionalidad, tristemente amortiguado por los bastardos intereses de añejos sistemas' [return to the Spanish people an apprehension of their nationhood, lamentably stifled by the illegitimate personal ambitions found in alien systems] (p. lxxiv). If these last phrases remind us of nothing so much as the strident pamphlets published some fifty years earlier by Böhl von Faber in his propagation of Schlegelian ideas, then we are not surprised to find the indefatigable German given honourable mention along with numerous other foreign writers whose labours, in Amador's words, 'no han podido menos de vencer y aun avasallar añejas preocupaciones, desvaneciendo la ojeriza, con que era antes vista fuera de España nuestra primitiva literatura' [could not but vanquish and indeed hold in thrall an alien set of concerns, thus putting an end to the bias against our ancient literature that had long been felt outside of Spain] (p. lxxxvii). These 'añejos sistemas' and prejudiced 'ojeriza' would naturally include, it goes without saying, neo-Classical formalism.

Among those young Spaniards who had flocked to the banner of Durán, meanwhile, Amador lists the historians Eugenio de Tapia and Fermín Gonzalo Morón — however extraordinary might seem to us the appearance of the latter beneath a banner of tolerance and moderation, and the more strictly literary names of Juan Eugenio Hartzenbusch, Antonio Gil y Zárate, Pedro José Pidal, Eugenio de Ochoa, and Mariano José de Larra. The last, it is interesting to note — and I feel that Amador's words here speak volumes — is singularly commended for two things: his ability to 'combatir el romanticismo fisiológico, que con los dramas franceses comenzaba a cundir en nuestro suelo' [confront that physiological Romanticism, which in the form of the French dramas was beginning to spread into our own land]; and his desire to effect, in *Macías*, a restoration of traditional Spanish theatre (p. lxxiv). The emphases typical of conservative historical Romanticism are once again transparent.

One further notable link with other areas of historiographical study is provided by Amador's castigation of neo-Classicists and Enlightenment thinkers alike for their excessive preoccupation with external form, with no more than the empirical reality of phenomena, with the consequent lack of appreciation of their spiritual or metaphysical content. Thus while the desire of 'el espíritu enciclopédico' [the spirit of the *Encyclopédie*] to seek inspiration exclusively in Classical antiquity had been an absurd pretension that could only lead 'a la negación y al abismo' [to utter rejection and to the void] (p. lxxvi), his own century now sought, in its characteristic spirit of tolerance, to 'penetrar los misterios de otras edades' [penetrate the mysteries of other ages] (p. lxxvii). At the same time critical inquiry, instead of being limited to a desultory examination and appraisal of external forms, had perceived 'real significación y trascendencia en el desarrollo de la civilización de los pueblos' [true transcendent meaning in the flowering of civilization and of peoples] (p. lxxvii). Once more, as the choice of 'trascendencia' most tellingly reveals, there is a degree of religious intentionality behind Amador's words; George Ticknor he regards as having been oblivious to the real significance of 'un pensamiento fecundo y trascendental' [a fertile and transcendent principle] that had guided the history of the Spanish Reconquest: that is, 'el santo fuego de la fe' [the sacred flame of faith] (p. lxxxix).

Amador de los Ríos therefore presents us with, in Juretschke's words, a broad Romantic perspective politically akin to a conservative Christian vision of an integrated and seamless world.[88] As Leonardo Romero has more recently stressed, the conservative roots of national literature are here located 'en un idealizado fondo cristiano de porosa base popular' [in an idealized Christian bedrock with a permeable popular foundation].[89] Amador's text is annotated on several occasions with reference to Friedrich Schlegel and is one in which the German theorist's influence is at many other points indirectly felt. In the broadest terms it adopts what the Vienna lectures designate 'the moral point of view', that perspective from which literature can be 'more easily contemplated' and 'more securely judged'; crucially, this outlook is commended as the exclusive means of discovering 'whether a literature be throughout national and in harmony with the national weal and the national spirit', and as a mode of deciding which, if adopted, will 'be found in favour of the Spaniards'.[90] What Amador's text exemplifies perhaps above all else, then, is the durability of the Schlegelian Romantic perspective in Spanish intellectual debate; the lease of life enjoyed by Romantic historicism is extended well into the second half of the century, after its survival of the fierce literary controversy prompted by the advent of Romantic radicalism and via its assimilation into a broad movement towards 'buenas ideas' in the wake of that same controversy.[91]

As we begin to draw conclusions from the textual material adduced here, it is possible to see that, in literary history as in wider historiographical method, most perceptions of the contemporary age were firmly anchored in a single defining set of ideas, a set of ideas that reveals a characteristically Romantic yet at the same time overwhelmingly conservative response. Vico's developmental framework, the nucleus of many an historical overview, would be effectively paralleled in the application to more strictly literary or intellectual history of the organicism deriving from Herder and the Schlegels. Whereas in broader histories, the eighteenth century was almost universally decried for having perverted and distorted the Providential ordering of things, for having removed the idea of God from humanity's cosmological vision, in literary terms the same century was almost without exception blamed for having corrupted the essential relationship between the intimate reality of a given culture and that same culture's most spontaneous and precious forms of expression. If the bond between God and humanity had been broken by the rationalist doctrines of the *philosophes*, we are led to conclude, then a similarly affective bond between the physiognomy of a people and that people's historically determined imaginative hypothesis might likewise be destroyed by the perceived anachronisms and incongruities of neo-Classicism. Specifically, as we expand the argument, French neo-Classicism as institutionalized in the higher echelons of eighteenth-century Spanish society had conspired to destroy Spain's native literary tradition in the same way that the pernicious doctrines of the *Encyclopédie* and of the French Revolution threatened to corrode — in their 'disolvente' effects — the moral certainties and close homogeneity of outlook of the Catholic people of Spain. French Romantic drama and its Spanish imitations had likewise threatened to pervert and distort the broadly accepted view of Romanticism; since this form of drama, if we continue to follow the seemingly irresistible logic of the period, had its fundamental origins in the doctrines of the French Enlightenment, it was now seeking to communicate the same moral depravity, the same despairing nihilism and the same formula of wanton destruction that for Spanish Catholics had characterized the thought-processes of the previous age. Inevitably then, what we now know as liberal Romanticism came to be seen as nothing less than the literary corollary of the earlier political Terror. Íñigo Sánchez Llama describes the application of the basic conservative perspective as a striking anachronism present in every area of the Isabeline experience, viscerally opposed to the idea of progress that stemmed from the Industrial Revolution and the Revolution of 1789 in France; a conservative reaction that spared not an ounce of effort in striving to countervail those aesthetic doctrines that might be associated with a liberal and reformist society.[92] An identical form of rhetoric, indeed a virtually identical vocabulary, in an identical attack upon a single perceived adversary; what we have then is an extraordinarily consistent expression of the same basic Manichaean outlook, in which literature constitutes, in José Escobar's words, an integrative part of the ideological reality of the age.[93] Where the detailed body of original textual evidence considered here reveals the internal contradictions of those more schematic approaches adopted by several modern critics is in its depiction of Romanticism — that is, the majority Schlegelian Romanticism pre-eminent in the period — not as a heterodox or subversive literary creed threatening the stability of society as traditionally conceived, but as a form of orthodoxy, a fundamentally reassuring and cohesive element in sharp contrast to the 'disolvente' prescriptions of the earlier Enlightenment.

Both August Wilhelm and Friedrich Schlegel had of course heaped the most extravagant praise upon Spain's native literary tradition as enshrined in the *romancero* and in Golden-Age drama. It can only be considered as natural, therefore, that their numerous Spanish followers would strike in their own writings such ringing notes of cultural nationalism; less surprising still, perhaps, that those writers should eventually lapse into such strident or even bombastic terms. More striking, possibly due to many modern critics' lack of acquaintance with the original texts and consequently to those critics' cursory reference to the exclusively literary components of Schlegelian ideas, is the fact that Friedrich Schlegel's work at least was not entirely lacking in the kind of invective contained in Spanish critical writing of the period we are examining. Friedrich Schlegel, it should be remembered, unlike Vico but in common with Spanish literary commentators later confronting the same issues, was writing in the wake not just of French cultural pre-eminence (a pre-eminence that would itself further increase in the decades after the Italian thinker's death in 1744), but also of what came to be widely regarded as the catastrophic end result of the work containing and projecting that pre-eminence: the Revolution and the Terror. He was also, and this is surely not without its own significance, writing just four years after his mature conversion to the Roman Catholic faith.[94] Two passages in particular from his lectures delivered in Vienna in 1812 emblematize his response in terms that have a notable affinity with later Spanish reactions to that object of unrestrained loathing 'el filósofo de Ferney'; that is, Voltaire. As rendered in John Gibson Lockhart's English translation of 1818, the French writer's 'perversity of genius' and 'aversion for Christianity' meant that 'his spirit operated as *a corrosive and destructive engine for the dissolving of all earnest, moral and religious modes of thinking*'. His view of history consisted 'in expressing, on every opportunity, and in every possible form, hatred for monks, clergymen, Christianity, and, in general, for all religion'.[95] The highlighted piece of phrasing communicates precisely, it goes without saying, the historical depiction of Voltaire and of the Enlightenment generally that was so to dominate later Spanish intellectual history. The very words chosen are exactly consonant with the vituperation of both Reformation and Enlightenment as 'disolvente' that was so strongly to characterize Spanish historiography of the period under discussion. What is more, Amador de los Ríos, who specifically cited Friedrich Schlegel's text on several occasions in the introduction to his *Historia crítica de la literatura española*, would himself reconstrue in more broad-based terms the German commentator's categorization of Voltaire's impious genius, feeling the entire cultural production of eighteenth-century France to have been inspired by a similarly malignant 'genio de la incredulidad'. While the passage quoted would undoubtedly have been music to the ears of men like Balmes, Donoso, Gonzalo Morón, Tejado, and the rest, Friedrich Schlegel's subsequent devastating attack on the republican outlook of Voltaire's writing would have struck an equally welcome chord with the Spanish defenders of throne and altar: 'In regard to politics, its prevalent spirit is a partial, and in the situation of modern Europe, an absurd predilection for the republican notions of antiquity, accompanied very frequently with an altogether false conception, or at least extremely imperfect knowledge of the true spirit and essence of republicanism'. Among the followers of Voltaire, he pinpointed 'a decided and bigoted hatred of all kingly power and nobility, and in general of all those modes of life and government which have been produced by what is called the feudal system'.[96] What we have in Friedrich Schlegel's Vienna lectures is then an extension of Romantic aesthetics into an openly ideological domain, with a political direction and ferocity of expression which anticipate in their motivation and rhetoric many of the Spanish texts I have been examining in detail here. The same transparent parallels between Romanticism and the spiritual ideals of Christianity and monarchy, between neo-Classicism and the aspirations of philosophical rationalism and political republicanism, dominate Friedrich Schlegel's text as they were to dominate so much of the writing of Donoso, Gonzalo Morón, Amador de los Ríos, and others. Francisco María Tubino, when he came to produce his broad overview of 'El Romanticismo en España' in the pages of the *Revista Contemporánea* in 1877, stressed the 'decidido carácter ultramontano' [decidedly ultramontane nature] of the Schlegels' literary doctrine; he remained apparently unaware, however, that his summary of the motivation and aims of Romanticism as conceived and expressed in Germany could equally stand as an admirable résumé of those ideas put forward by so many of his countrymen in preceding decades. In Tubino's terms:

> Nacía para los alemanes el romanticismo de un doble deseo: oponer a la influencia sensualista, anárquica y volteriana de la literatura francesa el contraste de un florecimiento creyente y conservador, nutrido en la savia nacional; y a la vez servir la causa del espiritualismo católico, oponiéndolo al naturalismo hueco y artificial del Consulado y del Imperio. De esta suerte, el romanticismo englobaba tres ideas capitales: la ética, la política y la religiosa, que armonizándose en una superior relación, la estética, negaba y combatía el neoclasicismo jurídico, filosófico y literario, encarnado en la Francia.[97]

> [For the Germans Romanticism stemmed from two complementary desires: to hold up against the sensualist, anarchical, and Volterian literature of France the contrasting blossoming of a conservative and devoutly religious tradition nourished by the sap of nationhood; and at the same time to serve the cause of Catholic spirituality that it upheld against the hollow and artificial naturalism of the Consulate and Empire. In this way, Romanticism contained three founding ideas: ethical, political, and religious respectively, which, joining in a transcendent harmony, in aesthetics, were able to refute and to counteract that legislative, philosophical, and literary Classicism personified by France.]

Tubino's words, I need hardly add, represent a remarkably accurate synthesis of the pattern of ideas assessed here; indeed it is difficult to read this passage without assuming it to be, in part at least, prompted by the tenor of much of the writing I have been examining, with much of which Tubino would surely have been familiar. While Tubino was himself keen to stress the very different Romantic prescriptions underlying the poetry of Espronceda,[98] his chosen expression in the passage cited is nevertheless intimately revealing; a form of expression consciously or unconsciously shaped, I would contend, by many of the Spanish texts of the previous generation: Tubino later acknowledges, for example, that a reaction in favour of German critical thought arose in the Iberian peninsula when France and French influence appeared to be at the height of their ascendancy.[99]

Spanish literary critics, after all, if we remind ourselves once more of the connection between aesthetic and political spheres, like Spanish cultural historians of the Romantic period, had been writing in the wake of an immediate and potent threat to the sovereignty and stability of their own country. Their preference for *lo castizo* is necessarily bound up with an almost paranoiac insistence upon the inherent dangers of admitting culturally alien and philosophically and politically subversive forms of literary expression. At the time of the introduction into Spain of those German theories of Romanticism that were to prove an important catalyst for forms of literary *casticismo*, meanwhile, French neo-Classical taste had been the preferred mode of expression of *afrancesados* and liberal patriots alike: not just Moratín, Javier de Burgos, and Lista but Quintana, Martínez de la Rosa, and the Duque de Rivas as well. Taking the broad historical perspective obtaining within the period, therefore, the *doceañistas* as much as the constitutional liberals of the *trienio* figure as imitators both in a literary sense, given the unconditional adherence of their most conspicuous literary intellectuals to neo-Classical canons of taste, and in a political one, given the prevalent view that their revolutionary inspiration had derived from the despised Enlightenment formulae. Men like Martínez de la Rosa and the Duque de Rivas, it should be noted, figure as Romantic writers at a moment in their lives when they act as political conservatives; the period of their greatest political radicalism coincides more or less exactly with that of their virtually unconditional adherence to neo-Classical standards. Attempts by certain modern critics to circumvent or distort this set of contextual parameters emerge as singularly unconvincing in the face of all the evidence to the contrary. As we shall see in the concluding chapter, their alternative interpretation is only possible via an adulteration of the term 'Romanticism' that detaches it from its particular and specific nineteenth-century context and allocates it instead to a politically partial late twentieth-century perspective. To cite Leonardo Romero's observation, interpretations of Romanticism amount to projections of intimate self-examinations made by the interpreters themselves, and are intensely revealing of the respective contexts in which such interpretations take place.[100] Vicente Llorens, for example, readily confessed to using, in his analysis of Spanish Romanticism, the kind of socio-political orientation characteristic of his own day.[101] This reading, one that equates Spanish Romanticism with Spanish political liberalism and demonizes an opposing and supposedly minority conservative Romanticism is a process that amounts, within Philip Silver's terms, to nothing less than a '"restitutional" spin', comparable to the earlier traditionalists' own manipulation of their historical past, and one that makes only a pretence of examining the full historical context. As Silver bravely contends, intimating the same kind of historical transference evident in the work of nineteenth-century writers: 'the Republicans and their disciples projected their own post-Civil War exiles backward onto the romantics; and young Marxist academics wouldn't touch the romantics unless they were at least Liberals. No one dared to question the Romantics' liberalism, their romanticism, or their eighteenth-century entailments'.[102] An acute example, we might reflect, is provided by Ricardo Navas Ruiz's transparently resentful assertion that there does not exist, despite claims to the contrary, any conservative Romanticism set upon upholding the traditions of throne and altar: this he views as an archaic and impossible political pipedream, an intellectual cul-de-sac that ended in failure and left behind it no valid or enduring literary testimony.[103] Navas Ruiz's perspective is, quite clearly, irreconcilable with the considerable body of evidence examined here upon which I have chosen to base my own very different thesis.

Finally, and within the broadest possible terms, the assessments of literary history considered in this chapter possess a remarkable degree of congruity with many of the ideas on historical development examined earlier. The majority conservative Romanticism of Spain projects a singularly united front, seeking for itself an uncomplicated picture and consequently formulating a polarized account with no difficult shading. It seemed to be taken as read that the moral requirements of a Christian and monarchical nation were perfectly straightforward, easily determined and objectively verifiable; in order to satisfy the 'necesidades morales' of its time, Spanish literature had simply to renew its imaginative subscription to the eternal ideals that had characterized it in the Middle Ages and Golden Age. This conception of a Romantic art containing specifiable features commensurate with a vision of man and the world resolutely opposed to that of mechanistic philosophy and the *Encyclopédie* was, as Giovanni Allegra makes admirably clear, rooted in Schlegelian aesthetics.[104] Yet, as Silver insinuates, the issues concerned were ultimately more far-reaching: this current of thought, he asserts, 'carried within it a peculiar catachresis of Herderian Romantic historicism', in which we find not just the idea that literature should reflect its era and nation but 'historicism as an ideological message of bogusly retrospective, essentialist, bourgeois romantic nationalism'. Silver consequently claims, with some justification, that 'the original romantic nationalism that first appeared within historical romanticism was not one content among others, but the *form* that held the thematics of historical romanticism together'.[105]

Within the largest terms, then, the connections are clear. On the one hand, the desire for a single, authoritative historical discourse able to explain with an unqualified degree of epistemological certainty the existence of a physical universe ordered by a beneficent God within the workings of a Providential design. Alongside it, an account of literary history that privileged the Christian — and specifically, for Spanish writers, the Catholic — ideal, the superior nature of monarchy as a temporal institution, and a coherent and indissoluble (I use the term calculatedly) alliance between the physiognomy of modern, i.e., Christian and monarchical, society and its mode of imaginative expression. While so many historical accounts had been geared towards the exclusion of philosophical rationalism, political radicalism and all other forms of secularism as desirable — or even admissible — intellectual alternatives, so contemporary interpretations of the history of Spanish literature were predicated upon the desire to exclude the literary expression of those same offending principles: namely neo-Classicism, tarnished by association with eighteenth-century republicanism; and radical forms of Romanticism, tarnished by association with the inevitable nihilistic consequences of eighteenth-century thought-patterns. Both had emanated from France, lair of the revolutionary beast so feared by Spanish commentators, and both were calculatedly suppressed in favour of a profoundly conservative Romantic orthodoxy that sought relentlessly to perpetuate its own chosen canon, a canon so remarkably different from that instituted by the previous neo-Classical age. It therefore seems to me apt to conclude this chapter with a representative summary offered by Gonzalo Morón, writing in *El Iris* in 1841 in just one brief instalment of his exhaustive 'Examen filosófico del teatro español', suggestively sub-titled 'relación del mismo con las costumbres y la nacionalidad de España'. The author here makes admirably explicit both the inspiration and direction of the prevailing conservative Romantic orthodoxy:

> hoy que los estudios históricos están haciendo una revolución en las ciencias morales y políticos, deben también extender sus consideraciones filosóficas a las bellas artes; y es indispensable decir a los preceptistas que éstas se hallan destinadas a satisfacer las necesidades morales de los pueblos, que ellas se dirigen a la imaginación y al corazón de los hombres, y que deben estar en relación con las creencias y vida moral de cada país, so pena de ser estéril e infecunda su elevada y sublime misión [...] ¿No sería por ello solemne anacronismo y profunda aberración pedir a la literatura moderna el fondo y las formas de la literatura

Baleares y Valencia in which he categorized essentially different forms of Romanticism: 'Los bandos partían ya la arena del romanticismo en creyente, aristocrático, arcaico y restaurador; y descreído, democrático, radical en las innovaciones y osado en los sentimientos' [The factions were already drawing a line in the sand between a Romanticism of religious faith, aristocracy, the historical past and the restoration of that past, and a Romanticism of religious scepticism and democracy, radical in its innovations and daring in its sentimental content]: *La viña y los surcos*, p. 145. Tubino's choice of 'aristocrático' and 'democrático' as contrasting poles of expression hint at a revision of some of the staple critical terminology between the Romantic period itself and the later part of the nineteenth century: 'popular', commonly used in the 1840s without 'progressive' ideological overtones to signify the expression of a collective imagination, and customarily seen as an inalienable feature of a conservative historical Romanticism, would, by the time Tubino was writing, have acquired an overtly political meaning, much closer to the 'democrático' he elects to employ as a characteristic of Romantic radicalism. Hence the choice, to counterpoint this last term, of 'aristocrático', seldom found in Romantic criticism as a form of literary designation.

 99. See *El romanticismo*, ed. by Gies, p. 77.
100. *Panorama crítico*, p. 79.
101. 'El siglo XIX en la Historia y en la Literatura', in *Aspectos sociales de la Literatura Española* (Madrid, 1974), p. 160; cited by Romero Tobar, *Panorama crítico*, p. 37.
102. 'Towards a Revisionary Theory of Spanish Romanticism', p. 297.
103. *El romanticismo español: historia y crítica*, p. 14.
104. *La viña y los surcos*, p. 90.
105. *Ruin and Restitution*, p. 13.
106. *El Iris*, 2 (1841), p. 281.

CONCLUSIONS

History Singular and Plural

What has emerged from the preceding chapters is that Romantic literary history as conceived and expressed in Spain, as much as the interrelated idealization of the Christian Middle Ages and Manichaean interpretations of the recent historical past, explicitly reveal — both in general terms and much more specifically — what Pérez-Bustamante Mourier and Romero Ferrer call the peculiar stylization according to which *casticista* prescriptions were characteristically configured in the first half of the nineteenth century. Their contention that intellectual, as well as popular, forms of *casticismo* stemmed from a deforming principle of manipulation, one that was systematically to produce a polarization of perspective,[1] is reinforced and expanded by a detailed assessment of Spain's Romantic philosophy of history; theirs is, I feel, a shrewd explanation of typical *casticista* procedures, one that helps to locate modes of expression that were not always blatant pronouncements so much as elusive but identifiable undercurrents permeating a large part of the intellectual activity of the Romantic period in Spain. The stylized accounts of the past that I have been examining here allow us to perceive the essence of the Romantic historical imagination in Spain above and beyond the inherited theological positions, defining aesthetic principles and informing ideological motivations in which those accounts have been seen to be grounded. For at the heart of this historical imagination is the most tenaciously held, virulently expressed and, at the same time, peculiarly Romantic form of *casticismo*.

Succinctly summarizing these historical prescriptions, D. L. Shaw comments that the idealization, by conservative Romantics, of the values of the Middle Ages and Golden Age was a process of mythification that provided a reconciliation with the cosmological vision professed by the national past; its ideological intentionality, as he subsequently stresses, resided in its determination to countervail any new and radical explanation of life and the world and roundly to deny the eighteenth-century rationalist conception of a world lacking any convincing metaphysical explanation. Shaw likewise pinpoints, at the core of this Romantic traditionalism, the desired return to an authoritarian and integrative cosmology.[2] It hardly needs to be stated how consonant are these judgements with the conclusions necessarily deriving from the material considered here. The full extent and significance of the said material, however, seems to be unsuspected by Shaw himself, given that he downplays both the efficacy of such positions in nineteenth-century Spain and the intellectual value of their legacy to our own age. I would suggest, on the basis of the foregoing chapters of this study, that the efficacy of the traditionalist argument can be proven to be beyond dispute both during the larger part of the nineteenth century and, as we are about to see, for a considerable part of our own.[3] The final piece of evaluation, meanwhile, is of a kind that is, it goes without saying, subjectively determined; as Hayden White put it, in words that will be seen to have a direct bearing on this concluding chapter, when placed before the alternative visions that history's interpreters offer for our consideration we are frequently driven to moral and aesthetic reasons for the choice of one vision over another.[4] Accordingly, it is not difficult to find assertions entirely to the contrary of that expressed by Shaw. José Vila Selma, for example, comments that the discovery, by the post-Napoleonic Restoration, of an antidote to revolutionary activity in the study of the past is one that has most profoundly affected the influence on modernity not just of history but of all the human sciences in a period of acute crisis in which societal and intellectual structures and models are once again subject to the threat of collapse;[5] he underlines, then, the relevance and transferential potential of that set of ideas in our own age of uncertainty. One lesson we might profitably draw, after all, from the uncompromising stance of so many nineteenth-century Spanish writers is that our conception of the relevance or otherwise of a given scale of values or a particular mindset to our own historical moment is rarely if ever able entirely to transcend our personal inclinations.

It is appropriate, meanwhile, that Shaw should, in the same piece, locate the early existence of dialectical interpretations of Romanticism in the work of Menéndez Pelayo; as I have already suggested, it is by framing the body of historical writing examined in this study, in the context both of the precedents offered by the earlier reactionaries and of the later evaluation of their endeavours by Don Marcelino, that we perceive the most fundamental continuities of outlook pervading nineteenth-century intellectual history and come to apprehend fully the central and indispensable function of forms of *casticismo* within the larger pattern. Such a process of framing leads, at the same time, to a perception of Romantic ideas as enunciated in Spain over nearly half a century that profoundly questions those critical positions that came to dominate the 1970s and 1980s. These positions I have elsewhere, principally with reference to literary theory and criticism, argued to be fundamentally flawed; while they can no longer be claimed to represent the same degree of consensus — as evidenced by important work by, amongst others, Hans Juretschke, María José Alonso Seoane, Leonardo Romero Tobar, and Philip Silver, they nonetheless continue to exert some considerable influence over the critical debate: they strongly inform, for example, Diego Martínez Torrón's formulation of the ideological origins of Spanish Romanticism, and reappear more recently still in Andrew Ginger's assessment of the thought-patterns of progressive liberalism. What the present study does, I would contend, by positing a re-location of Romantic thought within Spanish intellectual history, is to allow us to dispense definitively with the deceptively simple — indeed, demonstrably false — 'Romanticism equals liberalism' thesis. As should already be apparent, the pattern emerging here dovetails with the findings of Philip Silver's *Ruin and Restitution*. It will be evident, however, that I have followed significantly different emphases throughout, being more closely guided by strictly intellectual, as opposed to socio-political, history. The divergence in methodological approach is probably best encapsulated by the fact that while Silver, by way of foundation of his persuasively argued thesis, prioritizes those ideological factors underlying the historical emergence and consolidation of a *moderado* bourgeoisie, I have preferred to remain with the salient philosophical features of what amounts to a peculiarly Romantic *casticismo*.

In accordance with my chosen approach, and in beginning to formulate a series of overall conclusions, I would wish to stress what Javier Herrero pointedly refers to as the schism, in the whole of Don Marcelino's work, between 'heterodoxo' and 'antiheterodoxo', between 'extranjerizante' and 'tradicional': that is to say, between a culturally alien heterodoxy and true-blooded national tradition.[6] By identifying orthodoxy with the terms 'tradicional' and 'español', and, similarly, by linking the Enlightenment with the terms 'extranjero' and 'heterodoxo', Menéndez Pelayo was, as we know and as Herrero copiously documents, receiving and reinforcing an interpretation of the essence of Spain and Spanish nationhood originating in the work of the eighteenth-century reactionaries.[7] The great intellectual historian trusted, after all, in the world-view of these earlier traditionalists, whom he regarded as having been, in Herrero's words, dispossessed by the partiality of a triumphant liberalism.[8] In his *Historia de los heterodoxos españoles*, Don Marcelino suggested that a detailed study of Spanish resistance against 'el enciclopedismo y la filosofía del siglo XVIII' [the *Encyclopédie* and eighteenth-century philosophy] would provide both consolation and instruction. Meaningful appreciation of the work of these writers had, he felt, been suppressed by nineteenth-century liberalism since the vanquished can expect neither forgiveness nor mercy;[9] it begs the question whether Menéndez Pelayo himself was fully aware of the extent to which prominent traditionalists of the Romantic period effectively recycled their pattern of ideas.

Also charted by Herrero, meanwhile, is the re-emergence of Menéndez Pelayo's interpretation of events after the Nationalist victory in the Spanish Civil War, when we see a comparably partial and calculatedly ideological account stemming from a committed political perspective entirely inimical to the ideals of liberalism. It is nothing less than a twentieth-century corollary of earlier forms of *casticismo*, one in which Spain is figured as a 'reserva espiritual' [reserve of spirituality], as a 'pueblo dilecto de Dios' [chosen people].[10] As Marta Campomar Fornieles notes, Menéndez Pelayo, together with Franco himself, came to be seen as an important bastion of a unified Catholic Spain that had itself triumphed over heterodoxy in 1936 and whose opposition to liberalism was strictly non-negotiable.[11] Equally, as José Alvarez Junco has emphasized, Donoso Cortés himself owes much of his prestige to Francoist Catholic authoritarians who saw him as their historical precursor.[12] Thus the *Historia del tradicionalismo español* published in 1941 by Melchor Ferrer, Domingo Tejera, and José F. Acedo was to affirm that in the eighteenth century the Spanish tradition was abruptly severed and 'repentinamente nuestra Patria entera se extranjeriza' [our motherland suddenly and entirely turned foreign]; it was a period, they affirmed, when Madrid accepted all that came from outside while pointedly rejecting all that was traditionally Spanish. One of those poisons entering Spain was 'la Enciclopedia francesa, con sus deletéreas y desenfadadas teorías filosóficas' [the French *Encyclopédie*, with all its noisome and uninhibited philosophical theories]. As in Menéndez Pelayo, Spanish traditionalists like Zeballos are exalted as a bastion against heresy; Fray Fernando himself appears as 'el máximo paladín de la verdadera España' [the greatest paladin of the true Spain] combating valiantly 'las nuevas doctrinas de destrucción' [the new doctrines of destruction], while in the tumultuous days of the Cadiz Parliament, Alvarado, the *Filósofo Rancio*, 'siente el alma de España vibrar' [feels Spain's whole soul throb within him].[13] As recently as 1966, Francisco Puy's *El pensamiento tradicional en la España del siglo XVIII (1700–1760)* saw Spanish culture of the Golden Age and the later modern civilization born of rationalism, scientific analysis, and democracy as, respectively, St Augustine's City of God and City of Men. The modern state is conceived as a diabolical work hostile to a spiritual culture with transcendent aspirations. Due to the work of traditionalist thinkers, however, 'no se olvidó el edificio de la ciudad de Dios' [the structure of the city of God did not lay forgotten]; they determinedly sought to prevent 'la construcción de esta ciudad terrena que padecemos' [the construction of the earthly city that now besets us].[14] We detect then a striking coincidence, in terms of vocabulary and allusion, with Negro Pavón's view of Vélez's *Preservativo contra la irreligión*, which saw the Enlightenment, the French Revolution and the subsequent Napoleonic Wars from the perspective of a theologically defined history as a defined moment in the struggle between the forces of evil and God's divine plan, between the two cities, which he depicts as the conflict between philosophy and religion, and not necessarily between State and Church.[15] At the same time, and this is what I feel has remained largely unsuspected, there are irresistible and unnerving echoes here of much of the content of Spain's trenchantly conservative Romantic historiography; especially noteworthy, perhaps, is the parallel with Donoso's 1851 *Ensayo*, whose fundamentally orthodox and Providential account encapsulates the course of human history thus:

> Después del diluvio vuelve a comenzar la historia antediluviana; los hijos de Dios vuelven a combatir con los hijos de los hombres; aquí se levanta la ciudad divina, y enfrente la ciudad del mundo; en una se rinde culto a la libertad y en otra a la Providencia, y la libertad y la Providencia, Dios y el hombre, vuelven a reñir aquel gigantesco combate cuyas grandes vicisitudes son el asunto perpetuo de la Historia.

> [After the Flood, antediluvian history begins afresh; the children of God go into battle once more against the children of men; in one place there is raised the divine city, and facing it the wordly city; in one of them is worshipped liberty and in the other Providence, and liberty and Providence, God and man, fight again that colossal battle, the changing fortunes of which are the constant matter of History.][16]

There is certainly more than ample evidence, within the politically polarized modern history of Spain, to support Hayden White's celebrated contention that any and every assessment of the historical past carries with it its own specifiable ideological implications.[17] Within the period examined by Menéndez Pelayo, meanwhile, we do in effect find an abundance of precedents for his subsequent ideologically laden interpretation; as Campomar Fornieles observes of just one key term, the word 'tradicionalismo' carried with it from 1812 all the connotations of historical conflict between traditional Catholic Spain and reformist society, the latter of which was a liberal and secularizing enterprise that sought to expropriate the assets of the church, abolish the Inquisition, and open its doors to the ideals of the French Revolution.[18] Fernández de Valcarce, for example, had declared that the new ideas emanating from

France tended to disfigure the character of the nation.[19] We could equally mention Rafael de Vélez's *Preservativo contra la irreligión*, which contributed more than any other single work, according to Herrero, to disseminate the reactionary myth and to identify, in Spanish conservative thought, the concepts of 'moderno', 'europeo' and 'liberal' with 'lo antiespañol' [anti-Spain]; thus were created the 'two Spains' and the mantra of 'la anti-España' that were to occasion what Herrero representatively calls the bloody confrontation that would poison the collective life of Spain for more than a century.[20] Capmany's 1806 letter to Godoy, as Herrero again documents, identifies Spanish nationhood with a set of moral virtues deriving from the Roman Catholic faith that directly counterpoint a French-inspired degradation that the writer believed to have corrupted the soul of Spain for an entire century. Capmany's contention as summarized by Herrero is that 'we are still capable of regenerating ourselves if we can cast aside that alien Enlightenment and return to the true-blooded Spanishness into which we were born'.[21]

Meanwhile, those patriotic extremes that surfaced two years later in 1808, in the face of an insidious revolutionary threat, are admirably summarized by Manuel Moreno Alonso; tradition, nation, and religion, he emphasizes, will provide guarantees of continuity and afford an effective sense of identity.[22] Herrero himself refers to a nucleus of essential motifs relentlessly used by those figures hostile to the Enlightenment headed by Zeballos; those same motifs, he asserts, reappeared in the writings and pronouncements of *serviles*, backed by wide-ranging arguments, and effectively informed by the policies of Ferdinand VII.[23] Herrero felt that 'la desespañolización' [the disfiguring of Spain] amounted to a singular obsession of the *pensamiento servil*; he sums up thus the rationale underlying it: Spain had admitted, in the eighteenth century, a set of destructive ideas emanating from France; it had progressively renounced its distinctive way of life, its spiritual being; it now saw itself plunged into a fathomless decadence. Yet this French invasion had served a purpose: it had shown to all and sundry the true face of rationalism and the reality of 'las falsas ideas regeneradoras' [the sham ideas of regeneration]; it had convinced a generation of Spaniards of the necessity of returning to what was 'genuinely Spanish'.[24]

We are, then, on particularly firm ground. What has not been hitherto acknowledged, however, is the prevalence, within the Romantic period proper, of a comparably strident cultural nationalism, an equally virulent form of *casticista* rhetoric and a similarly uncompromising theocentric expression of the historical imagination. When Romantic traditionalists, in precisely the *casticista* vein detailed by Herrero in his examination of the forces of reaction and exemplified by Menéndez Pelayo in his account of the same period, conceive of the Counter-Reformation, consciously or unconsciously, as a struggle for the survival and ultimate salvation of humanity that was to be repeated in the Catholic response to the Enlightenment, then we begin to perceive a form of ideological chain reaction that was to recur throughout the seemingly interminable conflict between the two Spains. At the heart of the process, straddling the nineteenth and twentieth centuries, is the figure of Marcelino Menéndez Pelayo. His forthright rejection of 'la mitología progresista' [the mythology of progress] becomes, as Allegra sees it, the colossal reaffirmation by the Cantabrian writer of a pattern of thought, of a literature, and indeed of an entire civilization, an affirmation of a genuine national consciousness that a modern secular culture had placed in the dock.[25]

The conscious ideological preferences of Don Marcelino afford a parallel not just with divergent interpretations of history belonging to the earlier part of the nineteenth century but also with the competing mythologies of Nationalist and Republican narratives of history in the wake of the Spanish Civil War. Pro-Franco historical writing, as I have indicated, underlined — through another identifiably *casticista* prism — the relevance of earlier traditionalist thought to its own historical moment, seeking and eliciting satisfying righteous comparisons between the struggle against the revolutionary beast spawned by the Enlightenment and the authors' own commitment to the concept of a *Cruzada* [Crusade] against an atheistic and secular culture that they felt had already degraded the greater part of western society. Conversely, it is tempting for many reasons to echo Philip Silver's frank observation that the association of Spanish Romanticism with political liberalism stemmed directly from a comparable form of historical transference, one in which not just exiled Republicans and their disciples but also, one is inclined to add, younger academics immersed in a culture of liberal resistance to the Franco dictatorship, saw enticing parallels between the situation of idealistic nineteenth-century radicals and their own. Abellán, for example, comments that the problem of the two Spains is not just an intellectual one but the denial of 'patria' and 'tierra' to a large number of Spaniards who, in the name of patriotism and religion, had been dismissively labelled as 'antiespañoles';[26] it is hard to read these last comments without being aware of their potential application not just to the nineteenth-century origins of the conflict but also to those historical events occurring during and after the Spanish Civil War. Abellán's words irresistibly recall, in fact, the propagandistic nationalism of Franco, with its emphasis on the holy war fought by an inherently God-fearing people against the forces of international communism and freemasonry and with its insidious manipulation of past periods of history. The struggle for freedom in a nation benighted at different historical moments by comparable modes of political and ideological repression made for a passionate attachment to the cause of *doceañismo*, a sense of kinship that becomes, in the process, a form of self-projection inevitably colouring any critical account with a romantic tincture. In fact, in considering the past origins and future implications of Spanish Romantic historiography we become profoundly aware of the repeated phenomenon of history as mirror of the present attributed to the Spanish Romantic mind by Ricardo Navas Ruiz. It may be less of a coincidence than a pointed historical lesson that the emergence of a more impartial and pluralistic assessment of Spanish Romanticism, free of the kind of 'ideological imperialism' detected by Juan Luis Alborg in certain interpretations of the period,[27] has occurred after the consolidation of Spanish democracy, the historical reconciliation between hereditary monarchy and constitutional parliament, and the integration of the Spanish nation-state into the mainstream of western Europe.

The clear antagonisms I have detailed, meanwhile, are at the heart of ideological division throughout the history of modern Spain. Herrero's tracing of the links between earlier reactionary thought and the trenchant prescriptions of 'approved' historical writing under Franco, as revealed by the citations I have chosen to recall here, make for a singularly clear parallel. What I believe to be equally clearly shown by the corpus of historical material examined in the present study, however, is the dominant presence, in the form of an internally consistent and systematically argued set of values and principles, of precisely the same informing nucleus of ideas within the period of Spain's essentially conservative Romanticism; without a thoroughgoing apprehension of the extent and significance of these values and principles, the intellectual historian is inevitably left with only a partial picture. Hence Inman Fox's rigorous detailing of the 'invention of Spain' in modern times provides what is an incomplete, and hence ultimately misleading, contextualization of the evidence, in which a liberal hegemony dated between 1850 and 1936 is only partly counterweighted by an opposing traditionalist undercurrent.[28]

The continuity of traditionalist thought, embracing not just the immediate response to the French Enlightenment and the revolutionary events of 1789 and after but also the entire period of Spanish Romanticism, the work of arguably the most influential intellectual historian of the second half of the nineteenth century — Menéndez Pelayo, and almost the entirety of the period between 1939 and 1975, might suggest a rather different ideological balance. One problem with Fox's study, which is for so many reasons a particularly valuable one, is that the inavailability to his scrutiny of so substantive a portion of Romantic historiography leads him unwarily to attribute to what he defines as liberal histoirography of 1850 and after core concepts and intentions of the earlier traditionalist Romantic discourse. Thus in arguing for the existence in Spain of both a functional and politically pragmatic nationalism and a concomitant cultural nationalism that drew upon instinctive sentiment and that was in the service of political ideology, he attributes to such a nationalist thrust the affirmation of a democratic liberal nation-state and identifies as a fundamental principle of the liberal historiographical tradition the idea that language, literature, and art, in their combination and conjunction, articulate a configuration of the world commensurate with the workings of the popular collective imagination.[29] It should be evident that the intellectual phenomenon Fox is analysing had existed in an earlier, radically different, guise and came to the second half of the century with specifiable *casticista* credentials. As Fox himself states, the ideas of Herder, and especially his pioneering theories of collective imagination, came to exert a profound influence upon nineteenth-century cultural history; he indeed identifies the nucleus of Herder's framework as the concept of a collective identity residing in a shared cultural experience.[30] It is only in the form of a footnote, however, that he stipulates that an ideological Romanticism applied these Herderian ideas outside of their proper context, bestowing upon them a conservative reading that nonetheless profoundly contributed to the historical 'invention' of a distinctive Spanish culture.[31]

The historical writing that has been the subject of this study forces us entirely to revise, I would therefore contend, the assessment of the place of Romanticism within Spanish intellectual history that has been prevalent in recent decades. Firstly, in the light of the considerable weight of evidence to the contrary culled from contemporary sources, it seems nothing less than extraordinary that Abellán should proclaim *doceañista* liberalism to be one of the earliest and most significant manifestations of European Romanticism.[32] It is surely only possible to justify this thesis by manifestly distorting the contextual evidence, so that any form of liberalism that affirms the idea of national independence appears, by definition, Romantic, or at least pre-Romantic,[33] or by asserting, in what comes close to sophistry, that early nineteenth-century liberals, while politically and existentially Romantics, in a literary sense only remained bound to the values of neo-Classicism.[34] Abellán is clearly using the terms 'romántico' and 'romanticismo' in a sense entirely detached from their stricter meaning. His reference to the years between 1808 and 1814 as 'esa gran manifestación romántica' [that great romantic manifestation], as much as his declaration that nothing could be more romantic than the constitutionalist urges of the Cadiz Parliament,[35] may be felt to be lacking in academic rigour. While these may be examples of an acceptable usage commensurate with the employment in English of the traditionally lower-case 'romantic', they perhaps lead on inevitably to the much more questionable claim, founded as it is upon an understanding of upper-case 'Romantic' rooted in cultural history, that the Peninsular War is 'la primera expresión del Romanticismo' [the initial expression of Romanticism] with which the contemporary age truly begins.[36]

Not even the otherwise sober judgements of Manuel Moreno Alonso entirely escape this form of contagion: he sees fit to refer to 'la lucha por la libertad emprendida románticamente' [the struggle for liberty so romantically undertaken] by the liberal patriots of the Peninsular War; he subsequently affirms that 'El romanticismo es el principal elemento definidor del liberalismo de la generación de 1808' [Romanticism is the principal defining element of the liberalism of the generation of 1808], detecting a Romantic spirit present in Cadiz before the appearance of a more specific cultural movement, and goes on to claim that Romanticism is a fundamental and original characteristic of the struggle for liberty that began in 1808.[37] The same kind of distortion can equally be seen to bedevil Martínez Torrón's recent account. With the 'Romanticism equals liberalism' prior definition, then, Spain was 'un país romántico por excelencia' [a romantic country par excellence] from the initiation of the Peninsular War and the subsequent struggle of the emigrés against Ferdinand VII.[38] Martínez Torrón may or may not be aware of the irony produced here: he is in fact using the very same phrase that formed a defining part of August Wilhelm Schlegel's assessment of Spain's historical culture, an assessment that went a long way towards determining both the essential nature of the Romantic movement in Spain and the broadly accepted understanding of the term within the first half of the nineteenth century. Like Abellán and Moreno Alonso, however, Martínez Torrón is at best unwary in his employment of the terms 'romántico' and 'romanticismo': he effectively downgrades their academic meaning in claiming that the patriotic writings of the time of the Peninsular War all possess a romantic tincture[39] and in referring to 'la situación política del trienio, en donde el sentimiento romántico, que ya apareció durante la Guerra de la Independencia, se consolida' [the political situation of the constitutional government of 1820–23, in which the romantic spirit that made its first appearance during the Peninsular War became reinforced].[40] Faced with material evidence contrary to his thesis, Martínez Torrón blithely discards the issue of nomenclature as it affected the nineteenth-century context: whether writers describe themselves as 'Romantic' or 'anti-Romantic', he professes, was, in the period in question, of negligible importance; many writers were Romantics in spite of themselves, without knowing or understanding what the term meant.[41] These are again comments bordering on sophistry. Within this disconcertingly unreal perspective, Quintana, a trenchant adherent of neo-Classicism virtually throughout his writing career, is lauded as the figurehead of Spain's original and committedly liberal early Romanticism.

This sort of convoluted argument is rendered necessary, of course, by the existence of very specific contemporary declarations to the contrary, most famously by José Joaquín de Mora. As Philip Silver tersely puts it: 'liberal critics ever since [Mora] have resisted the notion that Spanish romanticism could be anything but liberal';[42] he goes on to comment: 'it is difficult to understand the general reluctance to acknowledge… that the *majority* romanticism was *essentially* conservative'.[43] Spanish writers *were* closely concerned with the question of definition, which contained inescapable ideological overtones, while their understanding of 'romanticismo' is more or less diametrically opposed to that defended by modern critics like Abellán, Martínez Torrón, Vicente Llorens, Ricardo Navas Ruiz, Susan Kirkpatrick, and Iris M. Zavala. One problem here is that we are often dealing, as I have intimated, less with 'Romantic' as a principally aesthetic concept than with the debased vulgar 'romantic' commonly used to denote any adventure or enterprise passionately undertaken or recalled. It is surely in this sense, for example, that Revuelta González writes of the priests who served with the Peninsular War guerrillas as irrational and explosive romantic figures, typical products of a people and society in which religion possessed an unwonted intensity and primitive force,[44] in words presumably unacceptable to those who would view Romanticism as inextricably bound up with political liberalism. Revuelta González is nonetheless undoubtedly aware of more profound processes at work, and there is no sense of his systematizing any simplistic interpretation. What he at once establishes is that to take on, as did nineteenth-century radicals, the 'problem of Spain' was to run up against the national religion and the national Church; thence any attempt at political, social, or economic reform became virtually by definition an attempted religious reform that opened a can of theological worms: it was inevitable, he concludes, that any and every attempt at reform become something of a religious controversy.[45] Or, as Juan Donoso Cortés expressed it, in words that exemplify the contemporary insistence upon the priority in human affairs of the spiritual rather than the profane: 'El conocimiento de lo sobrenatural es, pues, el fundamento de todas las ciencias, y señaladamente de las políticas y de las morales' [Experience of the supernatural is, therefore, the foundation all science and knowledge, and particularly in the realms of politics and morality].[46]

A further ongoing complication for ideologically committed commentaries such as those of Abellán and Martínez Torrón is that *doceañismo* has to be justified as the authentic, original, and Romantic expression of Spanish nationhood; if we pay close attention to the writing of the period, however, the opposite can be said to be true. Martínez Torrón is led to proclaim, for example, that the 1812 Constitution exemplifies 'un romanticismo peculiarmente español' [a peculiarly Spanish Romanticism], while the efforts of Böhl von Faber to acclimatize the ideas of A. W. Schlegel are demonized as not only a form of Romanticism that is reactionary but also an imported product, shrugged aside by Martínez Torrón as something that in 1814 could only be a pale reflection of what was going on in Germany, an isolated incident lacking in significance or influence.[47] The reality is entirely different, as a substantial body of recent criticism has made clear. Guillermo Carnero in particular, far from sympathetic towards Böhl's intransigent ideological positions, nevertheless acknowledges the import of what he calls a fundamental moment in the introduction of Romanticism into Spain, one without which it would be impossible fully to comprehend 'la significación ideológica que, mayoritariamente, tuvo en nuestro país el Romanticismo' [the ideological meaning which, in the main, Romanticism assumed in our country].[48] Heredia Soriano, meanwhile, looking at the period between 1808 and 1874, comments that in its beginnings that philosophy professed by early political liberalism bore little relation to the emerging cultural manifestations of Romanticism and had instead much more in common with the prescriptions of the Enlightenment.[49] This, as we have seen, was certainly the prevailing view in the first half of the nineteenth century, and, crucially, it cannot be said to have been definitively reversed in more recent times. Allegra, who uncannily preserves many of the distinguishing features of nineteenth-century reactionary thought in his own critical discourse, is adamant that the chaotic discussions taking place within the Junta Central surrounded political reforms that derived from 'el modelo "filosófico"' [the 'philosophical' model] and that bore no relation whatever to Spain's national traditions.[50] In the view of Carlos Seco Serrano, the 1812 Constitution was not based on what he calls the historical core of the nation but instead, as a result of 'el deslumbramiento producido por la gran Revolución francesa' [the bedazzling effects of the French Revolution], became a cluster of exotic innovations.[51] The phrasing here too is itself reminiscent of the age in question. As Seco Serrano then continues, the 'Manifiesto de los Persas', the political blueprint presented to the newly-restored Ferdinand VII, saw the work of the Cortes since 1810 as a break with the country's national traditions.[52] Javier Herrero likewise felt that the Manifiesto viewed political reform as rooted in what was specifically Spanish in opposition to the vision of radicals founded upon ideas which never sat comfortably with the Spanish people.[53] Seco Serrano himself then read the confrontation between the two Spains, and this is a verdict amply borne out by a mass of supporting evidence detailed in the present study, as one between a 'progresismo exaltado pero anticastizo' [heady but anti-national idea of progress] and a 'casticismo estricto pero inactual' [clearly defined but anachronistic nationalism].[54]

Setting aside unduly programmatic or evidently misleading definitions, the inner processes of Spanish Romantic thought might be said to project a complex but undoubtedly coherent pattern, in which the single most significant common denominator in expressions of the historical imagination was undoubtedly the idea of Providence, one that Menéndez Pelayo's view of history, particularly Spain's national history, effectively recreates. Allegra, in his encomiastic assessment of Menéndez Pelayo's thought, particularly of the *Historia de los heterodoxos españoles*, identifies the typically *casticista* terms of this providentialist outlook, which implied a belief in the existence of an ordering of events which, more than in any other nation, confirmed that the fortunes of humanity were dependent upon the workings of a metaphysical reality above and beyond the affairs of men.[55] Revuelta González, meanwhile, and adhering to nineteenth-century terminology, comments that one of the most distinctive characteristics of the Romantic movement had been the exaltation of religious feeling, in pointed contrast with 'la frialdad racionalista e intramundana de la Ilustración' [the cold earthbound rationalism of the Enlightenment].[56] If his words can be felt accurately to encapsulate the intimate outlook encountered in the various chapters of this study, then the essential hallmarks of Spain's Romantic historical discourse begin to emerge even more clearly from Heredia Soriano's summary of the intellectual activities of the Fernandine Restoration as the prioritizing of the metaphysical dimension of human life, the transcendent and organic nature of society, and the directing structural role of tradition and authority.[57] The dialectical intentionality of this mode of thought is transparently clear; Heredia Soriano identifies just some of the polarities in the following way: in opposition to the totalitarian power of reason, the living presence of mystery and the teachings of history; in opposition to the narrow and unyielding application of Enlightenment ideals, the flexible and persuasive pedagogy of faith; in opposition to a self-sufficient humanism, a metaphysical perspective and an awareness of man's fallen nature; in opposition to the supremacy of the State and temporal power, a recognition of the pre-eminence of the Church and of spiritual life; in opposition to the preponderance of science, the restoration of a sense of the sacred.[58]

Again, and as Allegra once more notes, the constants in Menéndez Pelayo's thought bear the unmistakable imprint of Schlegelian Romantic theory; Don Marcelino's championing of the German theorists at an historical moment dominated by their Positivist detractors, he declares, was to pave the way for their enthusiastic reception by Curtius and the later, more considered but equally positive, reading made by Wellek.[59] If we pursue the trail still further, we recognize the even more recent process by which an awareness of the full import within Spain of Schlegelian modes of thought has posited a fundamental re-reading of Spanish Romanticism. María José Alonso Seoane speaks for many in decrying any exclusive or limited definition of the term. What she chooses to highlight, though not to impose as some exclusive definition, is the 'planteamiento metafísico cristiano' [Christian metaphysical perspective] of the dominant Schlegelian model, which we have seen to be entirely commensurate with the salient distinctive features of the Romantic historical imagination as expressed in Spain; Alonso Seoane subsequently avers, in the most significant terms, that what was short-lived in Spain was the appeal of a radical and sceptical Romanticism; by contrast, the Schlegelian model, then and later, came to be considered 'único y auténtico "romanticismo"' [the single authentic expression of Romanticism].[60]

These words, more a faithful reflection of the ongoing nineteenth-century debate and less a programmatic response prompted by a twentieth-century ideological agenda, are representative of the recent shift away from exclusivist positions towards a more sympathetically focused and accurately contextualized appraisal. The dominant moment of so-called 'liberal Romanticism' only really extends from the first performance of *Don Alvaro* in March of 1835 to the latter part of the following year. As I have elsewhere indicated, Hartzenbusch's *Los amantes de Teruel*, premièred in January of 1837 and the last play to be reviewed by Larra before his untimely death less than a month later, is a text self-consciously exorcizing, in its dualities of structure and symbology, the demon of radical Romanticism, specifically of *Don Alvaro*, and calculatedly displacing it in favour of a markedly Christian and providentialist emphasis.[61] As a play consciously drawing upon a native dramatic tradition and invoking, in its ending, a harmonious and stable Christian cosmology within a framework of ultimate religious reliance, it can be said to belong to that category of literature projected by Romantic writers who, according to José Escobar, displaced contemporary socio-political concerns onto a transcendent imaginative plane.[62]

Events of that pivotal year of 1837 occurred, moreover, in conscious awareness of a pre-existing conceptual pattern that was in turn to last well into the *década moderada*. I am for many reasons unable to share Vicente Llorens's assertion that the *sargentada*, the army rising in favour of radical government in 1836, was a crucial event that prompted, by way of reaction, the most conservative tendencies in Spanish Romanticism, so that only from that specific moment could be traced the appearance of a more conservative Romanticism.[63] Events at La Granja had, in the first place, been preceded by the furious critical response to *Antony*, something rather more likely to have exerted a powerful effect. Far more significantly, Dumas's play was widely perceived, as we have seen, as a lamentable aberration that had little to do with what the majority of people felt Romanticism truly to represent; Lista's blunt comment that 'nada es menos romántico que esta depravación' [nothing is less Romantic than this kind of depravity] was an opinion shared by most of his contemporaries. Llorens's assertion that the reactionary traditionalism of Zorrilla is only explicable in the light of radical *progresista* policy with regard to the Church[64] ignores the fact that the young 'poeta nacional' was the natural representative of a majority Romanticism whose intellectual bases had been firmly established and whose values and principles were internally coherent and consistent. Even Martínez Torrón is disposed to comment that Zorrilla, whose work symbolized an enduring traditional order of things, perfectly reflected a broadly conceived but very specific ideological moment.[65]

Any number of citations may be used to locate Zorrilla squarely within the *casticista* ideological parameters of the Romantic historical imagination that I have been analysing here: in the preface to his second volume of poems, published in 1838, we find his celebrated proclamation of 'la patria en que nací y la religión en que vivo. Español, he buscado en nuestro suelo mis inspiraciones. Cristiano, he creído que mi religión encierra más poesía que el paganismo' [the country into which I was born and the religion that I live and breathe. As a Spaniard, I have sought my inspiration in our own soil. As a Christian, I have always believed my own religion to contain more poetry than paganism];[66] summoned to the stage after the first performance of *Cada cual con su razón*, Zorrilla would make his oft-quoted scathing reference to the 'monstruosos abortos de la elegante corte de Francia' [monstrous abortions of the elegant French court] and declare his preference for models nearer to the native Spanish tradition than to Hernani or Lucrezia Borgia;[67] finally, the verse prologue to his *Cantos del trovador* of 1840–41 professed: 'Lejos de mí la historia tentadora/ de ajena tierra y religión profana./ Mi voz, mi corazón, mi fantasía,/ la gloria cantan de la patria mía' [Away, away, alluring tales of strange realms and pagan faith. My voice, my heart, and my poetic fantasy shall sing the glories of my own land].[68] It will be readily evident how closely the imaginative vision of Zorrilla's verse narratives and historical dramas, like the comparable literary creations of so many of his contemporaries, tallies with the Romantic prescriptions of the broader mediaeval revival. Perhaps clearer still is the way in which *Don Juan Tenorio* exemplifies Spain's fundamentally conservative Romanticism in its sources, traditions, outlook, and conceptual pattern. Rather than, as David Gies alleges,[69] betray the very core of Spanish Romanticism, *Don Juan Tenorio*, read as the transcendent triumph of a conservative, restorative, and Christian Romanticism over the rationalism and religious scepticism of the Enlightenment, profoundly communicates the Spanish movement's essential ideological nucleus. It therefore sets the seal on Spain's traditionalist literary Romanticism at the very moment when its conservative and *casticista* historical imagination was being most potently expressed.

Looking further into the century, meanwhile, Bécquer, who has been identified by Philip Silver, amongst others, as Spain's quintessential Romantic poet, consistently displayed, according to the American critic, 'a late conservative, Catholic, medievalizing' variety of Romanticism.[70] Bécquer's conservatism, Silver affirms, was not only political but cultural, his artistic thought sitting in profound accord with the tenets of *moderantismo*; avowedly following Rubén Benítez, Silver goes so far as to claim that Bécquer's traditionalism made him 'a neo-Catholic, whose thought contains a clear Ultramontane strain', and an equally committed, though considerably more sophisticated and less intrusively dogmatic, Catholic writer and moralist than Fernán Caballero. Bécquer, although he never collected ballads and other popular poetry, nevertheless shared Cecilia Böhl's high estimate of their value as precious surviving remnants of a happier and more harmonious Christian society.[71] The work of Fernán Caballero herself, one might add, sits more than comfortably with the tenor of much of the historical writing examined here, as I have argued elsewhere.[72] It is tempting also to see Galdós's characterization of the bibliophile and archaeological historian Cayetano Polentinos, in *Doña Perfecta*, as based upon the *casticista* emphases of an earlier generation, especially in his reference to 'lo más venerando que existe en la conciencia de los pueblos: la fe religiosa y el acrisolado españolismo' [the most venerable things to be found in the hearts and minds of peoples: religious faith and a fervent Spanishness].[73]

Taking all of the evidence into account — that is, embracing not just literature and literary criticism but also, and particularly in the present context, the ideologically laden expression of the Romantic historical imagination as it appeared within Spain in the middle part of the nineteenth century–, it seems appropriate to affirm, with Jean-Louis Picoche, that the salient constant features of Spanish Romanticism were its religious emphasis and its dynamically intense patriotism, this last, as he put it, characteristic of the entire movement.[74] It is equally pertinent to share Javier Herrero's assertion that, across an enormously wide area of intellectual enquiry, that, in the Spain of the first half of the nineteenth century, historical Romanticism enjoyed almost unchallenged pre-eminence,[75] and to concur in Philip Silver's contention that a conservative literary Romanticism was 'disseminated as a nationalistic politico-literary ideology throughout the nineteenth century'.[76] On a final note, however, I should like briefly to pursue what Heredia Soriano calls the 'flexibility' of religiously orientated teaching, a turn of phrase that we might surely read euphemistically as intimating a common practice of calculated manipulation. Perhaps most telling is the insistent underlying sense of 'pecado', of a fallen humanity, noted also by Heredia

Soriano: so much of the material considered in this study, after all, derives ultimately from a fundamentalist apprehension of the human condition, of the sinful nature of humanity and its necessary subordination to a discernible divinely ordained pattern. The fact that so much of the rhetoric of Romantic historiography was culled from scripture, and most particularly from the book of Genesis and from the Revelation of St John the Divine, is unlikely to be coincidental. History is within these terms not an enigmatic narrative open to a plurality of nuances or to finer shades of interpretation but, at this its most fundamental level, a sacred text eliciting doctrinal explication, and the task of the historian one of assertive exegesis. It is therefore singularly appropriate that, after the revolutionary tumult of the early part of the century that so exercised the Romantic historical imagination, the greatest systematic threat to the hegemony of the traditionalists was to stem from the impact of Darwin's *Origin of the Species* and its iconoclastic evolutionary account of the descent of humankind.

Notes to the Conclusions

1. *Casticismo y literatura en España*, 'Presentación', p. 8.
2. 'El prólogo de Pastor Díaz', pp. 473–74.
3. See also in this context José Luis Molina Martínez, *Anticlericalismo y literatura en el siglo XIX* (Murcia, 1998), p. 14.
4. *Metahistory*, p. 433.
5. Juan Donoso Cortés, *Ensayo sobre el catolicismo, el liberalismo y el socialismo*, ed. by Vila Selma, 'Introducción', p. 13.
6. *Los orígenes del pensamiento reaccionario*, p. 14.
7. *Los orígenes del pensamiento reaccionario*, pp. 14–15.
8. *Los orígenes del pensamiento reaccionario*, p. 14.
9. *Historia de los heterodoxos españoles*, VI, 362.
10. See Pérez-Bustamante Mourier, 'Cultura popular, cultura intelectual y casticismo', p. 158.
11. 'Menéndez Pelayo en el conflicto entre tradicionalismo y liberalismo', *Boletín de la Biblioteca de Menéndez Pelayo, Estudios sobre Menéndez Pelayo. Número extraordinario en homenaje a don Manuel Revuelta Sañudo* (Santander, 1994), 109–34 (p. 111). See also Section III, 'El menendezpelayismo franquista', in Antonio Santoveña Setién, *Menéndez Pelayo y las derechas en España* (Santander, 1994), pp. 197–243.
12. 'Estudio preliminar', in Juan Donoso Cortés, *Lecciones de derecho político* (Madrid, 1984), pp. i–xxxvii; see Ginger, *Political Revolution and Literary Experiment*, pp. 33–34.
13. Cited by Herrero, *Los orígenes del pensamiento reaccionario*, pp. 18–19.
14. Cited by Herrero, *Los orígenes del pensamiento reaccionario*, p. 22.
15. *Historia de España Menéndez Pidal*, XXXV: I, 560.
16. *Ensayo sobre el catolicismo, el liberalismo y el socialismo*, ed. by Vila Selma, p. 169.
17. *The Tropics of Discourse* (Baltimore, 1978), p. 69.
18. 'Menéndez Pelayo en el conflicto entre tradicionalismo y liberalismo', p. 115.
19. See Herrero, *Los orígenes del pensamiento reaccionario*, p. 112.
20. *Los orígenes del pensamiento reaccionario*, p. 314.
21. *Los orígenes del pensamiento reaccionario*, p. 223.
22. *La generación española de 1808*, p. 72.
23. *Los orígenes del pensamiento reaccionario*, p. 115.
24. *Los orígenes del pensamiento reaccionario*, p. 220.
25. *La viña y los surcos*, p. 321.
26. *Historia crítica del pensamiento español*, IV, 151.
27. *Historia de la literatura española. IV: El romanticismo*, p. 61.
28. *La invención de España*, p. 12.
29. *La invención de España*, p. 12.

30. *La invención de España*, p. 46.

31. *La invención de España*, p. 47n.

32. *Historia crítica del pensamiento español*, IV, 64.

33. *Historia crítica del pensamiento español*, IV, 70.

34. *Historia crítica del pensamiento español*, IV, 223.

35. *Historia crítica del pensamiento español*, IV, 93.

36. *Historia crítica del pensamiento español*, IV, 96.

37. *La generación española de 1808*, pp. 209, 221–22.

38. *El alba del romanticismo español*, p. 19.

39. *El alba del romanticismo español*, p. 135.

40. *El alba del romanticismo español*, p. 169–70.

41. *El alba del romanticismo español*, pp. 111–12.

42. *Ruin and Restitution*, p. 4.

43. *Ruin and Restitution*, p. 10; author's italics.

44. *Historia de España Menéndez Pidal*, XXXV: I, 219.

45. *Historia de España Menéndez Pidal*, XXXV: I, 217.

46. *Ensayo sobre el catolicismo, el liberalismo y el socialismo*, p. 140.

47. *El alba del romanticismo español*, pp. 111–12.

48. *Los orígenes del romanticismo reaccionario español: el matrimonio Böhl de Faber* (Valencia, 1978), p. 19.

49. *Historia de España Menéndez Pidal*, XXXV: I, 332.

50. *La viña y los surcos*, p. 78.

51. *Obras de Martínez de la Rosa*, I, 'Estudio preliminar', p. xxiv.

52. *Obras de Martínez de la Rosa*, I, 'Estudio preliminar', p. xxxv.

53. *Los orígenes del pensamiento reaccionario*, p. 338.

54. *Obras de Martínez de la Rosa*, I, 'Estudio preliminar', p. xxiv.

55. *La viña y los surcos*, p. 326.

56. *Historia de España Menéndez Pidal*, XXXV: I, 219.

57. *Historia de España Menéndez Pidal*, XXXV: I, 349.

58. *Historia de España Menéndez Pidal*, XXXV: I, 349.

59. *La viña y los surcos*, pp. 330–31. In his *Historia de las ideas estéticas en España*, Menéndez Pelayo cited Madame de Staël's first-person account of how she had listened to A. W. Schlegel speak in Vienna in 1808, and commented of the published version of the famous lectures that 'todavía no ha envejecido el libro en sus partes esenciales' [the essential parts of the book have still not aged]: in the 1947 Edición Nacional, the citation from Vol. IV, 142. As most Spanish intellectuals of the nineteenth century came to do, however, Menéndez Pelayo preferred Friedrich Schlegel, notably his lectures on the history of literature — 'libro breve en volumen, pero rico de elevadísimos pensamientos' [a book that is small in content but mightily rich in its elevation of thought] — and his work on the philosophy of history: in the same edition, the citation from Vol. IV, 146.

60. See Francisco Martínez de la Rosa, *La conjuración de Venecia, año de 1310*, ed. by María José Alonso Seoane (Madrid, 1993), 'Introducción', pp. 75–77.

61. See my article 'The Romantic Theology of *Los amantes de Teruel*', *Crítica Hispánica*, 18 (1996), 25–34.

62. 'Romanticismo y revolución', in *El romanticismo*, ed. by Gies, p. 322.

63. See *El romanticismo español*, pp. 233, 270.

64. *El romanticismo español*, p. 229.

65. *El alba del romanticismo español*, p. 179.

66. See Narciso Alonso Cortés, *Zorrilla, su vida y sus obras* (Valladolid, 1943), p. 204.

67. Reproduced in *Obras completas*, ed. by Narciso Alonso Cortés, 2 vols (Valladolid, 1943), II, 2207.

68. See Alonso Cortés, *Zorrilla, su vida y sus obras*, p. 258.

69. See 'José Zorrilla and the Betrayal of Spanish Romanticism', *Romanistisches Jahrbuch*, 31 (1980), 339–46 (p. 346).

70. *Ruin and Restitution*, p. xiii.

71. See *Ruin and Restitution*, pp. 73–74.

72. See my 'Historia y pueblo en el costumbrismo romántico: Fernán Caballero y la capilla de Valme', in *Romanticismo 6: el costumbrismo romántico. Actas del VI Congreso del Centro Internacional de Estudios*

sobre el Romanticismo Hispánico (Rome, 1996), pp. 155–61, and my rather more extensive 'La historia que nos llega: Fernán Caballero y la poética de la tradición', in Milagros Fernández Poza (ed. by), *Fernán Caballero hoy* (El Puerto de Santa María, 1998), pp. 89–105. Virgil Nemoianu, it should be noted, views Fernán Caballero as Spain's most authentic representative of a European-wide *Biedermeier* Romanticism: see *The Taming of Romanticism: European Literature and the Age of Biedermeier* (Cambridge MA., 1984), 38–39. For the framing of Fernán Caballero's work as folklorist within traditionalist conceptions of Romantic historicism, see Montserrat Amores, *Fernán Caballero y el cuento folclórico* (El Puerto de Santa María, 2001).

73. Benito Pérez Galdós, *Doña Perfecta*, ed. by Rodolfo Cardona (Madrid, 1984), p. 291.

74. *Un romántico español: Enrique Gil y Carrasco* (Madrid, 1978), p. 156.

75. 'El naranjo romántico: esencia del costumbrismo', *Hispanic Review*, 46 (1978), pp. 343–54 (p. 354).

76. *Ruin and Restitution*, p. 3.

BIBLIOGRAPHY

A. Primary Sources

ALCALÁ GALIANO, ANTONIO, *Historia de España desde los tiempos primitivos hasta la mayoría de la reina doña Isabel II, redactada y anotada con arreglo a la que escribió en inglés el Doctor Dunham, por don Antonio Alcalá Galiano, con una reseña de los historiadores españoles de más nota por don Juan Donoso Cortés, y un discurso sobre la historia de nuestra nación por don Francisco Martínez de la Rosa*, 6 vols (Madrid, 1844–46)

—— *Historia de la literatura española, francesa, inglesa e italiana en el siglo XVIII: lecciones pronunciadas en el Ateneo de Madrid* (Madrid, 1845)

—— 'Reflexiones sobre la influencia del espíritu caballeresco de la edad media en la civilización europea', *Revista Cinetífica y Literaria*, 1 (1847), 193–202, 267–79

ALMAZÓN, M.V. Y, 'La sociedad actual', *El Reflejo* (1843), 145–46

ALVAREZ, FERNANDO, 'Memoria leída por el Secretario del Ateneo Científico y Literario de Madrid el día 29 de diciembre de 1842', *Revista de Madrid*, 3rd series, 4 (1842), 87–102

AMADOR DE LOS RÍOS, JOSÉ, 'Estudios históricos: el rey don Pedro', *El Laberinto*, 2 (1845), 150–51

—— 'Biografía: Torquemada', *El Laberinto*, 2 (1845), 209–11

—— 'Costumbres caballerescas de la edad media: El Paso Honroso', *El Laberinto*, 2 (1845), 217–19

—— 'Crítica literaria', *El Laberinto*, 2 (1845), 300–02

—— 'Tradiciones populares de España: Rodrigo Díaz de Vivar', *El Laberinto*, 2 (1845), 369–70, 377–78, 385–90

—— *Oración pronunciada en la solemne apertura del curso académico de 1850 a 1851, de la Universidad de Madrid, por el Doctor Don José Amador de los Ríos, catedrático de literatura española en los Estudios superiores de la Facultad de Filosofía* (Madrid, 1850)

—— 'Crítica literaria: *Historia general de España desde los tiempos más remotos hasta nuestros días*, por D. Modesto Lafuente. Madrid, 1850 y 1851', *Eco Literario de Europa*, 1 (1851), 226–40

—— *Historia crítica de la literatura española*, facsimile edn, 6 vols (Madrid, 1969)

ARMEDA, SABINO DE, 'Breves reflexiones sobre el socialismo', *El Laberinto*, 2 (1845), 351–52

ARNAO, VICENTE, 'Opinión de un jurisconsulto español sobre la constitución de Cádiz de 1812', in *Apuntes para una biblioteca de escritores españoles contemporáneos en prosa y verso*, ed. by Eugenio de Ochoa, 2 vols (Paris, 1840), pp. ??

BALMES, JAIME, *El Protestantismo comparado con el Catolicismo en sus relaciones con la civilización europea*, 2nd edn, 4 vols (Barcelona, 1844)

—— 'La civilización', *La Civilización*, 1 (1841), 3–13, 49–59, 97–108

—— 'La religiosidad de la nación española', *La Civilización*, 2 (1842), 193–213

—— (ed.), *El Pensamiento de la Nación* (Madrid, 1844–46)

—— *Obras completas*, 8 vols, Biblioteca de Autores Cristianos (Madrid, 1950)

BARALT, RAFAEL M., 'Estudios literarios: Chateaubriand y sus obras', *El Siglo Pintoresco*, 3 (1847), 121–27

—— *Obras literarias publicadas e inéditas de Rafael María Baralt*, ed. by Guillermo Díaz-Plaja, Biblioteca de Autores Españoles, 204 (Madrid, 1967)

BÉCQUER, GUSTAVO ADOLFO, *Obras completas*, ed. Ricardo Navas Ruiz (Madrid, 1995)

BERMÚDEZ DE CASTRO, SALVADOR, 'Crítica literaria: de la novela moderna', *Semanario Pintoresco Español*, 2nd series, 2 (1840), 150–51

—— 'Historia: el príncipe don Carlos de Austria. Artículo 20 ', *El Iris*, 1 (1841), 4–9, 25–31, 45–51

—— 'Literatura: movimiento dramático', *El Iris*, 1 (1841), 77–82

—— 'Literatura: movimiento dramático. Artículo 30.', *El Iris*, 1 (1841), 109–14

—— review of Antonio Gil y Zárate, *Un monarca y su privado*, *El Iris*, 1 (1841), 225–27

—— 'Reflexiones sobre Homero y la tragedia griega: caracteres distintivos de la literatura antigua y moderna', *El Iris*, 1 (1841), 340–42, 385–88

BLANCO Y CRESPO, JOSÉ MARÍA, *Letters from Spain, by Don Leucadio Doblado* (London, 1822)

BURGOS, JAVIER DE, 'Segundo discurso sobre el teatro español, pronunciado por el excelentísimo Señor Don Javier de Burgos, en el liceo de Granada, en la noche del 2 de abril', *El Panorama*, 3rd series (1841), 153–57, 161–63.Camus, Alfredo Adolfo, 'Homero y la Ciencia Nueva', *El Siglo Pintoresco*, 1 (1845), 49–54

CABALLERO, FERNÁN (pseud.), *Obras completas de Fernán Caballero*, ed. by José María Castro y Calvo, 5 vols (Madrid, 1961)

CANARIAS, OBISPO DE, 'Juicio crítico del Protestantismo comparado con el Catolicismo, en sus relaciones con la civilización europea, por el Doctor D. Jaime Balmes, Presbítero', *Revista de España y del Extranjero*, 4 (1842), 80–96, 107–15

—— 'Ensayo sobre la influencia del luteranismo en el gobierno de España en sus relaciones con la iglesia, desde Carlos I hasta la época constitucional', *Revista de España y del Extranjero*, 5 (1843), 47–56, 163–79

—— 'Ensayo sobre la influencia del luteranismo en la política de la corte de España', *Revista de España y del Extranjero*, 6 (1843), 156–64, 338–59

CANGA ARGÜELLES, FELIPE, 'Discurso del Excmo. Señor D. Felipe Canga Argüelles sobre la influencia de los institutos religiosos en los adelantos de la Historia',in *Discursos leídos en las sesiones públicas que para dar posesión de plazas de número ha celebrado desde 1852 la Real Academia de la Historia* (Madrid, 1858), pp. 45–63

CAÑETE, MANUEL, 'Crítica literaria: estado actual de la poesía lírica en España', *Revista de Europa*, 1 (1846), 39–50, 163–78

—— 'Estudios críticos: rápida ojeada acerca del rumbo que ha seguido la literatura dramática española en 1847', *Antología Española*, 1 (1848), 97–108

—— 'Crítica literaria: del neo-culteranismo en la poesía española. Zorrilla y su escuela', *Revista de Ciencias, Literatura y Artes*, 1 (1855), 34–46

CASTELAR, EMILIO, *La civilización en los primeros cinco siglos del cristianismo. Lecciones pronunciadas en el Ateneo de Madrid*, 3 vols (Madrid, 1858)

CASTRO Y OROZCO, JOSÉ, 'Carlos III considerado como reformador', *Revista de Madrid*, 2nd series, 3 (1840), 115–34

CAVEDA, JOSÉ, *Ensayo histórico sobre los diversos géneros de arquitectura empleados en España desde la dominación romana hasta nuestros días* (Madrid, 1848)

—— 'La poesía considerada como elemento de la historia', *Eco Literario de Europa*, 1 (1851), 361–77

COELLO Y QUESADA, DIEGO, 'Sobre la dominación en España de los reyes austríacos', *Revista de Madrid*, 2nd series, 3 (1840), 220–33

-- 'Revista dramática: consideraciones generales sobre el teatro y el influjo en él ejercido por el romanticismo', *Semanario Pintoresco Español*, 2nd series, 2 (1840), 198–200

CORTADA, JUAN, *Historia de España, dedicada a la juventud, por D. Juan Cortada, Catedrático y Director del Instituto de Barcelona. Adicionada y continuada hasta 1868 por D. Gerónimo Borao, Catedrático y Rector de la Universidad de Zaragoza*, 2 vols (Barcelona, 1872–73)

COSTANZO, SALVADOR, 'De las reformas que experimentó la poesía italiana después de mediado el siglo pasado, y de las poesías de Alejandro Manzoni', *Semanario Pintoresco Español*, 3rd series, 2 (1844), 389–91, 394–95

—— 'Breves indicaciones acerca de la cultura intelectual y del método que debe seguirse para escribir una historia literaria', *Revista Científica y Literaria*, 1 (1847), 511–16, 2 (1848), 22–27

Díaz, Nicomedes-Pastor, *Obras completas de don Nicomedes-Pastor Díaz*, ed. by José María Castro y Calvo, 3 vols (Madrid, 1969–70)

Donoso Cortés, Juan, 'España desde 1834. Artículo I: Consideraciones generales', *Revista de Madrid*, 1 (1838), 3–19

—— *Obras completas de don Juan Donoso Cortés, Marqués de Valdegamas*, ed. by Hans Juretschke, 2 vols, Biblioteca de Autores Cristianos (Madrid, 1946)

Durán, Agustín, 'Análisis crítico del drama de Tirso de Molina intitulado *El condenado por desconfiado*', *Revista de Madrid*, 3rd series, 2 (1841), 109–34

E., P., 'Sobre el antiguo drama nacional', *El Reflejo* (1843), 78–79

Fernández de los Ríos, Angel, 'Introducción', *El Siglo Pintoresco*, 3 (1847), 1–3

Ferrer del Río, Antonio, 'Bosquejo histórico. Minoría de Isabel II: declaración de su mayor edad', *El Laberinto*, I (1843–1844), 38–40

—— 'Biografía: Chateaubriand', *El Laberinto*, 1 (1843–44), 295–98

—— *Galería de la literatura española* (Madrid, 1846)

—— 'Meditaciones y estudios morales, por Mr. Guizot', *Eco Literario de Europa*, 2 (1851), 34–49

Ferrer y Subirana, José, 'De la nacionalidad', *La Civilización*, 2 (1842), 61–72

Flórez, V. M., 'Estudios históricos: sociedad pagana', *El Reflejo* (1843), 84–86

—— 'Estudios históricos: principio de la sociedad cristiana', *El Reflejo* (1843), 91–93

Forner, Juan Pablo, *Reflexiones sobre el modo de escribir la historia* (Madrid, 1816)

García Luna, Tomás, '¿Cuál es el provecho que puede reportarse de las investigaciones históricas acerca de Grecia y Roma? ¿Por qué es reciente la filosofía de la historia?', *Revista Científica y Literaria*, 1 (1847), 378–82

García y Tassara, Gabriel, 'De la influencia social de Francia en España', *El Pensamiento* (1841), 255–58

Gil y Carrasco, Enrique, 'Revista teatral: introducción', *Semanario Pintoresco Español*, 2nd series, 2 (1839), 342–43

—— 'Literatura contemporánea: colección de los viajes y descubrimientos que hicieron por mar los españoles desde fines del siglo XV, con varios documentos inéditos pertenecientes a la historia de la Marina Castellana, y de los descubrimientos españoles en Indias, por D. Martín Fernández de Navarrete. Tomo I y II', *El Pensamiento* (1841), 76–82

Gil y Zárate, Antonio, *Introducción a la historia moderna; o, Examen de los diferentes elementos que han entrado a constituir la civilización de los actuales pueblos europeos* (Madrid, 1841)

—— *Manual de literatura* (Madrid, 1842)

—— *Manual de literatura, por D. Antonio Gil de Zárate. Segunda parte: Resumen histórico de la literatura española* (Madrid, 1844)

—— *Resumen histórico de la literatura española. Segunda parte del Manual de literatura, por D. A. Gil de Zárate*, 4th edn corr. and aug. (Madrid, 1851)

Gironella, Gervasio (trans.), Charles du Rozoir, 'La historia considerada como ciencia de los hechos', *Revista de Madrid*, 2nd series, 1 (1839), 36–66, 222–37

—— 'Biografía contemporánea: Metternich (Príncipe de)', *Revista de Madrid*, 2nd series, 2 (1839), 97–116

—— 'Biografía contemporánea: Guizot (Francisco Pedro Guillermo)', *Revista de Madrid*, 2nd series, 2 (1839), 287–311, 383–94

—— 'La edad media', *Revista de Madrid*, 2nd series, 4 (1840), 117–32

Golmayo, Pedro Benito, 'La reforma protestante', *Revista de Madrid*, 3rd series, 1 (1841), 468–93, 2 (1841), 161–83, III (1842), 196–223

Gómez de la Cortina, José, *Cartilla historial o método para escribir la historia* (Madrid, 1829)

GONZALO MORÓN, FERMÍN, *Curso de Historia de la civilización de España, lecciones pronunciadas en el Liceo de Valencia y en el Ateneo de Madrid en los cursos de 1840 y 1841 por el profesor de historia en ambos establecimientos literarios*, 6 vols (Madrid, 1841–46)

—— *Ensayo sobre las sociedades antiguas y modernas y sobre los gobiernos representativos. Por Don Fermín Gonzalo Morón, Profesor del Ateneo y autor de la Historia de la Civilización de España* (Madrid, 1844)

—— 'Examen filosófico del teatro español, relación del mismo con las costumbres y la nacionalidad de España', *El Iris*, 2 (1841), 54–57, 72–75, 87–89, 103–07, 119–24, 134–38, 151–54, 166–71, 182–88, 200–02, 214–17, 231–33, 246–49, 263–64, 278–82

—— 'Examen crítico del teatro antiguo: Aguilar y Lope de Vega', *El Iris*, 2 (1841), 309–15, 326–31

—— 'Examen de los bienes y males producidos por la democracia. Reseña y juicio de la obra, de la democracia en América por Mr. Alexis Tocqueville. Instituciones políticas, gobierno y costumbres de los Estados-Unidos', *Revista de España y del Extranjero*, 1 (1842), 17–28, 71–91

—— 'Noticia de varias obras inglesas publicadas en este siglo sobre los árabes. Estado actual en Europa y en España de la literatura árabe. Deberes del gobierno españo, sobre la enseñanza de las lenguas orientales, protección de sus profesores y traducción de manuscritos árabes', *Revista de España y del Extranjero*, 1 (1842), 28–36

—— 'Reseña política de España. Artículo 120.', *Revista de España y del Extranjero*, 2 (1842), 241–53

—— 'Reseña política de España. Artículo 150.', *Revista de España y del Extranjero*, 3 (1842), 97–107

—— 'Las mil y una noches. Influjo de la literatura oriental sobre la árabe y de ésta sobre la de la edad media', *Revista de España y del Extranjero*, 3 (1842), 275–84

—— 'Movimiento intelectual de España: la Restauración, revista católica', *Revista de España y del Extranjero*, 6 (1843), 36–39

—— *Obras escogidas* (Madrid, 1875)

GOÑY [sometimes GOÑI], FACUNDO, *Tratado de las relaciones internacionales de España: Lecciones pronunciadas en el Ateneo de Madrid* (Madrid, 1848)

—— 'De la filosofía de la historia y sus principales escuelas', *Revista Española de Ambos Mundos*, 1 (1853), 613–25 and 2 (1854), 93–106

GUIZOT, FRANÇOIS, *Histoire de la civilisation en France depuis la chute de l'Empire Romain*, 4 vols (Paris, 1851)

—— *Histoire générale de la civilisation en Europe depuis la chute de l'Empire Romain jusqu'à la Révolution Française*, 4th edn (Paris, 1840)

—— 'H. F. C.' (tr.), François Guizot, *Historia de la civilización en Europa* (Barcelona, 1839)

HARTZENBUSCH, JUAN EUGENIO, 'Trozos del retrato histórico de don Enrique de Aragón, Marqués de Villena', *El Laberinto*, 1 (1845), 114–15

LAFUENTE, MODESTO, *Historia general de España, desde los tiempos más remotos hasta nuestros días*, 30 vols (Madrid, 1850–67)

LARRA, MARIANO JOSÉ DE, *Obras de D. Mariano José de Larra (Fígaro)*, ed. by Carlos Seco Serrano, 5 vols (Madrid, 1960)

LEÓN BENDICHO, JAVIER DE, 'Consideraciones sobre la religión católica y el protestantismo', *Revista de Madrid*, 3rd series, 1 (1841), 317–42

—— 'Instituciones monásticas', *Revista de Madrid*, 3rd series, 4 (1842), 5–24

LISTA, ALBERTO, *Ensayos literarios y críticos*, ed. by José Joaquín de Mora, 2 vols (Seville, 1844)

M., 'Teatros: *El paje*, drama en cuatro jornadas: su autor don Antonio García Gutiérrez', *Semanario Pintoresco Español*, 2 (1837), 165–66

MADRAZO, FERNANDO DE, 'Filosofía de la historia: caballería', *El Laberinto*, 2 (1845), 118–20.

MADRAZO, PEDRO DE, 'Bellas artes: génesis del arte cristiano', *El Renacimiento*, 28 March 1847, 17–18.

—— 'Bellas artes; sobre una de las causas de la decadencia del arte antiguo', *El Renacimiento*, 18 April 1847, 41-43.

MARTÍNEZ DE LA ROSA, FRANCISCO, '¿Cuál es el método o sistema preferible para escribir la historia?', *Revista de Madrid*, 2nd series, 2 (1839), 531–39

—— 'El sentimiento religioso', *Revista de Madrid*, 3rd series, 2 (1841), 313–22

—— *Obras de D. Francisco Martínez de la Rosa*, ed. by Carlos Seco Serrano, 8 vols (Madrid, 1962)

MEDRANO, DIEGO, 'Del progreso', *Revista de Madrid*, 3rd series, 3 (1842), 461–79

MESONERO ROMANOS, RAMÓN DE, 'Rápida ojeada sobre la historia del teatro español. Tercera época', *Semanario Pintoresco Español*, 2nd series, 4 (1842), 388–91

—— 'Rápida ojeada sobre la historia del teatro español. Conclusión: época actual', *Semanario Pintoresco Español*, 2nd series, 4 (1842), 397–400

MITJANA, RAFAEL, 'Estudios históricos sobre las bellas artes en la edad media. Arquitectura: Siglos XIII-XIV-XV', *El Siglo Pintoresco*, 1 (1845), 163–68, 193–202

MONTE, DOMINGO DEL, 'Literatura española del siglo XVIII', *Antología Española*, 2 (1848), 53–62

MORALES SANTISTEBAN, JOSÉ, 'Carácter distintivo de la sociedad antigua y moderna', *Revista de Madrid*, 1 (1838), 201–19

—— 'España cartaginesa y romana', *Revista de Madrid*, 1 (1838), 349–72

—— 'España goda', *Revista de Madrid*, 3 (1839), 55–74

MORENO LÓPEZ, MANUEL, 'Ensayo político y literario sobre la Italia desde el siglo XI hasta nuestros días, por don Salvador Constanzo', *Revista de España y del Extranjero*, 6 (1843), 397–401

PACHECO, JOAQUÍN FRANCISCO, *Historia de la regencia de la reina Cristina* (Madrid, 1841).

—— *D. Francisco Martínez de la Rosa* (Madrid, 1843)

—— *Literatura, historia y política* (Madrid, 1864)

PALLARÉS, JOSÉ MARÍA, 'Sobre la imparcialidad y divergencia histórica', *Revista de Madrid*, 3rd series, 1 (1841), 436–52

PÉREZ GALDÓS, BENITO, *Doña Perfecta*, ed. by Rodolfo Cardona (Madrid, 1984)

PI Y MARGALL, FRANCISCO, 'Una ojeada a la historia del arte monumental', *El Renacimiento*, 2 May. 1847, pp. 58–59

PIDAL, PEDRO JOSÉ, 'Literatura española: Poema del Cid — Crónica del Cid. — Romancero del Cid', *Revista de Madrid*, 2nd series, 3 (1840), 306–44

PINO, JOAQUÍN DEL, 'Reforma teatral', *Revista de Teatros*, 4 April 1841, 1–2

PRÍNCIPE, MIGUEL AGUSTÍN, *Guerra de la Independencia*, 3 vols (Madrid, 1844)

QUADRADO, JOSÉ MARÍA, 'Crítica literaria: Víctor Hugo y su escuela literaria', *Semanario Pintoresco Español*, 2nd series, 2 (1840), 189–92

—— prologue to Chateaubriand, *El último abencerraje. Atala. René* (Madrid, 1944)

REVILLA, JOSÉ DE LA, 'Ateneo de Madrid: cátedra de literatura española', *Semanario Pintoresco Español*, 2nd series, 1 (1839), 154–56

—— 'Estudios literarios: introducción', *Museo de las Familias*, 1 (1843), 1—— 5

ROCA Y CORNET, JOAQUÍN, 'La religión considerada como la base de la civilización', *La Civilización*, 1 (1841), 13–23

—— 'La divina epopeya', *La Civilización*, 1 (1841), 232–40

—— *Ensayo crítico sobre las lecturas de la época en la parte filosófica y social*, 2 vols (Barcelona, 1847)

ROSELL, CAYETANO, 'Creación de la orden de la Banda', *El Laberinto*, 1 (1843–44), 255–58

SAAVEDRA, ANGEL, DUQUE DE RIVAS, *Discurso del Excmo Señor Duque de Rivas sobre la utilidad e importancia del estudio de la Historia, y sobre el acierto con que le promueve la Academia*, in *Discursos leídos en las sesiones públicas que para dar posesión de plazas de número ha celebrado desde 1852 la Real Academia de la Historia* (Madrid, 1858), pp. 247–57

—— *Romances*, ed. Cipriano Rivas Cherif, 2 vols (Madrid 1911-1912)

SABATER, PEDRO, 'Curso de Historia de la civilización de España, por D. Fermín Gonzalo Morón', El Iris, 2 (1841), 22–26

SÁNCHEZ DE FUENTES, JOAQUÍN, 'Preliminares al estudio del derecho público', Revista de España y del Extranjero, 9 (1843), 267–86

SCHLEGEL, AUGUST WILHELM, A Course of Lectures on Dramatic Art and Literature, trans. by John Black, 2 vols (London, 1815)

SCHLEGEL, FRIEDRICH, Lectures on the History of Literature, Ancient and Modern, trans. by John Gibson Lockhart, 2 vols (Edinburgh, 1818)

SIMONDE DE SISMONDI, J. C. L., De la littérature du Midi de l'Europe, 3rd edn, 4 vols (Paris, 1829)

TAPIA, EUGENIO DE, Historia de la civilización española, desde la invasión de los árabes hasta la época presente, 4 vols (Madrid, 1840)

TEJADO, GABINO, 'Poesía popular', El Laberinto, 2 (1845), 134–36

—— 'Poesía dramática', El Laberinto, 2 (1845), 201–03, 214–15, 222–23

—— 'Poesía lírica', El Laberinto, 2 (1845), 246–47, 270–72, 278–79

—— 'Escritores contemporáneos: el Duque de Rivas', El Siglo Pintoresco, 1 (1845), 220–26

—— 'Ensayo crítico sobre algunas épocas de la literatura española', Revista Española de Ambos Mundos, 1 (1853), 281–302

—— 'Noticia biográfica' [1854], Obras de don Juan Donoso Cortés, marqués de Valdegamas (Madrid, 1891), pp. xix–cx

TORENO, CONDE DE, Historia del levantamiento, guerra y revolución de España, Biblioteca de Autores Españoles, 64 (Madrid, 1872)

VICENTE Y CARABANTES, JOSÉ, Historia general de la civilización europea, por Mr. Guizot, traducida al castellano conforme a su última edición, y anotada por D. J. V. C., 3 vols (Madrid, 1839)

—— 'Literatura religiosa', El Arpa del Creyente, 2 (1842), 9–10; reproduced in José Simón Díaz, El Arpa del Creyente (Madrid, 1842), Colección de Indices de Publicaciones Periódicas, 7 (Madrid, 1947), 3–5

ZARAGOZA, JOSÉ DE, Discursos leídos en la Real Academia de la Historia el día 12 de abril de 1852 con motivo de la admisión de D. José de Zaragoza (Madrid, 1852)

ZORRILLA, JOSÉ, Obras completas, ed. by Narciso Alonso Cortés, 2 vols (Valladolid, 1943)

B. Secondary Material

ABELLÁN, JOSÉ LUIS, Historia crítica del pensamiento español. IV: Liberalismo y romanticismo (1808–1874) (Madrid, 1984)

ALBORG, JUAN LUIS, Historia de la literatura española. IV: El romanticismo (Madrid, 1980)

ALLEGRA, GIOVANNI, La viña y los surcos: las ideas literarias en España del XVIII al XIX (Seville, 1980)

ALONSO CORTÉS, NARCISO, Zorrilla, su vida y sus obras (Valladolid, 1943)

ALONSO SEOANE, MARÍA JOSÉ (ed.), Francisco Martínez de la Rosa, La conjuración de Venecia, año 1310 (Madrid, 1993)

AMORES, MONTSERRAT, Fernán Caballero y el cuento folclórico (El Puerto de Santa María, 2001)

ARANGUREN JOSÉ LUIS L., Moral y sociedad: la moral social española en el siglo XIX (Madrid, 1966)

ARTOLA, MIGUEL, Partidos y programas políticos, 1808–1936 (Madrid, 1975)

BANN, STEPHEN, 'Romanticism in France', in Romanticism in National Context, eds Roy Porter and Mikulás Teich (Cambridge, 1988), 240–59

BENÍTEZ, RUBÉN, Bécquer tradicionalista (Madrid, 1971)

BERLIN, ISAIAH, Vico and Herder: Two Studies in the History of Ideas (London, 1980)

BURKE, PETER, Vico, Past Masters Series (Oxford, 1985)

CAMPOMAR FORNIELES, MARTA, 'Menéndez Pelayo y el conflicto entre tradicionalismo y liberalismo', in *Boletín de la Biblioteca de Menéndez Pelayo, Estudios sobre Menéndez Pelayo. Número extraordinario en homenaje a don Manuel Revuelta Sañudo* (Santander, 1994), pp. 109–34

CARNERO, GUILLERMO, *Los orígenes del romanticismo reaccionario español: el matrimonio Böhl de Faber* (Valencia, 1978)

—— (ed.), *El siglo XIX (I)*, vol VIII of Víctor García de la Concha, *Historia de la literatura española* (Madrid, 1997)

CARNICER, RAMÓN, *Vida y obra de Pablo Piferrer* (Madrid, 1963)

CARR, RAYMOND, *Spain 1808-1939* (Oxford, 1966)

CATTANEO, MARÍA TERESA, 'Gli esordi del romanticismo in Ispagna e *El Europeo*', in *Tre studi sulla cultura spagnola* (Milan, 1967), pp. 75–137

CEÑAL, RAMÓN, 'La filosofía de la historia de Donoso Cortés', *Revista de Filosofía*, 11 (1952), 91–113

—— 'J. B. Vico y Juan Donoso Cortés', *Pensamiento*, 24 (1968), 351–73

CHANDLER, ALICE, *A Dream of Order: The Medieval Ideal in Nineteenth-Century Literature* (London, 1971)

CHAO ESPINA, ENRIQUE, *Pastor Díaz dentro del romanticismo*, *Revista de Filología Española*, 46 (1949)

COLLINGWOOD, R. G., *The Idea of History* (Oxford, 1946)

CROSSLEY, CERI, *French Historians and Romanticism* (London, 1993)

DÍAZ, JOSÉ PEDRO, *Gustavo Adolfo Bécquer: vida y poesía* (Madrid, 1971)

ELORZA, ANTONIO, *La modernización política en España*, Ensayos de historia del pensamiento político (Madrid, 1990)

ESCOBAR, JOSÉ, 'Romanticismo y revolución', *Estudios de Historia Social*, 36–37 (1986), 345–51; reproduced in *El romanticismo* ed. by David T. Gies (Madrid, 1989), pp. 320–35

FERNÁNDEZ CARVAJAL, R., 'El pensamiento español en el siglo XIX', in *Historia general de las literaturas hispánicas*, V (Barcelona, 1969)

FERNÁNDEZ SEBASTIÁN, JAVIER, 'La recepción en España de la *Histoire de la civilisation* de Guizot', in *La imagen de Francia en España (1808–1850)* ed. by Jean-René Aymes y Javier Fernández Sebastián (Paris/Bilbao, 1998), pp. 127–49 (p. 127)

FLITTER, DEREK, *Spanish Romantic Literary Theory and Criticism* (Cambridge, 1992)

—— 'Zorrilla, the Critics and the Direction of Spanish Romanticism', in, *José Zorrilla, 1893–1993: Centennial Readings*, ed. by Richard A. Cardwell and Ricardo Landeira (Nottingham, 1993), pp. 1–15

—— 'The Romantic Theology of *Los amantes de Teruel*', *Crítica Hispánica*, 18 (1996), 25–34

—— 'Historia y pueblo en el costumbrismo romántico: Fernán Caballero y la capilla de Valme', in *Romanticismo 6: El costumbrismo romántico. Actas del VI Congreso del Centro Internacional de Estudios sobre el Romanticismo Hispánico* (Rome, 1996), pp. 155–61

—— 'La historia que nos llega: Fernán Caballero y la poética de la tradición', in *Fernán Caballero hoy. Homenaje en el bicentenario del nacimiento de Cecilia Böhl de Faber*, ed by Milagros Fernández Poza (El Puerto de Santa María, 1998), pp. 91–105

—— 'Ideological Uses of Romantic Theory in Spain', in *Romantik and Romance: Cultural Interanimation in European Romanticism*, ed. by Carol Tully, Strathclyde Modern Language Studies, 4 (Glasgow, 2000), pp. 79–107

—— 'Hacia una poética ideológica de la historia: romanticismo y medioevo', in *La poesía romántica. Actas del VII Congreso del Centro Internacional de Estudios sobre el Romanticismo Hispánico*, edited by Piero Menarini (Bologna, 2000), pp. 69–80

FOX, E. INMAN, *La invención de España: nacionalismo liberal e identidad nacional* (Madrid, 1997)

GARCÍA CASTAÑEDA, SALVADOR, *Las ideas literarias en España entre 1840 y 1850* (Berkeley, 1971)

GIES, DAVID T., *Agustín Durán: A Biography and Literary Appreciation* (London, 1975)

—— 'The Plurality of Spanish Romanticisms', *Hispanic Review*, 49 (1981), 427–42

—— 'José Zorrilla and the Betrayal of Spanish Romanticism', *Romanistisches Jahrbuch*, 31 (1980), 339–46

—— *The Theatre in Nineteenth Century Spain* (Cambridge, 1994)

—— 'A modo de conclusión: la poesía romántica y la creación de una nación', in *La poesía romántica. Actas del VII Congreso del Centro Internacional de Estudios sobre el Romanticismo Hispánico*, ed. by Piero Menarini (Rome, 2000), pp. 99–105

—— (ed.), *El romanticismo* (Madrid, 1989)

GIL NOVALES, ALBERTO, 'Las contradicciones de la revolución burguesa', in *La revolución burguesa en España* (Madrid, 1985), pp. 45–58

GINGER, ANDREW, *Political Revolution and Literary Experiment in the Spanish Romantic Period (1830–1850)* (Lewiston, 2000)

HALSTED, JOHN B. (ed.), *Romanticism: Selected Documents* (London, 1969)

HEREDIA SORIANO, ANTONIO, 'La filosofía', in *Historia de España Menéndez Pidal, XXXV: La época del romanticismo (1808–1874), I: Orígenes, religión, filosofía, ciencia*, ed. by Hans Juretschke (Madrid, 1989)

HERRERO, JAVIER, *Fernán Caballero: un nuevo planteamiento* (Madrid, 1963)

—— *Los orígenes del pensamiento reaccionario español* (Madrid, 1971)

—— 'El naranjo romántico: esencia del costumbrismo', *Hispanic Review*, 46 (1978), 343–54

—— 'Romantic Theology: Love, Death and the Beyond', in *Resonancias románticas: evocaciones del romanticismo hispánico en el sesquicentenario de la muerte de Mariano José de Larra*, ed. by John R. Rosenberg (Madrid, 1988), 1–20

JOHNSON, DOUGLAS, 'Historians', in *The French Romantics*, ed. by D. G. Charlton, 2 vols (Cambridge, 1984), II, 274–307

JOVER ZAMORA, JOSÉ MARÍA, 'Prólogo', in *Historia de España Menéndez Pidal, XXXIV: La era isabelina y el sexenio democrático (1834–1874)* (Madrid, 1981), pp. ix-clxii

—— *Realidad y mito de la Primera República. Del "Gran Miedo" meridional a la utopía de Galdós* (Madrid, 1991)

—— *La civilización española a mediados del siglo XIX* (Madrid, 1992)

JURETSCHKE, HANS, 'El problema de los orígenes del romanticismo español', in *Historia de España Menéndez Pidal, XXXV* (see Heredia Soriano, above), pp.

KIRKPATRICK, SUSAN, *Larra: el laberinto inextricable de un romántico liberal* (Madrid, 1977),

—— 'Spanish Romanticism', in *Romanticism in National Context*, ed. by Roy Porter and Mikulás Teich (Cambridge, 1988), 260–83

LLORENS, VICENTE, *El romanticismo español* (Madrid, 1979)

MARTÍNEZ TORRÓN, DIEGO, *Ideología y literatura en Alberto Lista* (Seville, 1993)

—— *El alba del romanticismo español* (Seville, 1993)

MENÉNDEZ PELAYO, MARCELINO, *Historia de las ideas estéticas en España*, 5 vols (Santander, 1947)

—— *Historia de los heterodoxos españoles*, 7 vols (Buenos Aires, 1951)

—— *Estudios y discursos de crítica histórica y literaria*, 7 vols (Santander, 1941–42)

MOLINA MARTÍNEZ, JOSÉ LUIS, *Anticlericalismo y literatura en el siglo XIX* (Murcia, 1998)

MONTESINOS, JOSÉ F., *Introducción a una historia de la novela en España en el siglo XIX*, 2nd edn (Madrid, 1966)

MORENO ALONSO, MANUEL, *Historiografía romántica española: Introducción al estudio de la historia en el siglo XIX* (Seville, 1979)

—— *La revolución francesa en la historiografía española del siglo XIX* (Seville, 1979)

—— *La generación española de 1808* (Madrid, 1989)

—— *Blanco White: la obsesión de España* (Seville, 1998)

NAVAS RUIZ, RICARDO, *El romanticismo español: historia y crítica* (Salamanca, 1970)

—— (ed.), *El romanticismo español: documentos* (Salamanca, 1971)

NEGRO PAVÓN, DALMACIO, 'El pensamiento político', in *Historia de España Menéndez Pidal,. XXXV* (see Heredia Soriano, above), pp.

NEMOIANU, VIRGIL, *The Taming of Romanticism: European Literature and the Age of Biedermeier* (Cambridge, MA., 1984)

PÉREZ-BUSTAMANTE MOURIER, ANA-SOFÍA, and ALBERTO ROMERO FERRER (eds), *Casticismo y Literatura en España* (Cadiz, 1992)

PICOCHE, JEAN-LOUIS, *Un romántico español: Enrique Gil y Carrasco* (Madrid, 1978)

PRAWER, SIEGBERT (ed.), *The Romantic Period in Germany* (London, 1970)

REVUELTA GONZÁLEZ, MANUEL, 'Religión y formas de religiosidad', in *Historia de España Menéndez Pidal,* XXXV (see Heredia Soriano, above), pp.

ROMERO TOBAR, LEONARDO, *Panorama crítico del romanticismo español* (Madrid, 1994)

—— (ed.), *El siglo XIX (II),* Vol. IX of Víctor García de la Concha, *Historia de la literatura española* (Madrid, 1998)

SÁNCHEZ LLAMA, ÍNIGO, *Galería de escritoras isabelinas: la prensa periódica entre 1833 y 1895* (Madrid, 2000)

SANTOVEÑA SETIÉN, ANTONIO, *Marcelino Menéndez Pelayo: revisión crítico-biográfica de un pensador católico* (Santander, 1994)

—— *Menéndez Pelayo y las derechas en España* (Santander, 1994)

SCHURLKNIGHT, D., '*La conjuración de Venecia* as/in Context', *Revista de Estudios Hispánicos,* 32 (1998), 537–55

SHAW, D. L., 'Towards the Understanding of Spanish Romanticism', *Modern Language Review,* 58 (1963), 190–95

—— 'The Anti-Romantic Reaction in Spain', *Modern Language Review,* 63 (1968), 606–11

—— 'Spain: Romántico-Romanticismo-Romancesco-Romanesco-Romancista-Románico', in '*Romantic' and its Cognates: The European History of a Word,* ed. by Hans Eichner (Toronto, 1972), pp. 341–71

—— 'El prólogo de Pastor Díaz a las poesías de Zorrilla (1837): contexto y significado', in *De místicos y magos, clásicos y románticos: homenaje a Ermanno Caldera* (Messina, 1993), pp. 471–83

—— 'En torno al Rivas de los *Romances históricos*', in *La poesía romántica. Actas del VII Congreso del Centro Internacional de Estudios sobre el Romanticismo Hispánico,* ed. by Piero Menarini (Bologna, 2000), pp. 185–91

SIEDENTOP, LARRY, 'Introduction' to François Guizot, *The History of Civilization in Europe,* trans. by William Hazlitt (Harmondsworth, 1997), pp. vii–xxxvii

SILVER, PHILIP W., 'Towards a Revisionary Theory of Spanish Romanticism', *Revista de Estudios Hispánicos,* 28 (1994), 293–302

—— *Ruin and Restitution: Reinterpreting Romanticism in Spain* (Liverpool, 1997)

TUBINO, FRANCISCO MARÍA, 'El romanticismo en España', *Revista Contemporánea,* 1877, 78–98, 184–98; reproduced in *El romanticismo,* (see Escobar, above), pp. 66–97

URIGÜEN GONZÁLEZ, MARÍA BEGOÑA, *Origen y desarrollo de la derecha española en el siglo XIX,* 2 vols (Madrid, 1981)

VARELA, JOSÉ LUIS, 'La autointerpretación del romanticismo español', in *Los orígenes del Romanticismo en Europa* (Madrid, 1982), 123–36; reproduced in *El romanticismo,* (see Escobar above), pp. 252–68

VILA SELMA, JOSÉ (ed.), Juan Donoso Cortés, *Ensayo sobre el catolicismo, el liberalismo y el socialismo* (Madrid, 1978)

WELLEK, RENÉ, *A History of Modern Criticism 1750–1950,* I: *The Later Eighteenth Century* (London, 1955)

WHITE, HAYDEN, *Metahistory: The Historical Imagination in Nineteenth-Century Europe* (Baltimore, 1973)

—— *The Tropics of Discourse* (Baltimore, 1978)

ZAVALA, IRIS M. (ed.), *Romanticismo y realismo. Primer suplemento,* Historia y crítica de la literatura española, ed. by Francisco Rico, 5.1 (Barcelona, 1994)

INDEX